The Soviet
Administrative
Elite

The Soviet Administrative Elite

Kenneth C. Farmer

PRAEGER

New York
Westport, Connecticut
London

Library of Congress Cataloging-in-Publication Data

Farmer, Kenneth C.
    The Soviet administrative elite / Kenneth C. Farmer.
        p.   cm.
    Includes bibliographical references and index.
    ISBN 0-275-94139-6 (alk. paper)
    1. Elite (Social sciences)—Soviet Union. 2. Political
leadership—Soviet Union. 3. Government executives—Soviet Union.
I. Title.
HN530.Z9E434   1992
305.5'2'0947—dc20   91-33599

British Library Cataloguing in Publication Data is available.

Library of Congress Catalog Card Number: 91-33599
ISBN: 0-275-94139-6

First published in 1992

Praeger Publishers, One Madison Avenue, New York, NY 10010
An imprint of Greenwood Publishing Group, Inc.

Printed in the United States of America

The paper used in this book complies with the
Permanent Paper Standard issued by the National
Information Standards Organization (Z39.48-1984).

10 9 8 7 6 5 4 3 2 1

To Lorene

Contents

Tables and Figure

TABLES

FIGURE

Preface

This study began as a quantitative study of the careers of post-Stalin Central Committee members. It turned out that the amount of truly significant information that could be obtained from that database was limited. My aim grew, then, from a small quantitative study to a larger qualitative analysis, with the database only one source of data. The methodology is eclectic and synthetic. I have based the approach on an effort to integrate the work of four classical theorists—Gaetano Mosca, Vilfredo Pareto, Max Weber, and Alexis de Tocqueville—with more contemporary theorists, notably John A. Armstrong and Suzanne Keller, and with the structuralist approach and anthropological approach to theory. As I imagine that many scholars do, I am left, upon its completion, with a vague sense of dissatisfaction with the result. All projects must come to closure, however, or they will never see the light of day.

For the transliteration of Russian words and names, I have employed a modified Library of Congress system, omitting diacritical marks. For names that have become part of the Western vocabulary, I have employed *Yu* or *Ye* rather than *E*, as in *Yurii* and *Yel'tsin*. Unless otherwise credited, all translations from the Russian are my own; quantitative generalizations, unless otherwise credited, are derived from my own databases.

I am indebted to a number of institutions and individuals for assistance and advice in the course of this project. The Graduate School of Marquette University provided a Summer Faculty Research Fellowship

(1987), and several Faculty Development grants, which provided needed time and resources for this work. I am grateful to the Hoover Institution at Stanford University for a National Fellowship during the 1987–88 academic year. Without the time thus afforded, and access to the Hoover Institution's incomparable library, this work could not have been done.

The following individuals provided invaluable advice to me in the course of researching and writing this work: John A. Armstrong, Mikhail S. Bernstam, Bill Bishop, Stephen Burant, Gerald Dorfman, Bohdan Harasymiw, John McAdams, James Rhodes, and John P. Willerton. I also acknowledge the help of my graduate research assistants, Toni Dembski, Lai Hongyi, and Kathy Schalow. Much of the administrative inconvenience of research and writing was ably smoothed by our department's administrative assistant, Ms. Jo Morstatter. Finally, I thank Mary E. Glenn and Stephen A. Hatem of Praeger Publishers, for their encouragement and assistance.

I would not dream of disavowing final responsibility for the book's errors and shortcomings.

The Soviet
Administrative
Elite

Chapter 1

Introduction:
The Theoretical Context

Cupido dominandi cunctis affectibus flagrantior.

Tacitus

IDENTIFYING ELITES

Human collectivities seem naturally to divide into leaders and the led, and this has been the case throughout all of human history.[1] Indeed, it is also true of most animals that live and travel in groups. Collective action, of men or animals, requires focus if it is not to be simply random and incoherent, and so the most elemental function of leadership is to coordinate in some way the individual actions of group members so that they are directed to the same end. At this elemental level, strength and cunning are what set leaders apart from the masses of the led. Authority—the right to lead—is always gained through some type of intramural competition that tests these qualities—often in the past an actual fight. The desire to dominate, and the expectation of the rewards that accompany domination, presumably are what motivate individuals to enter this competition.

Competition for preeminence in all areas of endeavor is characteristic of human societies. The possession of some characteristic highly valued by the community, then, defines elite status. Elites are those who have the most of what there is to have. Artistic elites, thus, are those possessing the greatest artistic gifts and skills, and political elites are those having the most political power. This is essentially Gaetano Mosca's definition of the elite—a minority set off from the masses by the possession of some prized quality.[2]

Although leadership by elites and the moral justification for it no doubt predated written human history, the philosophical origins of the Western tradition of elitism lies with the Greeks, ironically also the authors of democracy. Plato put forth an unabashed apology for political rule by intellectual elites.

Speaking still of elites in general, rather than political elites specifically, I propose that there are three characteristics of elites: exclusivity, superiority, and domination. "Exclusivity" simply means separateness; they are separate and apart from the larger society. The degree of exclusivity of elites can be assessed in terms of artificial boundary maintenance, gatekeepers of the recruitment process, and symbols of exclusiveness in lifestyle.[3] In keeping with Mosca, "superiority" denotes material, intellectual, or moral qualities or traits markedly above the level at which such qualities appear in the society. Finally, "domination" means just that: elites dominate the sector of human life with which they are associated. Suzanne Keller wrote that "elites are ultimately responsible for the realization of major social goals and for the continuity of the social order."[4]

The larger argument that Keller is making is that there is not a ruling class, at least in industrial societies. Such societies are so differentiated, and there are so many areas of human activity, that no one particular social group can dominate every aspect. Life has become highly compartmentalized in modern societies, and as a result there are many "strategic elites" that dominate different areas of life in modern societies.

A political elite, then, is a group that dominates the political life of a society, is superior in political skills (keeping in mind that the types of skills valuable for politics vary and can include duplicity and murderousness as well as rhetorical skill and persuasiveness), and insulated from everyday contact with the larger society. A considerable literature exists around the problem of defining the boundaries of the political elite, drawing the line between the elite and the nonelite, and distinguishing among elites and leaders.[5]

Without gainsaying that precision is important, there must be a point beyond which the search for precision is simply carried too far, in endless and irritating rumination over defining leadership, for example. In general, political science is more parsimonious than sociology, or at least that sociological literature dealing with elites. Sociological literature chews up and analyzes and overanalyzes minute concepts—in meticulous definition of what constitutes a "role," for example. One is inclined to wonder whether political science is more parsimonious because our concepts are taken predigested from sociology, or because political scientists deal less with "conceptual atoms" and more with "molecules" or "compounds"—macroconcepts such as voting behavior, for example, rather than "atoms" such as roles.

I will join this argument in greater detail in Chapter 3. I have, in this book, chosen a positional definition of the Soviet political elite: the political elite are those who hold high political office. Some authors prefer, and there is good reason for it, to identify the elite as the members of the *nomenklatura*, patronage lists controlled by the Communist Party.[6] Most of the national political elite so defined are members of the Communist Party of the Soviet Union (CPSU) Central Committee,[7] and this is a fortunate circumstance for Soviet elite studies, since Central Committee members (and Supreme Soviet members, with much overlap) are the only groups for which detailed career information is easily accessible.

The Soviet elite is an institutionalized power elite—eliteness inheres in the office, not in the person. The power elite are the men who hold institutional positions of power—no assumption is made of a shadowy cabal behind them. A focus on the political elite alone is not sufficient, however; following Keller, we have to make some effort to locate "strategic elites." This has been of less importance in the past in the Soviet context than it is going to be in the future: No account of the genesis of Gorbachev's policies will be complete without an account of the role of the Novosibirsk economists, for example, and other influentials.

A distinction should, to my mind, be drawn here between "natural" and "artificial" elites. Natural elites emerge "naturally" under conditions of unregulated competition, that is, their elite position flows from their own possession of certain qualities. "Artificial" elites occupy an elite position without regard to their own qualities—hereditary aristocracies certainly fall into this category: history abounds with powerful, aristocratic idiots. The Soviet institution of *nomenklatura* certainly maintains an artificial elite.[8]

At a general theoretical level, I postulate four general criteria that govern recruitment and promotion in a system that fosters an artificial elite. These are not alternatives to one another; all of them are likely to be operative, to varying degrees.

I. REPRESENTATIVENESS

    A. Work to create an elite that is representative of the population

    B. Work to create a political elite that is characteristic of the social elite

        1. Co-opt "strategic elites" into the political elite

    C. Work to create an elite representative of the Party

II. EFFICIENCY
   A. Technocratic: Work to create an elite that has the skills to get the job done
      1. Technocracy, meritocracy
   B. Paretian: Work to rejuvenate the elite by drawing in the younger generation

III. SYMBOLIC
   A. Work to create an elite that corresponds to the ideology
      1. *vydvyzhenie*: promotion of workers

IV. PATRIMONIAL
   A. Work to create an elite structure in which the position and privileges of oneself and one's cronies are protected
      1. Clientelism

In this introductory chapter I shall lay a broad theoretical basis or, perhaps, context, which will inform the remainder of this study. More particular knotty theoretical problems will be dealt with as they arise. In this chapter, as they impinge on the study of the Soviet political elite, I shall discuss the tenets of a structuralist approach to elite studies, the question of the relative strength and autonomy of the state, and the appropriateness of and insights that can be gained from the work of four classical elite theorists: Gaetano Mosca, Vilfredo Pareto, Max Weber, and Alexis de Tocqueville. The study will make liberal and eclectic use of these men's work. Finally, I shall describe the study's methodology and the sources of its data.

STRUCTURALISM

Valerie Bunce argues that "because scholars have found so little evidence for elite impact and so much evidence in support of environmental effects, they should have been persuaded more than they have been by a structuralist view of social reality."[9]

Theda Skocpol agrees:

One can begin to make sense...of such complexity only by focusing simultaneously upon the institutionally determined situations and relations of groups within society and upon the interrelations of societies within world-historically developing international structures. To take such an impersonal and non-subjective viewpoint—is to work from what may...be called a structural perspective.[10]

There are actually two separate strains of structuralism. The first is that associated with neo-Marxist thinkers such as Nicos Poulantzas and

Louis Althusser. In this materialist tradition of structuralism, human motivation and, by implication, culture count for little in explaining history. One student of structuralism remarks, for example, that the important factor in understanding human society is "not the conscious activities of the human subject, but the unconscious structure which these activities presupposed."[11] For Althusser, culture is merely the vehicle for "ideologies" that justify existing structural arrangements.[12]

The other, nonmaterialist strain of structuralist thought allows greater autonomy to culture and emphasizes "deep structures." Richard Merelman writes that

whole countries embody particular cultures in the form of deep structures, and ... these deep structures of culture predispose individuals to shape institutions and movements of a particular kind. Thus, the deep structures of national culture incline institutions and movements towards particular forms, even as institutions and movements attempt to control the preferences of their members.[13]

Structuralists in the Levi-Strauss tradition hold that deep structures constitute sets of paired opposites between which there is a psychological tension: the cooked and the raw, the social and the natural, and so on. In Russian (and not only in Russian) peasant culture, the most crucial such set of paired opposites is ingroup versus outgroup, or we versus they. The peasant views life, if not as a zero-sum game, then certainly as a finite-sum game. George Foster has captured this peasant outlook in the notion of the limited good: the peasant has learned over the generations that all the desirable things in his life, tangible or intangible, are in short supply and can usually be gotten only at someone else's expense.[14]

The famous Leninist political question, *kto-kogo*,[15] betokens political action as a zero-sum game, as does Marxism itself, with its Manichaean image of the final struggle between the bourgeoisie and the proletariat. This image does not envisage a negotiated settlement.

A society experiences collapsed development when a modernizing elite "collapses" the process of development, jumps over "stages," and attempts to superimpose the institutions of a modern society on a traditional feudal society. Under such circumstances, when deep structures are not allowed to evolve, a crypto-modern society results, that is, one that superficially has modern characteristics but retains a feudal structure beneath the surface. Authority relations in such a society will be predominantly patrimonial and/or charismatic, rather than rational-technical. Hence, the deep structure of Russian society is peasant/feudal.

The concept of deep structure has a respectable pedigree. As I am using the term, it refers to underlying mental conceptions of the structure of social reality, somewhat similar to Pareto's residues. It is deeper than culture or political culture—in fact, it informs these. Culture is readily accessible; without great difficulty, individuals can recognize that their behavior is in conformity with cultural norms.

Leon Trotsky turned out to be wrong about Soviet culture when he wrote that "essentially the Revolution means the people's final break with the Asiatic, with the Seventeenth Century, with Holy Russia, with icons and cockroaches."[16] Josef Stalin's purges and subsequent upward mobility meant a vast influx of peasants into administration. Quoting Boris Pilniak's line "The dark waters of *muzhik* Russia have swept and swallowed the Petrine empire,"[17] Nicholas Vakar observes that "the decimated intelligentsia could be replaced only by recruits from peasant homes."[18] Looking at the persistence of traditional cultural patterns in the Soviet elite's political style, Stephen Burant found considerable continuities of form (not content) with the Russian peasant tradition and the style of elites of the Brezhnev administration, and attributes this to the primary socialization experiences of individuals in the elite,[19] as do also Marshall Shatz[20] and Robert Tucker.[21]

Structuralism deals with models of the nature of reality that underlie the "social construction of reality" on which culture is built. It is not equivalent to culture or political culture, for these are phenomena that are on the surface and so are more or less easily accessible both to individuals within them and to outside analysts. Nor is it *mentalités*, which are individual, not collective, mental models of reality.[22] Deep structure underlies both of these. Claude Levi-Strauss warns that

it can only be said that when the structure of a certain type of phenomenon does not lie at a great depth, it is more likely that some kind of model, standing as a screen to hide it, will exist in the collective consciousness. For conscious models, which are usually known as "norms," are by definition very poor ones, since they are not intended to explain the phenomena but to perpetuate them. Therefore, structural analysis is confronted with a strange paradox well known to the linguist, that is: the more obvious the structural organization is, the more difficult it becomes to reach it because of the inaccurate conscious models lying across the paths that lead to it.[23]

Soviet Communist political culture is just such a screen, or inaccurate conscious model. Beneath it lies the Paretian "residue" of a centuries-old, mainly peasant, outlook. It is real in the sense that it helps shape more superficial attitudes and outlooks, and to some extent, action. No argument is made, however, that it is strictly determinative; rather, it is predisposing.

Structuralism thus deals with something that has no empirical existence. Its reconstruction, therefore, proceeds almost intuitively: the successive testing of partial hypothetical models until one is found that is subjectively convincing. Beyond that, there is no way of proving that it is the right one, or even that it exists. Any attempt to treat it as an independent variable and test it in a precise way is likely to be futile. It merely helps explain, qualitatively.

A structural approach to the explanation of political phenomena assumes that social and political structures play the predominant role, and human volition and choice a lesser role, in shaping broad political outcomes. Although the structural approach is a kind of determinism, it does not deny the reality of free will so much as it assumes the relative irrelevance of free will in explaining the behavior of individuals within a structured social matrix.

Whether an individual actor's free volition matters or not depends on the potential scope of the consequences of that person's action. It is clearly more important whether Stalin had free will than whether a local *gorkom* secretary did. This is to say that the *gorkom* secretary is more constrained by structure. Power can be defined somewhat loosely as relative freedom from structural restraint, or, to say much the same thing, as relative autonomy. This concept is the same as the concept of power defined as the ability to influence outcomes.

In adopting an approach informed by structuralism, we are not, for example, interested so much in Stalin or other top leaders themselves, but in the *structure* of Stalinism within which the elite had to move, and how it set parameters for them, and the mentalized *deep structure* of peasant-defined reality that set the parameters of their individual behavior. One scholar attributes instability in developing countries today to incongruities between an inoculated political structure and the traditional political culture.[24]

Far from being a totalitarian monolith, Soviet society—even, or especially, under Stalin—was highly compartmentalized. The mental structure of reality was one divided into corporate groups, each of which had its own norms and set of expected behavior. That reality is so structured is a world view carried over from peasant society. In a society most of whose members are separated from the peasantry by a generation or less, the persistence of a peasant ontology is not surprising. If one's parents had moved to the city, the socialization the child receives is rooted in peasant orientations; if it was one grandparents, even, who moved up to worker status, the influence probably persisted due to the important role of *babushkas* (grandmothers) in child raising. What the child learns about how reality is structured at his mother's, or his grandmother's, knee, is folk wisdom; and in a society so recently removed from feudalism, folk wisdom is peasant wisdom.

Ironically, this has been facilitated, not hindered, by Marxist ideology. As Kenneth Jowitt observes, "In Communist countries a charismatic political organization acting as the *purposive* and *dominant* agent of change has generated a *neotraditional* ethos and institutional pattern at both the social and regime levels."[25]

This is a "status society," as opposed to a "class society," in Weber's conception. As the Soviet Union continues to modernize and urbanize, and the urban nuclear family replaces rural ties, this *mentalité* will gradually fade away. But it does so only very gradually. Relationships *within* these corporate groups are highly personalized; relationships *between* groups are formal and impersonal, and often, in practice, mediated by gatekeepers. Individuals do not seek interactions that cross the boundaries of these corporate groups, and when such interactions are unavoidable, they tread cautiously.

Granted, the state could impinge on people's lives rudely and abruptly, particularly under Stalin. What is more important here is that the state itself is one of these autonomous, corporate groups. So is the Party. And most importantly of all, so are the cliques, patron-client networks, and "family circles" that are so characteristic of contemporary Soviet political life.

The persistence of this deep structure manifests itself in the pervasive importance—and ready acceptance—of the collective in Soviet society. The important point is not whether a particular collective or type of collective is carried over from the peasant past; the important point is the organization of life around such compartmentalized communes, as it had been in the peasant past. Relationships within the collective are personal, face to face, nurturing, and warm. They are also, at least from a Western perspective, despotic. They enforce conformity with an effectiveness the secret police could not match. Alexander Zinoviev sees the lowly primary collective, not the state, as the real "totalitarian" force in Soviet society. It dominates all aspects of people's lives:

This communal life is reflected in all the other bits and pieces of their lives; it dominates them; it paints them in its own colours. It has an overwhelming influence on the lives of the members of their families. And even afterwards when they do leave the collective and get their old-age pension, they bear the imprint of their former communal life to the very end of their days.[26]

Attitudes and orientations resulting from this deep structure include the Soviet citizen's habit of making sharp distinctions between insiders and outsiders (or we and they, ours and theirs)—with a marked suspicion and distrust of outsiders; this extends to xenophobia. Related is a distinctively Soviet combination of public unfeeling aloofness, even coldness, with unmatched warmth and hospitality at the primary-group level. It perhaps accounts as well for the unflattering but common ascription to Soviet people of a too ready submissiveness, along with other aspects of a subject-participant political culture; deep social and cultural structures shape and inform political culture.

A society oriented to personal, rather than impersonal, norms of social interaction will naturally be one in which due process of law is underdeveloped and weak, corruption flourishes, and bureaucracy has decidedly non-Weberian characteristics. The social structure of the Soviet Union is not that of an industrial society at all; I submit that it is crypto-modern and essentially feudal.

The unit of analysis in this study is the elite as a whole, not individuals within it. Stalinism and post-Stalinism set a context within which the elite structurally evolved. It is the failure of the Soviet Communist elite to adapt to changing circumstances that more than anything else accounts for the failure of communism. The elite did not adapt because it did not have to; it has been insulated from societal pressures because its commanding position, and the exclusion of other groups from that position, has been *structurally* guaranteed. The Party's monopoly on positions of political power has prevented the kind of competitive mechanism that would ensure a proper circulation of elites—that is, a situation in which groups or individuals with different skills or approaches are successively allowed to fail until some such group manages to succeed sufficiently to maintain the system. It is only in this concrete sense that a system "selects" elites that can maintain it, and it is only in this concrete sense—not in some unspecified metaphysical sense—that a system maintenance function is operative in societies.

It will be appropriate in this context to say something about structural-functionalism. I will make a number of functional arguments in this book. I do not disavow functionalism or structural-functionalism, but I do have doubts about what I shall call strong structural-functionalism. Strong structural-functionalism suggests that system requisites bring forth the structures that are necessary to fulfill them, and extremely strong structural-functionalism implies that it brings out the structures best adapted to fulfill that need. A weaker and more realistic structural-functionalism would be somewhat Darwinian—or perhaps, Simonian—in that, in effect, a system need elicits the first structure that "satisfices," in the sense of minimally fulfilling the function. It may be far from an optimal arrangement, and in fact the structure that does fulfill the particular function in an emergency may actually be harmful to the system in the long run, for it may contribute to the system's eventual demise. There is nothing implicit in the systematic requisite for maintaining order that will prevent the rise of a police force or a paramilitary organization or a Nazi Party that gets a head start but in the long run brings the system down. There is nothing in the notion of a system requisite that is going to guarantee that the structure that fulfills it is also simultaneously going to fulfill a system maintenance function. One would search long and hard to find a systemic requisite for which the Nazi holocaust was the best available structure. In fact, a number of factors—instability, high inflation, class conflict, industrial strife, and so on—created a need, and as it turned out the Nazis were there and fulfilled the immediate need of restoring order. But in the longer run they did not preserve the system but, rather, contributed to its demise. The Nazi Party was *dysfunctional* for any imaginable need except that of restoring and maintaining order in the 1930s. By the same logic, we cannot make sense of the Great Purges of 1936–1938 in systemic functional terms; the only needs they met were Stalin's. This is not to gainsay that they destroyed an older generation to make way for a new Soviet intelligentsia—but this was a need defined by Stalin, not one necessitated by industrialization. Because an institution has latent functions—even latent functions that bolster the system—does not imply that that is why the institution came about. This is a form of teleological fallacy; it confuses latent function with manifest purpose.

The biological sciences, from which, via anthropology, structural-functionalism entered the social sciences, has ironically taken the lead, not so much in abandoning the paradigm as in relegating it to a distinctly second place. Hannah Arendt quotes Adolf Portmann: "Prior to all functions for the purpose of preservation of the individual and the species ... we find the simple fact of appearing as self-display that makes these functions meaningful."[27] Arendt adds, "Moreover, Portmann demonstrates ... [that] the enormous variety of animal and plant life, the very richness of display in its sheer functional *superfluity*, cannot be accounted for by the common theories that understand life in terms of functionality."[28]

In the early Soviet state, during the civil war and after, there was no identifiable system; the Bolsheviks were navigating unchartered waters in the 1920s and making up the system as they went along; the only needs that were met were immediately discernible needs relating to defense, civil order, and production. Any notion of long-term system requisites is inapplicable because the system was inchoate and undefined and the class structure was fluid and labile. Any systemic needs of more than *immediate* relevance are identifiable *ex post facto* only, and if they had more than theoretical existence, they were not being met.

If one posits and insists upon a system maintenance function, one can find structures that contribute to the maintenance of the system, but the only way one can know that is because the system is seemingly being "maintained." It is not altogether clear how the system might stop being maintained and go out of existence, other than through defeat in war or revolution; in the very, very long cycle, one can see the decline of civilizations (but "system" has a much more immediate signification than this); other than that, the positing of a system maintenance function is in the first place a little metaphysical and in the second place not empirically justifiable.[29] The structure and operation of modern society are in fact *perpetuating* conditions (environmental destruction, astronomical debt in the Third World, and indeed in advanced countries like the United States, the extraordinarily wasteful economy of the Soviet Union that takes no account of inputs, only outputs) because they do fill an immediate need, but these conditions could well eventually destroy us.

THE AUTONOMY OF THE STATE

Until recently both liberal and neo-Marxist scholars, at least in the Anglo-American academic community, have traditionally avoided according an important role to the state in their analyses of political systems. Both academic traditions have been largely society oriented. To Marxist writers, this was largely because it is axiomatic in Marxism that the state is merely the instrument of the ruling class's domination. For the non-Marxist, it was because of the turn away from the study of institutions, particularly state institutions, and toward society-centered approaches such as structural-functionalism. Continental European scholars, particularly Germans such as Max Weber and Otto Hintze, have been more inclined to give an important role to the state.[30]

Neo-Marxists in the 1960s and non-Marxists in the late 1970s began debating the relative autonomy of the state as an actor in the political process. The more recent view is to regard the state as an actor, just as other institutions are actors—it is an actor with roles of its own, and with goals and interests that are not necessarily coterminous with those of the citizens, and for that matter, the classes that comprise it. Most of these analyses have emphasized the capitalist state.[31]

Marxism unambiguously attributes the necessity for the state to class conflict. The state, in Karl Marx's view, is the instrument of one class for oppressing another. Friedrich Engels had a less stark theory: it is necessary to moderate irreconcilable class conflicts and keep them within bounds of order. Soviet leaders have always had to find justification for the state's survival after it should have withered away. During the early Stalin period, the reason given was the survival of hostile classes and the intensification of class struggle; later in the Stalin period, capitalist encirclement was the justification. By the Brezhnev period, the idea of the withering away of the state was no longer taken seriously. Ironically, under Gorbachev's reforms, the state has become the vehicle of popular democracy as against the Party.

Montesquieu constructed his typology of states in part on the basis of their autonomy: the republic was the least autonomous, followed by aristocracies. Only despotic states were totally autonomous from society.

The state's autonomy rested on its monopoly of the machinery of domination, the bureaucracy and the army.[32] The recent emphasis on the autonomy of the state is essentially a rejection of the Marxist notion that the state is an epiphenomenal structure, merely an arena for the class struggle. Skocpol, for example, points out that the state is comprised of administrative and coercive machinery to extract resources from society and deploy them.[33]

Relatively few scholars have focused on the role of the state as actor in Communist countries.[34] Two reasons for this suggest themselves. First, it was because of aversion to the now generally discredited totalitarian model, with a monolithic and all-powerful state at its center. The second reason parallels the earlier Marxist neglect of the state: that it is merely the instrument of domination of the Communist partocracy. The first model uncritically accepts the autonomy of the state as total; the second regards state autonomy as totally lacking: the state is seen as totally in thrall to the Communist Party. Ironically, Marx and the earlier Bolsheviks likewise so saw it. This "thrall" was nothing more or less than the "dictatorship of the proletariat," after which the state would wither away.

Both liberals and Marxists, then, ascribe low autonomy to the state itself. Scholars in the realist tradition, by contrast, regard the state as an autonomous actor that can act in its own interests externally[35] and internally—and in this latter regard it is not merely the arena for the pluralistic interaction of interest groups. In this tradition, and not in the other two, it makes sense to speak of the state as an actor along with other actors; the state could even be regarded as a "juristic person," in the same way that a corporation is.

It seems to me that the autonomy of the state—its ability to act in its own interests—is a separate question from the relative strength or weakness of the state. A strong state is one that is able to resist its co-optation by autonomous groups within the society; a weak state, though it may retain some autonomous ability to act, is vulnerable to such co-optation—to becoming the "tool," if you will, of another group. A weak state's autonomy is considerably more limited, to be sure, than that of a strong state. I make this distinction, however, because I wish to characterize the Soviet state as of but limited autonomy and weak.

This is basic to the question of whether one is to consider the Communist Party to be a "ruling class." A ruling class exists prior to its capture of the state, and the basis of its dominance in the society is independent of the state—it dominates the economy. The situation in Communist countries is the reverse: the ability of the Party to dominate the economy is derivative of its domination of the state and could not exist outside that framework. The Party-state bureaucracy may—indeed, does—exercise all the privileges of a more traditional capitalist ruling class, but its ability to do so rests on its mastery over the state. Except by controlling the state, it would have no means of dominating the society.[36] To be sure, the Communist Party has autonomous strengths that contribute to maintaining its dominance of the state apparatus, most notably its impressive organization.

Uniquely in state-socialist systems, the state's power is shared with the Party, and the two are sometimes inseparable. This raises a conceptual question about the actual autonomy of the state. The state's machinery must be manned by someone. The Communist Party in the USSR is extremely jealous of its domination of the state and has gone to great length to protect it. It would not do so if its domination were assured. It is just not true that there are no competing elites that could potentially challenge the Party's monopoly of the state machinery, most notably, the military. In Poland in the 1980s, the challenge, ultimately successful, came from an independent labor union. This, and not any millenarian hope of transforming society, accounts for the Soviet Communist Party's insistence on controlling all social organizations and co-opting their leaderships. Strategic elites are potential counterelites.

Conceived, then, as an organization separate from, and dominated by, the Party, the Soviet state is a rather pathetically weak structure, and not very autonomous. Conceived on the other hand as a party-state, and vis-à-vis the rest of society, it is quite the contrary. The Communist state conceived in this way—as coextensive with the ruling party—is highly autonomous. It can formulate its own goals and extract resources from the society for their implementation, and no societal group can impose demands on it against its will. Such political systems are sui generis, a type unto themselves, and distinct from other types of states, democratic or authoritarian, economically developed or underdeveloped. I will call such regimes "state-socialist" societies.

The state-socialist structure of Soviet society is among the targets of Gorbachev's restructuring program. He has shifted the base of his own authority from his role as Party general secretary to his role as president in a strengthened state system. There were sentiments leaning in this direction even during the Brezhnev period. As Neil Harsing writes:

The potentially dangerous theoretical fiction of the dictatorship of the proletariat—that it was a temporary and transitional institution fated to wither away when the stage of developed socialism had been attained—has been the most significant casualty of recent theoretical developments. The state has now, quite unambiguously, been allotted a *permanent* role as *the* directing agency of all political, economic and social life.[37]

PARETO AND THE "CIRCULATION OF ELITES"

Vilfredo Pareto was born in 1848 in Paris, where his father, a Genoese nobleman, was in exile for his revolutionary activities as a Mazzinist, returning to Italy only with the amnesty of 1858. Pareto became an engineer, rising soon to a responsible position with the Italian railways. He was active politically, too, a liberal and an impassioned public advocate of free trade. His criticisms of the protectionist and corrupt government led to reprisals that ultimately forced him to retire from public and professional life. In 1894 he accepted appointment to a chair in mathematical economics at Lausanne University in Switzerland, and there, from 1896 until 1919, his written output in economics and sociology became increasingly prolific, culminating in the publication between 1915 and 1919 of his massive *Trattato di Sociologia Generale*.

During this period, he turned away from his earlier liberalism, becoming convinced that only force and suppression, on behalf of authority and religion—neither of which he personally believed in—could reverse the anemic stagnation of the Italian polity. He came thus to the attention of Benito Mussolini, who acknowledged an intellectual debt to him and showered him with honors. Shortly before his death in August 1923, Pareto for the first time publicly endorsed fascism, at the same time calling on Mussolini to respect freedom of opinion and expression, particularly in the university classroom. The unpopularity of Pareto today may be due as much to this accident of historical contingency as to the shortcomings of his theories. The rise of fascism in Europe was unquestionably a takeover by "lions" of political systems manned by not overly cunning "foxes." He did not live long enough to see what fascism developed into, and he was far from the only notable person initially to greet fascism as a welcome infusion of vigor and forcefulness into an effete age.

Still, there is little of a democratic ethos in Pareto's major writings. They abound with disgust and contempt for democracy, republicanism, humanitarianism, progress, and idealism. Franz Borkenau argues that as these were the ideals of Manzzinism, which his father presumably held dear, there may have been more than a hint of filial rejection involved.[38] This reaction came only near the end of his life and could well have been—as it was for the whole generation—a reaction to the general failure of liberalism.

Pareto's sociology has serious flaws. His concept of residues and derivations is ingenious, but his exposition and classification of residues is not satisfactory at all. To a degree it rewards patient consideration, but in many cases it is difficult to make sense of and leaves one wondering what he might have been thinking of. His neologisms are obscure and irritating more than helpful, and his scheme of nomenclature is not consistent. His theory of residues seems more appropriately a matter for psychoanalytic theory than for sociology; Pareto, oddly in 1919, seems to have been completely unaware of Sigmund Freud or his theories. Throughout his *Trattato* it is unclear whether his concepts apply to individuals or to social aggregates; he uses them in both ways. His major contribution to elite studies, the "circulation of elites," sometimes refers to the gradual movement of individuals into the elite, and at other times to the displacement of one elite by another, as in his assertion that history demonstrates a constant pattern of circulation between "lions" and "foxes." Finally, like many system builders in social science, he tries to make his theory do too much; residues become a single factor by which he wishes to explain the totality of human individual and collective action.

Pareto makes a distinction between logical and nonlogical actions. The distinction is no more than that between rational and arational motivation. Logical actions have a clear relationship between means and ends that is obvious to both the agent and the observer. There are not very many of these—Pareto concedes they exist only in science and economics—and it is really nonlogical actions that he is interested in. He totally rejects Enlightenment rationalism, the conviction that reason is humanity's predominant characteristic, insisting instead that most human action is based on residues, which are groups of nonlogical actions deriving from one common underlying "sentiment." The use of the term "sentiments" here is identical, it would seem, with the term "instincts," although Pareto does not exactly say that and at times indicates that they are learned by "imitation." Whatever their origin, they are universal, unchanging over time, and resistant to any further attempts at explanation. They are just there, as a sort of collective unconscious fixture.

All of people's conscious explanations for their actions, which they mistakenly believe are rational, are but "derivations" of residues. Residues are constant and timeless, but derivations can and do take myriad forms at different ages and in different societies and even in different individuals. Religion, ideologies, indeed all rationales that people offer for their own or others' actions, are derivations, similar to, but vaster in scope than, Marx's notion of false consciousness. A very troubling corollary follows from this. There can be no coherence to social life, nor to the lives of individuals, if all human action consists just in virtually automatic responses to randomly occurring residues. In arguing that residues are meaningless in themselves, Pareto ignores the entire principle of functionalism, which lies at the heart of modern sociology. Many, if not most, of human activities and outlooks, which Pareto attributes merely to residues, in fact do have meaning for the people who practice them and are part of an adaptive response to perceived or real necessities.

With respect to derivations, it is true that people do frequently act for reasons entirely other than the ones they give for their actions. Marx's concept of ideology as a rationalization for class interests does not presuppose that such individuals are unaware of their duplicity (although individuals who act in a manner inconsistent with their interests but in accord with an ideology are said by Marx to have false consciousness). Individuals acting in defense of an interest they would prefer to conceal are nonetheless acting rationally, and their actions are not based on any kind of residue; it seems clear that these are "logical actions" in Pareto's meaning. It is not explicit in Pareto, but it seems logically necessary to confine "derivations" to "false consciousness," that is, to suppose that people actually believe that the derivations are the real reasons for their own and others' actions.

Although there are six categories of residues, with many subcategories, Pareto uses only the first two in his theory of the rise and fall of elites, and these are the two for which he is known. Type 1 residues he calls the "instinct of combinations." The word "combinations" in Italian encompasses originality, ingeniousness, and scheming.[39] They are so called because Pareto detects here a preoccupation with "similar and dissimilar things," a desire to combine things, and in particular a tendency to combine dissimilar things—a disposition toward novelty. Individuals whose behavior derives from Type 1 residues are "foxes." They are progressive, inventive, and imaginative, but they are also selfish and aggressive, tricky, short-sighted, prone to take risks; they are "speculators," squeamish about the use of force. These attributes tend to occur together. Governments dominated by an elite in which Type 1 residues prevail will be marked by fraud, graft, and corruption.[40]

Type 2 residues Pareto calls "persistence of aggregates." "Aggregates" here refers to aggregates of sensations or phenomena, and the Type 2 tendency is to consolidate them into "group-persistences" in the desire to make them permanent through time. It is by this process that civilizations are built. "Lions" are conservative, stolid consolidators. Their instincts tend toward the preservation of relationships among like things rather than to novel combinations of unrelated things. Type 2 residues tend toward preservation, continuity, and tradition. Rather than being devious and cunning, people in whom these residues predominate are straightforward and forceful, and they are quite prepared to use violence to achieve their ends. In his own usage, when he comes down to cases, Pareto tends to simplify Type 1 residues as predisposing to a spirit of change and Type 2 residues as predisposing to continuity and conservatism.

The ideal state is one in which the governing elite exhibits a balance between lions and foxes, but this happy condition never prevails for long. Gatekeepers can be expected to recruit into the elite individuals like themselves; and if they do so, without care to co-opt potentially rebellious lions from the society, Type 1 residues become concentrated in the governing elite, while an energetic counterelite with Type 2 attributes remains among the masses, whom it can lead in revolution against a governing elite in disarray and unwilling to use force to maintain its position.

The long-run prospects of the lions in power are no better. They typically employ coercion at first in reasoned ways, but in time they become too conservative and stultified, lose touch with the masses, resort too readily to violence, and find themselves in need of foxes who are experts at generating consent through maneuver. These infiltrate the governing elite, gradually transforming and then replacing it.

History, then, is merely cyclic, alternating between foxes and lions, and "the graveyard of aristocracies," in Pareto's own graphic phrase. There is no Hegelian progression through stages. Both Mosca and Pareto were consciously concerned with refuting Marx's conception of human history as a progression toward an ultimately classless society. Elite rule was inevitable, and for Pareto the fall of one elite merely occasioned the rise of another. Pareto's scheme is more clearly relevant to what I shall call a Hobbesian elite culture (one in which power motives are dominant and power is an end in itself) than to a Lockean one (in which motives of cooperation are dominant and power is seen as a means to other ends).[41]

GAETANO MOSCA AND THE RULING CLASS

Gaetano Mosca (1858–1941) was a contemporary of Pareto; both men were Italian, although Pareto was Frenchified and spent the most productive part of his career in Switzerland. Both were system builders, aspiring to create a general theory of sociology, in Pareto's case, or the "elements of a science of politics," in Mosca's case. Nonetheless, Pareto's system is much more sweeping and comprehensive, while Mosca's, in spite of the original Italian title of his book, can more properly be called middle-range theory.

Mosca has generally enjoyed the better reputation of the two, partly because, as indicated earlier, Pareto is wrongly identified as an exponent of fascism, whereas Mosca denounced it or, more accurately perhaps, pointedly failed to endorse it. It is perhaps also due to the fact that unlike Pareto's coldly dispassionate scientific stance, Mosca seems more human by letting his normative concerns show constantly. Whatever their numerous other dissimilarities, both Mosca and Pareto share a decisive refutation of both liberal democracy and Marxism, and the insistence that elites rule—now, at all times in the past, and in the future.

Mosca was born in Palermo in Sicily but pursued his career in Rome, serving both as a public servant and an academic. He was a member of the Chamber of Deputies in 1908–1918, subsequently becoming a senator for life (although he ceased significant participation in 1925). He served as a lecturer (without salary) in constitutional law at the University of Palermo in 1881–1886, and in Rome in 1887–1895. He became a professor of constitutional law at the University of Turin in 1895, returning to Rome in 1923, where he served as a professor of political theory until 1935.

Mosca was a comparativist in that he believed that the systematic study of history could yield laws with general applicability. What he discovered from his study was that at all times, and at all places, a small elite ruled the larger society. This elite possessed some quality esteemed by the society, or at least influential in the society, and that elites used this to ensure their domination. Such attributes might include sheer coercive power or administrative talent, priestly power, and even ownership of the means of production. In addition to this, the ruling class manipulates the political formula—the ideology—to cement and legitimize its rule. Elites lose power to competing elites (never to the masses) seeking to replace them, if they fail to adapt their policies or to rejuvenate their ranks with fresh blood from competing elites.[42]

MAX WEBER

Whereas Mosca and Pareto may be a bit obscure, Max Weber (1864–1920) needs little introduction to a Western readership. His contributions to Western social science are broad and crucial, and they defy facile generalization. His theories of bureaucracy, on the types of domination, and on authority, in particular, are germane to this work, and I will make frequent appeal to him.

Weber lived a difficult, even somewhat tragic, life. He was born in Erfurt (in what subsequently became East Germany), but early in his life the family moved to Berlin. His father, Max, was a lawyer, a politician in the National Liberal Party, and a member of the Reichstag. The elder Weber's circle of intimate friends included prominent intellectuals and politicians, and so throughout his youth Max, Jr., was exposed to the most influential political, social, and philosophical ideas of the time. His father was pragmatic and not overly concerned with morality, while his mother Helene was pious and unremittingly moralistic, and politically devoted to the Christian reform and social welfare movements increasingly sponsored by liberal Protestant churches.

Weber studied law at Berlin and Heidelberg (not failing to obtain the important facial dueling scar), after which he devoted a year to military service. In 1889 he finished his doctoral work, and in 1891 he submitted his *Habilitationsschrift* at Göttingen on classical Roman agrarian arrangements. He became a lecturer in Berlin and later in Freiburg, and in 1896, with the help of a family friend, the historian Theodor Mommsen, he acquired a distinguished faculty position at Heidelberg. In 1893 he had married his cousin Marianne Schnitger, who was later to become a prominent feminist leader.

In 1897 Weber suffered a crippling nervous breakdown. Severe depression making it impossible for him to work, he resigned his academic position and withdrew from political activity. The occasion was apparently the death of his father, shortly after a stormy argument in which Weber had defended his mother's rights to visit her children alone and without Max, Sr.'s, permission. He began to work again in 1903, producing after his recovery the bulk of his best work. His self-inflicted guilt over his father's death continued to trouble him, however, and it does seem that there were other difficulties of a psychological nature. His young wife apparently despised sex (an attitude he did not discourage); some writers maintain that the marriage was never consummated,[43] and Marianne Weber hints of this, too, in her biography of Weber.[44]

One Freudian study of Weber argues that Weber suffered from sexual repression, due in part to his ascetic mother and his reaction against his freewheeling father.[45] Beginning around 1907, it appears that Weber did begin to have extramarital affairs, and in particular with Else von Richthofen (a distant cousin of the famous baron), whose sister Frieda married the novelist D. H. Lawrence.[46] After World War I, Weber decided to enter politics again. He tried (to his great hurt, unsuccessfully) to win the nomination for a Frankfurt constituency by the newly formed German Democratic Party. Having turned back to scholarship, he died of pneumonia in Munich on June 14, 1920, at the age of 56.

Weber's prodigious scholarly output ranged over a wide variety of topics, including comparative religion, the ancient city, the origins of capitalism, social and economic organization, and the philosophy of the social sciences.[47] Reviewed here are only those elements of work most germane to this study: sociological method, bureaucracy, and types of domination.

Three elements of Weber's sociological method comprise his distinctive contribution to modern social science: *Verstehen* (understanding), the importance of human individual choice in structuring social action, and the concept of ideal types. By *Verstehensoziologie*, Weber intends a sociology premised on the assumption that social events are caused by voluntary human choices; it is possible, therefore, to reconstruct the world as the actor saw it and gain an almost intuitional understanding of the meaning the actor projected onto reality, and the subjective reasons for his choices.[48] Weber does not intend the *Verstehen* approach to supplant or supplement, but rather to inform, more positivistic approaches to social science. Ultimate ends or values must be understood in their own terms, not taken for granted, and this is especially important when such ends or values differ radically from our own.[49]

Weber emphasized a hypothetically postulated "pure form" of social action, as a base from which to assess the degree of deviation of social action from pure rationality.[50] These postulated pure forms Weber called ideal types: "They state what course a given type of human action would take if it were strictly rational, unaffected by errors or emotional factors and if, furthermore, it were completely and unequivocally directed to a single end."[51] Weber goes to great lengths to stress that ideal types are not empirical generalizations from reality, and that in no case does reality correspond to any ideal type. They are tools with which to measure the effect of various nonrational and non-self-conscious factors or motives that are present.[52]

One of Weber's most famous ideal types is that of bureaucracy. A bureaucracy, whether in the private or public sphere, is a permanent agency with a fixed jurisdiction ordered by rules, characterized by mon-ocratic hierarchical organization that completely segregates bureaucratic office from the private household and budget of the officeholder.[53] Governmental bureaucracy in Weber's conception occurs only in modern states, and in the private sphere only late in the development of capitalism. When its forms but not its functions are imitated, I will refer to non-Weberian, or crypto-Weberian, bureaucracy. I will engage Weber's theory of bureaucracy in much greater detail in Chapter 5.

Bureaucracy is the form taken by a rationally regulated system of domination. Other types of domination are traditional, encompassing patriarchalism and patrimonialism, and charismatic encompassing individual authority based neither on rational legitimacy nor tradition.[54] Weber despairs of providing a precise definition of domination (*Herrschaft*), but he ties it to power (the ability to impose one's will on the behavior of others) and distinguishes between two types of domination: "domination by virtue of a constellation of interests . . . and domination by virtue of authority, i.e., power to command and duty to obey."[55] Weber's conceptualizations of domination go further than theories of totalitarianism in explaining Soviet politics. Patrimonialism in particular is essential to the proper understanding of authority relationships and the exercise of power in the Soviet system.

ALEXIS DE TOCQUEVILLE

I will begin by acknowledging that Tocqueville was only in an oblique sense an elite theorist. Tocqueville was a master sociologist of class, refining his conception of class as his writing matured. He preceded Marx in the explanation of events using class analysis. Like that of many great intellectuals, Tocqueville's work was woven around a single idea: once called the "Prophet of the Mass Age,"[56] equality (*démocratie*) was almost an obsession with the aristocratic thinker.

Tocqueville goes in and out of vogue; his relevance to the particular age has been debated in every era, with detractors and champions alike marshaling impressive arguments for their viewpoint.[57] He has been dismissed as relevant only to "agricultural or commercial societies,"[58] on the one hand, and praised as "keenly aware of the social impact of the new industrialism,"[59] on the other. There is little consensus as to whose tradition can claim him: political scientists, historians, sociologists, philosophers, anthropologists, liberals, even conservatives.

Alexis Charles Henri Clerel de Tocqueville was born in Paris in 1805 to a long-established family whose estate was at Verneuil. His father, Hervé de Tocqueville, who barely survived the French Revolution, later worked as a prefect under the restored Bourbons. Alexis was raised in a noble family, then, with a marked nostalgia for the Old Regime, and he received a Catholic primary education from the Abbé Lesueur. While his father was prefect in Metz, Alexis attended the *lycée* in that city. Biographers differ on his academic record there. J. P. Mayer, a particular admirer of Tocqueville, writes that "his career at school was a brilliant one, a special prize and two first prizes being awarded to him," but he adds that on the whole Tocqueville did not read much.[60] Irving Zeitlin, on the contrary, states that at the *lycée*, "he was an undistinguished student who developed little interest in books, failed the classics, and excelled only in . . . rhetoric and French composition."[61] He apparently read enough of the *philosophes*, however, to become an agnostic in his late teenage years.

After studying law in Paris, Tocqueville was appointed a magistrate in the court of Versailles. He aspired to a political career, however, and his political views increasingly became sympathetic to the liberals. In 1830 Tocqueville and his friend Gustave de Beaumont swore an oath to the Orleanist regime, fearing that the only alternative would be "republic and . . . anarchy."[62] Tocqueville viewed the political world in terms of the "paired-opposites" aristocracy versus democracy/anarchy. He was convinced of the inevitability of democracy (in fact, he was the first to interpret the French Revolution as a bourgeois revolution); he regarded it his duty to help the French nation adapt to it to avoid the disaster of anarchy or despotism. Tocqueville and Gustave de Beaumont undertook their trip to the United States in 1831 to study at first hand a society they believed was already far along the road upon which France was then embarking. The first of Tocqueville's two great contributions to social science, *Democracy in America*, was written after this journey, at the beginning of his career. The second, *The Old Regime and the French Revolution*, was written near the end of his life.[63] In between, he led an active political life, serving as minister of foreign affairs after 1848 and retiring from politics after the accession of Louis Napoleon.

Tocqueville was not explicit or self-conscious about his methodology, and this has prompted some—notably sociologists, perhaps among social scientists the most conscious of methodology—to deny him the status of a theorist. Talcott Parsons, for example, remarks that Tocqueville was more of a talented political and social commentator than the "originator of major theoretical schemes for analysis."[64] That Tocqueville was so infrequently wrong in his assessments and prognoses makes this seem a bit mingy, but it is true that he was not engaged in theoretical system building. He was concerned about the proper understanding of events of his generation, and even in *The Old Regime* he was concerned to show his contemporaries the proper paths to liberty without anarchy.

It is not true, however, that he had no method; although he did not label it explicitly as such, his method was comparative historical analysis, and he employed it skillfully. His method was "concomitant variation," as it was formalized later by Tocqueville's friend and contemporary John Stuart Mill.[65] He compared Canada and the United States to seek the correlates of centralized and decentralized administration.[66] He employed diachronic comparison of France at intervals over history to correlate increasing centralization with the decrease of freedom and authority.[67]

Whitney Pope does a masterful job of reconstructing the formal theory that is implicit in Tocqueville's work, rather more complex than I can do justice to here in short summary. Briefly, however, he concludes that the correlates of freedom include religion, morality, decentralized administration, authority based on legitimacy deriving from a healthy sense of community and a social contract in which the government returns to the community in the form of protection and services what it extracts in the form of taxes, and a high-level mass energy and activity generating material prosperity. The correlates of tyranny are centralized administration, the use of force as a substitute for legitimate authority, egoism rather than a sense of community, and the stifling of individual and collective energy and initiative, resulting in lower prosperity.[68]

If we step outside Marx's deterministic agenda for human progress and assume that the "proletarian revolution" of 1917–1936 was sui generis, the result of a unique confluence of events and social forces, and if it is granted, as I have argued above, that the social structure of the Soviet Union is essentially quasi-feudal, it takes only a little imagination to interpret what is happening in Gorbachev's Soviet Union today as a bourgeois revolution in Tocqueville's understanding. The nearest model (much abstracted, of course) of the Soviet Union in 1991 is France of 1789. I shall return to this argument in Chapter 8.

METHODS AND APPROACHES

Carl Beck and his associates argued that "one must be able in elite studies to do three things: (1) describe the type of the elite; (2) explain how a particular pattern hangs together and maintains itself; (3) and explain how patterns change and new patterns emerge."[69]

I intend in this study to do that, and more. By employing classical elite theorists, I want also to interpret the experience of the Soviet political elite in a manner consistent with the broad mainstream of Western thought on political elites and political leadership. I do not aspire to grand theory, however. I confine the study to middle-level questions and middle-level theory. The unit of analysis throughout is the elite *as a whole*, rather than individuals.

I will make frequent reference in this book to leadership cohorts. This is a useful approach to studying variables over time. Individuals can be aggregated into cohorts according to various criteria; the criterion the analyst will choose will be some significant event that then defines the cohort. Birth is the event most often used, and most cohort studies are of age cohorts. I will use a different criterion: cohorts will be defined according to the time period in which a person first accepts a full-time Party or government post; that is, I will refer to recruitment cohorts. Many models of social change assume that an individual's political consciousness is formed during early adulthood, between the ages of about 18 to 25. The prevailing political ethos at that time is a factor common to all members of that cohort, and only to it.[70] This age range also corresponds to the time when most individuals in the Soviet system begin their careers. My reasoning for the use of recruitment cohorts is that this event, rather than, say, joining the Party, is the truly critical choice the individual makes, and the political environment at the time this choice is made is relevant to the individual's selection and self-selection. The prevailing political environment will be called a "regime"; as I use it, the term is not coextensive with the rule of a top leader; rather, it refers to a particular time period when particular and identifiable selection criteria appear to be operative. These cohorts are as follows:

Cohort 1: 1900–1916, Prerevolutionary. Self-selection into full-time illegal Party activity.

Cohort 2: 1917–1921, Revolution and Civil War. Dominated largely by Old Bolsheviks.

Cohort 3: 1922–1927, New Economic Policy (NEP). A period of stabilization; elite still dominated by Old Bolsheviks, but a large "Lenin Enrollment."

Cohort 4: 1928–1935, First Five-Year Plan, Collectivization. Stalin's consolidation of power. In the ascendancy, because of industrialization, are elites who received technical educations either before the revolution or during the NEP.

Cohort 5: 1936–1940, Purge. Massive purges of Party elites and technical intelligentsia, creating unprecedented opportunities for advancement for persons who received technical educations in the early 1930s. This cohort is the notorious "Class of 1938."

Cohort 6: 1941–1945, War. The war took its draconian toll not so much of men already established in the elite (even the relatively new Cohort 5 could protect itself), as of men born around 1920–a missing cohort that was not available to step into power in the 1970s as Cohort 5 began noticeably to age.

Cohort 7: 1946–1952, High Stalinism. Again, there is a missing cohort here: men who might otherwise have joined the elite later but were deprived in this time period of the requisite higher education because of the needs of postwar reconstruction.

Cohort 8: 1953–1964, Khrushchev period. A vigorous period of recruitment and lateral entry into the elite, marked by high turnover and insecurity of elite tenure as Nikita Khrushchev tinkered endlessly with the apparatus.

Cohort 9: 1965–1969, Collective Leadership. As always following a succession, men paid with their careers for their past loyalties, as Brezhnev slowly consolidated his personal power and undercut that of his rivals. At high levels, this continued into the 1970s.

Cohort 10: 1970–1982, "Stability of Cadres." This stability gradually disintegrated into stagnation as the Brezhnev generation clung to their posts. As a result, there was considerable "bunching up" of aspirants at middle levels of the hierarchy.

Cohort 11: 1982–present, Smena. A *smena*, or generational change, as the old Brezhnev elite dies or is forced into retirement, to be replaced by people 20 years their juniors.

The principle methodology in this study is the analysis of collective biography, or prosopography, as it has been called.[71] The principle quantitative databases for this are several computer files containing demographic and career data on all full and candidate CPSU Central Committee members and Auditing Commission members since 1917. The first, containing 552 names (through the Seventeenth Party Congress), is scanty, as we have little information on the careers of these people. The second, containing 1,501 names, consists of full demographic data on all full and candidate Central Committee members and Auditing Commission members for the Eighteenth through the Twenty-seventh Party Congress. The third contains full *career* data on full Central Committee members for the Nineteenth through the Twenty-sixth CPSU Congresses. The fourth contains (often incomplete) demographic and career data for the 412 members of the Twenty-eighth Central Committee. Finally, there is a file of demographic and career characteristics for the members of the Congress of People's Deputies as of January 1, 1991, and within that a subfile consisting of the members of the newly revamped Supreme Soviet. The problems presented by this database are discussed in the chapters in which they are used, Chapters 3, 6, and 8.

The method of organizing the presentation is primarily analytical, rather than chronological. Chapter 2 discusses the elite's educational experiences, from the earliest years to the present. Chapter 3 is concerned with elite structure (structure, in this case, in the sense of morphology). Chapter 4 deals with the first postrevolutionary wholesale transformation of the elite under Stalin in the 1930s. Under the rubric of elite-society relations, Chapter 5 examines the question of bureaucracy (and offers a theory of non-Weberian bureaucracy), the problem of technocracy, and the question of whether the Party or the Party elite constitute a "ruling class." Chapter 6 is concerned with elite recruitment and mobility. Chapter 7 discusses three problems under the label of venality: corruption, clientelism, and elite style. Chapter 8 discusses the Gorbachev transformation, well under way, and the emergence of strategic elites in Soviet society, and it contains the concluding remarks.

NOTES

1. Thus states perhaps Mosca's most quoted passage: "In all societies . . . two classes of people appear—a class that rules and a class that is ruled." Gaetano Mosca, *The Ruling Class: Elementi di Scienza Politica*, ed. and rev., with an introduction by Arthur Livingstone, trans. Hannah D. Kahn (New York: McGraw-Hill, 1939), p. 50.

2. Ibid., p. 53.

3. George E. Marcus, " 'Elite' as a Concept, Theory, and Research Tradition," in George E. Marcus, ed., *Elites: Ethnographic Issues* (Albuquerque: University of New Mexico Press, 1983), pp. 11–12.

4. Suzanne Keller, *Beyond the Ruling Class: Strategic Elites in Modern Society* (New York: Random House, 1968), p. 4.

5. See, for example, Peter Y. Medding, "Ruling Elite Models: A Critique and an Alternative," *Political Studies* 30, no. 3 (September 1982):393–412; Jack Bielasiak, "Elite Studies and Communist Studies," in Ronald H. Linden and Bert A. Rockman, eds., *Elite Studies and Communist Politics: Essays in Memory of Carl Beck* (Pittsburgh: University of Pittsburgh Press, 1984), pp. 103–24; A. Giddons, "Elites and the British Class Structure," in P. C. Stanworth and A. Giddons, eds., *Elites and Power in British Society* (Cambridge: Cambridge University Press, 1974), p. 4; Paolo Zannoni, "The Concept of Elite," *European Journal of Research*, no. 6 (1978):1–30; Jerzy J. Wiatr, "Political Elites and Political Leadership: Problems and Selected Hypotheses for Comparative Research," *Indian Journal of Political Science*, no. 7 (1973): 139; Harold D. Lasswell, Daniel Lerner, and E. Easton Rothwell, *The Comparative Study Of Elites: An Introduction and Bibliography* (Stanford, CA: Stanford University Press, 1952).

6. For example, Bohdan Harasymiw, *Political Elite Recruitment in the Soviet Union* (London: Macmillan Press, 1984), p. 11; Mervyn Matthews agrees: "The upper layers of the *nomenklatura*, particularly at the level of the All-Union and Republic CCs, could themselves serve as an excellent basis for delineating the elite in the USSR. . . . The Soviet elite is virtually state-registered." *Privilege in the Soviet Union: A Study of Elite Life-Styles under Communism* (London: Allen & Unwin,

1978), p. 34; T. B. Bottomore, *Elites and Society* (New York: Basic Books, 1965), p. 37.

7. Seweryn Bialer maintained that the Central Committee *is* the elite: "How Russians Rule Russia," *Problems of Communism* 13, no. 5 (September-October 1964):48–51.

8. E. H. Suleiman posits a similar concept when he refers to "state-created elites." E. H. Suleiman, *Elites in French Society: The Politics of Survival* (Princeton, NJ: Princeton University Press, 1978).

9. Valerie Bunce, "Of Power, Policy, and Paradigms: The Logic of Elite Studies," in Ronald H. Linden and Bert A. Rockman, eds., *Elite Studies and Communist Politics: Essays in Memory of Carl Beck* (Pittsburgh: University of Pittsburgh Press, 1984), p. 22.

10. Theda Skocpol, *States and Social Revolutions* (Cambridge: Cambridge University Press, 1979), p. 18.

11. David McLellan, *Marxism after Marx: An Introduction* (New York: Harper & Row, 1979), p. 298. As will be seen below, this is not a statement with which Weber could agree.

12. Louis Althusser, *Lenin and Philosophy, and Other Essays* (London: New Left Books, 1971), p. 170.

13. Richard M. Merelman, "On Culture and Politics in America: A Perspective from Structural Anthropology," *British Journal of Political Science* 19, no. 4 (October 1989): 477.

14. George M. Foster, "Peasant Society and the Image of Limited Good," *American Anthropologist*, no. 65 (April 1965):293–315.

15. Literally "who-whom?" The sense of it is "who is hurting, backstabbing, doublecrossing, whom?"

16. Leon Trotsky, *Literature and Revolution* (New York: International Publishers, 1925, but Ann Arbor, MI, 1960), p. 94.

17. Boris Pilniak, *The Naked Year* (Ann Arbor, MI: Ardi, 1975).

18. Nicholas Vakar, *The Taproot of Soviet Society* (New York: Harper & Brothers, 1961), p. 16.

19. Stephen R. Burant, "The Influence of Russian Tradition on the Political Style of the Soviet Elite," *Political Science Quarterly* 102, no. 2 (Summer 1987):273–93.

20. Marshall Shatz, "Stalin, the Great Purge, and Russian History: A New Look at the 'New Class,' " *Carl Beck Papers in Russian and East European Studies* (University of Pittsburgh), Paper no. 305 (1984).

21. Robert C. Tucker, *Political Culture and Leadership in Soviet Russia: From Lenin to Gorbachev* (New York: W. W. Norton, 1987), p. 95.

22. A fascinating study in the reconstruction of *mentalités* is Giulia Calvi, *Histories of a Plague Year: The Social and the Imaginary in Baroque Florence*, trans. Dario Biocca and Bryant T. Ragan, Jr. (Berkeley: University of California Press, 1989).

23. Claude Levi-Strauss, *Structural Anthropology* (New York: Basic Books, 1963), p. 281.

24. Rakhahari Chatterji, "Structural Concepts in Aristotle's Politics," *Indian Journal of Political Science* 34, no. 1 (January-March 1973):81.

25. Kenneth Jowitt, *The Leninist Response to National Dependency* (Berkeley: Institute of International Studies, University of California, 1978), pp. 69–70.

26. Alexander Zinoviev, *The Reality of Communism* (New York: Schocken Books, 1984), p. 113.

27. Adolf Portmann, *Das Tier als soziales Wesen* (Zurich, 1953), p. 252. Cited by Hannah Arendt, *The Life of the Mind* (San Diego: Harcourt Brace Jovanovich, 1978), p. 27.

28. Ibid., pp. 27–28.

29. John Armstrong argues similarly that "utilizing these conceptual approaches [conflict models], one does not seek to explain the adoption or persistence of a structure by reference to its (essential) functional position in the total society, but by its utility to a specific societal segment." *The European Administrative Elite* (Princeton, NJ: Princeton University Press, 1972), p. 8.

30. Theda Skocpol, "Bringing the State Back In: Strategies of Analysis in Current Research," in Peter B. Evans, Dietrich Rueschmeyer, and Theda Skocpol, eds., *Bringing the State Back In* (Cambridge: Cambridge University Press, 1985), pp. 5–7.

31. See, for example, Martin Carnoy, *The State and Political Theory* (Princeton, NJ: Princeton University Press, 1984); Fred Block, "The Ruling Class Does Not Rule," *Socialist Revolution* 7, no. 3 (1977):6–28; Bob Jessup, *Theories of the State* (New York: New York University Press, 1983); Goran Therborn, *What Does the Ruling Class Do When It Rules? State Apparatuses and State Power under Feudalism, Capitalism, and Socialism* (London: New Left Books, 1978).

32. William Doyle, *The Old European Order, 1660–1800* (London: Oxford University Press, 1978), p. 222.

33. Theda Skocpol, *States and Social Revolution* (Cambridge: Cambridge University Press, 1979), p. 29.

34. An exception, however, is Sheila Fitzpatrick, "The Bolsheviks' Dilemma: Class, Culture, and Politics in the Early Soviet Years," *Slavic Review* 47, no. 2 (Winter 1988):599–613. Also see in the same issue Ronald Grigor Suny, "Class and State in the Early Soviet Period: A Reply to Sheila Fitzpatrick," pp. 614–19.

35. John A. Hall and G. John Ikenberry, *The State* (Minneapolis: University of Minnesota Press, 1989), p. 12.

36. I will deal in detail with the question of whether the Party is a ruling class in Chapter 5.

37. Neil Harding, in "Conclusion" in *The State in Socialist Society* (Albany: State University of New York Press, 1984), p. 304.

38. Franz Borkenau, *Pareto* (New York: John Wiley, 1936), p. 11.

39. Vilfredo Pareto, *The Mind and Society*, ed. Arthur Livingston (London: Jonathan Cape, 1935), editor's footnote on p. 519.

40. Ibid., p. 1515.

41. Pareto's major work is *The Mind and Society*, 4 vols. (New York: Harcourt Brace & World, 1935); this is an English translation of *Trattoro di Sociologia Generale*, first published in 1915–1919. Also see Vilfredo Pareto, *Sociological Writings*, ed. S. E. Finer (New York: Praeger, 1966); and Vilfredo Pareto, *The Rise and Fall of the Elites: An Application of Theoretical Sociology* (Totowa, NJ: Bedminster Press, 1968). Good secondary studies include Norberto Bobbio, *On Mosca and Pareto* (Geneva: Droz, 1972); Franz Borkenau, *Pareto*; Morris Ginsberg, "The Sociology of Pareto," in Morris Ginsberg, ed., *Reason and Unreason in Society*

(Cambridge: Harvard University Press, 1948); Ferdinand Kolegar, "The Elite and the Ruling Class: Pareto and Mosca Re-examined," *Review of Politics* 29 (1967):354–69; Robert A. Nye, *The Anti-democratic Sources of Elite Theory: Pareto, Mosca, Michels* (Beverly Hills, CA: Sage Publications, 1977); Alan Zuckerman, "The Concept Political Elite: Lessons from Mosca and Pareto," *Journal of Politics* 39 (1977):324–44; and S. E. Finer, "Pareto and Pluto-Democracy: The Retreat to Galapagos," *American Political Science Review* 62, no. 2 (June 1968):440–50.

42. Mosca's major work is *The Ruling Class*. Secondary works, in addition to those on both Mosca and Pareto cited above, include Ettori A. Albertoni, *Mosca and the Theory of Elitism* (Oxford: Basil Blackwell, 1987); H. Stuart Hughes, "Gaetano Mosca and the Political Lessons of History," in H. Stuart Hughes with Myron P. Gilmore and Edwin C. Rozwenc, eds., *Teachers of History: Essays in Honor of Laurence Bradford Packard* (Ithaca, NY: Cornell University Press, 1954), pp. 146–67; Fritz Morstein-Marx, "The Bureaucratic State: Some Remarks on Mosca's Ruling Class," *Review of Politics* 1 (October 1939):457–72; James H. Meisel, *The Myth of the Ruling Class: Gaetano Mosca and the "Elite"* (Ann Arbor: University of Michigan Press, 1958); James H. Meisel, ed., *Pareto and Mosca* (Englewood Cliffs, NJ: Prentice-Hall, 1965); Renzo Sereno, "The Anti-Aristotelianism of Gaetano Mosca and Its Fate," *Ethics* 48, no. 4 (July 1938); Renzo Sereno, "Note on Gaetano Mosca," *American Political Science Review* 46, no. 2 (June 1952).

43. See, for example, Arthur Mitzman, *The Iron Cage: An Historical Interpretation of Max Weber* (New York: Knopf, 1970), p. 291.

44. Marianne Weber, *Max Weber: A Biography*, trans. and ed. Harry Zohn (New York: John Wiley, 1975), p. 189.

45. Randall Collins, *Max Weber: A Skeleton Key* (Beverly Hills, CA: Sage Publications, 1986), pp. 18–20.

46. Martin Green, *The von Richthofen Sisters: The Triumphant and the Tragic Modes of Love* (New York: Basic Books, 1974), p. 170 and passim. After Marianne Weber's death in 1954, Else Jaffe turned Weber's letters, confirming Weber's great love for her, over to Professor Eduard Baumgarten for publication: Eduard Baumgarten, *Max Weber: Werk und Person* (Tübingen: J.C.B. Mohr, 1964).

47. Weber's most important works in English translation include *The Protestant Ethic and the Spirit of Capitalism*, trans. Talcott Parsons (New York: Charles Scribner's Sons, 1958); *The City*, trans. Don Martindale and Gertrud Neuwirth (New York: Free Press, 1958); *Ancient Judaism*, trans. Hans H. Gerth and Don Martindale (New York: Free Press, 1952); *The Agrarian Sociology of Ancient Civilizations*, trans. R. I. Frank (Atlantic Highlands, NJ: Humanities Press, 1976); *The Methodology of the Social Sciences*, trans. Edward A. Shils and Henry A. Finch (Glencoe, IL: Free Press, 1949); *Roscher and Knies: The Logical Problems of Historical Economics*, trans. Guy Oakes (New York: Free Press, 1975); *The Theory of Social and Economic Organization*, trans. A. M. Henderson and Talcott Parsons (New York: Oxford University Press, 1947); *Economy and Society: An Outline of Interpretive Sociology*, ed. Guenther Ross and Claus Wittich, 2 vols. (Berkeley: University of California Press, 1978); the latter contains some of the other cited works. There are several anthologies containing excerpts from Weber's work; the most useful is *From Max Weber: Essays in Sociology*, ed. H. H. Gerth and C. Wright Mills (New York: Oxford University Press, 1971). There are hundreds of secondary works

on Weber; accessible and useful are Reinhard Bendix, *Max Weber: An Intellectual Portrait* (Garden City, NY: Doubleday, 1960); Dennis Wrong, ed., *Max Weber* (Englewood Cliffs, NJ: Prentice-Hall, 1970); Frank Parkin, *Max Weber* (Chichester, England: Ellis Horwood, 1982); Dirk Kasler, *Max Weber: An Introduction to His Life and Work*, trans. Philippa Hurd (Chicago: University of Chicago Press, 1988).

48. Weber discusses the *Verstehen* method in *The Theory of Social and Economic Organization*, pp. 88–105.

49. Ibid., p. 91.

50. Ibid., p. 92.

51. Ibid., p. 96.

52. Ibid., pp. 111–12.

53. Weber, *Economy and Society*, vol. 2, pp. 956–58.

54. Ibid., p. 954.

55. Ibid., pp. 942–43.

56. Jacob P. Mayer, *Prophet of the Mass Age: A Study of Alexis de Tocqueville*, trans. M. M. Bozman and C. Hahn (London: J. M. Dent & Sons, 1939).

57. A useful and well-documented review of the debates over Tocqueville's contemporary relevance is in Whitney Pope, *Alexis de Tocqueville: His Social and Political Theory* (Beverly Hills, CA: Sage Publications, 1986), pp. 11–17.

58. T. A. Tilton, "Alexis de Tocqueville and the Political Sociology of Liberalism," *Comparative Social Research* 2 (1979):284–85.

59. R. A. Nisbet, "Alexis de Tocqueville," in D. L. Sills, ed., *International Encyclopedia of the Social Sciences*, vol. 16 (New York: Macmillan and Free Press, 1968), p. 93.

60. J. P. Mayer, *Alexis de Tocqueville: A Biographical Study in Political Science* (New York: Harper & Brothers, 1960), p. 3. This is a reprint of *The Prophet of the Mass Age*.

61. Irving M. Zeitlin, *Liberty, Equality, and Revolution in Alexis de Tocqueville* (Boston: Little, Brown, 1971), p. 2. The discrepancy lies in the earlier sources on which these scholars rely: Zeitman relies mainly on George Wilson Pierson, *Tocqueville and Beaumont in America* (New York: Oxford University Press, 1938), although, oddly, he cites Mayer on the same page. Mayer's principle source is Antoine Redier, *Comme Disait M. de Tocqueville* (Paris: Perrin, 1925).

62. Quoted in Zeitlin, *Liberty, Equality, and Revolution*, p. 5.

63. Alexis de Tocqueville, *Democracy in America*, ed. J. P. Mayer and Max Lerner, trans. George Lawrence (New York: Harper & Row, 1966); *The Old Regime and the French Revolution*, trans. Stuart Gilbert (Garden City, NY: Doubleday, 1955). Other important works by Tocqueville include *The European Revolution and Correspondence with Gobineau*, trans. and ed. John Lukacs (Garden City, NY: Doubleday, 1959); *The Recollections of Alexis de Tocqueville* ed. J. P. Mayer, trans. Alexander Teixeira de Mattos (New York: Meridian Books, 1959); a useful short collection of excerpts is *Alexis de Tocqueville on Democracy, Revolution, and Society*, ed. John Stone and Stephen Mennell (Chicago: University of Chicago Press, 1980); the complete works in French are in *Oeuvres Complètes*, ed. J. P. Mayer (Paris: Gallimard, 1951).

64. Talcott C. Parsons, "The Sociological Tradition," *American Sociological Review* 32 (1967):641.

65. John Stuart Mill, *A System of Logic, Ratiocinative and Inductive*, ed. J. M. Robson (Toronto: University of Toronto Press, 1974).

66. Tocqueville, *The Old Regime*, pp. 253–54.

67. Pope, in *Alexis de Tocqueville*, pp. 32–43, provides a thorough discussion of Tocqueville's incisive use of the comparative method.

68. Ibid., pp. 52–76.

69. Carl Beck, William A. Jarzabek, and Paul H. Ernandez, *Political Succession in Eastern Europe: Fourteen Case Studies* (Pittsburgh: University Center for International Studies, University of Pittsburgh, 1976), p. 35.

70. Karl Mannheim, *Ideology and Utopia: An Introduction to the Sociology of Knowledge* (New York: Harcourt, Brace & Co., 1954); Norman Ryder, "The Age Cohort as a Concept in the Study of Social Change," *American Sociological Review* 30, no. 4 (November 1965):843–61; Ronald Inglehart, "The Silent Revolution in Europe: Intergenerational Change in Post-industrial Society," *American Political Science Review* 65, no. 4 (December 1971):991–1017.

71. Lawrence Stone, "Prosopography," *Daedalus* 93, no. 4 (Winter 1971):46–79.

Chapter 2

Educating the Elite

Nam et ipsa scientia potestas est.

Francis Bacon

It has been said that to know who is educated is to know who will rule. Of all the characteristics that differentiate a political elite from the masses, the possession of higher education is the most consistently predictable one; indeed, it is a nearly universal characteristic of the ruling stratum, both geographically and temporally. Imperial China did not differ from any present-day state in this respect. The percentage of national political elites possessing higher education in 1970 ranged from 88 percent in the United States and the USSR to between 60 percent and 76 percent in Western Europe, whereas the percentage of their respective populations with higher education was less than 5 percent everywhere except in the United States, where it was 11 percent.[1]

This relationship between education and elite status has held true throughout modern history (the last three centuries) and of course was true not only in China but in the young American republic, as well as the Russian Empire. It is even more pronounced in underdeveloped countries.

The relationship between education and elite status is complicated by the relationship of social class to both. Gaetano Mosca notes well that even a putatively "open" elite may in fact be closed if there are class, gender, and national or other inequalities in access to higher education.[2]

Due to Soviet efforts to manipulate *both* access to education and entry to the elite on a class basis in the 1920s, the Soviet experience diverged for a time from this historical trend, but as shall become clear below, it very soon mirrored this virtually universal tendency once again.

In some societies the relationship among high school status, access to higher education, and entry into the elite is so marked that specific educational institutions have come to serve the purpose of training the elite for rule. This includes Great Britain's "Oxbridge," the French *grandes ecoles*, Germany's *Juristenmonopol*, Mexico City's National University, Tokyo University in Japan, and, though the relationship is less marked, the American Ivy League schools.[3]

By contrast, there are no schools in the Soviet Union that have a monopoly on training future elites, except, of course, the system of Party schools. However, most graduates of the Party schools do not enter the central- or even the middle-level elite. I shall argue in Chapter 6 that in most cases, a Party education is remedial in nature, of low prestige, and a handicap to political mobility. The Soviet elite are for the most part trained in technical institutes and universities, of the former of which there are hundreds, most having only one alumnus among the central elite, and few having more than three or four. (Table 2.8, later in this chapter, gives a list of the higher-education institutions that contributed the largest number of graduates [six or more] to the database of members of the post-Stalin central elite.)

In this chapter, after a brief discussion of the structure of contemporary Soviet higher education, I will examine from a historical standpoint first the development of non-Party, mainly technical, education from 1917 to the present, and second, the development of Party education in the same time period. I will conclude with a profile of the educational characteristics of the contemporary elite.

THE STRUCTURE OF SOVIET HIGHER EDUCATION

Soviet higher-education institutions are commonly referred to as VUZy (the acronym for *vysshie uchebnie zavedanii*, VUZ in the singular). The administration and supervision of the Soviet Union's VUZy lies with the central USSR Ministry of Higher and Secondary Specialized Education (*Ministerstvo vysshego i srednego spetsial'nogo obrazovaniia SSSR*), frequently shortened to *MinVUZ*; the minister in 1988 was Gennady A. Yagodin. Authority extends downward from *MinVUZ* to corresponding ministries in each of the 15 Union Republics, and from there to the higher-education institutions themselves.

MinVUZ directly administers only 351 of the Soviet Union's 828 VUZy.[4] The Ministry of Education (*Ministerstvo prosveshcheniia*, often translated "the Ministry of Enlightenment") administers 176. Other

USSR and union republic ministries administer schools that fall within their substantive jurisdiction: the Ministry of Agriculture administers 99; Health, 81; and Culture, 51. The remaining 70 VUZy are administered by various ministries and state committees.[5] Most educational institutions also come under the authority of the USSR State Planning Committee (*Gosplan*), exercised through the state planning committees of the union republics.

There is a system of Party supervision as well, with authority extending from the Science and Educational Institutions Department of the CPSU Central Committee—the department chief in 1988 was Valentin A. Grigor'ev—through similar departments in republican Central Committees, down to Party committees within the educational institutions themselves.

There are four types of VUZy in the Soviet Union today:

1. *Universities*. Universities offer a wide range of courses, with specializations similar to those available in Western universities, and which enjoy considerable prestige; the term of study ranges from four to five years, depending on specialization. In 1983 there were 67 universities, with a total enrollment of 339,739 students, and an additional 230,890 enrolled in correspondence and evening division courses.[6]

2. *Institutes*. Institutes train individuals in very narrow specializations, with few electives and, except for the social sciences,[7] very little in the way of liberal arts. The term of study ranges from four to six years, depending on the specialization. In 1981 there were 816 institutes.[8]

3. *Military institutes and academies*. Some of these, such as the General Staff Academy, accept only military officers, whereas others accept civilians preparing for military careers. By no means do all graduates of military academies pursue military careers. Thirty-one members of the database attended military schools but did not pursue a military career. There were 22 military schools in 1959–60.[9]

4. *Party and government schools*. Party schools continue a tradition that dates from before the revolution, training and retraining full-time Party apparatus workers at all levels. There are a variety of state schools operated by various agencies, such as the Higher School of the Trade Union Movement and the Ministry of Foreign Affairs' Higher Diplomatic School.

Evaluation of student work takes the form of periodic course "tests" (quizzes, exams, and papers), final exams in courses, a supervised diploma project (which will culminate in a lengthy paper), and state exams at the end. Upon graduation from the VUZ, students are awarded a *diplom* (diploma) along with a certificate of qualification in the specialization, specifying a job title according to the classification system discussed below. Available in most VUZy is graduate work (called *aspirantura*), the successful completion of which requires a dissertation and leads to the award of the Candidate of Sciences degree (so called in all specializations), approximately the equivalent of the Western Ph.D. The title "Doctor" (*doktor*) is not usually awarded until later in the individual's career, and it requires the publication of substantial and high-quality research work.

The total number of students enrolled in VUZy (excluding military and Party schools) in the 1981–82 academic year was 5,284,000.[10] Forty-three percent of enrollments were part time, evening, or correspondence.[11]

The curricula in Soviet VUZys are carefully and rigorously specified, leaving the student little (though some) latitude for elective courses. *MinVUZ* has developed a comprehensive classification of specializations, which changes periodically. At the time of Josef Stalin's death, there were approximately 900 narrow specializations. By 1954 it was decided these were too narrowly defined, and a new classification was promulgated containing 274 specializations.[12] In 1956–57 the classification was again revised, producing 356 specializations, this time introducing a comprehensive decimal classification code to delineate subspecializations.[13] By 1979 there were 449 specializations.[14]

Soviet pedagogical theorists are very precise in their specification of not only the content of curricula but also the precise proportion of time to be spent in each area, as this quote from the *Bol'shaia sovetskaia entsiklopediia* shows:

In the mathematics specialization 42.3% of the time planned for classes is taken up by lectures, 13.3% by laboratory work, 22.6% by practical work, and 11.3% by seminars. In...engineering, the corresponding figures are 31.6%, 17.6%, 45.9%, and 4.9%; in law the corresponding figures are 44.4%, 9.3%, 34.4%, and 11.6%.[15]

The student workload is very heavy. Four thousand instruction hours are scheduled for the arts, 5,000 for the sciences, in addition to practical work and study outside of class. Students devote 8–11 hours per day to classroom work and study.[16] In addition, there are military training and obligatory Komsomol activities. Social activities and recreation have to be fitted into the interstices.

A constant in the curriculum of every VUZ is social science. During the Stalin era, "Fundamentals of Marxism" (for which the required text was Stalin's awful *History of the VKP(b): Short Course*) was required. Under Khrushchev, the requirements were revised, and a course on dialectical and historical materialism was added. Stalin's text was dropped and replaced by *History of the CPSU*, which has been retained but subsequently revised several times to fit the version of history preferred by the current leadership. In June 1963 another new course, "Scientific Communism," was added. Each regime has tinkered with and worried over the social sciences curriculum in VUZy.[17]

The breakdown of the curriculum in subdisciplines for engineering technical specializations in 1970 was as follows:[18]

Social sciences and economics	11.8%
General science	26.1%
General engineering	28%
Special courses (the "major")	24%
Physical education and sports	3.1%
Electives	2.5%

Throughout the Brezhnev period, the distribution of VUZ students among specializations has been quite stable. The reason for this stability is that the distribution reflects not so much student choices as the decisions of central planners in *Gosplan* and the ministries, including *MinVUZ*. After extensive consultation with the administrative apparatus to determine the needs for specialists, quotas are established for each specialization and communicated to the VUZy. The authorities also manipulate entrance requirements to affect the profile of enrollments by specialization; if fewer students than required are enrolling in a particular specialization, entrance qualifications for that specialization are lowered in VUZy that offer it.[19] Presumably, then, the brightest students will have the greatest degree of choice with respect to their specialization; marginal students take what they can get. According to Mervyn Matthews, "An analysis of 4,000 Leningrad engineering students in the mid-1960s showed: while 45% said they entered a VUZ out of interest in the subject matter, 62.2% entered a VUZ just to get a higher education—presumably *any* higher education—11.4% were prompted by the desire to improve their material position."[20]

Indeed, it is difficult to see how any 18-year-old could have very ardent an interest in Specialty No. 0905, Technology of Wood Flakes and Plastics, or have a genuine motivation to get into the Leningrad Refrigeration Institute.[21] Although I do not have data on the question, it is reasonable to wonder whether the less attractive specializations get marginal students who have little effective choice, resulting systematically in less competent specialists in some areas. It would not be the only dysfunctional side effect of the Soviet passion for planning and predictability.

HIGHER EDUCATION UNDER *NARKOMPROS*

The tsarist higher-education system enjoyed considerable world prestige. This applied not only to the traditional humanistic and literary-oriented universities, but to the technical and engineering schools that were being opened before and after the turn of the twentieth century.

Undoubtedly the best of the tsarist engineering schools was the Petersburg Polytechnical Institute. It had exceptionally modern facilities for its time. Its entrance requirements were very high—its division of shipbuilding, for example, accepted only students with a gold medal from the *gymnasium* (secondary school). Two members of the shipbuilding division, A. N. Krylov and I. G. Bubnov, published books on shipbuilding that were translated and used in all the navies of the pre–World War I world.[22] Russia was in a leading world position in railroad transport engineering at the time of the revolution. After the revolution, a number of such engineers came to the United States and contributed to the development here of new types of locomotives.[23] By 1917 Russian higher technical institutes had graduated around 15,000 engineers.[24]

The Russian Empire (within its present-day boundaries) had 105 institutions of higher learning, about half of them private. Figures on enrollment vary. Alexander Korol cites 117,000 students in the 1913–14 academic year, or about 8.3 persons per 10,000 total population.[25] Mervyn Matthews cites a higher figure of 127,000 for the same year,[26] and *Bol'shaia sovetskaia entsiklopediia* gives 127,400 for the 1914–15 academic year.[27]

Unfortunately, tsarist higher education (like secondary education) was elitist in nature. I. I. Khodorovsky, a member of the Soviet government's Commissariat of Enlightenment (*Narkompros*) wrote that the tsar's minister of enlightenment (he could not refrain from interjecting that it was not a Ministry of Enlightenment but a ministry of keeping people in the dark) had said that the tsar's government would never admit "cook's children" (*kukharkinye deti*) to higher education, and that by "cook's children" he of course meant the children of workers and peasants. With a somewhat less than original phrase, Khodorovsky quips that under the tsar "you might say it would be easier for a camel to pass through a needle's eye, than for a peasant or a worker to get a higher education."[28]

Although the tsarist education system was indeed sharply elitist, some progress toward democratization was being made in the last years of the empire. According to Nicholas Hans, 36 percent of university students in 1914 were from the aristocracy and civil-service origins, 39 percent from the middle class, petty bourgeoisie, and working class, and 14 percent from the villages.[29] It is regrettable that Hans does not specify a percentage for the working class alone, but its inclusion in the large figure of 39 percent, as well as 14 percent for the villages (which must include many peasant children) belies Khodorovsky's implication that these classes were completely excluded. If Khodorovsky's reference is to the last tsarist minister of enlightenment, Count P. Ignat'ev, then the aspersion is unfair as well as incorrect, since Ignat'ev in 1915–16 sponsored a comprehensive school reform and modernization plan that envisaged wider access.[30]

There was no fully developed Marxist theory of education. The Bolshevik Party program of 1919 set the Party's educational policy in terms very general, but still to the point: education was to be transformed "from the weapon of bourgeois class domination into a weapon for the total destruction of class divisions within society, into a weapon for the Communist regeneration of society."[31]

Lenin's wife, Nadezhda Krupskaia, had made some effort to formulate an educational program for the Bolshevik Party. Her program, influenced by progressive educational theorists in the West, emphasized a unified school system with compulsory attendance, elimination of obstacles to access to education, and encouragement of the full development of the child's personality.

There is, as will be seen, a sharp dividing line between Soviet educational policies during the NEP, New Economic Policy (1922–1927), and those after 1928. The latter date, of course, corresponds to Stalin's victory over the Right Opposition, his consolidation of his personal dictatorship, and the beginning of the policies that came to be known as the cultural revolution.

In the new government he constructed after the October revolution, Lenin included a People's Commissariat of Enlightenment (*narodnyi komissariat prosveshcheniia*, virtually universally referred to, then as now, as *Narkompros*).[32] As RSFSR commissar, he appointed the widely respected literary and cultural figure Anatolii Lunacharsky; Krupskaia and Ivan Khodorovsky were also appointed to *Narkompros*. By a decree of the Council of People's Commissars (*Sovnarkom*), signed by Lenin and issued December 11, 1917, all educational institutions in the country were transferred to the jurisdiction of *Narkompros*.

Most of the priorities and strategies of *Narkompros* would be recognizable and quite congenial to progressive educational theorists in democratic countries today. Much of *Narkompros*'s orientation to education was in reaction to the faults of the tsarist system. In the Bolshevik view, in addition to the problem of elitism discussed above, tsarist educational practices had been formalistic, authoritarian, and intellectually stultifying.

Under Lunacharsky, *Narkompros*'s first priority was equality of access to education—so called, though in practice efforts were made to give preferential treatment to workers and peasants.

In reaction to the perceived scholasticism and classical orientation of education under the old regime, *Narkompros*'s second emphasis was on relevance—and relevance particularly to industrial production.[33] The key concept here, almost a shibboleth, was "polytechnical" training. The spirit of polytechnical training was to give students broad grounding in the principles of science and technology, rather than a narrow vocationalism.[34]

New universities were opened in 1918 in Nizhnyi Novgorod (now Gor'ky), Dnepropetrovsk, Voronezh, Irkutsk, Tbilisi, Tashkent, Baku, Erevan, Sverdlovsk, Minsk, and other cities. In August of the same year, on Lenin's initiative, a Bolshevik decree proclaimed open admission to Soviet VUZy for all Soviet citizens over 16 without regard to nationality or sex, and without the encumbrance of entrance examinations. It was understood that working-class and peasant admissions were to be encouraged, and those of former capitalist and bourgeois elements discouraged, although this was not admitted until later. In any event, these people had been deprived of civil rights by the 1918 Constitution. The regime had no choice but to retain the old tsarist professors in the VUZy, after dismissing those who were most openly and avowedly anti-Bolshevik. In the spirit of egalitarianism, academic ranks in the VUZy were abolished.

The result of open admissions was predictable enough. The higher-education institutions were flooded with a mass of applications from persons who were simply not qualified to pursue higher education, and who in some cases were barely literate. To deal with this situation, the institution of "workers' faculties" (*rabochie fakul'tety*, or more commonly, *rabfaki*) was created in February 1919. The *rabfak* was a remedial school for factory workers; its goal was to provide them with the minimal knowledge necessary to allow them to enter the VUZy for higher education. They were established at existing VUZy, and the teachers were for the most part VUZ professors. Entrance requirements were nominal: entrants were required to have basic literacy (writing ability) and familiarity with basic arithmetic.[35] The term of instruction was three to four years.

The *rabfaki* were extremely popular with the workers and had strong support within the Party. *Narkompros* was less enchanted with them, since preferential treatment was given to *rabfak* graduates in admissions to VUZy over graduates of *Narkompros*'s general secondary schools, even though the qualifications of the secondary school graduates were higher. Preferential admissions also violated the ethos of equality that pervaded *Narkompros*.[36] Lenin, too, was hostile to the idea of what he called caste schools, though he tolerated the *rabfaki*,[37] probably because of their immense popularity.

Not surprisingly, students of the general secondary schools were hostile to the *rabfakovtsy*, as *rabfak* students and graduates were called, because they hindered their own prospects for admission to higher education. An interesting exchange took place in the press on this question. Using the pseudonym "Professor," someone had published an article in issue 1 of the journal *Novaia Rossiia*, urging that the "fratricidal war" between *rabfakovtsy* and regular VUZ students be ended; that these two groups would find much in common were they to fraternize. His article dripping with sarcasm, a Mikhail Korbut of Kazan responded in the pages of the official *rabfak* magazine:

Inasmuch as the majority of higher-school students, especially in the senior classes, belong to the bourgeois and petty bourgeois classes, the struggle taking place between the regular students and the *rabfakovtsy* is a class struggle, the struggle of "two worlds,"...and the real basis of this struggle, as "Professor" strangely fails to see from the heights of his lectern, is the class contradictions between the bourgeoisie (and those who share its ideology) and the proletariat, taking place within the walls of the higher school.[38]

By the year 1927, there were 122 *rabfaki*, enrolling 48,000 students, the vast majority of whom were workers and peasants. It can probably be assumed that most of the *rabfak* teachers did not serve voluntarily and had a low opinion of the *rabfakovtsy*. Consider this excerpt from the letter of a certain Matveev, a *rabfak* student and employee of the Podol'sk Mechanical Plant, to the *Narkompros* official journal:

In one class, a *batrak* [poor peasant] gave an incorrect answer to the teacher's question. The teacher asked, "And just who might you be?" ["Kto ty takoi?" using the condescending familiar form of "you"]. The lad answered, "I am a *batrak*." The teacher said, "What fool sent *you* to the *rabfak*?"[39]

As a further measure to augment proletarian admissions into VUZy, a system of quotas (*razverstka*) was established, whereby official organizations (the Party, the trade unions, the Komsomol [the Communist League of Youth], the *rabfaki* themselves, and others) could nominate a certain number of students for VUZ entry on the understanding that they were of worker or peasant origin. A small percentage of openings was left for nonfavored classes, who alone were also required to pay tuition. In Table 2.1, showing percentages of accepted applications to VUZy broken down by the source of applications for the 1924–25 academic year, it can be assumed that nonfavored classes make up most, if not all, of the "not nominated" category.

Thus, out of 6,810 applications from *rabfakovtsy*, only 190, or 2.8 percent, were turned down. Acceptance rates for *rabfakovtsy* ranged from 88.3 percent to 99.4 percent (88.3 percent is for arts; the remainder is above 94 percent). Acceptance rates for applicants nominated by Party and state organizations ranged from 51.3 percent to 86.7 percent, whereas those for unnominated applications ranged from 12.4 percent to 46.3 percent. The Bolsheviks' educational priorities emerge very clearly from these figures.

The 1924–25 academic year—in many ways, from the regime's point of view at least, *Narkompros*'s best—showed dramatic improvement. In

Table 2.1
Percentage of Applications Accepted, 1924–25

VUZ Type	Type of Nomination		
	I	II	III
Pedagogical	94.8	70.7	32.0
Industrial	97.0	57.6	16.3
Agricultural	98.4	66.9	26.9
Economic	99.4	86.7	26.6
Medical	98.8	74.3	12.4
Arts	88.3	51.3	32.2
University	96.8	77.2	46.3
Total	97.2	69.5	29.0

I: *Rabfak* graduates
II: Nominated by an organization
III: Not nominated

Source: Adapted from *Narodnoe prosveshchenie*, No. 11-12, 1924.

the RSFSR the combined proletarian and peasant component of the enrollment climbed from 24.2 percent in 1923 to 49.6 percent; the proportion of Party and Komsomol members in the student body rose from 26.9 percent to 48.8 percent.[40]

It cannot really be argued convincingly, however, that these priorities were consistently met in the 1920s. After the initial increase in the worker composition of first-year admissions, that fluctuated, and the proportion of workers in the student body increased only modestly. Peasant gains were even more unremarkable. Although first-year admissions of students in the "employee" category were indeed cut sharply at first, this is the only category whose proportion of the student body consistently increased. The category "other" can be presumed to include "undesirable" classes; although their proportion of the student body steadily declined, their proportion of first-year admissions increased.[41] The explanation for the anomalous relationship between admissions and composition of the student body probably lies in the series of student purges in the 1920s, discussed below.

These figures, like all data pertaining to social class in Soviet literature, have to be accepted with some caution. The three categories of worker, peasant, and employee, with "other" referring to bourgeoisie (arranged from most desirable to least), were artificial and derived from ideology rather than empirically. Almost certainly, students and others misrepresented their social origins if they could. The slightest excuse for calling oneself a worker was seized, and so school authorities were faced with the necessity of clarifying criteria for class membership. In 1925, and again in 1928, the Central Committee published guidelines on the determination of social status. In particular, a "worker" (*rabochii*) was a person engaged in manual hired labor, *without owning any of the means of production*. A "peasant" (*krest'ianin*) and "employee" (*sluzhashchii*) were similarly defined. All others were classified as "other" (*prochii*).[42]

Other schools were also opened for workers and peasants, though for the purpose of raising their production skills rather than to prepare them for admission to VUZy. Among these were factory apprenticeship schools (*shkoly fabrichno-zavodskogo uchenichestva*, or FZU). Teachers came to the factory and spent several hours with the workers every day for two years; the third and fourth year were spent in practical supervisory work in the plant. In 1925, there were 100,000 students participating.[43]

There were also "Schools for Peasant Youth" (*Shkoly krest'ianskoi molodezhi*, or simply ShKM). The ShKM were created as Komsomol initiative toward the middle of the NEP period; *Narkompros* had the same objection to ShKM as it did to the FZU: they were "caste" schools training peasant and worker youth to follow the occupations of their fathers. The schools were of low quality and did little to channel peasants into higher education. According to James McClelland, at middecade it was 28 times as likely for a student from a nonmanual family to attend a VUZ than for a peasant, and five and one-half times more likely for a worker than for a peasant.[44] McClelland's principal purpose in this article is to refute, not quite convincingly in my view, the widely accepted belief among Western scholars that *Narkompros* had failed to proletarianize the student body in the 1920s, just as Stalin and others maintained. Graduates of ShKM were eligible to enter the *rabfaki* but, according to Sheila Fitzpatrick, in fact most of them attended agricultural or pedagogical technicums (the latter refers to secondary schools, not higher schools) or took white-collar jobs in the countryside. Thus, it was a "small but effective channel for the promotion of peasant youth into white collar and professional employment."[45]

Ever concerned about preparing cadres for production work, the Central Committee in late 1924 gave its backing to a *Sovnarkom* resolution of May 23, 1923, requiring bringing VUZ and other students closer to the production process.[46] This meant placing students directly into production practice in factories. Industry was subsequently required to find "places" for VUZ students in factories. There were 7,694 "places" found in Moscow in 1924, and 2,901 in Leningrad.[47] Later, production practice evolved into the student diploma project in most VUZy and VTUZy (VTUZy referred to higher technical education institutions).[48]

Among all the categories of students discussed above, members of the Communist Party comprised about 22.5 percent of the student body at middecade, and Komsomol members made up another 25.5 percent.[49] These Communist students were regarded as the Party's future elite, the *smena* (roughly "the change" or "the succession"). Fitzpatrick, however, quoting Soviet sources, finds that as many as half, and sometimes as many as three-fourths, of these Komsomol and Party students may have been proletarian by conviction but in fact came from white-collar origins.[50]

Part of the problem was that bourgeois children did better in elementary and secondary schools than proletarian or peasant children because of a home environment more conducive to academic success and access to better schools and teachers, a problem not unfamiliar to lower-class children in the United States and elsewhere today. Bourgeois children were also more likely to finish secondary school and hence had an advantage; the proletarian component dropped off radically after fourth grade.[51] The system of preferential admission of *rabfakovtsy* and nominees of organizations was designed to counter this. In 1924 only 650 VUZ places were available for 30,000 general secondary school graduates, the remaining 12,850 going to *rabfakovtsy* and nominees.[52]

In a further attempt to increase the proletarian component of the student body, a series of purges were carried out. At the time of the October revolution, by far the majority of students were anti-Bolshevik, and after Lenin's death, a very high proportion of them were Trotskyites. A purge in 1922 was directed against Kadets (members of the liberal Constitutional Democratic Party).[53] In 1923–24, as part of a larger purge, as many as one-fourth of the Communist students in the VUZy were expelled from the Party (and from school), their "alien" and "bourgeois" social origins given as the reason.[54] In the spring of 1924, a massive purge of the student body was again carried out, again the grounds being the social origins of the students. *Narkompros* attempted to downplay this aspect of the purge, preferring to call it academic "verification" (*proverka*), but its political purpose was well understood. According to I. I. Khodorovsky's report on the purge to VUZ rectors:

As a result . . . about 18,000 persons in the RSFSR were dismissed from school, approximately 13–14% of the student body in VUZy. Looking at separate cities and regions, this number can be broken down as follows: in Moscow, in round numbers, 7,000 were dismissed; in Leningrad 5,000, and in the provinces 6,000. A minimum percentage of the dismissals were of workers or the children of workers.[55]

As a result of the purge, of 12,713 students in 69 RSFSR VUZy, 24.6 percent were workers, 11.5 percent children of workers, 11.5 percent peasants, and 20.1 percent children of peasants. The working-class contingent after the purge was thus 36.1 percent, compared to 21.2 percent the previous year, and the peasant contingent was 31.6 percent, compared to 25.4 percent the year before. *Rabfak* graduates made up 48.6 percent of the enrollment.[56]

Table 2.2
**Percentage of Total Population with Higher or Incomplete or Complete
Secondary Education (by social class)**

YEAR	% of total population			% with education			M: Index of Malproportion		
	Wrkr	Empl	Psnt	Wrkr	Empl	Psnt	Wrkr	Empl	Psnt
1939	33.7	16.5	49.8	08.7	54.6	01.8	0.70	4.30	0.10
1959	50.2	18.1	31.7	40.0	91.1	22.6	1.00	1.90	0.50
1970	57.4	22.1	20.5	59.0	95.6	39.3	0.94	1.50	0.60
1985	60.0	27.6	14.9	82.5	98.7	69.5	0.95	1.10	0.80

Source: Calculated from data in *Narodnoe khoziaestvo SSSR v 1984 g.* (Moscow,
1985).

Not surprisingly, there followed a decline in academic performance
in the 1925–26 school year. In June 1926 the Central Committee ordered
a reform of VUZ admittance procedures for the fall 1926 enrollment.
The quota system of nominations by state and Party organizations was
dropped. Entrance exams were made tougher, and although preference
was still given to *rabfak* graduates, they were no longer exempt from the
exams. A consequent 21 percent drop in the enrollment of *rabfakovtsy*
led to a 3.8 percentage-point decline in proletarian composition of the
student body.

We can conclude this section by looking at overall figures for educational attainment by social class. Unfortunately, Soviet statisticians have
an irritating habit of aggregating data in inconvenient categories for
analysis. It would be preferable to have data on completion of higher
education by social class, but in all sources that give data on this, higher-
education attainment is aggregated with complete and incomplete secondary education: no distinction is made between high school dropouts
and college graduates! But even with this limitation, it will be useful to
examine the class distribution of educational attainment. The index of
malproportion used here assumes that if social class (or any variable)
has no effect on educational attainment, then educational attainment
would be distributed exactly according to the particular class's distribution in society. The index of malproportion, M, is simply the ratio of
actual attainment to "expected" attainment. M is in fact the percentage
of the expected number that the actual number represents. Thus, an M
of 1.0 would be perfect proportionality, an M less than 1 is underrepresentation, and an M greater than 1 signifies overrepresentation. Table
2.2 shows very dramatic leveling of access to partial and complete secondary and higher education.

Table 2.3
Higher Education by Urban and Rural Residence, 1939–1984

YEAR	Percent with Higher Education		M: Index of Malproportion	
	Urban	Rural	Urban	Rural
1939	01.9	0.2	2.5	0.27
1959	04.0	0.7	1.7	0.31
1970	06.2	1.4	1.5	0.35
1984	11.1	2.5	1.4	0.32

Source: Calculated from data in *Narodnoe khoziaestvo SSSR v 1984 g.* (Moscow, 1985), pp. 6, 30.

The table shows that, disregarding a slight loss to the working class in 1970, the indices of malproportion for each class are, over time, converging on 1. The sharp decline in overeducation of the "employee" class may be misleading; it is very likely that most of the leveling apparent in this table is due to leveling of access to *secondary* schooling and that higher education is dominated by the white-collar class. Indeed, it was found that children's choices for what they will do after the eighth year of school is closely related to their parents' level of education. More children of the intelligentsia opt for the ninth grade of general education school (the pathway to VUZ entry) than do the children of specialists or workers. It was found that all children aspire to some upward mobility, but only by increments; the children of the intelligentsia sought to achieve the same status for themselves, whereas the children of unskilled workers or lower-level employees sought to transcend their parents' status by moving up a few notches, entering a technicum, perhaps, and becoming a specialist.[57]

The urban-rural dichotomy does not neatly fit the distinctions among the social strata. Peasants working on state farms (*sovkhozy*), for example, are counted as "workers" but are listed as rural residents. Similarly, there is a large component of the "employee" category living in rural areas. In 1985, for example, 34 percent of the rural population of the USSR were engaged in nonagricultural occupations.[58]

Keeping this in mind, we can compare the indices of malproportion over time for the two categories with regard to higher education alone (see Table 2.3).

The malproportion of city residents in higher education has declined from two and a half times their expected share to one and a half times. At the same time, though, the proportionality of improvement of rural residents has hardly improved at all. At the base of these figures is a vastly increasing urban population (from 63.1 million in 1939 to 177.5 million in 1984) and an equally vastly shrinking rural population (from 131 million in 1939 to 96.3 million in 1984). Possibly the same individuals are listed, but certainly many of the children of those listed as rural in earlier years are urban in later years; if individuals listed earlier as rural and later as urban also acquired higher education, this in part would account for the low *M* for rural groups over the 45-year time period.

It will be fitting before moving on to the cultural revolution to examine two additional sources of unequal access to education that *Narkompros* faced during the NEP: gender and nationality. The liberation of women was of course a long-standing Marxist and Bolshevik programmatic goal.[59] Before the revolution, women were underrepresented in secondary and higher education, making up 30.5 percent of the student body in 1914. In the first decade after the revolution, enrollment of women in higher education barely held its own and in fact declined somewhat, so that by the 1926–27 academic year women comprised 27.3 percent of VUZ admissions (5,443 individuals). In that year, women accounted for 49.2 percent of admissions to pedagogical institutes, 50 percent to medical institutes, 29 percent to arts institutes, 21.3 percent to socioeconomic institutes, 17.6 percent to agricultural institutes, and 10.7 percent of admissions to industrial-technical schools. Seventeen percent of admissions to *rabfaki* in the same year were women.[60] At the secondary level in the same year 46.9 percent of admissions to technicums and an estimated 40 percent of admissions to factory apprenticeship schools (FZU) were women.[61] The same source notes that the dropout rate for women declined a bit in 1926–27, but it does not give figures. In fact, the representation of women in higher education did not begin to show significant improvement until the 1930s. By 1928 the proportion of women was 28.3 percent, but by 1935 it had increased to 39.5 percent, subsequently rising to 56 percent in 1940.[62]

Unlike the question of preferential treatment on the basis of social class, there was general consensus on the importance of admitting more women to higher education. However, some cultural prejudices remained concerning the types of occupation appropriate for women, and the pattern became underrepresentation of women in some occupations and overrepresentation in others. The percentages of women enrolled in FZUs, technicums, and vocational schools by specialization were as follows in 1926–27:[63]

FZUs

Printing industry	68.2
Chemical industry	50.4
Metalworking	12.7

Leather industry	14.2
Paper industry	34.5
Sewing and textiles	80.8

Technicums

Pedagogical	64.5
Agricultural	19.0
Industrial-technical	8.7
Medical	93.6
Industrial-economic	44.6
Art	57.7

Vocational Schools

Industrial	18.7
Socioeconomic	81.0
Sewing-textile	96.7
Arts	49.0

One sees from these figures a trend toward the concentration of women in socioeconomic trades, teaching, medicine, and textiles and their relative exclusion from industrial occupations, and this has continued to the present day. These occupations have become "feminized" in the Soviet Union. Soviet schoolgirls tend to shun vocations involving manual labor, while boys are attracted to them; as a result, girls tend to opt for general secondary education leading to VUZ entry or choose specialized secondary institutions teaching manual trades.[64] Status in the Soviet Union depends almost solely on occupation, and occupation is determined by education. The question is important because occupation is also closely related to entry into the elite. To the extent that a technical or a Party education is a prerequisite to elite recruitment, to that extent will women be excluded from the elite as long as they are underrepresented in those occupations.

Since 1940 women have been underrepresented among those with higher educations, but over the intervening four decades their situation has consistently improved, as can clearly be seen in Table 2.4. This table gives the percentage of the total population having higher education by sex, employing an index of malproportion, M—calculated by taking the ratio of actual numbers of men and women having higher education to the "expected" number according to each sex's proportion of the population in the given year.

Nationality was another bar to access to education to which *Narkompros*

Table 2.4
Percentage with Higher Education, Percentage of Population, and Index of Malproportion (by sex)

	With Higher Education		Percent of Population		M: Index of Malproportion	
YEAR	Men	Women	Men	Women	Men	Women
1940	1.1	0.5	47.9	52.1	1.4	0.6
1959	2.7	2.0	45.0	55.0	1.3	0.7
1970	4.8	3.7	46.1	53.9	1.2	0.8
1979	7.5	6.2	46.6	53.4	1.2	0.8
1984	8.8	7.7	46.9	53.1	1.1	0.9

Source: Calculated from data in *Narodnoe khoziaestvo v SSSR v 1984 g* (Moscow, 1985).

addressed itself. The non-Slavic Soviet nationalities lagged far behind the Slavs in cultural development, literacy, and education. Ukrainians, Belorussians, and Baltic nationalities lagged behind the Russians, but not by so great a magnitude. The Communist Party and the Soviet regime prides itself on having brought literacy and enlightenment to national minorities (*natsmen*); leaving aside the question of attendant Russification of national cultures, for the most part this pride is justified. The magnitude of the task facing *Narkompros* in the 1920s was immense. One contemporary author made a revealing observation: "Nowhere, among a single nationality other than Jews, does the percentage of workers with complete secondary education exceed forty, and among the Cossacks it drops to thirteen."[65]

The number of schools for members of national minorities in the RSFSR grew considerably in the mid–1920s, from 3,018 in 1923–24 to 5,336 in 1926–27.[66] The enrollments of national minority children in these schools ran about 30-35 percent, twice as low as that of children in Russian schools; all the deficiencies of Russian schools—lack of textbooks or visual aids, frequent absence, the presence of children of greatly varying age and ability in a single class—were not only worse in *natsmen* schools, but getting worse with time.[67]

A more serious problem was the lack of qualified native teachers. A. Rozin provides data on minority teachers in Latvia for the late 1920s. His data draw a simplified portrait of the *natsmen* teacher: he or she was in his or her late twenties, had less than three years' experience, was either a Party or Komsomol member, and had not finished high school. Rozin asserts that the figure of 30 percent with no teaching experience was typical of all *natsmen*. Commenting bitterly on the low level of preparation of teachers in minority schools, Rozin remarks that "if at the beginning of last academic year, *Pravda* reported humorously on the ignorance of teachers of Greek, Armenian and other nationalities (M. Kol'tsov, *"Golye fakty, fel'eton"*[The Naked Facts: A Satire], today the *nats-men* teacher has outdone even the anecdote."[68]

A distinction was made in the early Soviet regime between "cultured" nationalities and "culture-lacking" nationalities, a straightforward if not an altogether felicitous term. "Cultured" nationalities were those (such as Germans, Poles, and Jews) which had a written language at the time. "Culture-lacking" nationalities (Turko-Mongols, Ugro-Finns, and *Gortsy*) did not have a written language—under the Soviet regime their languages were transliterated into the Roman alphabet. By the 1926 census 26 percent of the population of the RSFSR was made up of various national minorities, of whom 10 percent were "cultured" and 14 percent were "culture-lacking."[69] A. Rakhimbaev reports that, not surprisingly, "culture-lacking" nationalities accounted for fewer of the students enrolled in the various educational institutions administered by the Main Administration for Professional-Technical Education of *Narkompros* (*Pro-fobr*) in 1929, and of those that were, far more were in trade schools than in the more desirable *rabfaki* and VUZy. As a further example, Rakhimbaev wrote that Mordvinians, Tatars, and Chuvash made up 20 percent of the population of Srednaia Volga *oblast* in 1928, but the percentage of these enrolled in lower trade schools was 33.5.[70]

Some progress was made in the later 1920s and early 1930s. One author reports that whereas there were only 3,500 students in VUZy in the Central Asian republics in 1928, by 1930 there were over 20,000.[71] There was not a single VUZ in 1928 in Turkmenistan or Tadzhikistan. In Transcaucasia (a republic that no longer exists, comprised then of Azerbaidzhan, Armenia, and Georgia) there were 2 industrial VUZy with 4,000 students in 1928, a number that rose by 1931 to 12 VUZy and 11,900 students.[72]

Table 2.5 provides data on the representation of nationalities among Soviet people enrolled in institutions of higher education in the 1980–81 academic year, arranged in decreasing order of their overrepresentation. It is important to keep in mind that these data refer to members of nationalities, wherever they are located, and not to union or autonomous republics or *oblasts*.

The number of enrollees listed in this source total 5,098,400, rather than the total number of enrollees in the USSR, 5,235,200. Not listed are 136,800 VUZ enrollees of other nationalities, or 2.6 percent. Some of the omissions are curious. The smallest nationalities listed in the table are Balkars (66,000) and Abkhazians (91,000), yet Germans, Jews, and Poles, each with a population in excess of one million, are omitted. In addition, 12 nationalities with populations in excess of 100,000, and 3 with popula-

Table 2.5
Malproportion in VUZ Enrollments by Nationality, 1980–81

Nationality	Percent of USSR Population	Actual VUZ Enrollments	Expected VUZ Enrollments	M
USSR TOTAL	100.00	5,235,200	5,235,200	1.00
Overrepresented:				
Buriats	0.13	16,000	7,329	2.18
Abkhazians	0.03	2,600	1,571	1.66
Kalmyks	0.06	5,100	3,141	1.63
Iakuts	0.13	9,200	6,806	1.35
Balkars	0.03	2,000	1,571	1.27
Georgians	1.36	90,000	71,199	1.26
Kazakhs	2.50	155,500	130,880	1.19
Ossets	0.24	14,900	12,565	1.19
Lithuanians	1.09	64,700	57,064	1.13
Russians	52.42	3,016,400	2,744,292	1.10
Armenians	1.58	89,500	82,716	1.08
Kirgiz	0.73	39,800	38,217	1.04
Kabardins	0.12	6,300	6,282	1.00
Estonians	0.39	20,400	20,417	1.00
Underrepresented:				
Azeris	2.09	102,000	109,416	0.93
Peoples of Dagestan	0.63	30,600	32,982	0.93
Belorussians	3.61	167,900	188,991	0.89
Latvians	0.55	25,600	28,794	0.89
Ukrainians	16.16	701,600	846,008	0.88
Komi	0.13	6,000	6,805	0.88
Ingush	0.07	3,200	3,665	0.87
Bashkirs	0.52	22,200	27,223	0.82
Tatars	0.82	120,200	146,062	0.82
Uzbeks	4.75	199,600	248,672	0.80
Tuvinians	0.07	2,900	3,665	0.79
Turkmen	0.77	29,700	40,311	0.74
NOT LISTED	3.60	136,800	188,467	0.73
Tadzhiks	1.11	42,000	58,111	0.72
Karelians	0.05	1,800	2,618	0.69
Udmurts	0.27	9,800	14,135	0.69
Chuvash	0.67	23,900	35,076	0.68
Moldavians	1.13	38,300	59,158	0.65
Mordovians	0.45	15,300	23,558	0.65
Chechens	0.29	9,500	15,182	0.63
Mari	0.24	7,800	12,565	0.62

Source: Calculated from data in *Narodnoe khoziaestvo SSSR v 1984 g.*,
(Moscow, 1985), p. 517 and pp. 26-28.

tions larger than the Balkars, are also omitted. This group of omitted nationalities together occupies 0.73 percent of the VUZ places they merit; only 8 other nationalities have indices of malproportion lower than this. There could be any number of reasons for this. The only nationalities that might be politically sensitive (either much higher or much lower than expected enrollments) are Germans, and, of course, Jews.

About two-thirds of the nationalities listed (21 of 35) are underrepresented to varying degrees of severity, with Chechens, Mari, Mordovians, and Moldavians at the bottom, occupying 65 percent or fewer of the VUZ places to which their proportion of the population would entitle them. The least well represented nationalities tend to be autonomous Soviet Socialist Republics (ASSRs) or autonomous *oblast* nationalities; of the union republic titular nationalities, only the Moldavians, Tadzhiks, and Turkmen have indices lower than 0.80. The peoples of Dagestan, it should be noted, are not a single nationality; rather, they are comprised of ten nationalities, and in the aggregate they are slightly underrepresented, but data on the individual nationalities is not available.

The patterns of overrepresentation are interesting as well. The pronounced overrepresentation of Buryats (2.18) is astonishing; I have no explanation for it—it could well be the result of intentional affirmative action. Other overrepresented nationalities of the traditionally undermobilized groups are the Yakuts (1.35), the Kalmyks (1.62), the Balkars (1.27), and the Kazakhs (1.19). It is surprising to find Armenians, traditionally well educated, to be only modestly overrepresented (1.08). As recently as 18 years ago, the Georgian SSR led the entire country in the proportion of its population with higher education.[73] Georgians are still overrepresented, though by a smaller factor (1.26), and it is noteworthy that two of the smaller nationalities that are overrepresented (Ossets and Abkhazians) are located in Georgia.

Problems still remain in quality of instruction, poor preparation of applicants, and finding sufficient VUZ seats for aspirants. The proportion of *natsmen* in VUZy lags behind their proportion of the total population in all republics. National minority women in particular are underrepresented in higher education, and severely so in Islamic republics, where patriarchal attitudes about the proper role of women persist.

Another serious problem for national minorities in higher education today is language. The language of instruction in the best VUZy, wherever they are located, is Russian; Russian is also the language of scientific discourse throughout the country. Whatever the law may provide for in terms of the right to education in one's native tongue, a serious *natsmen* student who wishes to go far must become fluent in Russian, as must any aspirant to central elite status.

THE FIRST FIVE-YEAR PLAN AND AFTER

The beginning of the First Five-Year Plan in 1928 saw a dramatic change in Stalin's educational priorities. Collectivization of agriculture and rapid, forced-pace industrialization could go forward only on the basis of a firm consensus on goals and methods among the political elite and the technical intelligentsia. Stalin's effort to create such a consensus over the next three years comprised a constellation of policies referred to then as now as the cultural revolution. Stalin intended nothing less sweeping than to create an entirely new technical intelligentsia, drawn from a more reliable social background, namely, from the working class.

Among the earliest victims of the new orientation was *Narkompros* and its commissar, A. V. Lunacharsky. *Narkompros* was accused of failure to understand class warfare and of failure in particular to proceed energetically enough in creating a proletarian intelligentsia. In fact, the line went, the entire state and Party bureaucracy had, under the baneful influence of the Right Opposition, retreated from Communist goals and was conciliating the class enemies of the proletariat.[74] Embattled, Lunacharsky resigned in 1929, and *Narkompros*, a shadow of its former self, began progressively to lose significant jurisdiction over higher education.

To implement the new policy of rapid, forced-pace industrialization, Stalin had to overcome not only objections from the more moderate right in the top leadership but also the objections (on technical, not political grounds) of virtually all the existing technical intelligentsia. It seems abundantly clear in retrospect that their objections—that the proposed policies would be wasteful, inefficient, and counterproductive—were valid; Stalin, however, purported to overcome the manifest difficulties through a combination of harsh taxation of the rural sector and Bolshevik enthusiasm. To accomplish his goals, Stalin sought first to discredit or intimidate the "bourgeois specialists" by means of a series of show trials (see Chapter 4) and then through creating a new technical intelligentsia to promote from the working class. This ambitious goal was to be realized by sending thousands of workers and Communists to institutes of higher education.

Stalin's campaign to replace bourgeois technicians with Communist, proletarian ones was embodied in a resolution of the July 1928 Central Committee plenum. The resolution provided that no less than 65 percent of admissions in the fall of 1928 were to be workers, and it was foreseen that this percentage would rise to 80 percent within a few years. A thousand experienced Communists were to be sent to the VTUZy in addition, and the *rabfaki* were instructed to admit an additional 3,000 workers.[75]

To accomplish this, a radical overhaul of the educational system was necessary. As Sergo Ordzhonikidze said in 1928 in response to a Central Committee discussion of "overtaking and passing" the capitalist states in the graduation of engineers, "to overtake and pass them, we'll need not a decrepit old horse [*kliacha*] but an express train."[76]

There were new purges of "alien" elements in the student body commencing in 1928, and in 1929 there was a purge of the "reactionary professoriate" in the VUZy and VTUZy. Twenty percent of a total of 1,062 professors were purged.

Other changes were made as well. A number of VUZy were transferred to the jurisdiction of *Vesenkh* (the Supreme Council of the National Economy). Specializations were narrowed, and the course of study was reduced from four to three years. The production element of higher education was enhanced. Compensation for VUZ teachers was doubled, and the stipends paid to students more than tripled.[77] The number of VUZy vastly increased, but this was due less to building new ones than to splitting up existing VUZy and VTUZy into narrowly specialized institutes.[78] Enrollments in higher education skyrocketed, rising to a half million by 1932, and by 1940 to 812,000 students in 817 VUZy.[79]

The workers and Communists who were sent to school in the First Five-Year Plan were referred to as *vydvizhentsy*, meaning roughly the "promoted ones," or the "ones put forward." Of the *vydvizhentsy*, adult Communist Party members who were selected and dispatched in groups of 1,000 to higher education by Party and government organizations became known as "Party thousanders" (*parttysiachniki*), or simply "thousanders" (*tysiachniki*). To be eligible for selection as a thousander, Party members were required to be 35 or younger and have five years of Party experience. By far, most of them were sent to engineering schools, many in Moscow. In all, in the course of the First Five-Year Plan, approximately 20,000 *tysiachniki* were sent to VUZy and VTUZy.[80]

Like all campaigns, the cultural revolution eventually ran its course and began to die down after the 1931–32 academic year. There were only so many individuals intellectually capable of joining the *vydvizhentsy*, and so the qualifications of entering classes dropped drastically in 1931–32. The hasty technical education of the *vydvizhentsy* also had its predictable effect, and once again there were complaints from industrial managers about the poorly trained engineers. So the organized mobilization of workers and Party members ended in 1932.

For several years industrial managers had been protesting the persecution of the bourgeois technicians, and Josef Stalin yielded in the summer of 1931 and rehabilitated them. In fact, public discussion of class origins diminished considerably with the promulgation of the 1936 Constitution, which declared all citizens equal, and social-class criteria for admission to VUZy ended; thenceforth, the only objective criterion was entrance exams. De facto discrimination in favor of upper-class children resulted, however, from the introduction of fees in 1940, which remained in effect until 1956. This effectively benefited youth from higher-income families.

Stalin was aware of the growing predominance of white-collar students in higher education and encouraged it. This is not as contradictory or uncharacteristic of Stalin as might be imagined. The cultural revolution and the Great Purges of 1936–1938, the latter particularly, accomplished their purpose of eliminating the old intelligentsia class from industry, the Party, and the government. Stalin now had his "proletarian intelligentsia," and so the issue of social class was no longer of interest to him. Now, the majority priority was improving the qualifications of graduate specialists. Perhaps because this might be publicly embarrassing, the rich availability of sociological studies on the social backgrounds of students that characterized the 1920s dried up after 1931.

Furthermore, after Stalin's virtual declaration of war on the peasantry in collectivization, they were in fact, if still not in theory, no longer a favored class and, like the proletariat, could no longer count on preferential treatment with respect to education.

Working-class and peasant youth began to be channeled into vocational schools rather than the ten-year general education school; the latter became the sole path to higher education. This channeling began as early as age 14, so that in 1940 alone, up to one million peasant and working-class youth were effectively bound to manual occupations.[81] By the late 1930s 45 percent, and by the time of Stalin's death, 60 percent to 70 percent of the students in the better VUZy came from white-collar families. Some working-class students could pay the fees (up to 200 rubles per year) and, if they were bright, gain admittance to a VUZ. Peasants could not, and virtually the only rural youth admitted to VUZy were the children of the rural intelligentsia: collective farm chairmen, Party secretaries, and the like.[82]

Khrushchev did periodically voice his concern about the dominance of children of white-collar families in higher education, but neither he nor the Brezhnev leadership did much to change it. Khrushchev's 1958 reform—requiring secondary school graduates to work in industry for two years before being admitted to VUZy—did not change anything and was disliked by students, families, and industrial managers. Hence, Brezhnev dropped it.

All VUZy were never equal. The larger, better, and more prestigious institutes were those located in republican capitals, and in Moscow and Leningrad. Not unsurprisingly, the better schools came to serve the more privileged students, and still do. Stalin may have even encouraged this trend, according to Mervyn Matthews, because the scholarships that were granted in his and other leaders' names could be used only at certain VUZy, the better ones.[83] Close to the bottom of the VUZ prestige hierarchy are pedagogical, medical, and agricultural institutes.[84] Near the top are the various technical, industrial, and engineering institutes, and at the top are the major universities, especially those in Moscow, Leningrad, and Kiev. Some state schools, notably Institute of World Economics and International Relations (IMEMO) in Moscow, are very prestigious and therefore difficult to get into.

THE DEVELOPMENT OF PARTY EDUCATION

Party education is unique to Communist countries; there are no analogous institutions anywhere else. Their primary purpose is instruction or indoctrination in Marxist-Leninist ideology or, as it is often called in the Soviet Union, the "social sciences." The structure of Party education ranges from the postgraduate Academy of Social Sciences in Moscow, through republican and inter-*oblast* higher Party schools, to soviet-Party schools at the middle level for rural Party cadres—with terms of instruction ranging from a single seminar through seminars of several months or up to one year's duration—to primary political schools at the bottom to instill basic "political literacy" in the most unsophisticated. Party education, particularly at the lower and middle levels, is not confined to Party members; a little more than one-third of enrollees are non-Party personnel.[85]

At the present time, there are over one-quarter of a million persons enrolled in Party education courses at all levels. Our principal concern here, however, is with higher Party education, since that is directly relevant to the educational qualifications of the political elite.[86]

Writing in 1971, one Soviet scholar reported:

At the present time almost half the secretaries of union republic central committees and *kraikom* and *obkom* committees, and more than 50% of the secretaries of *gorkoms* have a higher Party-political education. Graduates of higher Party schools include almost 60% of the chairmen of union republican and ASSR Supreme Soviets, and *krai, oblast*, city and district executive committees. There is an increasing number of workers with higher Party-political education among department heads, instructors of Party committees, and secretaries of PPOs.[87]

Ascertaining the number of students who pass through Party schools is difficult and inexact because Soviet published statistics on the matter either lump categories of Party schools together or fail to provide dates, or both. *Bol'shaia sovetskaia entsiklopediia* (1970) states that (for an unspecified time period), the Higher Party School of the CPSU Central Committee (henceforth CC CPSU HPS) graduated 10,000 Party and state workers, and that 14,500 took retraining courses there.[88] Tatjana Kirstein has estimated, calculating from a number of ambiguous reports, that the CC CPSU HPS graduated an average of 300 persons per year.[89]

A Soviet writer reports that for the period 1946–1966 the CC CPSU Academy of Social Sciences graduated almost 3,000 people; CC CPSU HPS (both the in-residence and correspondence divisions) graduated nearly 40,000; republic, *oblast*, and *krai* higher Party schools graduated almost 25,000; and the middle-level soviet-Party schools graduated more than 31,000.[90]

The development of Party education in the twentieth century was less controversial than that of technical higher education, but it underwent a number of changes in importance, purpose, prestige, and institutions. The tradition of Party education actually began before the revolution. The main method of training revolutionary cadres was illegal circles and schools; one organized in St. Petersburg by Vladimir Ilyich Lenin later became the "Union for the Struggle for Liberation of the Working Class."[91]

In 1909 a revolutionary school was opened on the Isle of Capri by A. V. Lunacharsky, Maksim Gorky, and others of the *Vpered* movement who were opposed to Lenin's "Bolshevik Center." In an effort to disrupt the school, Lenin invited the students to Paris in November-December 1909, where he lectured them on the contemporary political situation and Peter Stolypin's agricultural policy.[92] This merely prompted the *Vpered* group to open a second school in Italy in November, 1910. Lenin responded by opening another school in Longjumeau, France, which he directed himself. Sergo Ordzhonikidze was among the students, who numbered less than two dozen.[93]

After the revolution, in June 1918, a two-week (later expanded to six-week) agitation-propaganda course was organized by the All-Union Central Executive Committee (VTsIK), to be conducted by local soviets. In January 1919 these courses were reorganized into a school for soviet and Party workers, with a six-week term of instruction. From June 1918 to November 1919 this school graduated 5,805 persons, of whom 3,253 were dispatched to the front.[94]

In the same month, by order of VTsIK, a Communist Academy was created; its purpose was, not to teach, but eventually to become the successor of the Russian Academy of Sciences. Its work was of low quality, however, and the regime managed to take over control of the Academy of Sciences without its help. In 1936 it was abolished and its resources given to the Academy of Sciences.[95]

The Eighth Congress of VKP(b), meeting March 18–23, 1919, instructed the Central Committee to organize a central CC higher Party school, which among other things would work out curricula for and send lecturers to local Party schools.[96] Accordingly, the VTsIK school was reorganized in the second half of 1919 into the Sverdlov Communist University in Moscow, the regime's first Communist VUZ (KOMVUZ).

Sverdlov Communist University was envisaged as a center of theoretical education for cadres of the Party, the soviets, and the trade unions, and for the training of highly qualified propagandists and lecturers. During the civil war, the course of instruction had to be shortened to 6 to 8 months, but in 1921 it was lengthened to two years, then to three, and in 1924 to four years. Preferential admission was given to Party members of working-class background.

The school's namesake, Ya. M. Sverdlov, worked out the curriculum and invited prominent people to lecture. The first program of instruction included the following:

"Labor, Capital, and History of the Class Struggle" (V. I. Lenin)

"The Agrarian Question" (E. M. Yaroslavsky)

"Organization of Soviet Rule" (M. F. Vladimirsky)

"Food Production" (A. D. Tsiurup)

"Parliamentarism and the Dictatorship of the Bourgeoisie" and "Soviet Construction" (M. N. Pokrovsky)

"The National Question" (J. V. Stalin)

"The Soviets and Popular Education" (A. V. Lunacharsky)[97]

The Thirteenth Party Congress (May 23–31, 1924) mandated that the central purpose of the KOMVUZ was to train Party workers and that all instruction should be geared toward the problems of the day.[98] Accordingly, the curriculum at Sverdlov and other KOMVUZy was changed to emphasize traditional university coursework: mathematics, physics, chemistry, geography, statistics, geology, history, and the like. Each student also was required to study a foreign language. After Sverdlov became a four-year institution and began to enroll Party members who had a secondary education (1924), the curriculum was changed to include fewer general education courses and more courses of an ideological nature, such as Party history, Marxist-Leninist philosophy, political economy, and Party and soviet construction.

Leading figures lectured there: Kliment A. Timuriazev, Lenin, Stalin, Valerian Kuibyshev, Nikolai Bukharin, Mikhail Pokrovsky, Mikhail Kalinin, Maksim Gorky, and others. In its first ten years, Sverdlov Communist University graduated more than 19,000 persons, and in 1933, on its fifteenth anniversary, it was awarded the Order of Lenin.[99] Unlike higher Party schools of the future, Sverdlov graduates enjoyed considerable prestige and developed a certain esprit, referring to themselves and each other with pride as *sverdlovtsy*.[100]

Sverdlov Communist University became the model for other KOMVUZy that began to appear in 1921 in all the major cities of the country. Some of the more important ones were the following:

Artem Ukrainian Communist University (Khar'kov)

Belorussian Communist University (Minsk)

North Caucasian Communist University (Rostov)

Transcaucasian Communist University (Tbilisi)

East Siberian Communist University (Irkutsk)

Far Eastern Communist University (Khabarovsk)

Urals Communist University (Sverdlovsk)

Zinoviev Communist University (Leningrad)

There were also KOMVUZy in Leningrad, Saratov, Kazan, and Omsk. In addition to Sverdlov Communist University in Moscow, there were three KOMVUZy specifically established for national minorities: the Communist University of Toilers of the East (KUTV), the Communist University of Toilers of the West (KUTZ—with a branch in Leningrad for Baltic nationalities—and the Chinese Toilers' Communist University (KUKT). In addition, there was a Central Asian Communist University in Tashkent.[101] According to a resolution of the Thirteenth Party Congress, the Communist University of Toilers of the East was established to train Party and soviet cadres for the "treaty" republics (*dogovornye*: referring to those that were negotiating for inclusion in the USSR) and ASSRs.[102]

The most important KOMVUZ for preparing school teachers, political education workers, and journalists was the Krupskaia Academy of Communist Education. This was originally established in Moscow as the Academy of Social Education, renamed after Lenin's wife Nadezhda Krupskaia in 1923, and in 1928 moved to Leningrad, where it was renamed the Krupaskaia Leningrad Political Education Institute (LPPI im. Krupskoi). There were also Communist Institutes of Journalism in Moscow, Leningrad, and the Ukraine.

Additional KOMVUZY were authorized by Central Committee resolutions in 1928 and 1930. Many of these were in national *oblasts* and republics; although these were regarded as higher Party schools, they did not have the right to grant their graduates a Party education diploma, as could the central and all-union KOMVUZy. There were 19 KOMVUZy with 8,400 students in 1928; by 1932, there were 53, with 30,500 students.[103] In 1927, they were all renamed Higher Party Schools (HPS).

In November of 1935 the Central Committee opened its own higher school for propagandists, taking students under age 32 with incomplete higher education and experience in Party work. After the Eighteenth Party Congress (1939), this school was upgraded and reorganized as the Higher Party School of the CC VKP(b), accepting students with higher education for a two-year term of study. After World War II, by a Central

Committee resolution of August 2, 1946,[104] the system of HPSs was again reorganized. The Central Committee HPS was to train Party and soviet workers at the republican, *krai* and *oblast* levels, with initially a three-year, later a four-year, term of instruction. In 1947 an HPS attached to the Central Committee of the Ukrainian Party was created. For training cadres at the *raion* (mainly rural) level, two-year (later three-year) soviet-Party schools were attached to *obkoms, kraikoms*, and the central committees of the union republics.[105] By 1958, there were 75 such schools, but as the level of education of rural functionaries increased, their number again declined, to 16 in 1976 with about 4,000 students.[106]

The subjects taught in the HPSs were almost exclusively ideological ones: Party history, political economy, Marxist-Leninist philosophy. Later, courses in scientific communism were added. From the beginning, the system of HPSs was poorly staffed, poorly coordinated, and constantly the subject of Central Committee criticism. Finally, in April 1978, the CC CPSU HPS was abolished as an individual entity and combined with the Academy of Social Sciences, considered later in this chapter.[107]

In the immediate postrevolutionary years, there was also the problem of the "bourgeois professoriate." As late as 1924 the Thirteenth Party Congress could still complain that "in the majority of VUZy, old bourgeois professors still hold even chairs of social sciences."[108] Lenin had recognized this problem earlier and signed a decree of the RSFSR *Sovnarkom* establishing Institutes of Red Professors (IKP)[109] for the purpose of training young Communists with a higher education to become professors of the social sciences.

A number of prominent Communist scholars were invited to help create the institute: M. N. Pokrovsky (who was to become the rector), V. V. Adoratsky, V. P. Volgin, Yu. Markhlevsky, and others. The instructional program was hammered out between March and August of 1921, and faculty were recruited. Among the prominent Communist scholars who taught at the institute were N. N. Baransky, A. S. Bubnov, E. S. Varga, A. V. Lunacharsky, and V. I. Nevsky.[110] The institute was placed under the administrative jurisdiction of *Narkompros*, but general direction of its activities lay with the Agitation-Propaganda Department of the VKP(b) Central Committee.

Next was the problem of recruiting students. At first there was apprehension that enough suitable young Communist candidates might not be found, but in fact there were 289 applications for admission.[111] Applicants had to be individuals with a higher education and Communist Party membership of at least three years' standing; in 1925 the minimum *partstazh* was increased to five years. In order to increase the proportion of working-class Communists in the student body, a preparatory department was opened at the Institute in 1929. By 1930 there were 530 entrants, the majority of them claiming working-class status.[112] The term of instruction was three years, increased at the end of 1923 to four years.

In 1931, IKP took over the *aspirantura* program of the nearly defunct Communist Academy, and in the same year it was reorganized into ten separate and independent IKPs: economic, agrarian, world economy and politics, philosophical, historical, soviet construction and law, natural science, literature, technology, and Party history IKPs. In 1932 enrollment reached a combined total of 1,035 students. In 1936 the technology and natural science IKPs were closed, leaving eight.[113]

Some prominent state and Party figures of the time were IKP graduates, including N. A. Voznesensky, Ya. Eh. Kalnberzin, A. Ya. Pelshe, B. N. Ponomarev, P. N. Pospelov, and M. A. Suslov. Graduates who became prominent academicians or professors included B. M. Kedrov, I. I. Mints, M. B. Mitin, A. N. Pankratova, P. F. Yudin, N. L. Rubinshtein, and A. L. Sidorov.[114]

Many of the *ikapisty* ("IKP-ers," as they were referred to) were sent to the countryside in the early 1930s to assist in the difficult collectivization process.

Given its nature, it was natural that IKP would become a rather politicized institution in the 1930s. There were bitter ideological rivalries among the professoriate and the students, and of course the inevitable purges.[115]

By 1938 the social science faculties of the universities and other VUZy had been sufficiently strengthened that the need for the Institutes of Red Professors was obviated, and by an order of the Central Committee their doors were closed that year.

The successor to the Institute of Red Professors is the CC CPSU Academy of Social Sciences (known by its Russian initials AON), created in 1946 by the same Central Committee decree that established the HPS. Whereas the HPS was placed under the operational administration of the Central Committee Cadres Administration, AON fell to the jurisdiction of Agitprop. The services of IKP were apparently missed, for the mission of AON was very similar: to provide postgraduate education in the social sciences for leading Party and state officials, as well as for others in ideologically oriented work.

EDUCATIONAL CHARACTERISTICS OF THE SOVIET POLITICAL ELITE

Without judging whether the policy was necessary or appropriate, we can judge that Stalin's effort to create a new proletarian intelligentsia was successful on its own terms. The *vydvizhentsy*—the first class of which graduated in 1930[116]—and the thousanders enjoyed immense occupational and political mobility, since in the purges to come in 1936–1938, they were to step into the shoes of purged industrial managers and political leaders. The *vydvizhentsy* themselves survived the purges almost intact,[117] evidence if any is needed that they were the darlings of Stalin. Sometimes called the "class of 1938," this was the Brezhnev generation. Leonid Brezhnev graduated in 1937 from the Dneprodzerzhinsk Metallurgical Institute; Aleksey Kosygin graduated in 1934 from the Kirov Textile Institute in Leningrad; Dmitry Ustinov finished the Leningrad Mechanical-Military Institute in 1934. Other well-known *vydvizhentsy* included Nikita Khrushchev, Frol Kozlov, Mark Mitin, Valery Zorin, Gennady Sizov, Arvid Pelshe, and Petr Shelest.

There is no way to identify thousanders in our database, but the *vydvizhentsy* can be approximately identified. The list of these people who achieved central elite status will of course vary with the operational criteria used to identify them, and any criteria are likely to be inaccurate to some degree. Employing the criterion that a *vydvizhenets* is a person who joined the Party before 1929 and graduated from a VUZ between 1929 and 1936, we have the following numbers of *vydvizhentsy* for the central committee elected at each congress. Members subsequently reelected are counted only once.

18th Congress:	5
19th Congress:	46
20th Congress:	17
22nd Congress:	14
23rd Congress:	4
24th Congress:	3
25th Congress:	1
26th Congress:	1
TOTAL:	91

There was a curious pattern to the mobility of the *vydvizhentsy*: almost all of those who undertook political careers advanced to near the top. There were not enough of them to fill all posts. In a study of the dominance of *vydvizhentsy* in Party and government posts in 1952, Fitzpatrick also noted that at middle levels—a sample of 70 *obkom* first secretaries who were not in the Central Committee—more than half lacked any kind of higher or secondary education.[118]

Communist Party members have consistently over time been six to eight times as well educated as the general population. In terms of secondary education (complete and incomplete) the general population is rapidly approaching the level of Party members. In 1941 Party mem-

Table 2.6
Higher Educational Attainment of Central and Regional Elites

	Central Elites		Regional Elites	
YEAR	Party	Soviet	Party	Soviet
1946	41.0	27.8	12.1	07.3
1952	67.7	58.0	18.4	12.8
1956	86.0	71.7	25.7	22.2
1961	92.0	87.7	67.8	55.8
1966	97.0	94.1	89.4	79.5
1971	98.9	96.9	96.4	91.8
1976	99.4	98.8	99.2	96.5
1981	99.9	99.4	99.7	99.3

Source: Adapted from data in *Partiinoe stroitel'stvo: uchebnoe posobie* (Moscow, 1981), pp. 294-97.

bers collectively had only 70 percent of the higher-education experiences expected from their proportion of the population, but by 1961 they had 470 percent. Since then the malproportion, though still quite high, has been steadily decreasing as the educational level of the population increases.

If the educational level of Party members is high relative to the general population, the educational level of political elites, particularly central elites, is higher still. In the period from the end of World War II to 1981, the educational level of both central and regional elites has risen dramatically, both approaching 100 percent. In Table 2.6, "central elites" refers to secretaries of *obkoms*, *kraikoms*, and the central committee of union republics, and to soviet executive committee chairmen at the same levels. These are on the CPSU Central Committee *nomenklatura*. Regional elites in this table refer to secretaries of *raikoms*, *gorkoms*, and *okruzhkoms* and to executive committee chairmen at these levels; of these, all but the larger *gorkoms* are on the *nomenklatura* of union republics and *obkoms*. In general, Party executives are better educated than soviet executives, and central executives are better educated than regional elites, although since the beginning of the 1970s, the differences have been small.

In terms of its educational characteristics, the Soviet elite has been predominately trained in technical areas. Taking the entire period of the Nineteenth through the Twenty-seventh Party Congress, the types of institutions attended by the central elite were distributed as follows:

Industrial institutes	35.5%
Agricultural institutes	13.7%
Higher Party Schools	23.1%
Universities	7.4%
Pedagogical institutes	6.7%
Economic-financial institutes	3.7%
Military academies	2.6%
Government schools	1.5%
Arts and science institutes	1.4%
Law institutes	1.1%
Other	3.3%

Thus, 72.3 percent of post-Stalin central elite educations were attained at industrial or agricultural institutes or a HPS. The miniscule percentage of law school graduates among the political elite dramatizes one of the major differences between elite mobility in the United States and the USSR. Since many elite members attended more than one institute, usually two (of my database, 302, or 27 percent, did) these figures refer to educational experiences rather than to individuals.

Just under one-half of the full and candidate Central Committee members elected in 1952 were trained in the engineering and industrial fields (see Table 2.7). By 1956 the proportion exceeded 50 percent, where it has remained. At every post-Khrushchev Party congress, between 56 percent and 57 percent of full members have been technically trained, as have been between 47 percent and 48 percent of candidate members. The next largest category is agricultural specialists, which had a low of under 6 percent under Stalin, steadily rose to a high of 18 percent in 1971, then declined to less than 15 percent in 1986. The only other large category of specialization is "ideological." This category includes VUZ graduates in philosophy, journalism, and history; graduates in these areas, when they pursue a political career, do so almost exclusively as ideological officials. From more than 10 percent of full members at the Nineteenth Congress, the proportion of individuals in this category declined over the intervening three decades among full members to 6.6 percent in 1986. Among candidate members and Auditing Commission members, the percentage has fluctuated. When the proportion of full members in this category goes down, it rises among candidates and Auditing Commission members.

There are other differences as well in the distribution of educational characteristics among full, candidate, and Auditing Commission members. Among candidate members, the proportion of industrial specialists is lower and other categories are more evenly distributed. They are even

Table 2.7
Specializations of Political Elites in the CPSU Central Committee, by Party Congress (in percentages)

	Congress							
Specialization	19th	20th	22nd	23rd	24th	25th	26th	27th
Agriculture	5.7	13.7	16.1	20.1	18.3	19.3	17.1	15.7
Industry	50.0	56.8	56.6	56.0	57.1	57.1	56.4	57.9
Economics	8.6	6.3	6.3	4.4	4.7	4.6	5.4	3.7
Law	4.3	1.1	0.7	0.6	1.0	1.3	1.6	2.5
Ideological	10.0	8.4	9.1	5.7	5.2	5.5	7.4	6.6
Arts, Sciences	4.3	3.2	2.8	2.5	2.1	1.3	1.2	2.9
Pedagogy	15.7	7.4	7.7	10.1	9.4	9.7	9.3	7.0
Untrained	1.4	1.1	0.0	0.0	1.0	0.8	0.8	3.3
Military	0.0	2.1	0.7	0.6	1.0	0.4	0.8	0.4
N	106	123	159	172	203	249	270	249
Valid N	070	095	143	159	191	238	257	242

Source: Author's database (full members only).

better distributed among Auditing Commission members; whereas among full members categories other than industry, agriculture, and ideology do not exceed 10 percent, and often are far below that, many more categories among Auditing Commission members approach and often exceed 10 percent. Since the Auditing Commission is a politically impotent organization and membership in it is essentially honorary, the tendency to overrepresentation of agricultural, industrial, and ideological officials is less.

The higher-education characteristics of the elite also deviate somewhat from the educational specializations of the general population. The proportion of students in agricultural institutions in 1981–82 was 10.3 percent, whereas at the same date 17.1 percent of the central elite had agricultural training. The corresponding figures for the arts were 0.93 percent *versus* 1.2 percent; for economics and law combined, 7.2 percent as against 7.0 percent; a larger proportion of the elite (56.4 percent) had industrial training, whereas only 45.5 percent of students were studying in industrial VUZy; many more students were studying in pedagogical institutes (28.8 percent) than the proportion of the elite with pedagogical training.[119]

My sample of the central elite graduated from 534 different VUZy, and with the exception of Party schools, no one institute graduated more than 3 members of the elite. Most VUZy graduated only one or two. This is a remarkable dispersion, quite unlike the situation in Western Europe, where only a few higher-education institutions graduate most of the elite. This cannot but hinder elite integration, since there is little opportunity for something similar to the "old school tie" to develop,[120] although there are other integrative forces that more than make up for it.

Party schools are, of course, the largest category of VUZ, having graduated 308 members of the central elite. The question is how to interpret this. M. B. Sverdlovtsev reports:

Over the last 25 years [1946–1971] AON trained more than 3,800 theoretical workers, of whom more than 400 were comrades from fraternal Communist and workers parties. At the present time, more than 50 graduates of AON are secretaries of republican central committees, and *kraikoms* and *obkoms* of the CPSU. Hundreds of graduates are engaged in propaganda work. Nearly 250 graduates have been promoted to responsible work in the Party and state *apparat*, and ministries and departments of union and autonomous republics. A large group of graduates is engaged in leading work in publishing houses, magazines, newspapers, and other press organs, in scientific research institutions, and in VUZy. Among AON graduates are presidents of Academies of Sciences of union republics, rectors of universities, and heads of major scientific research institutes.[121]

In other words, 300 of these 3,800, or 7.9 percent, found positions in the political elite. At an average of 152 graduates per year (and it no doubt increased rather than decreased), the total number of graduates since 1946 would be at least 6,384, 7.9 percent of which is 504, of which only 308 attained central elite status. This is an astonishingly small number. From a sociological perspective, Tatjana Kirstein interprets it to mean that the activities of the vast ideological apparatus have come to serve the purposes of its own self-preservation, since the number of graduates of these schools that are engaged in practical work in politics or science is so vanishingly small, and so many are writing and propagandizing.[122] Apparently, trained theoreticians need work, too.

In the 1920s, graduates of the Communist Universities, particularly Sverdlov Communist University, enjoyed a certain prestige. After the turn of the decade, however, the prestige attached to graduation from Party schools declined considerably,[123] and graduates have experienced markedly slow political mobility, relatively few reaching the central elite.[124] The greater percentage of HPS graduates are in the teaching profession—until 1978, many in the Party schools themselves—and in press, radio, and television work. Of those that go into politics, most are concentrated in lower-level positions in the state, rather than the Party, apparatus. They can be found most often as chairmen of autonomous republic, *krai, oblast, gorod,* and *raion* soviets.[125] There is also impressionistic evidence, at least, that a Party education came to be considered remedial.[126] It is doubtful that mere attendance at a Party school accounted for slow mobility; some other variable no doubt explains both Party school attendance and mobility. A little more than half the Party school graduates attended the Party school after having graduated from a technical institute; and in their case, at least, it cannot be argued that their selection for the HPS were remedial in terms of education alone. Lack of management skills or lack of ideological sophistication suggest themselves as possible explanations. For those who did not have a technical degree before attending the HPS, and who did not acquire one afterward, lack of technical sophistication may account for their slower mobility.

Nine of 59 full politburo members (15.3 percent) since the Nineteenth Party Congress attended Party schools, all in residence, 5 as their only educational experience; of the other 4 who received a Party education as their second educational experience, all but 1 were by correspondence. A higher proportion of candidate politburo members (7 of 26, or 27 percent) had a Party education, 2 in residence as their only educational experience; of those for whom the Party school was their second experience, all but 1 were by correspondence.

Beginning in the 1950s, part-time study became prevalent in the form of correspondence courses and evening divisions at VUZy. The part-time sector has always been understaffed and underfunded, however,[127] and the time pressure on students is great. One tends to suspect that the quality of a higher education gained by correspondence is rather low.[128]

In the database of 1,117 members of the central elite, 92, or 8.2 percent, of the first higher-education experience of elite members was gained by corrspondence. Of the 302 who had a second higher-education experience, 141, or nearly half, were by correspondence. Seventeen of the first educational experiences were through evening division; significantly, none of the second experiences were. One hundred thirty-three individuals had a Party education as their first experience, 34 of which were by correspondence; of 183 Party educations as the second experience, nearly half were by correspondence.[129]

There is some impressionistic cause to doubt the quality of the higher education acquired by a political leader after assuming a position in the elite. Into this category fall 140 (13 percent) of the members of the database, who on average commenced their higher education nine years after joining the elite. Even in the case of ordinary, nonelite VUZ students, the pressure on professors to pass them is immense because it is regarded as a deficiency of the teacher if his students fail to learn (a kind of fallacious reasoning not confined to the Soviet Union). The motivation not to give offense to a local Party leader by failing him—or even by making very many intellectual demands on him—is surely high and probably not unfounded. Indeed, Michael Voslensky has called the Academy of Social Sciences a diploma mill, where the professors' principal responsibilities are to write dissertations for the *nomenklaturists*.[130]

There is considerable evidence that the political elite use their influence to gain admission for their children to the best institutes of higher education. One means of doing this is to place them in the very best general education secondary schools, especially foreign-language schools and schools for the gifted.[131] This, along with bribes and influence, facilitates their entry into the best VUZy. According to Ilya Zemtsov:

When sociological researchers questioned students accepted in 1971 to the Institute of International Relations, it was found that 312 of them were the children of important Party officials, 210 were children of high-level Soviet government bureaucrats, 180 were children of senior officers, and 50 were children of academicians and professors, while only 8 were children of workers and 2 were children of peasants.[132]

Calling it the "migration to academe," Alexander Yanov has a different interpretation of the phenomenon. He sees the recent fad for academic titles among the elite as one of a number of channels of aristocratization of the elite. Academic titles confer the only status that guarantees privilege and high income for life in an egalitarian society and, by creating the essentially closed schools discussed above, a surrogate means of passing privilege on through inheritance.[133]

Interestingly, however, even though elite parents are able to channel their offspring into the elite, they do not channel them into the *political* elite, and in elite families Party-governmental work is not highly respected. There is considerable aversion to the concept of nepotism at high elite levels, and the elite are also sensitive, for historical and ideological reasons, to the implication that they are becoming a ruling class. Matthews collected data on the careers of the children of 51 men who were Politburo members between 1953 and 1975. He finds that these children and their spouses occupy the "upper ranks of the intelligentsia," but not the very highest ranks.[134]

NOTES

1. Robert D. Putnam, *The Comparative Study of Political Elites* (Englewood Cliffs, NJ: Prentice-Hall, 1976), p. 27; Ilya Zemtsov, *The Private Life of the Soviet Elite* (New York: Crane Russak, 1985), p. 72; *Itogi chislennost' i sostav naseleniia SSSR* (Moscow, 1984), p. 26.
2. Gaetano Mosca, *The Ruling Class* (New York: McGraw-Hill, 1939).
3. Between 6 percent and 11 percent of U.S. business and political elites

attended these schools. See Thomas R. Dye and John W. Pickering, "Governmental and Corporate Elites: Convergence and Differentiation," *Journal of Politics* 36 (November 1974): 914.

4. There were actually 842 VUZy in 1974: A. B. Dainovsky, *Ekonomika vysshego obrazovaniia* (Moscow: 1974), p. 101. According to Mervyn Matthews, 14 of the 842 are probably "closed" institutes with restricted admission, administered by the KGB and the Ministries of Defense, Internal Affairs, and Foreign Affairs, and rarely mentioned in public sources. Mervyn Matthews, *Education in the Soviet Union* (London: Allen & Unwin, 1982), p. 109.

5. Dainovsky, *Ekonomika*, p. 101.

6. Calculated from data in D. J. Aitken, ed., *International Handbook of Universities and Other Institutions of Higher Education*, 9th ed. (Berlin: DeGruyter, 1983), pp. 943–59.

7. The term "social sciences" has quite a different meaning in the Soviet Union than it does in the West. In VUZ curricula, it refers exclusively to indoctrination courses in Marxism-Leninism, Party history, scientific communism, political economy, and the like.

8. *Partiinoe stroitel'stvo: uchebnoe posobie* (Moscow, 1981), p. 294. This assumes that 67 of the 883 VUZy actually reported there are actually universities. This does not include state or Party schools or military academies.

9. Nicholas DeWitt, *Education and Professional Employment in the USSR* (Washington, DC: National Science Foundation, 1961), pp. 711–12.

10. *Narodnoe khoziaestvo SSSR 1922–1982* (Moscow, 1982), p. 499.

11. This figure is for 1980. Calculated from data in George Avis, "Access to Higher Education in the Soviet Union," in J. J. Tomiak, ed., *Soviet Education in the 1980s* (New York: St. Martin's Press, 1983), p. 201.

12. Matthews, *Education in the Soviet Union*, pp. 116–17.

13. DeWitt, *Education and Professional Employment*, provides a listing of these codes, pp. 659–77, and a list of "divisions of instruction" (*fakul'tety*) for all Soviet VUZy in 1959–60, pp. 658–711. This dated but detailed and comprehensive work is still very useful. A more recent list of specialization codes is provided by Seymour M. Rosen, *Education in the USSR: Current Status of Higher Education* (Washington, DC: National Science Foundation, n.d., but ca. 1979), pp. 35–49.

14. Matthews, *Education in the Soviet Union*, p. 117.

15. *Bol'shaia sovetskaia entsiklopediia* (henceforth *BSE*), 3rd ed., vol. 5, p. 556.

16. Matthews, *Educatiion in the Soviet Union*, p. 119.

17. For the latest set of concerns, see V. I. Zubarev, V. N. Donchenko, V. G. Kremen', eds., *XXVII s"ezd KPSS 1 zadachi kafedr obshchestvennykh nauk* (Moscow, 1986).

18. *BSE*, vol. 5, p. 556.

19. Even so, at the Central Committee plenum of February 17–18, 1988, convened to discuss educational reform, Egor Ligachev complained about imbalances in the output of different kinds of specialists and noted an acute shortage of economics specialists and managerial specialists. Sergei Voronitsyn, "The Central Committee Plenum: Ligachev's Blueprint for Soviet Education," *Radio Liberty Research Report* 66/88 (February 22, 1988), p. 3.

20. Matthews, *Education in the Soviet Union*, p. 161.

21. Indeed, Matthews reports that only 20 percent of the students at that

institute reported being there out of interest in the subject matter: *Education in the Soviet Union*, p. 161.

22. Stephen P. Timoshenko, "The Development of Engineering Education in Russia," *Russian Review* 15, no. 3 (July 1956):180.

23. Ibid., p. 184.

24. *Sovetskaia istoricheskaia entsiklopediia* (Moscow, 1961), vol. 6, p. 117.

25. Alexander Korol, *Soviet Education for Science and Technology* (Cambridge: Technology Press of Massachusetts Institute of Technology, 1957), p. 131.

26. Matthews, *Education in the Soviet Union*, p. 97.

27. *BSE*, vol. 5, p. 555.

28. I. I. Khodorovsky, *Narodnoe obrazovanie v sovetskoi respublike* (Moscow, 1925), pp. 28–29. Khodorovsky provides no documentation.

29. Nicholas Hans, *History of Russian Educational Policy, 1701–1917* (New York: Russell & Russell, 1964), p. 239.

30. Khodorovsky probably did not have Ignat'ev in mind; otherwise he would have said so, since the more recently the quote was made, the stronger would Khodorovsky's case be. On Ignat'ev, see Oskar Anweiler, "Educational Policy and Social Structure in the Soviet Union," in Boris Meissner, ed., *Social Change in the Soviet Union: Russia's Path toward an Industrial Society* (Notre Dame: University of Notre Dame Press, 1972), pp. 173–210.

31. *KPSS v rezoliutsiiakh i resheniiakh s"ezdov, konferentsii i plenumov TsK* (henceforth *KPSS v rezoliutsiiakh*), 7th ed., vol. 1 (Moscow: Politizdat, 1954), p. 419. Cited by Gail Warshofsky Lapidus, "Socialism and Modernity: Education, Industrialization, and Social Change in the USSR," in Paul Cocks, Robert V. Daniels, and Nancy Whittier Heer, eds., *The Dynamics of Soviet Politics* (Cambridge: Harvard University Press, 1976), pp. 195–220.

32. *Prosveshchennie* can be translated as "enlightenment" or as "education." For many years now, Enlish-speaking scholars at least have used the literal translation "enlightenment," partly to distinguish it from *obrazovanie*, also meaning "education," and partly, I suspect, because the word has a rather droll quality to it.

33. *KPSS v rezoliutsiiakh*, vol. 1, p. 419.

34. Gail Warshofsky Lapidus, "Educational Strategies and Cultural Revolution: The Politics of Social Development," in Sheila Fitzpatrick, ed., *Cultural Revolution in Russia, 1928–1931* (Bloomington: Indiana University Press, 1984), p. 84.

35. See *Ezhenedel'nik Komissariata po prosveshcheniiu RSFSR*, no. (1924):10.

36. Sheila Fitzpatrick, *Education and Social Mobility in the Soviet Union, 1921–1934* (Cambridge: Cambridge University Press, 1979), pp. 49–50.

37. Ibid., p. 9.

38. Mikhail Korbut, "K voprosu ob edinenli mezhdu rabfakami i osnovnikami," *Znamia rabfakovtsa*, no. 1 (May 1922):6. I do not have a citation for "Professor's" original article beyond what is given in the text.

39. *Narodnoe prosveshchennie*, no. 2 (1930):4.

40. I. I. Khodorovsky, "Itogi priema v VUZy v 1924 godu i nekotorie perspektivy budushch," in I. I. Khodorovsky, *Na fronte prosveshchennie, Stat'i i rechi* (Moscow: Gosudarstvennoe izdatel'stvo, 1926), p. 142.

41. *Narodnoe prosveshchenie v RSFSR k 1928/29 godu: otchet NKP RSFSR za 1927/28 uchebnyi god* (Moscow: 1929), p. 65.

42. James C. McClelland, "Proletarianizing the Student Body: The Soviet Experience during the New Economic Policy," *Past and Present* (Great Britain), no. 80 (August 1978): 133. McClelland notes that the 1928 decree and instructions are in Smolensk Archives, WKP 213, pp. 113–14.

43. Khodorovsky, "Itogi priema," p. 24.

44. McClelland, "Proletarianizing the Student Body," p. 135.

45. Fitzpatrick, *Education and Social Mobility*, p. 61.

46. "TsK RKP o vysshei shkoli," *Narodnoe prosveshchennie*, no. 8 (1924):32.

47. "Vtoroi god letnei proizvodstvennoi praktiki studentov VUZ," *Narodnoe prosveshchennie*, no. 8 (1924):76–91.

48. For a detailed description of a VUZ student's practicum in the late 1920s, see the biography of Sergei Korolev: P. T. Astashenkov, *Glavnyi konstruktor* (Moscow: Voennoe izdatel'stvo, 1975).

49. I. Ryzhkov, "Itogi priema v VUZy na 1924/25 akademicheskii god," *Narodnoe prosveshchennie*, nos. 11–12 (1924):125.

50. Fitzpatrick, *Education and Social Mobility*, pp. 92–93.

51. V. Kasatkin, "Kak obsluzhivaiutsia nashei shkoloi deti rabochikh?" *Narodnoe prosveshchennie*, no. 10 (October 1928):28.

52. Fitzpatrick, *Education and Social Mobility*, p. 50.

53. Ibid., p. 89.

54. Ibid., p. 97.

55. "Soveshchanie rektorov VUZ, 21–23 October 1924," *Narodnoe prosveshchennie*, nos. 11–12 (1924):105. Also see "Itogi akademicheskoi proverki studenchestva vysshikh uchebnykh zavedenii," *Narodnoe prosveshchennie*, no. 8 (1924):73–75.

56. "Soveshchanie rektorov VUZ," p. 106.

57. Murray Yanowitch and Norton Dodge, "Social Class and Education: Soviet Findings and Reactions," *Comparative Education Review* 12, no. 3 (October 1968):252–54.

58. *Narodnoe khoziaistvo SSSR v 1984 g.* (Moscow, 1985), p. 5.

59. A sophisticated discussion of Marxist and Bolshevik thinking on this question is A. Zalkind, "Polovoi vopros i sovetskaia pedagogika," *Narodnoe prosveshchennie*, nos. 11–12 (November-December 1924):127–36.

60. Ol'ga Anikst, "Professional'noe obrazovanie zhenshchin," *Narodnoe prosveshchennie*, no. 3 (March 1927):56.

61. Ibid., p. 57.

62. McClelland, "Proletarianizing the Student Body," p. 123n.

63. Anikst, "Professional'noe obrazovanie zhenshchin," explains that the large percentage of women engaged in the chemical industry is an artifact of the Central Statistical Administration's inclusion of the rubber industry, where women predominate, in that category (p. 57). The author gives no breakdown of women by specialization in higher-education institutions.

64. George Avis, "Access to Higher Education in the Soviet Union," in J. J. Tomiak, ed., *Soviet Education in the 1980s* (London: Croom Helm, 1983), pp. 199–239. On social inequalities of access to education, also see Eh. K. Vasil'eva, *Sem'ia i ee funktsii* (Moscow: "Statistika," 1975), esp. pp. 132ff.

65. A. Rozin, "Sostoianie prosveshcheniia natsional'nykh men'shinstv," *Narodnoe prosveshchennie*, nos. 8–9 (August-September 1927):53.

66. M. Taitsh, "Pervyi s"ezd perestroennogo *Tsentrosovnatsmena*," *Narodnoe prosveshchennie*, nos. 8–9 (August-September 1927):60.

67. Ibid., p. 60.

68. Rozin, "Sostoianie prosveshcheniia," p. 53.

69. A. Rakhimbaev, "O podgotovke kadrov natsional'nykh men'shinstv," *Narodnoe prosveshchennie*, no. 3 (March 1930):12.

70. Ibid., p. 12.

71. A. I. Lutchenko, "Rukovodstvo KPSS formirovaniem kadrov tekhnicheskoi intelligentsii (1926–1933 gg.)," *Voprosy istorii KPSS*, no. 2 (February 1966):41–42.

72. *Norodnoe Khoziaistvo SSSR: statisticheskii spravochnik za 1932 g.* (Moscow, 1932), pp. 512–13.

73. Richard B. Dobson, "Georgia and the Georgians," in Zev Katz, Rosemarie Rogers, and Frederic Harned, eds., *Handbook of Major Soviet Nationalities* (New York: Free Press, 1975), p. 167.

74. Sheila Fitzpatrick, "The 'Soft' Line on Culture and Its Enemies: Soviet Cultural Policy, 1922–1927," *Slavic Review* 33, no. 2 (June 1974):267. On the purge of *Narkompros*, see V. G. Rudnitsky, "Kak prokhodiat proverka i chistka apparata narodnogo obrazovaniia," *Narodnoe prosveshchennie*, no. 6 (June 1930):15–16; and Ia. Bauer, "Itogi chistki Narkomprosa RSFSR," *Narodnoe prosveshchennie*, no. 6 (June 1930):12–14.

75. Lutchenko, "Rukovodstvo KPSS formirovaniem kadrov," p. 32.

76. G. K. Ordzhonikidze, *Stat'i i rechi* (Moscow, 1927), p. 35. The reference to *kliacha* is part of an old Russian proverb.

77. B. Panfilov, "Obshchie orientirovki po piatiletke kadrov," *Narodnoe prosveshchennie*, no. 5 (May 1930):19.

78. Korol, *Soviet Education for Science and Technology*, p. 133.

79. Matthews, *Education in the Soviet Union*, p. 99.

80. Lutchenko, "Rukovodstvo KPSS formirovaniem kadrov," p. 36; Fitzpatrick, *Education and Social Mobility*, p. 186.

81. Anweiler, "Educational Policy and Social Structure," p. 185.

82. Jeremy R. Azrael, "Fifty Years of Soviet Education," *Survey*, no. 64 (July 1967):52.

83. Mervyn Matthews, *Privilege in the Soviet Union: A Study of Elite Life-Styles under Communism* (London: Allen & Unwin, 1978), pp. 117–18.

84. Armstrong in one study refused to consider any kind of training in agricultural institutions as "higher education" because the quality of training was low and terms in agricultural institutes, like those in Party schools, were often interludes in adult careers. John A. Armstrong, "Tsarist and Soviet Elite Administrators," *Slavic Review* 31, no. 1 (March 1972):10n.

85. Ibid., p. 310.

86. The best source on Party education of adults below the level of higher education is Ellen Propper Mickiewicz, *Soviet Political Schools* (New Haven, CT: Yale University Press, 1967).

87. I. I. Pronin, "Sovershenstvovanie sistemi podgotovki partiinykh i sovetskikh kadrov," *Voprosy istorii KPSS*, no. 9 (1971):40. One could, of course,

question whether the cup is half full or half empty with respect to these figures, and in a subsequent chapter I shall.

88. *BSE*, vol. 5, p. 553.

89. Tatjana Kirstein, "Das Sowjetische Parteischulsystem," in Boris Meissner, Georg Brunner, and Richard Lowenthal, eds., *Einparteisystem und Burokratische Herrschaft in der Sowjetunion* (Cologne: Markus Verlag, n.d., but ca. 1978 or 1979), p. 220n.

90. F. Agafonenkov, "Podgotovka i perepodgotovka partiinykh i sovetskikh kadrov (1946–1950 gg.)," *Voprosy istorii KPSS*, no. 11 (1970):108.

91. M. P. Fil'chenkov, "Iz istorii partiinykh uchebnykh zavedenii," *Voprosy istoril KPSS*, no. 1 (1958):108.

92. Ibid., p. 108. For Lenin's appraisal of the Capri school, see *Sochineniia* (Moscow, 1925), vol. 16, p. 518.

93. Katz, *Handbook of Major Soviet Nationalities*, p. 246n.

94. Fil'chenkov, "Iz istorii partiinykh uchebnykh zavedenii," p. 109.

95. Katz, *Handbook of Major Soviet Nationalities*, p. 239.

96. *KPSS v rezoliutsiiakh*, vol. 1, p. 444.

97. Fil'chenkov, "Iz istorii partiinykh uchebnykh zavedenii," p. 110. The term "soviet construction" did not mean what it sounds like in English. It referred, then as now, to establishing and strengthening *sovety* (literally, "councils," with elected members). The same is true of the term "Party construction."

98. *KPSS v rezoliutsiiakh*, vol. 1, p. 877.

99. Fil'chenkov, "Iz istorii partiinykh uchebnykh zavedenii," p. 114.

100. Kirstein, "Das Sowjetische Parteischulsystem," p. 220.

101. Fil'chenkov, "Iz istorii partiinykh uchebnykh zavedenii," p. 112; Katz, *Handbook of Major Soviet Nationalities*, p. 243.

102. Kirstein, "Das Sowjetische Parteischulsystem," p. 223.

103. *Sotsialisticheskoe stroitel'stvo v SSSR* (Moscow, 1934), p. 406.

104. *KPSS v rezoliutsiiakh*, vol. 3, pp. 476–84.

105. Fil'chenkov, "Iz istorii partiinykh uchebnykh zavedenii," p. 119.

106. *BSE* (1976 ed.), vol. 1, p. 38.

107. See *Partiinaia zhizn'*, no. 7 (1978):3.

108. *KPSS v rezoliutsiiakh*, vol. 1, p. 891.

109. *Sobranie ukazanii i rasporiazhenii raboche-krestianskogo pravitel'stva*, no. 12 (Moscow, 1921), p. 79.

110. M. B. Sverdlovtsev, "Podgotovka teoreticheskikh kadrov KPSS," *Voprosy istorii KPSS*, no. 1 (January 1972):90.

111. T. Dubinia and A. Pankratova, "Desiat' let Instituta krasnykh professorov," *Bor'ba klassov*, nos. 8–9 (August-September 1931):22.

112. Fil'chenkov, "Iz istorii partiinykh uchebnykh zavedenii," p. 114.

113. Ibid., p. 114.

114. Sverdlovtsev, "Podgotovka teoreticheskikh kadrov KPSS," p. 92.

115. For example, on the struggle with the Trotskyite-Zinovievite Opposition within IKP, see A. L. Sidorov, "Nekotorye razmyshleniia o trude i opyte istorika," *Istoriia SSSR*, no. 3 (1964):123. For a version of the events with quite different nuances, see Abdurakhman Avtorkhanov, *Stalin and the Soviet Communist Party: A Study in the Technology of Power* (New York: Praeger, 1959).

116. For a discussion of the numbers and assignments of the 1930 class, see

I. Bulatnikov, "Rabochii-vydvizhenets v shkole," *Narodnoe prosveshchennie*, nos. 7–8 (July-August 1930):46–47.

117. Fitzpatrick, *Education and Social Mobility*, p. 245.

118. Ibid, p. 248.

119. Calculated from my database and from information in *Narodnoe khoziaistvo SSSR v 1984 g.* (Moscow, 1985), p. 509.

120. Although Patolichev reports in his memoirs that considerable comaraderie did develop among classmates at the Military-Chemical Academy he attended, and that these ties persisted throughout his career, N. S. Patolichev, *Measures of Maturity: My Early Life* (Oxford: Pergamon Press, 1983), pp. 56–60.

121. Sverdlovtsev, "Podgotovka teoreticheskikh kadrov KPSS," p. 95.

122. Kirstein, "Das Sowjetische Parteischulsystem," p. 223.

123. Ibid., p. 220.

124. This will be discussed further in Chapter 3.

125. Kirstein, "Das Sowjetische Parteischulsystem," pp. 221–22.

126. For example, there is the case, reported in a different context by Werner Hahn, of Stavropol' *kraikom* first secretary A. L. Orlov, who was fired by the Central Committee in 1946 for failure to perform his duties and was then sent to study at the HPS; Werner Hahn, *Postwar Soviet Politics* (Ithaca, NY: Cornell University Press, 1982), p. 60n. In a previous study, I found reason to believe that a higher "price" for political advancement is exacted of non-Slavs than of Slavs in the form of postgraduate education and attendance at the HPS. Kenneth C. Farmer, "Consociational Dictatorship or Imperium? Non-Russian Political Elites and Central Decision-Making in the USSR," *Nationalities Papers* 13, no. 1 (Spring 1985):52.

127. Matthews, *Education in the Soviet Union*, p. 136.

128. This has been corroborated in conversations with a number of present and former Soviet citizens.

129. *Partiinoe stroitel'stvo: uchebnoe posobie* (Moscow: izdatel'stvo politicheskoe literatury, 1978), pp. 310–11.

130. Michael Voslensky, *Nomenklatura* (Garden City, NY: Doubleday, 1984), p. 220.

131. Ilya Zemtsov, *The Private Life of the Soviet Elite* (New York: Crane Russak, 1985), pp. 64–65. Similarly, there have been a number of recent articles in the Soviet press on this very problem, some of which are translated in *Current Digest of the Soviet Press* 39, no. 8 (March 25, 1987):1–5, 14.

132. Zemtsov, *Private Life*, p. 67.

133. Cited in ibid., p. 64.

134. Matthews, *Privilege in the Soviet Union*, pp. 159–63.

Chapter 3

Elite Structure

We few, we happy few, we band of brothers.

Shakespeare
King Henry V

Raymond Aron wrote that "one of the most characteristic features of any society's structure is the structure of the elite, that is, the relationship between the groups exercising power, the degree of unity or division between these groups, the system of recruiting the elite and the ease or difficulty of entering it."[1]

The received wisdom on the structure of the Soviet elite is that it is (1) monolithic, not differentiated; (2) monopolistic, not pluralist; (3) one-dimensional (ideological), not multidimensional; (4) exclusive, not open; and (5) integrative rather than competitive.[2] For the most part, this is accurate. In this chapter, I want to go beyond these descriptive categories to explore why the Soviet elite exhibits these characteristics.

The term "elite structure" is used today by most analysts in a different sense than I use it in the context of "structuralism" and "deep structures." The alternative to living with the imprecision of the English language is the proliferation of neologisms. The term "elite structure" as used in the literature of elite studies means *morphology*, and I will use it in that sense in this chapter. Elite structure refers to the morphological characteristics of the political elite body as a whole, as well as to patterned relationships among elite members.[3] Usually, these elite characteristics are subsumed under the term "elite integration."[4]

ELITE INTEGRATION

The term "elite integration" refers to the internal characteristics of the elite body. This is a far-ranging definition, to be sure, and can include a wide variety of dimensions, depending on the aims of the analyst and the data available. For our purposes, we can identify five important dimensions of elite integration: (1) Elite boundaries: identifying the elite; (2) the institutional context: the structure of opportunity; (3) the size of the elite; (4) group solidarity and consciousness; and (5) social homogeneity: social and background characteristics of elite members.

Some authors, notably Robert Putnam, include recruitment patterns as a dimension of elite integration. Although this is reasonable, I have devoted a separate chapter to recruitment and mobility of elites.

Elite Boundaries

The term "elite" is notoriously imprecise, even when the discussion is limited to the political, or governing, elite.[5] In pluralistic countries, the problem of defining elite boundaries is complicated by the necessary inclusion of "influentials," that is, individuals who do not occupy an explicitly political position but whose influence on political outcomes requires their inclusion. A mitigating factor is that divergences between formal and informal power structures tend to be greater in local communities, whereas at the national level they tend to converge. Hence by concentrating the bulk of attention, as I do, on the central elite, the distortion resulting from ignoring nonpolitical influentials will be minimized.

More so in the Soviet Union than in any other country, perhaps, political authority is contingent on position—political authority being loosely defined as the right of an individual officeholder independently to make a decision on a matter in some jurisdiction (however circumscribed) and expect that it will be carried out. I use the word "authority" rather than "power" to emphasize that I am referring to a legal right; political power extends beyond this, to be sure. The political elite are those who have the ability to make authoritative decisions (thus I exclude "influentials" from my definition of the elite). In the highly structured Soviet hierarchy, this right or ability is conferred by incumbency in a formal position and cannot be exercised without it.

It will, of course, be necessary to take account of influentials, and to "alternative elites," since Soviet political leaders do consult—in a variety of ways—with other "strategic elites" in the society, and this will become increasingly the case under Mikhail Gorbachev's newly restructured governmental system. Consultation, however, will be treated simply as consultation, and nonpolitical strategic elites are not included in my definition of political elites proper. Political elites are a subset of strategic elites. It will prove necessary in subsequent chapters to examine the degree to which, and the ways in which, nonpolitical strategic elites play a political *role* in Soviet society.

There is little disagreement within the discipline that political elitehood in the Soviet context can be defined in terms of position.[6] A number of other elite studies outside the Soviet field also define the elite in terms of position.[7] Sometimes, however, the elite has been rather narrowly defined to include the top leadership alone: the Politburo and the Sec-' retariat of the CPSU.[8] Other analysts have widened the net to include Central Committee full members, or regional first secretaries, or the government apparatus at the central or regional level.[9]

Jack Bielasiak suggests that the elite should not be conceived in exclusive terms such as the Politburo or the Central Committee, "but rather as a continuum subdivided into different strata ranging from the top political leadership to lower positions in the hierarchy."[10] Basic levels in the hierarchy, then, would be the uppermost level, consisting of the top leaders, divided into two strata, the Politburo and Secretariat, and below that, members of the Presidium of the Council of Ministers and of the Supreme Soviet Presidium not in the first stratum. The middle-level hierarchy, in Bielasiak's conceptualization, consists of Central Committee members and holders of positions such as regional first secretaries— these constitute the most important reserve for promotion to top positions. At the lower level, Bielasiak would include the general Party membership, insofar as it constitutes the ultimate pool for selection to all elite positions and because Party members are also an elite with respect to the rest of the society.[11] In my conceptualization, the latter is an elite, but only potentially a political elite, and will be considered in a later chapter.

J. H. Miller makes a very interesting distinction between the "top fifty" in Soviet politics—comprised of the members and candidate members of the Politburo, the secretariat of the Central Committee, the members of the Presidium of the Council of Ministers, and the heads of Central Committee departments—and the "top 500," consisting of full, candidate, and Auditing Commission members of the CPSU Central Committee.[12] T. H. Rigby, with qualifications, suggests that for some purposes, at least, one can take "at face value the Party leadership's own identification of its "best people" at each level, as it manifests this by having them elected (i.e., co-opting them) as congress and conference delegates and Party committee members. The former I identify as the 'broad elite' . . . and the latter as the corresponding 'inner elite.' "[13]

I take exception to identifying congress and conference delegates as any form of elite, insofar as they do not occupy a leadership role merely by virtue of being a delegate (although, of course, they may be members of the elite by other criteria).

It will be useful to make a distinction between my *conception* of the Soviet political elite and my *operationalization* of the elite for the purpose of quantitative analysis. As indicated earlier, my operationalized central elite consists of full, candidate, and Auditing Commission members of the CPSU Central Committee.[14] Unless qualified by an adjective ("full" or "candidate" members, e.g.), the use of the term "Central Committee" in this book is inclusive of all three. Some Central Committee members are excluded from the analysis if they do not occupy a political post: routinely excluded are "honorary" workers and peasants, military personnel (depending on the context of the discussion), and other nonpolitical persons who constitute the leadership of nonpolitical "strategic elites." By the same token, there manifestly are political elites—holders of Party or state political posts—who do not have Central Committee membership; although they are included in my conception of the political elite, they are not included in the operational definition. There are not large numbers of these at the national level. Since the Central Committee includes most, but not all, members of the national political elite, in this sense and only in this sense, Central Committee membership represents a sample of the political elite. This distinction will become important when I turn to statistical analysis.

The political elite is only one of the specialized elites in any society. Suzanne Keller's concept of strategic elites has acquired general acceptance in sociology and political science since it was introduced in 1963.[15] Keller defines strategic elites as "leadership groups which have a general and sustained social impact . . . [individuals] whose judgments, decisions, and actions have important and determinable consequences for many members of society."[16] Keller distinguishes strategic elites from merely segmental elites in that the former include moral and cultural leaders as well; a significant impact on many members of the society is the criterion that defines strategic elites.[17]

To my knowledge the analytical concept of strategic elites has not been systematically applied to the Soviet Union, though there are, of course, studies of nonpolitical elites such as lawyers, writers and artists, scientists, and industrial managers. In most cases these have been singularistic studies of a specific group. Some of them have specifically addressed the role of such groups in politics, as well. One reason for the lack is almost certainly the not inaccurate perception of the Communist Party's traditional stranglehold on all forms of public association and expression, so that the impact of nonpolitical elites seems minimal. This is not the result of inactivity or apolitical orientations on the part of strategic elites; rather, it is the result of the Party's co-optation—through the Writers'

Union, the Composers' Union, and so on—of the leadership of strategic elites. With the reduction in the Party's role and the legislation of forms of private voluntary association and activity under Gorbachev, the importance of nonpolitical strategic elites will increase.

I would propose as a useful conceptualization the system of *nomenklatura* as a means of identifying "strategic" elites (not merely political elites) in Soviet society. The system of *nomenklatura* in a very real sense identifies all those persons *the Party* at least regards as important in Soviet society. There may be people important in society who are not on *nomenklatura* lists (especially cultural elites), but there are not many of them. The political elite, then, can be defined as those who control *nomenklatura* lists.

The term *"nomenklatura"* has entered into common usage in the West, particularly among journalists, as a synonym for the Soviet elite.[18] This is not strictly correct. Although the term is sometimes also used by Soviet citizens with the same meaning, it is done in the knowledge that this is a metaphorical usage. In its strictly correct usage, *nomenklatura* does not refer to persons but to a list of positions over which the Party reserves the right to supervise appointments and dismissals. No one can be appointed to or dismissed from a position on a *nomenklatura* list without the permission of the Party organization on whose *nomenklatura* the position appears. There are "accounting" (*shchetnaia*) *nomenklatura* lists as well, made up of less important positions for which the Party expects to be informed of appointments and dismissals but does not have to approve them.

Every Party organization at every administrative level has its own *nomenklatura* lists, and generally speaking, the more important the post, the higher the administrative level in the Party that will supervise the position through its *nomenklatura*. *Nomenklatura* is administered *only* by the Party—its *raison d'être* is to ensure *Party* supervision over personnel appointments. Hence it is incorrect to refer to the *nomenklatura* list of a state organization. A Party organization within a state organization will exercise *nomenklatura* rights for the organization.

At every administrative level of Party organization—that is, all-union, union republic, province or territory (*oblast* or *krai*), city, and urban or rural district (*raion*)—responsibility for the exercise of *nomenklatura* rests with the secretariat at that level.[19] Within the secretariats are departments (often "Party Organizational Work" departments or, more recently, "Party Construction and Cadres Work" departments) that supervise the appointment and dismissal of personnel within their jurisdiction. This jurisdiction is not limited to Party posts; all positions that entail independent decision making (in Soviet parlance, "responsible" posts) are included on *nomenklatura* lists. It also includes state and government posts, economic posts, and responsible personnel in social organizations.

It should also be noted that the exercise of *nomenklatura* does not imply that only Party members can be appointed to these posts, only that the Party must approve all appointments or dismissals.

The origins of the *nomenklatura* system go back to the early 1920s, when the Party institutionalized, and claimed as a right, its power to "distribute forces."[20] (The origins of *nomenklatura* will be explored more fully in Chapter 4.) The system took its present form after being extensively redesigned, on Stalin's direction, by N. S. Patolichev in mid-1946 to mid-1947.[21]

It is true that the term "*nomenklatura*" is rarely mentioned in the USSR publically or in print. But it is occasionally mentioned. *Partiinoe stroitel'stvo* in 1981 gave a definition:

Nomenklatura is a list of the most important jobs, the candidates for which must undergo preliminary investigation, recommendation, and confirmation by a given Party committee [*raikoms, gorkoms, obkoms,* etc.]. Individuals being relieved of duties, and belonging to the *nomenklatura* of a Party organization, can likewise be removed only with the committee's approval.[22]

Nomenklatura has been the key institutional factor in the Party's effort to maintain a "leading role" in society by enabling it to control the placement of personnel in all important positions in the society. By claiming a "leading role" and exercising it in this manner, the Party in fact set for itself the task of preventing the emergence of strategic elites—functionally differentiated, autonomous, and influential within their sector—where attempts to co-opt such individuals proved fruitless. This accounts for the noteworthy prevalence of mediocrity among the Party establishment at the top of all sectors of Soviet society and the frustration and resentment of talented individuals in all walks of life who might otherwise have assumed cultural, economic, and indeed political positions of leadership. *Nomenklatura* is an artificial mechanism that thus prevents the emergence of natural elites or, otherwise stated, inhibits the natural "circulation of elites" that Vilfredo Pareto would have expected.

Bohdan Harasymiw—who among Western scholars has perhaps done the most to reconstruct *nomenklatura* arrangements—points out several other well-known characteristics of Soviet leadership that are clarified by the institution of *nomenklatura*:

The fact that the CPSU functions more as a simple "transmission belt" than as a political Party in the accepted sense; the ability of one man with authority over a *nomenklatura* to build a power base in the Party and elsewhere and consequently the necessity for purges; and the tendency for Soviet leadership as a whole to become inbred and conservative.[23]

The boundaries of strategic elite status, then, correspond to institutional positions that appear on actually existing *nomenklatura* lists, which are actually implemented, and which do carry with them the real power to make binding decisions at given levels of jurisdiction. Hence, it would be appropriate to operationalize these boundaries in terms of actual political posts. *Nomenklatura* lists are not published, however, and are rarely referred to. Western scholars have nonetheless reconstructed much of the *nomenklatura* system, partly through inference and partly through reports from Soviet émigrés.

Ilya Dzhirkvelov, for example, gives an account of the distribution of *nomenklatura* posts by administrative level that does not differ in significant respects from those available from other sources.[24] Dzhirkvelov also provides an interesting comment on relative status in the hierarchy:

The head of a department of the Central Committee is the equal in status of a minister in the Soviet government and indeed is more important than some ministers. The head of a sector has the status of a deputy minister. Heads of departments, who are also secretaries of the Central Committee, constitute the top elite, more powerful than the government itself.[25]

The inferential method of reconstructing *nomenklatura* lists rests on the assumption that Central Committee secretaries attend local Party meetings where "organizational questions," the ubiquitous codeword for personnel changes, are discussed and which involve Party functionaries holding posts falling within the *nomenklatura* of the Central Committee. This is seen most continuously and consistently, for example, in reports in *Pravda* of *obkom* meetings, attended by Central Committee secretaries, in which the *obkom* first secretary is replaced. There is no question that *obkom* first secretaryships are on the Central Committee's *nomenklatura* lists. As another example, if in fact it were not known for other reasons, it could be inferred that the chairman of the RSFSR Council of Ministers and the chairman of the Presidium of the RSFSR Supreme Soviet are on the Central Committee *nomenklatura*, since the candidates for each were introduced "on behalf of the CPSU Central Committee" by Central Committee secretaries Egor Ligachev and Nikolai Ryzhkov.[26]

Similarly, at a lower level *Pravda* reported on an *obkom* meeting in Perm': Gennady Konoplev, the first secretary, after discussing problems of high turnover and low qualifications of collective and state farm chairmen in various *raions* in the *oblast*, said that "these facts indicate . . . that the secretariat of the *obkom* and its department of agriculture and the food industry are guilty of serious errors in work with the branch's personnel." This implies that collective and state farm directors are on the *nomenklatura* list of the *obkom*.[27]

Robert Blackwell reports that "Of the RSFSR's 76 *obkoms*, those in the 6 *krais*, 49 *oblasts* and 16 autonomous republics are directly subordinate to Moscow. The *obkoms* in the 5 autonomous *oblasts* are subordinated to

Table 3.1
CPSU Central Committee *Nomenklatura* **List**

(1)	Politburo and Secretariate members
(2)	Responsible members of Central Committee *apparat*
(3)	Editors of central Party and government press organs
(4)	ministers; deputy ministers; chiefs and deputy chiefs of Main Administrations; directors and deputy directors of collegia; heads and deputy heads of state committees and administrations
(5)	Ambassadors and responsible workers in the Ministry of Foreign Affairs
(6)	Secretaries of *krai, oblast, raion* and union republic party committees; secretaries and department heads of union republic central committees; chairmen and presidium members of the Councils of Ministers of union republics
(7)	Members of the USSR Supreme Court; USSR Procurator General and deputies; union republic and *oblast* procurators; chairman and deputy chairmen of USSR, union republic, and *oblast* state security committees (KGB)
(8)	Responsible personnel of the Presidium of the USSR Supreme Soviet and of the Supreme Soviet
(9)	Military personnel down to the rank of division commander
(10)	Heads and deputy heads of All-Union Central Council of Trade Unions, All-Union Komsomol, and social organizations
(11)	Chairmen and secretaries of professional unions
(12)	Directors of central scientific institutes; directors and teachers of central and republican Party schools
(13)	Directors of major industrial enterprises and trusts

Source: Adapted from data in Abdurakhman Avtorkhanov, *The Communist Party Apparatus* (Cleveland: Meridian Books, 1968), pp. 211-12.

the Party committee of the respective *krais* in which the autonomous *oblasts* are located."[28]

In the 1960s Abdurakhman Avtorkhanov published a full *nomenklatura* list for the CPSU Central Committee, without, however, ascribing a source. Possibly he got it from memory. In any event, nothing discovered in the intervening years, to my knowledge, contradicts anything in Avtorkhanov's reconstruction.[29] The tabulation in Table 3.1 is adapted from Avtorkhanov.

These, then, are formal appointments to or dismissal from which requires the approval of the CPSU Central Committee. A glance at the list shows that political elites dominate it, but not exclusively. It also contains military leaders, cultural leaders, scientific and educational leaders, and others. It is not unreasonable to argue that the incumbents of positions on the Central Committee *nomenklatura* list constitute national strategic elites, at least as conceived by the political leadership.

The political elite is a strategic elite, too, but it is more: it dominates the others and in fact exercises a veto over who occupies strategic elite roles. Therefore, with some qualifications, it can be argued that the Central Committee *is* the political elite at the national, or all-union, level.

My attention here is focused on national political elites, but it is clear that individuals on the *nomenklatura* lists of union republics parties, *obkoms* and *raikoms*, and cities and districts constitute respectively republican, regional, and local strategic elites, dominated in each case by the political elites. Hence, the political elite at any level are political officeholders who are members of the central committees or Party committees at that level.

To be sure, high formal rank is not necessarily indicative of great political power. Before the 1989 reforms, the position of president (chairman of the Presidium of the USSR Supreme Soviet) was largely honorific and devoid of effective political power. But great political power in the Soviet Union is always associated with high formal rank. This is not true, it bears noting, of all Communist political systems. In China, for example, Deng Xiaopeng—clearly the most powerful politician in China over the last decade—never held an exalted *formal* post, nor did Mao before him.

The Institutional Context

One of the useful functions of a complex governmental system in the USSR is that it concentrates power while diffusing accountability. This is the great accomplishment of Soviet-type political systems: the divorce of accountability from effective power means that some can be forced to pay the price of others' mistakes. The institutional context, that is to say, the morphology of the administrative hierarchy, makes a difference: it constitutes the structure of opportunity for the elite. A given position in the political system carries with it a defined competence and a publicly recognized authority, in addition to the "deep structural" aspects of domination patterns discussed earlier. A brief discussion of the institutional system during the post-Stalin years is in order, along with a brief description of the institutional changes of 1989.

There are four main geographic/administrative levels at which both Party and state posts are organized, and essentially each structure is replicated at each level. These are all-union, union republic, province or territory (*oblast* or *krai*), and city (*gorod*) or rural district (*raion*). Most cities are further divided into districts as well.

In the Party hierarchy, the body of highest authority is the All-Union CPSU Congress, consisting of over 5,000 delegates and meeting usually once every five years. The congress elects a CPSU Central Committee, consisting, after the Twenty-eighth Party Congress in 1990 of 412 members. The Central Committee in turn elects a Politburo (24 members), and a Secretariat (13 secretaries, plus five "Secretariat members," a category newly created at the Twenty-eighth Congress in 1990). Until September 1988 the secretaries supervised 20 departments of the Central Committee. The number of departments was reduced to eight, and the powers of the Secretariat transferred to six Central Committee commissions—a move apparently intended to weaken Ligachev and his allies. The Secretariat was restored to its powers at the Twenty-eighth Congress.

Each of the fourteen union republics has an identical top Party structure—a Republican Party Congress, a Central Committee, a Politburo, and a Secretariat. The Russian Republic does not have a Party organization separate from the CPSU. An RSFSR Buro was created in December 1989; conservatives were pushing in the spring of 1990, without success, for the creation of a Russian Communist Party.

At the regional level, there are 154 provinces (*oblasts*) and territories (*krais*), each of which conducts a regional Party conference. Regional committees (*obkoms* and *kraikoms*) in turn elect *buros* and secretariats. Finally, there are 4,243 city and district Party conferences, electing the same number of committees (*gorkoms* and *raikoms*), each with its *buro* and secretariat. At the very grass-roots level, and quite outside the formal governing structure, there are over 460,000 Primary Party Organizations (PPO), organized at enterprises, factories, institutes, and apartment houses—indeed, wherever people live and work.

The state hierarchy parallels the Party hierarchy. It will be useful to describe first the state structure before the 1988 reorganization and then the new state system. The state structure is based on the institution of the "soviet" (*sovet*), or popularly elected council. The first soviets arose during the 1905 revolution to coordinate strikes. They reappeared at the time of the February 1917 revolution, dominated at first by Mensheviks, and in some ways rivaling the authority of the provisional government on the local level. On October 25, 1917, Lenin proclaimed the seizure of power, not in the name of the Bolsheviks, but in the name of the soviets. They had little choice, then, but to set up a governmental system organized around the soviets.[30]

In the pre-1988 system, there was a soviet at each geographical/administrative level, just as there are Party organizations at each level. The highest constitutional organ of state authority was the bicameral Supreme Soviet, with 1,500 deputies. From among its members was elected a Presidium, consisting of some 39 members, comprising a collective head of state; the chairman of the Presidium, a post last held by the late Andrei Gromyko, was informally called the president. In addition, it elected a Council of Ministers, whose chairman (until 1991, Ryzhkov) was the head of government, or premier. Each republic had its republican Supreme Soviet, with Presidium and Council of Ministers. Provincial, city, and district levels also had soviets, each with an executive committee (*ispolkom*) and a chairman. Altogether, there were over 50,000 soviets at various levels, with 2.2 million elected deputies.

The soviet structure was a sham: the soviets exercised no meaningful power, and it would be misleading to consider deputies to soviets as political elites on the basis of their membership in the soviets (however, many people who were political elites by virtue of holding other posts were also Supreme Soviet deputies). Real governmental power lay in the ministries of the USSR and the union republics.

Gorbachev's state restructuring at the all-union level has produced a Congress of Peoples' Deputies, consisting of 2,250 members elected for five-year terms, 70 percent of the seats being contested. The congress elects a president with a five-year term, a post now held by Gorbachev and, unlike the old presidency, exercising genuine executive power. It also elects a Supreme Soviet of 544 members, virtually in continuous session and demonstrably able to exercise real legislative power.

Size of the Elite

Elites are always a minority. Speaking of strategic, not political, elites, Keller estimates that few would exceed 3 percent of the population.[31] She cites a calculation by Chester Barnard that 100,000 individuals held executive positions in the United States in 1950, or one-tenth of 1 percent of the population.[32] This includes business executives as well as political ones. Gaetano Mosca, too, maintains that a small elite can rule a large society by virtue of the former's ability, and the latter's inability, to organize itself.[33]

Gaetano Mosca quotes Machiavelli to the effect that "in any city whatsoever, in whatsoever manner organized, never do more than forty or fifty persons attain positions of command."[34] In a provocative hypothesis, Mosca further suggests that the larger the size of a community, the smaller will be the proportion of the governing minority to the governed majority; this is the same as stating that the absolute size of the political elite is constant without regard to system size.[35] Lewis Edinger and Donald Searing argue that the political elite usually exceeds no more than about 5 percent of a political community.[36] John Armstrong likewise prefers to posit a small elite, of no more than 1,000.[37]

On this scale, to consider the entire membership of the Communist Party as an elite, or along with their families as a ruling class, would give—at nearly 10 percent of the population—an elite far larger than usually supposed for a society. Specifying the size of the Soviet elite has always been problematical. This has been due to lack of clarity in definitions of elite boundaries, and these, as indicated above, have been none too precise. The most famous estimate of the size of the Soviet elite, itself equally of spurious precision, is Josef Stalin's 1937 statement:

In our Party, if we have in mind its leading strata, there are about 3,000 to 4,000 first-rank leaders whom I would call our Party's corps of generals. Then there are about 30,000 to 40,000 middle-rank leaders who are our Party's corps of officers. Then there are about 100,000 to 150,000 of the lower Party command staff who are, so to speak, our Party's noncommissioned officers.[38]

Hough estimates that the Moscow city and district Party committees in 1958 were responsible for 17,000 positions, including 9,000 in the Party, 3,000 in economic administration, and 1,200 in the soviets. He attributes 662 positions to the Riga city Party committee in 1966, distributed as follows: Party organization and soviets, 253; industry, 107; administration and finance, 85; ideological work, 83; education, 71; construction and municipal services, 61.[39] George Fischer estimates 240,000 officials in 1956, and 180,000 officials in 1961.[40] Boris Meissner estimates the Soviet "power elite" at around 700,000.[41] Victor Kravchenko, writing of the 1940s, gives a somewhat larger estimate of the total size of the elite, but he includes nonpolitical elites: "I was now, overnight, transformed into one of the *elite* of the Soviet society, one of the million or so top Party officials, industrial managers and police functionaries who are, taken together, the new aristocracy of Russia."[42]

One of the problems here is definition, and I suspect that estimates of the size of the political elite, when they are very large, include in the count rank-and-file administrative personnel along with decision makers.

Some indication of the size of the Party elite at various levels was given in a recent Party publication listing CPSU members elected by leading Party organs; all figures given here are for the year 1981. The tabulation shows 31,400 individuals elected to *obkoms, kraikoms*, and Central Committees of union republics. It seems safe to assume that these are on the CPSU Central Committee's *nomenklatura*. There were 398,000 individuals elected to *okrugkoms, gorkoms*, and *raikoms*, presumably on union republic *nomenklatura* lists. There were 2,043,000 persons elected to *parkoms, partburos*, and as secretaries and deputy secretaries of PPOs. The final category shows 2,379,800 individuals elected to the same posts; the logic of the organization of the tabulation strongly suggests that the third category corresponds to *oblast nomenklatura* lists and the fourth to city and district patronage lists, although this is not indicated in the source.[43]

The political elite, of course, includes government as well as Party officials. Qualifying as central elites would be the entire membership of the USSR Council of Ministers (115 ministers and 40 some chairmen of state committees and other state bodies without ministerial status, and 15 chairmen of union republic Councils of Ministers). Arguably, first deputy ministers could be included, tripling or quadrupling that number, for a *central* state elite of between 510 and 680 individuals. This is not excessive for a system that has assumed responsibility for economic activities.

Albert Weeks estimates the number of "top tier, highest-ranking no-menklaturists" as about 100,000, a number that includes Party, government, military, Komsomol, and other public bodies' personnel at both the central and local level.[44] This seems a reasonable estimate, keeping in mind that Weeks is casting the net wide.

Group Solidarity and Consciousness

Keller writes that "what is required for effective social life is moral accord among strategic elites.... As societies become more differentiated a considerable degree of cohesion and consensus is needed at the top."[45] Because they are subjective, attitudes in general are difficult to assess, especially so when—before the Gorbachev period—access to elites for meaningful, in-depth interviews was not permitted. Some notable efforts have, of course, been made to infer attitudes from speeches and written articles and have found differences in attitudes among elites in different sectors or of different generations.[46] Efforts to infer attitudes from demographic and background factors have had more limited success. Joseph Schlesinger denied any connection between U.S. congressmen's origins and their voting behavior.[47] Donald Matthews, however, disagrees and shows that voting in Congress on some issues is predicted quite well by the social backgrounds of congressmen.[48] More recently, Searing and Edinger deny any significant connection between background factors and political attitudes.[49]

John Higley and Gwen Moore (dealing not merely with political elites) measure the integration and fragmentation of elites in terms of value consensus and personal ties among elites:

A national elite may be said to be integrated when there is (a) comparatively widespread value consensus, cooperation and trust among the different factions that make it up, and (b) comparatively extensive and inclusive personal interaction ties among all these factions. The absence of value consensus and interaction ties among factions indicates a fragmented elite.[50]

Higley and Moore further see two types of integrated national elites: ideologically integrated elites and consensually integrated elites. The former they explicitly attribute to Communist countries, the latter to democratic ones.[51]

There are structural factors that make a high degree of group solidarity and consciousness among the Soviet elite very likely. The Communist Party has always regarded itself as exclusive and apart from society and, at various stages of its history, even embattled. This attitude is even more pronounced among political leaders. The structuralist we-they dichotomy mentioned in Chapter 1 applies as much to leaders as to the led. At middle to higher levels of the leadership, there is almost no contact at all between elites and masses. At lower levels, where there is more contact, the tendency is still for local Party secretaries and soviet chairmen to be somewhat aloof. The Soviet political system has produced a few populists.[52]

The institution and practice of *nomenklatura* and clientelism exert pressure, in different ways, in the direction both of integration and fragmentation. *Nomenklatura* without question permits a selectorate to co-opt and promote like-minded people, if not their friends. Clientelism certainly has the same integrative effect. The Brezhnev policy of encouraging promotion from within sectors and geographical areas enhanced this. This integrative effect, however, is local. Looking at the elite as a whole, their effect is to create local cliques and to compartmentalize the elite both by sector and geographically. Insofar, however, as patron-client ties extend across geographical and functional boundaries, they are integrating, of course.

Social Homogeneity

Harold Lasswell proposed two contrasting models of political elite composition. The first of these, the "independence" model, holds that there is only a negligible correlation between political elite status and socioeconomic status; that is, it holds that the political elite is highly representative of the larger society. I know of no modern society this model fits, and its usefulness probably lies in highlighting the opposing, and more accurate, "agglutination" model. The latter assumes a high correlation between socioeconomic status and political elitehood, that is, that political power is dominated by a socioeconomically privileged group.[53] The term as used by Lasswell suggests the agglutination, or fusion together in a single group, of different social-value rankings; as Putnam states it, the "powerful are also the healthy, wealthy, prestigious, and (presumably) wise."[54] All the existing evidence, Putnam notes, supports the conclusion that political leaders are disproportionately drawn from upper social class family backgrounds, that the social backgrounds of the administrative elite are as exclusive as those of political leaders, and (supported by scattered evidence), that other strategic elites are also drawn from exclusive backgrounds.[55]

The classical elite theorists, Gaetano Mosca, Vilfredo Pareto, Max Weber—and, for that matter, Aristotle—were convinced that wealth, status, and political power naturally go together.[56] We can posit a "law of exclusivity" to refer to the tendency of elite characteristics to diverge from the same categories of characteristics in the general population. Furthermore, a "law of increasing disproportion" seems to increase the exclusivity of elite characteristics at successively higher levels of administration.[57]

The "law of increasing disproportion" leaves unanswered the question of which comes first: Do the rich and prestigious arrogate political power to themselves, or does political power bring access to riches and other concomitants of social elite status? Almost certainly, in Western pluralist societies, the advantages of high socioeconomic status open political doors to those who have them—and in fact political careers are not usually disproportionately lucrative. In the Soviet Union and other Communist societies, however, the relationship is more complex. Although access to elite status is restricted to an exclusive group (the male, the highly educated, and the Russified), the Soviet elite is more permeable than Western elites in purely socioeconomic terms, *and* political elite status carries with it definite economic and status rewards that are not otherwise accessible.

In large part, this difference is due to a difference in the nature and role of "gatekeepers" in Communist societies. Gatekeepers, or the selectorate, in Communist societies exercise control over political recruitment and mobility through *nomenklatura*, whereas in democratic countries their control is sharply attenuated.

Identifying the selectorate in the Soviet system presents no serious difficulty. It is those who select, that is to say, those who exercise the Party's right, through *nomenklatura*, to approve appointments. These are Party first secretaries at the various administrative levels of the Party.

I cannot offer a quantitative analysis of the social-class origins of the current elite because published biographical sketches of leaders long ago ceased including this data. Even when this information was included, it was of dubious reliability: the overwhelming majority listed working-class or peasant background. There was a premium on such credentials, as opposed to "employee," or white-collar, background. Some biographies listed the father's class background, and some reflected the person's earliest gainful employment. We can, however, discuss the gender and ethnic background of elites with some precision.

Gender

The path to the top in Soviet politics unquestionably begins with being born male. Only two women, Ekaterina Furtseva during the Khrushchev period, and Galina Semenova (as of July 1990) have served on the CPSU

Politburo. The same Semenova is on the Secretariat, as was Aleksandra Biriukova in the late 1980s. In the earliest years of the revolution, Aleksandra Kollontai had served as Commissar of Social Welfare, and Lenin's widow Nadezhda Krupskaia served as a member of the Central Control Commission and later in the Commissariat of Education. No woman has ever served as a first or second secretary of any Party organization at the level of *oblast* or higher.[58] In September 1987 Zoia Novozhilova, who had from 1981 been RSFSR deputy minister of education, was appointed the ambassador to Switzerland, only the second woman since Kollontai to be given as ambassadorship.

Reflecting the regime's concern about gender balance in the leadership, Kyamran Bagirov told the March 25, 1985, plenum of the Azerbaidzhan Party Central Committee that

a key component of personnel policy is the promotion of women to executive posts.... At present, one-quarter of the secretaries of the republic's city and district Party committees are women. Women head one-third of primary and shop Party organizations and Party groups.... But there are still very few women among the top officials and executives of ministries and departments. Even in those branches of the economy where the overwhelming number of workers are women, they are very seldom promoted to executive posts. Take the system of public education, for example. There women account for 53 percent of employees, but they comprise only 15 percent of the heads of *oblast*, city, and district departments of education.[59]

Ethnic Structure of the Elite

I propose that there are three models—or ideal types—of the governance of multinational societies: the independence, imperial, and consociational models. The independence model would suggest that political mobility is independent of ethnic identity or attainment of high office: the society is fully integrated. The imperial model has one nationality dominating the leadership. In the consociational model, each nationality has its own national leadership below the national, or federal, level, but at the top, the various national leaders—each on a par with the others—cooperate to govern the society as a whole.

The model that definitely is not a reflection of the Soviet system is the independence model. The Soviet system does have some aspects of consociationalism, but it is probably more accurately classified as imperial. Russians, and thoroughly Russified national elites, have the prerogative of rule. Ideologically, the Soviets would prefer to say their system always resembled the independence model. What it is evolving into, if Gorbachev's ideal of a looser federation becomes reality, is consociationalism.

Of the 45 full members of the CPSU Politburo in the period 1956–1976, only 11 (24 percent) were non-Russians. Of these, 5 were Ukrainians and 1 was Belorussian; thus, only five (11 percent) were non-Slavic. Of 11 who were candidate members (i.e., never became full members), 4 were non-Russian, and 2 were non-Slavic. Of the total population of the USSR, Russians comprise about 51 percent, and East Slavs (Russians, Ukrainians, Belorussians) about 75 percent.

Some positions in some union republics appear to be "entitled" to *ex officio* CPSU Politburo membership. The first secretaries of the Ukrainian and Kazakh parties appear to be entitled (the latter only since 1971). The first secretaries of Uzbekistan, Belorussia, and Georgia appear regularly as candidate members, as does the Azerbaidzhan Party chief since 1976. The only other *ex officio* position associated with the union republics has been that of the chairman of the Council of Ministers of the Ukrainian SSR. However, in all instances this has been Vladimir Shcherbitskii, a Brezhnev protege. When Shcherbitskii assumed the post of CC Communist Party of the Ukraine (CPUk) first secretary, the post of Ukrainian premier ceased to be represented on the Politburo. This was clearly an entitlement by person, rather than by post.

With only a few exceptions, most non-Russian Politburo members made their careers in the central Party or government apparatus, rather than in their home republics. Although Politburo members with full-time positions in their republic apparatus can be said, in a formal way, at least to "represent" their republics in the center, the ethnic background of other non-Russian elites—so far as the consociational model is concerned—is probably an irrelevant datum. It is likely that through Russification and commitment to central regime goals, these elites' policy influence is structured away from the representation function. This is probably a virtual prerequisite of continued Politburo membership; the dismissal in 1972 of the excessively autonomist Petr Shelest' is a case in point.

The Central Committee Secretariat was a crucial body. It appears to have had no symbolic functions (it certainly was not representative), and it exercised real power in the Soviet system. It was comprised of a small number of men (around a dozen) whose responsibility was the supervision of the 21 or so departments of the Central Committee (these departments were replaced in 1988 by six "commissions," a move meant by Gorbachev to emasculate the Secretariat). As these Central Committee departments supervised a wide range of government ministries and other agencies, the Central Committee secretaries sat at the apex of institutional power in the Soviet system. It would not be unreasonable to assume that consociationalism would require significant representation of non-Russian elites on a body so powerful.

In fact, however, of the 37 men who have served on the CPSU Central Committee Secretariat during 1956–1976, only 5 were non-Russians, and of these, only 2 were non-Slavic. From 1965 to 1976 there were *no* non-Russians on the Secretariat, and there have been no non-Slavs on that body since the death of the Finnish Old Bolshevik Otto Kuusinen in 1964.

Looked at another way, of 273 appointments in 1956–1976 (i.e., many of which were reappointments of the same individuals), only 25 (11 percent) were of non-Russians and 134 (5 percent) were of non-Slavs. Of the non-Russian Slavs, one was a Belorussian, the rest Ukrainians. The domination of the Secretariat by Russians and Ukrainians (a dominance in which the Ukrainians are very junior partners at that) has been close to complete throughout the post-Stalin period.

Furthermore, the non-Russians who have reached this post did not do so as the "representatives" of a national minority. Their careers were largely in the central Party and government apparatus; their political fortunes were tied to the center, not (with the possible exception of V. N. Titov) to their native republics, and they were denationalized in attitude and outlook. Nikolai Podgorny's career and political orientations are well known. Otto V. Kuusinen was an Old Bolshevik and Comintern functionary who was Finnish only in the biological sense. N. A. Mukhitdinov did indeed serve most of his career in Uzbekistan, right up to his appointment to the Secretariat. He rose to the top under Nikita Khrushchev's patronage, only to lose his position in the purges following the weakening of Khrushchev's influence in the spring of 1960.

The case of V. N. Titov is particularly instructive. Titov was a protege of Podgorny, having been second secretary under Podgorny and later in his own right first secretary of the Kharkov *obkom*. Titov was CPSU Central Committee secretary in charge of organizational Party work and simultaneously second secretary of the Ukrainian Party—both positions associated with cadres selection. Titov's fall came with Brezhnev's move against Podgorny and the Kharkov organization in 1965.[60]

Finally, Mikhail Zimyanin, whose early career was in Belorussia, has since 1953 been associated with the USSR Council of Ministers (primarily in foreign affairs) and was chief editor of *Pravda* from 1965 to 1976. His career for nearly three decades has been associated with the center rather than with the Belorussian republic. In the one case where there was a close tie to the republic—that of Titov—it was less in the character of representation of periphery interests at the center than of a factional struggle for advantage at the center.

Central control over cadres selection in the union republics has been maintained through the republican Party second secretaries. The second secretary in the republic seems to have complete control over the republic-level *nomenklatura*.[61] Under Khrushchev, it became more or less the rule that the republic Party *first* secretaries (as the more visible) were to be members of the republican titular nationality, symbolic of republican autonomy. The second secretary remained the voice of the center;

and under Brezhnev, the pattern emerged whereby the republics had a national first secretary and a Russian second secretary.[62]

Turning to the CPSU Central Committee, the consociational model would call for proportionality of ethnic membership in that body, and some equality of opportunity for elites of advancement to that level. The analysis that follows is based on background and career data available in Soviet sources. These are rather sterile categories of biographical information, as noted, and much is missing that is surely of great importance: personality attributes, patron-client ties and other personal associations, and contingencies of circumstance and fortune. Nonetheless, on the basis of these, generalizations can be made about differential career mobility of various ethnic groups.

A profile of ethnic representation on post-Stalin Central Committees is presented in Table 3.2. As a profile, these figures speak for themselves. On average, about 86.6 percent of seats have gone to Slavs—63 percent to Russians, 17 percent to Ukrainians, and 4 percent to Belorussians. Non-Slavs (roughly 25 percent of the USSR population) get about 13 percent of the seats.

When the proportion of Central Committee seats allotted to the various nationalities is compared to nationality share in the total population, and to the proportion of the total CPSU membership made up these nationalities, it is found that they are closely related. The correlation between Central Committee representation and proportion of Party membership is very high (over .995), and the correlation between Central Committee representation and population proportion is also high (.986). These two variables are, of course, themselves highly correlated with each other. The conclusion that emerges is that the CPSU Central Committee is highly representative of the ethnic makeup of CPSU membership, and less (but still highly) representative of the ethnic makeup of the Soviet population. This proportionality is so nearly perfect that it must be the result of conscious design: the Central Committee is intended to reflect the ethnic composition of the Party, and the latter to reflect the ethnic makeup of the population.

The question remains of where the cutoff point lies for representation on the Central Committee at all. An idea can be gained from Table 3.3. In this table, I have calculated an index of malproportion, M, which is the ratio of actual Central Committee representation to "expected" representation, the latter obtained by multiplying the proportion of the ethnic group in the CPSU by the number of members of the given Central Committee. An M of 1.0 would be perfect proportionality; a negative M indicates underrepresentation, and a positive M indicates overrepresentation. An "expected" representation of about .50 appears on inspection to be the cutoff point: an ethnic Party large enough to merit "half a person" on a given Central Committee presumably will get

Table 3.2
Ethnic Profile of Selected Post-Stalin Central Committees

Congress	20th		23rd		25th		28th	
Nationality	No.	%	No.	%	No.	%	No.	%
Russian	96	72.18	126	64.62	188	65.51	156	38.0
Ukrainian	14	10.53	34	17.44	52	18.12	40	9.7
Belorussian	3	2.26	10	5.13	12	4.18	9	2.2
Moldavian	–	—	1	0.51	1	0.35	7	1.7
Estonian	1	0.75	1	0.51	2	0.70	5	1.2
Latvian	1	0.75	3	1.54	4	1.39	5	1.2
Lithuanian	1	0.75	1	0.51	1	0.35	4	1.0
Georgian	2	1.50	2	1.03	1	0.35	9	2.2
Armenian	3	2.86	3	1.54	3	1.05	11	2.7
Azeri	2	1.50	1	0.51	1	0.35	9	2.2
Kazakh	1	0.75	4	2.05	6	2.09	7	1.7
Kirghiz	–	—	1	0.51	1	0.35	5	1.2
Turkmen	1	0.75	1	0.51	1	0.35	7	1.7
Uzbek	3	2.26	3	1.54	4	1.39	15	3.6
Tadzhik	1	0.75	1	0.51	1	0.35	9	2.2
Tatar	1	0.75	1	0.51	1	0.35	—	—
Bashkir	–	—	1	0.51	2	0.70	1	0.2
Komi	–	—	—	—	1	0.35	—	—
Buryat	–	—	—	—	1	0.35	—	—
Finn	1	0.75	—	—	—	—	—	—
Karelian	–	—	—	—	1	0.35	—	—
Jewish	–	—	1	0.51	1	0.35	—	—
Avar	1	0.75	1	0.51	—	—	—	—
Yakut	–	—	—	—	1	0.35	—	—
Tuvinian	–	—	—	—	—	—	1	0.2
Daghestani	–	—	—	—	1	0.35	1	0.2
Unknown Slavic	—	—	—	—	—	—	62	15.1
Unknown Asian	—	—	—	—	—	—	5	1.2
Unknown	—	—	—	—	—	—	36	8.8
TOTAL:	133	99.24	195	100.5	287	100.0	411	100.0
NON-RUSSIAN:	37	27.82	69	35.38	99	34.49		
SLAVIC:	113	84.96	170	87.18	252	87.80		
NON-SLAVIC:	20	15.04	25	12.82	35	12.20		
CC EXPANSION:	—	—	20	11.43	46	19.09		
% OF EXPANSION TO NON-SLAVS:	—	—	17	4.0	3	6.52		

Source: Author's database.

a whole person. If this rule is valid, then continued expansion of the size of the Central Committee over time will provide additional smaller nationalities with representation, and this has in fact occurred over the period under study. Nevertheless, smaller nationalities in the aggregate remain underrepresented.[63]

Table 3.3
Malproportion of Ethnic Representation in Central Committee Membership,
1961–1976

Nationality	22nd Congress M	23rd Congress M	25th Congress M
Russian	0.998	1.048	1.081
Ukrainian	1.285	1.116	1.131
Belorussian	1.342	1.531	1.162
Uzbek	1.158	0.890	0.677
Kazakh	0.369	1.307	1.156
Georgian	0.647	0.621	0.210
Azeri	1.039	0.400	0.235
Lithuanian	1.299	0.917	0.813
Moldavian	0.000	1.389	0.826
Latvian	1.631	3.947	4.348
Kirghiz	0.000	1.667	0.848
Tadzhik	1.681	1.389	0.232
Armenian	1.026	0.974	3.371
Turkmen	2.044	1.818	1.124
Estonian	2.285	1.695	2.174
Other	0.190	0.234	0.376

Source: Author's database.

The age structure of non-Russian Central Committee members does not differ to any great extent from the Central Committee norm. Among the ethnic groups, however, the data show that Balts and Caucasians were somewhat older than the norm, and RSFSR ASSR elites somewhat younger. The latter fact may reflect delayed mobilization among these nationalities. The Baltic elite includes a number of men who had been Bolsheviks before these nations were annexed, and this may explain their age in republics where loyal elites are more difficult to recruit than in the Slavic areas of the country.

Year of Party entry reveals some interesting variations. The mean year of Party entry for Slavs is the purge year 1939. The mean year for Balts, on the other hand, is 1933, well before the purges. Balts especially, and also Central Asians and RSFSR nationalities, entered the Party at a somewhat younger age than Slavs, but the differences are not great. More interesting is age at the time of election to the Central Committee. Here, Balts were on average five years older than Slavs at the time of election, while Central Asians were about four years younger.

Longer terms of Party membership (which I will call apprenticeship) were required of Balts and RSFSR nationalities before election to the Central Committee: 45.7 percent of Slavs served an apprenticeship of

24 years or less, whereas all Balts and 92.3 percent of RSFSR minorities served apprenticeships of 24 years or longer. Nearly half (46.7 percent) of Caucasians and 72.7 percent of Central Asians served apprenticeships of 24 or fewer years.

The length of service in full time Party-government posts before reaching the Central Committee (which I term seniority) is considerably longer for Balts (90 percent waited more than 20 years) than for Slavs (65 percent of whom waited *less* than 20 years). Finally, although Central Asians are of about average age, and seniority does not deviate far from the average, they reached the Central Committee at a younger age than most (age 47, compared to mean age of Central Committee election of all nationalities of 51). Thus Central Asians experience somewhat faster career progression. This can no doubt be explained in terms of a smaller pool of qualified elites in relatively undermobilized Central Asia than elsewhere.

The type of educational institution attended shows some variations. A much higher percentage of non-Slavs than of Slavs attended Higher Party Schools—as though an HPS education "compensates" in part for being non-Slavic in terms of career advantage. A higher percentage of Slaves than non-Slavs attended technical institutes and universities in their home republics—simply because fewer and less prestigious such institutes are available in the less-developed non-Slavic republics.

A higher percentage of Slavs (76 percent) than of non-Slavs (ranging from 30 percent to 61 percent) appear to have been able to advance to Central Committee status with only the four-year course in higher education. Thus, a higher price in the form of an advanced degree or attendance at a Party school is in effect exacted of non-Slavs for advancement to the Central committee elite.

There are some differences in the position held at the time of first election to the Central Committee. The largest category is first secretary of the home republic Communist Party organization. The Central Asians, however, stand out with a large percentage of members holding the position of republic premier, or chairman of the Council of Ministers. This is probably due to a combination of the economic development process in some of these republics and the simple fact that many of these republics have had Russian first secretaries during much of the post-Stalin period.

Finally, there are variations among the nationalities in the mode of recruitment. This refers to Frederic Fleron's distinction between "adaptive" (or recruited) elites and "co-opted" elites. The distinction is between two alternative methods by which a political elite can obtain the specialized skills it needs to maintain its effectiveness *and* the Party's leading role in an increasingly complex, differentiated, and sophisticated society. "Recruitment" refers to entry into the Party elite at a very early stage in the individual's career—elites are recruited and then trained, or existing elites are retrained. "Co-optation" refers to entry into the elite relatively late in the individual's career: the Party co-opts established specialists. The former strategy is thought to have the advantage of ensuring commitment to regime goals, but is expensive and risks mediocre technical ability and thus loss of effectiveness. The latter mode ensures a high degree of technical expertise and is cheaper but risks lukewarm ideological commitment and hence decline in the Party's leading role.[64]

Fleron employs seven or more years in the specialization before entering full-time Party work as the operational dividing line between co-optation and recruitment. Using that convention, my data show that recruitment is by far the dominant mode for all ethnic groups except the Slavs, who are divided about evenly. In the highly developed Baltic area, recruitment leads by a factor of 3 to 2; in the less developed Caucasian and Asian areas, it leads by 2 to 1. Among the relatively unmobilized ASSR minorities, recruitment is five times as prevalent as co-optation.

The explanation probably lies in relative levels of economic development. Up to a point, a higher level of development favors greater resort to co-optation simply because a larger pool of specialized elites is available. The anomaly is the Baltic area, more developed than the Slavic areas. Two explanations are possible. It may be that beyond a certain level of economic development, the attractiveness of a Party career begins to decline because of ample opportunities for advancement to positions in the nonpolitical sector. Alternatively, it may simply reflect antipathy to the CPSU among educated people in these areas so recently annexed by the Soviet Union. The first condition may in fact facilitate the second.

To conclude, differential advancement of ethnic elites to central decision-making posts appears to be explained by regime needs and the level of economic development of the union republic. On the one hand, a "higher price" in terms of proven qualifications and commitment to regime goals is demanded of non-Russians than of Russians; the regime has less implicit trust in non-Slavs than in Slavs. If the prerogative of rule has not belonged solely to Russians, it has belonged to Russians or thoroughly russified non-Russians. Secondly, non-Slavs appear to rise to the top faster. This is explained in terms of a smaller pool of qualified elites in economically less developed regions. For the same reason, these elites seem to enjoy longer tenures. The same phenomenon of long tenures in the more developed Baltic regions is explained by a smaller pool of *interested* elites.

CONCLUSIONS

The arguments in this chapter point to a highly integrated Soviet elite. In subsequent chapters, some forces, such as clientelism, that discourage integration will be discussed, but these are weaker than those structural factors that are integrating in their effects. One of the effects of this, at least in the post-Stalin period, has been relative political stability. Putnam notes that the argument that elite integration fosters stability is a widespread one.[65] A high degree of elite integration, some argue however, also facilitates the elite's domination of the society and reduces the ability of ordinary citizens to influence policy. Scholars of underdeveloping countries, on the other hand, suspect that too much diversity incapacitates elites.[66] At least in advanced industrial countries, elite theorists agree that an integrated elite contributes to political stability.[67]

Without question, however, the ideological and value consensus of the Soviet elite has disintegrated since the mid-1980s, and the elite has begun to fracture and fragment. Without doubt, this is a generational phenomenon. John Nagle emphasized that the "managerial modernizer" generation (the Brezhnev generation, born between 1900 and 1918) has dominated the elite for most of the post-Stalin period, and that it was the "last political generation which achieved a consensus among itself on the basic framework for Soviet society."[68] This second great transformation of the Soviet elite, now ongoing, will be discussed in Chapter 8.

NOTES

1. Raymond Aron, "Social Structure and Ruling Class," *British Journal of Sociology* 1, nos. 1–2 (1950):141.

2. Roy Macridis, *Modern Political Regimes* (Boston: Little, Brown, 1985), pp. 143–44.

3. Carl Beck and James M. Malloy, "Political Elites: A Mode of Analysis," Paper delivered at the Sixth World Conference, International Political Science Association, Geneva, 1964, pp. 2–3; cited by William A. Welsh, *Leaders and Elites* (New York: Holt, Rinehart & Winston, 1979), p. 29.

4. Robert D. Putnam, *The Comparative Study of Political Elites* (Englewood Cliffs, NJ: Prentice-Hall, 1976), Chap. 5.

5. On some problems of defining the boundaries of the elite, see James L. Paynbe, "The Oligarchy Muddle," *World Politics* 20 (April 1980):439–53.

6. Jack Bielasiak, "Elite Studies and Communist Systems," in Ronald H. Linden and Bert A. Rockman, eds., *Elite Studies and Communist Politics* (Pittsburgh: University of Pittsburgh Press, 1984), p. 111; Bohdan Harasymiw, *Political Elite Recruitment in the Soviet Union* (London: Macmillan, 1984); Richard M. Mills, "The Soviet Leadership Problem," *World Politics* 33, no. 4 (July 1981):590–613.

7. These include F. W. Frey, *The Turkish Political Elite* (Cambridge, MA: MIT Press, 1965); Masa'aki Takane, *The Political Elite in Japan: Continuity and Change in Modernization* (Berkeley, CA: Center for Japanese Studies, 1981); George E. Schueller, "The Politburo," in Harold D. Lasswell and Daniel Lerner, eds., *World Revolutionary Elites: Studies in Coercive Ideological Movements* (Cambridge, MA: MIT Press, 1966), pp. 97–178; Lester G. Seligman, *Leadership in a New Nation: Political*

Development in Israel (New York: Atherton Press, 1964); P. C. Lloyd, ed., *The New Elites of Tropical Africa* (London: Oxford University Press, 1966); a major study that explicitly eschews that definition is Marvin Zonis, *The Political Elite of Iran* (Princeton, NJ: Princeton University Press, 1971).

8. For example, T. H. Rigby, "The Soviet Politburo: A Comparative Profile, 1951–1971," *Soviet Studies*, no. 24 (July 1972):3–23, and "The Soviet Leadership: Towards a Self-Stabilizing Oligarchy," *Soviet Studies*, no. 22 (October 1970); Graeme Gill, "The Soviet Leader Cult: Reflections on the Structure of Leadership in the Soviet Union," *British Journal of Political Science*, no. 10 (1980):167–86.

9. For example, Frederic J. Fleron, Jr., "System Attributes and Career Attributes: The Soviet Political Leadership System, 1952–1965," in Carl Beck et al., eds., *Comparative Communist Political Leadership* (New York: David McKay, 1973), pp. 66–77; Robert H. Donaldson, "The 1971 Soviet Central Committee: An Assessment of the New Elite," *World Politics* 24, no. 3 (April 1972); Robert V. Daniels, "Office Holding and Elite Status: The Central Committee of the CPSU," in Paul Cocks et al., eds., *The Dynamics of Soviet Politics* (Cambridge, MA: Harvard University Press, 1976), pp. 77–95; Robert E. Blackwell, "Elite Recruitment and Functional Change: An Analysis of the Soviet Obkom Elite," *Journal of Politics*, no. 34 (February 1972):124–52; and other studies of *obkom* first secretaries by Blackwell; there are, of course, many others.

10. Bielasiak, "Elite Studies and Communist Systems," p. 114.

11. Ibid.

12. J. H. Miller, "How Much of a New Elite?" in R. F. Miller, J. H. Miller, and T. H. Rigby, eds., *Gorbachev at the Helm: A New Era in Soviet Politics?* (London: Croom Helm, 1987), pp. 61–89.

13. T. H. Rigby, "The CPSU Elite: Turnover and Rejuvenation from Lenin to Khrushchev," *Australian Journal of Politics and History* 16, Nos. 1–3 (1970):11.

14. For justifications of the use of the Central Committee as an operationalization of the elite, see Robert V. Daniels, "Office Holding and Elite Status: The Central Committee of the CPSU," in Cocks et al., *The Dynamics of Soviet Politics*, pp. 77–95.

15. Suzanne Keller, *Beyond the Ruling Class: Strategic Elites in Modern Society* (New York: Random House, 1968).

16. Ibid., p. 20.

17. Ibid.

18. For example, Michael S. Voslensky, *Nomenklatura: The Soviet Ruling Class*, Trans. Eric Mosbacher. (Garden City, NY: Doubleday, 1984).

19. Bohdan Harasymiw, "*Nomenklatura*: the Soviet Communist Party's Leadership Recruitment System," *Canadian Journal of Political Science* 2, no. 4 (December 1969):496.

20. See E. H. Carr, *Socialism in One Country, 1924–1926* (Harmondsworth, England: Penguin Books, 1970), vol. 2, pp. 221, 223. Also see *Deviatyi s"ezd RKP(b), Mart 1921 goda, stenograficheskii otchet* (Moscow, 1963), pp. 425–26.

21. B. A. Abramov, "Organizational-Party Work of the CPSU during the Years of the Fourth Five-Year Plan," *Voprosy istorii KPSS*, no. 3 (1979):58–63.

22. *Partiinoe stroitel'stvo: uchebnoe posobie*, 6th ed. (Moscow, 1981), p. 300. *Nomenklatura* has also been discussed in *Partinnaia zhizn'*, no. 5 (1975):68–73, and no. 20 (1975):41; and *Kommunist*, no. 14 (1977):49–61.

23. Harasymin, "*Nomenklatura*," p. 494. I will have occasion later and in subsequent chapters to return to how *nomenklatura* facilitates building power bases.

24. Ilya Dzhirkvelov, *Secret Servant: My Life with the KGB and the Soviet Elite* (London: William Collins' Sons, 1987), p. 125.

25. Ibid., p. 124.

26. *Sovetskaia Rossiia*, March 27, 1985, p. 1.

27. *Pravda*, March 28, 1985, p. 2.

28. Robert Blackwell, "Cadres Policy in the Brezhnev Era," *Problems of Communism* 28, no. 2 (March-April 1979):35n.

29. Abdurakhman Avtorkhanov, *The Communist Party Apparatus* (Chicago: Henry Regnery, 1966), pp. 211–12. Avtorkhanov's list, first published in 1965, has reappeared several times, notably in Andrei Lebed, "The Soviet Administrative Elite: Selection and Deployment Procedures," *Studies on the Soviet Union* 5, no. 2 (1965):47–55; and Harasymiw, "*Nomenklatura*," p. 497.

30. On the earliest governmental system, see T. H. Rigby, *Lenin's Government: Sovnarkom, 1917–1922* (Cambridge: Cambridge University Press, 1979).

31. Keller, *Beyond the Ruling Class*, p. 78.

32. Chester I. Barnard, *The Functions of the Executive* (Cambridge, MA: Harvard University Press, 1950), p. 289.

33. Gaetano Mosca, *The Ruling Class* (New York: McGraw-Hill, 1939), p. 53.

34. Mosca cites *Deca*, XVI.

35. Bruce Mayhew, "System Size and Ruling Elites," *American Sociological Review* 38, no. 4 (August 1978):468–75. Also see Thomas W. Casstevens and James R. Ozinga, "Research Update: Exponential Survival on the Soviet Central Committee," *American Journal of Political Science* 24, no. 1 (February 1980):175.

36. Lewis J. Edinger and Donald D. Searing, "Social Background in Elite Analysis: A Methodological Inquiry," *American Political Science Review* 61, no. 2 (June 1967):428.

37. John A. Armstrong, *The European Administrative Elite* (Princeton, NJ: Princeton University Press, 1973), p. 15 (emphasis added).

38. I. V. Stalin, *Socheneniia* (Moscow, 1950), vol. 13, pp. 107–8.

39. Jerry Hough, *The Soviet Prefects: The Local Party Organs in Industrial Decision-Making* (Cambridge, MA: Harvard University Press, 1969), p. 151.

40. George Fischer, *The Soviet System and Modern Society* (New York: Atherton Press, 1968), p. 162n.

41. Boris Meissner, "Der Soziale Strukturwandel im bolschewistischen Russland," in Boris Meissner, ed., *Sowjetgesellschaft im Wandel* (Stuttgart, 1966), pp. 27ff. Also see George Fischer, "The Number of Soviet Party Executives," *Soviet Studies* 16, no. 3 (January 1965):432–37.

42. Victor Kravchenko, *I Chose Freedom: The Personal and Political Life of a Soviet Official* (New York: Charles Scribner's Sons, 1946), p. 174.

43. *Partiinoe stroitel'stvo: uchebnoe posobie*, 6th ed. (Moscow, 1981), p. 113.

44. Albert L. Weeks, *Nomenklatura: A Comprehensive Roster of Soviet Civilian and Military Officials*, 2nd ed. (Washington, DC: Washington Institute Press, 1989), p. 1.

45. Keller, *Beyond the Ruling Class*, p. 146.

46. See, for example, A. H. Barton, "Determinants of Leadership Attitudes in a Socialist Society," in A. H. Barton, B. Denitch, and C. Kadushin, eds.,

Opinion-Making Elites in Yugoslavia (New York: Praeger, 1973), pp. 220–62; George Breslauer, "Is There a Generation Gap in the Soviet Political Establishment? Demand Articulation by RSFSR Provincial Party First Secretaries," *Soviet Studies* 36, no. 1 (January 1984):1–25; Milton Lodge, *Soviet Elite Attitudes since Stalin* (Columbus, OH: Charles E. Merrill, 1969); Philip D. Stewart, "Attitudes of Regional Soviet Political Leaders toward Understanding the Potential for Change," in Margaret C. Hermann, ed., *A Psychological Examination of Political Leaders* (New York: Free Press, 1977).

47. Joseph Schlesinger, *Ambition and Politics: Political Careers in the United States* (Chicago: Rand McNally, 1966).

48. Donald R. Matthews, *The Social Background of Political Decision Makers* (New York: Doubleday, 1962), p. 40.

49. Edinger and Searing, "Social Background in Elite Analysis," pp. 428–45. Also see Donald D. Searing, "The Comparative Study of Elite Socialization," *Comparative Political Studies* 1, no. 4 (January 1969):471–500; and Lewis J. Edinger, "Political Science and Political Biography: Reflections on the Study of Leaderships," *Journal of Politics* 26, nos. 2 and 3 (May and August 1974):423ff and 648ff.

50. John Higley and Gwen Moore, "Elite Integration in the United States and Australia," *American Political Science Review* 75, no. 3 (September 1981):582.

51. Ibid., pp. 582–83.

52. See the interesting study by Stephen Sternheimer, "Communications and Informal Power Networks in Soviet Cities: Who Talks to Whom, to What Effect, and Why" (Washington, DC: U.S. Department of State, International Communications Agency, 1980).

53. Harold Lasswell, *World Revolutionary Elites: A Study in Coercive Ideological Movements* (Cambridge, MA: MIT Press, 1965), p. 9.

54. Robert D. Putnam, *The Comparative Study of Political Elites* (Englewood Cliffs, NJ: Prentice-Hall, 1976), pp. 21–22.

55. Ibid., pp. 22–26.

56. Of course, not all members of higher social strata enter the elite: "Only a fraction of those eligible for elite status actually enter the elite: in most countries at most times, most people of great wealth and status do *not* enter the highest political stratum." Putnam, *Comparative Study*, p. 39.

57. The "law of increasing disproportion" is developed by Putnam, *Comparative Study*, p. 33.

58. Helene Carrere d'Encausse, *Confiscated Power: How Soviet Russia Really Works* (New York: Harper & Row, 1982), p. 134.

59. *Bakinskiy rabochii*, March 25, 1985, pp. 1–3. On women in Soviet politics, see Kenneth N. Ciboski, "A Woman in Soviet Leadership: The Political Career of Madame Furtseva," *Canadian Slavonic Papers*, no. 14 (Spring 1972):1–14; Bohdan Harasymiw, "Have Women's Chances for Political Recruitment in the USSR Really Improved?" in Tova Yedlin, ed., *Women in Eastern Europe and the Soviet Union* (New York: Praeger, 1980), pp. 140–85; Gail Warshofsky Lapidus, "Political Mobilization, Participation, and Leadership: Women in Soviet Politics," *Comparative Politics* 8, no. 1 (October 1975); Ellen Mickiewicz, "Regional Variation in Female Recruitment and Advancement in the Communist Party of the Soviet Union," *Slavic Review* 36, no. 3 (September 1977); Joel C. Moses, "Women in

Political Roles," in Dorothy Atkinson, Alexander Dallin, and Gail Lapidus, eds., *Women in Russia* (Stanford, CA: Stanford University Press, 1977), pp. 333–53.

60. Michel Tatu, *Power in the Kremlin* (New York: Viking Press, 1968), p. 50.

61. Helene Carrere d'Encausse, *Decline of an Empire* (New York: Newsweek, 1979), p. 142.

62. J. H. Miller, "Cadres Policy in the Nationality Area," *Soviet Studies* 29, no. 1 (January 1977):3–36.

63. On cadres policies in the non-Russian republics, see Kenneth C. Farmer, "Consociational Dictatorship or Imperium: Non-Russian Political Elites and Central Decision-Making in the USSR," *Nationalities Papers* 13, no. 1 (Spring 1985):45–69; Mary McAuley, "Party Recruitment and the Nationalities in the USSR: A Study in Centre-Republican Relationships, "*British Journal of Political Science* 10, 4 (October 1980):146–87; John H. Miller, "Cadres Policy in Nationality Areas—Recruitment of CPSU First and Second Secretaries in Non-Russian Republics of the USSR," *Soviet Studies* 29, no. 1 (1977):3–36.

64. Fleron, "System Attributes and Career Attributes," pp. 66–67.

65. Putnam, *Comparative Study*, p. 128.

66. Ibid., p. 43.

67. G. Lowell Field and John Higley, *Elitism* (London: Routledge & Kegan Paul, 1980).

68. John D. Nagle, *System and Succession: The Social Bases of Political Elite Recruitment* (Austin: University of Texas Press, 1977), p. 210.

Chapter 4

The Stalinist Transformation

For us Bolsheviks, democracy is no fetish.

Lazar Kaganovich

For a concept that is so central to his theory, Vilfredo Pareto is ambiguous about what precisely he means by "elite circulation." He uses it in at least two different ways: to refer to mobility of individuals in and out of the political elite and to refer to the rise and fall of particular kinds of people—that is, of social categories. Harold Lasswell and his associates refer to the latter as "personal circulation," distinguishing it from "social circulation," which refers to the social and personal characteristics of those passing through a specified position during a given interval.[1] Gaetano Mosca and Pareto agree that even though an elite may be firmly entrenched, if it is to remain dynamic, it must be permeable enough occasionally to permit talented individuals from the lower classes to replace the "degenerate elements" in the elite.

So the concept of elite circulation goes beyond the replacement of incumbents by new individuals. The latter process is really a category of elite mobility, either up or down, without any suppositions regarding the aggregate characteristics of the new leaders. Elite circulation as used by the classical elite theorists thus implies the emergence into the elite of individuals who differ in some essential respect from those they replace—perhaps different backgrounds or cohort socialization experiences, or even generation. The dimensions along which they differ from their predecessors, to be significant, should be such that they would imply at least the possibility of different attitudes, orientations, or policy preferences. If the new elites are merely clones of the old, nothing of importance can be expected to change.

Unlike pregnancy, then, elite circulation can exist to greater or lesser degrees among societies or within the same society over time. A high rate of elite circulation, so defined—whether brought about consciously and artificially in a short period of time or whether it occurs naturally as a process of adaptation to new conditions—will result in *transformation* of the elite. Transformation can be defined as a radical, general, and unambiguous change in whatever aggregate characteristics of the elite the analyst is interested in. It can be assumed that this will involve new people.

Elite circulation and transformation were of central concern to the classical elite theorists. Karl Marx's deterministic theory defined the ruling elite as the class that owns the means of production at a particular historical stage; transformation would come only with their dispossession by the previously exploited socioeconomic class. Consciously eschewing economic determinism, Mosca believed that "the whole history of civilized mankind comes down to a conflict between the tendency of dominant elements to monopolize political power and transmit possession of it by inheritance, and the tendency toward a dislocation of old forces and an insurgence of new forces."[2]

Pareto, as discussed, was distinct in his approach from Mosca in the former's emphasis on the psychological traits of leaders. His famous image of foxes and lions explains elite transformation in terms of an elite having come to power through cunning, which grows decadent, becomes squeamish about using coercion to maintain its dominance (a factor that was rather important to Pareto), and perforce cedes rule to more dynamic and forceful lions. Through their incompetence, however, the lions eventually give way once again to wily foxes. Pareto's image of the alternation of foxes and lions is a graphic and attractive metaphor, but though it may nicely explain some short-term changes in elites such as revolutions and coups d'etat, for longer-term explanations it is too simplistic and too deterministic, and, resting as it does on the psychological characteristics of leaders, essentially untestable.

A dilemma lies here, of course. In the final analysis, what we wish to understand about a particular political elite has to do with what is in their minds; we wish to explain past, or predict future, policy and behavior. To a greater or lesser degree, depending on our access to the elite, we are forced to rely on indirect indicators of what is in their minds. In the case of an inaccessible elite such as the Soviet one, we are forced to a very great degree to rely on inference from their aggregate characteristics, and of course on what they say publicly.

An aspect of political elites that is central to elite circulation and transformation is the skills of particular governing elites and the relationship of these to the society's needs at the time. While both Mosca and Pareto emphasize the suitability of elites to their tasks, Pareto gives pride of place to an elite's ability to maintain its position against counterelites, using force if necessary. Mosca, by contrast, makes the possession of ruling skills a criterion on which elites can rise or fall. A healthy society for Mosca is one in which the process of elite circulation constantly rejuvenates the governing stratum with energetic individuals from below who have skills appropriate for the tasks facing them; when these individuals can no longer serve these functions, they go into decline.[3]

Suzanne Keller, speaking not merely of political elites but of elites in all sectors of society, explains elite circulation in functional terms very evocative of Mosca: "Strategic elites move into ascendancy when their functions do likewise. . . . The rank order of elites, therefore, is generally determined by the types of problems confronting a society, the priority accorded to these, and the functional and moral solutions proposed to solve them."[4]

Mosca and Keller differ from Marx and Pareto in that the former offer functional explanations for changes in the elite, while the latter, strictly speaking, do not. Marx and Pareto, whatever other methodological objections we may have to their theories, offer clear structural causal chains. For Marx, technological change leads to socioeconomic change, which leads to dispossession of the elite by another socioeconomic group. For Pareto, elites undergo predictable psychological changes that render them vulnerable to displacement by counterelites.

A common failing of functional explanation in the social sciences is that it often seems to assume that if a societal need exists, then some mechanism will automatically appear to meet that need, so as to maintain the system. In fact, such a mechanism may or may not appear, and its appearance may fulfill a short-term need but in the long run contribute to the system's destruction or—much the same thing, actually—its transformation into something else entirely. At least, a theory of elite change based on functionalism must specify the hypothesized system needs and demonstrate that they exist without reference to the characteristics of the new elite that allegedly has emerged to meet them. To do otherwise is to offer a circular, nonfalsifiable explanation.[5]

There are several theoretical contexts within which elites in Communist societies are often discussed: that of revolutionary and postrevolutionary elites, in the tradition of the Hoover school of elite studies initiated by Lasswell and his associates, for example; there is also the impact of modernization and industrialization on elite composition and task orientation. Both of these perspectives bear importantly on the first great transformation of the Soviet elite carried out by Stalin in the 1930s.

THE REVOLUTION AND NEP

Revolution is certainly elite circulation carried to an extreme and involves, at least ideally, not so much a transformation of the ruling elite as its complete replacement by another. The structure of the Russian imperial elite was, of course, centered around the Romanov autocracy, but its real sinew lay with its large civil service, made up primarily of nobles. Legally, the population of European Russia consisted of three estates: noble, townspeople, and peasants. Elite status was formally defined by the tsarist Table of Ranks, dating from the time of Peter the Great. Perhaps half the educated people of Russia—themselves making up only a tiny stratum consisting of no more than three million people, including their families—belonged to the *chinovnichestvo*, that is, the ranks of the tsarist bureaucracy. In placing its faith in the permanence of this centuries-old organic stratification, the autocracy was unable to appreciate the dramatic changes in the feudal social structure that had begun in Russia in the latter half of the nineteenth century with the arrival, in however limited a form, of capitalism and industrialization. New classes of people were forming; townspeople were no longer homogeneous artisans, but workers, merchants, a handful of capitalists, even a few millionaires. Some ex-serfs had become landowners or businesspersons themselves. A distinct middle class was emerging, consisting of teachers, doctors, clerks, and the like. On an admittedly small scale, but increasingly, the universities were opening their doors to commoners, who could rise in the civil service or army and become nobles themselves. Finally, the nobility itself, the bulwark of the autocratic system, was changing its complexion. More or less betrayed by the autocracy in the emancipation of the serfs in 1861, many had lost their fortunes, many had emigrated, some held on pitifully to the remnants of their status, and a number became socially and politically active, the repentant noble intelligentsia in whose diverse midst the seeds of the revolutionary movement germinated.

The head was cut off the autocracy in the February 1917 revolution, but by no means did its massive body—the bureaucracy at all levels—simply abdicate; even in the midst of war and a revolutionary situation, the functions of government had in some way to be carried out from day to day. The new regime unavoidably had to rely on holdovers from the tsarist bureaucracy, at least initially. The highest ranks of the tsarist bureaucracy were held by nobles, men who were not inclined to join the Bolshevik bureaucracy and who were not welcome there anyway. Specialists in the tsarist bureaucracy were of lower social status and faced limited opportunities for advancement. These were the holdovers, as Don Rowney emphasizes: "The most important source of officials who were holdovers from the tsarist years was the socially inferior subelite that possessed special skills of use to the new government. For these segments of Russian society, revolution created opportunities for advancement that had been unthinkable under the Old Regime."[6]

A census of the state bureaucracy in 1928 showed that holdovers accounted for 27.8 percent of administrative personnel; but, according to one scholar, this is misleadingly high, since many of these may have held administrative jobs under tsardom but had not actually held a rank (*chin*), and only about 4 percent of Soviet administrative personnel by the mid–1920s were former *chinovniki*.[7]

In Crane Brinton's imagery, governmental power after a revolution moves progressively to the left; as each revolutionary party or faction seizes power, it finds the country ungovernable, and the next, more radical faction steps confidently forward, only to learn the same dismal lesson.[8] The process proceeds ineluctably to the only predictable solution, a bloodbath.

The liberal Kadets failed, having no significant constituency among the populace and doggedly pursuing an immensely unpopular war. Most of the socialists, and most markedly the Mensheviks, were unable to transcend the Marxist framework, which led them deterministically to interpret the February revolution as a "bourgeois" revolution—which should by doctrine be followed by a period of capitalist rule—and so they were most reluctant to seize power or take other decisive action. The social revolutionaries had a large peasant constituency, and with bolder leadership they might have altered the outcome.

It was Lenin's genius to see clearly that the Russian middle classes were far too small and important to serve as a political constituency for any political party, and so he refused to cooperate with them, content to watch them demoralize and even destroy themselves. Lenin realized, as few among the socialists did, that the real revolutionary, destructive force in Russia at the time was not the middle class but the *temnyi narod*, the "dark masses"—the small urban proletariat, but more especially the peasantry, making up nearly 90 percent of the country's population. By placing the Bolsheviks in front of this group, already on its destructive march, Lenin could ensure his victory.

In a relatively effortless coup d'etat, planned and executed by Lenin and Leon Trotsky, the Bolsheviks took over the key offices of government in St. Petersburg on the evening of October 25, 1917. Governmental power was taken, however, not in the name of the Bolsheviks, but in the name of the soviets, or councils, the territorially organized bodies of popularly elected deputies. The soviets were powerful symbols of self-government, having originated at the grass-roots level in the revolution of 1905. This legitimating device was so potent that the soviets have remained the central, though until recently politically emasculated, institution of the government structure.

Largely, the bureaucracy acceded to the new government, many fearing perhaps that if they failed to provide services they would be lynched. Resistance was put up by the Central Strike Committee of Government Institutions, and for several weeks the new government was unable to make use of state funds or state communications facilities; subsequently the Strike Committee agreed to return to work pending the Constituent Assembly.

Governmental authority thus fell to the countrywide system of soviets. Not having worked out in advance any detailed administrative structure for the new socialist state, the Bolsheviks had little choice but to allow the executive committees of the soviets to assume power at all levels and to concentrate their own energy on assuring that the Party's best people got themselves elected as the chairmen of these committees. For a time it appeared as though the Party were fading into the background. In addressing this problem, the Eighth Party Congress defined the Party's role as one of guiding and controlling the soviets, without becoming mired in day-to-day administration. To fulfill this role effectively, it would be necessary to increase the personnel and other resources available to the Party, that is, to create a large staff, or *apparat*, beginning with the Central Committee itself.

It fell to the Central Committee to create, nearly overnight, a national, regional, and local administrative structure and to man it with capable and reliable people. For this purpose, two departments were established within the Central Committee apparatus: the Organization and Instruction Department (*Orgotdel'*) and a Records and Assignment Department (*Uchraspred*). *Orgotdel'* became the more important of these and gradually included in its mission the issuance of instructions and guidance to local Party and soviet organizations, clarifying and reconciling the innumerable resolutions and decrees emanating from the center. It also served as arbiter in interagency disputes until the establishment in 1920 of the Party Control Commission.

Lenin created two additional organizations to conduct the day-to-day business of the Central Committee, the Organizational Bureau (*Orgburo*), and the Secretariat. The latter grew up somewhat by default; prior to 1920, there had been only one Central Committee secretary, with purely administrative tasks: first Ya. M. Sverdlov, and after his death in 1919, Nikoili Krestinskii. In 1920, two additional secretaries, Leonid Serebriakov and Evgeny Preobrazhenskii, were appointed, joined in 1922 by Josef Stalin as general secretary. Lenin had no doubt created and nourished these bodies to enable him to bypass the contentious Central Committee, but the complex structure and overlapping jurisdictions of these four agencies—the Central Committee, the Politburo, the *Orgburo*, and the Secretariat—created the opportunity for a sufficiently cunning and devious man to gradually and quietly extend his control throughout the political apparatus. The only individual who held membership on all four bodies from 1922 on was Josef Stalin.

In May 1921 *Orgotdel* was provided with a staff of Central Committee instructors, whose task was the inspection of the operations of local Party organizations. Shortly after Stalin's assumption of the post of general secretary of the Central Committee on April 2, 1922, his loyal ally Lazar Kaganovich became the head of *Orgotdel*, and at the same time the department received additional staff and resources. Almost certainly with Stalin's encouragement, *Orgotdel'* began to encroach on the jurisdiction of *Uchraspred*, taking a heightened interest in matters of personnel assignment. The bureaucratic agency responsible for major cadre assignments was the Central Committee's *Orgburo*. Naturally, in the years immediately following the revolution and civil war, the Central Committee had to make thousands of personnel assignments, and so it is not illogical that this responsibility was in large part delegated to the better-staffed *Uchraspred*.

The pool of available appointees to responsible posts throughout the country was limited to the membership of the Communist Party, and this fluctuated dramatically in the years between the revolution and 1922. Party membership grew from 115,000 in January 1918 to 250,000 a year later,[9] reflecting the Bolshevik victory. The Eighth Congress, fearing the Party ranks were being swelled with opportunists, directed a purge that reduced the membership to about 150,000. But in October-December 1991 the Party enrolled about 200,000 new members, and by 1920 it numbered 611,978 members.[10] Given the magnitude of the task of staffing the new socialist state, however, this was not a large pool of eligibles. In addition, they were not all potential leaders. The majority were youthful (only 10 percent were over 40) and inexperienced. A substantial portion of the 1919 enrollment were peasants; only one-third came from white-collar and intelligentsia origin.[11] Leonard Schapiro estimates that two-thirds of all Party members in 1922 occupied positions of some authority and prestige.[12]

Uchraspred's resources for dealing with this task were minuscule at the beginning. Personnel records were sparse, and indeed early assignments were often made in the aggregate: areas of weakness were identified, and all available cadres were assigned to these areas, with no investigation of their qualifications. By the end of 1921, responsibility for lower-level assignments began to be delegated to lower Party organs, and the nucleus of the *nomenklatura* system began to emerge. The potential significance of this organizational tool was not lost on Stalin, and within a year, Kaganovich's *Orgotdel'* had taken over *Uchraspred*.

The origins of the *nomenklatura* system lay in the weakness of the Bolshevik regime in the years immediately following the revolution. In the period after the civil war the regime had not to any significant degree established itself in the countryside. For good reason, the leaders in Moscow lacked trust in rank-and-file Party members and in the ability or willingness of the local Party leadership to carry out central policies. Without firm central control during those dangerous times, central Party leaders in Moscow, Lenin included, did not believe that the regime could survive.[13] Party personnel records in the 1920s and 1930s were haphazard and incomplete in the extreme. Appointments below the national level were made more often than not by local Party committees, with the CPSU Central Committee exercising only the power of confirmation or, occasionally, veto over selections. Local Party organizations began to regard their autonomy as a right.

In an effort to ensure coherence and coordination, the CPSU Central Committee began to dispatch reliable individuals to leadership positions in the periphery. To some extent, this practice was tolerated by local Party organizations, which acknowledged the necessity of some central coordination. There were complaints, however, and, as Sheila Fitzpatrick notes, intraparty debates during the civil war over the practice of filling responsible local Party posts with appointees from Moscow rather than by nominations and elections at the local level.[14] In any event, this practice clashed with the right of lower bodies to elect their leaders; the resolution of this contradiction was achieved by rules that required that lower-level Party officials be "confirmed" in office by the center. In practice, this meant that candidates were "recommended" for "election," and these recommendations were binding.[15] This, then, was the origin of *nomenklatura*: official lists of positions that various Party committees had the right to fill were drawn up in 1923 and again in 1926.[16]

Since Party records could not ensure the competence of candidates, resort was usually taken to assigning people on the basis of personal acquaintance. This created a presumption of loyalty and facilitated and encouraged the use of appointment power to build a personalized political machine. Excessive vulnerability of lower-level cadres to attach and blame from above, and absence of any institutionalized means of defense, meant that the only defense was the protection of a powerful patron.[17]

From the beginning, then, the convention was that the Central Committee exercised the right to make appointments to important Party posts in the periphery. This was codified in the first version of the Party rules as the Central Committee's power to "distribute forces."[18] This rule remained in effect until it was replaced by a reformulated version of the same provision in the 1961 Party rules.[19]

The central governmental and Party structure devised and put into place by Lenin before and during the civil war (1918–1920) persisted, with only minor modifications in institutions, through 1988. At the very top, membership in the Politburo was held by the makers of the October revolution. The "Bureau for the Political Guidance of the Insurrection," elected at the Central Committee meeting of October 10, 1917, consisted of Lenin, Trotsky, Grigorii Zinoviev, Lev Kamenev, Stalin, G. Y. Sokol'nikov, and Andrei Bubnov. After the seizure of power, the Politburo as a separate institution actually ceased to exist, being reconstituted only at the Eighth Congress in March 1919. The core membership of the Politburo remained quite stable until well after Lenin's death, consisting (as either full or candidate members) of Stalin, Trotsky, Lev Kamenev, Grigorii Zinoviev, Viacheslav Molotov, Mikhail Kalinin, and Nicolai Bukharin and later including Aleksel Rykov, Mikhail Tomsky, and Valerian Kuibyshev. All of these men except Trotsky were Old Bolsheviks, having joined the Bolsheviks well before 1917, and all were participants in the revolution, though not all had been close collaborators of Lenin. Of the 22 full Central Committee members elected in August 1917, all were Bolsheviks, although a number of them had, again, not worked closely with Lenin in the underground. Enlarging the picture to the men in key jobs in the Party apparatus, however, it appears that the majority of these had indeed been loyal followers of Lenin for years before the revolution.[20]

The Central Committee had been the decision-making body of the Russian Social Democratic Workers' Party since long before the revolution. Elected by the Party Congress, it was empowered to make policy between congresses, and—in line with Lenin's principle of "democratic centralism"—its decisions were binding. Genuine elections determined Central Committee membership up until the Tenth Congress; that is, other than expected factional conflict not inconsistent with democracy, there was no attempt on the part of the leaders to determine Central Committee membership prior to or independently of the elections at the Congress. The men and women who had made the revolution were assured of election only by the sheer weight of their prestige.

At the Tenth Party Congress in 1921, for the first time a slate of candidates was presented to be voted on as a group by the Congress, a practice subsequently institutionalized. At the time, however, this change in practice inspired tremendous opposition, not only on the part of Trotsky and the Workers' Opposition but outside the Party as well; there were peasant uprisings over it, and it triggered the naval mutiny at Kronstadt,[21] and these had to be forcibly suppressed. The purpose of this shift was, of course, Lenin's desire to suppress the left opposition's constant criticisms and obstructions, but it also established a precedent of awarding Central Committee membership to loyal but little-known regional Party leaders.

The key to the Party's initial and continued success was organization— quite consistent with Mosca's tenet that it is organization that enables a minority to rule a much larger, but unorganized, majority. The essence of Lenin's contribution to twentieth-century politics was his early conception of the monolithic party, thoroughly organized and in indisputable command of itself, from the top down, and tolerating no other autonomous organizational entities in competition with it. Hence, as early as 1921, the same year that the NEP was inaugurated, there began the forging of a totalitarian Party from within. The Tenth Party Congress, meeting March 8–16, 1921, passed a resolution "On the Unity of the Party":

The Congress prescribes the immediate dissolution of all groups, without exception, forming themselves on this or that platform, and instructs all organizations to insist strictly on the inadmissability of any kind of factional activities. Nonfulfillment of this decision must entail immediate and unconditional expulsion from the Party.[22]

The Tenth Congress gave full power to the Central Committee to exercise this discipline upon Party organizations and their members, and although this was not published until 1924, it gave the Central Committee the right—with a two-thirds majority—to impose this discipline on its own members.[23] Increasingly, from that time forward, powers vested in the Central Committee came to be de facto vested in the Politburo and, later, the Secretariat. To an increasing extent, beginning with the Tenth Congress, the Party's top leadership relied on the *CheKa* (the first secret police organization), working through the Party Control Commission, to locate and identify dissidents.[24]

Having created the mechanism for stifling organized dissent and factionalism within the Party, Lenin proceeded to outlaw extra-Party organized opposition in the spring of 1921 as well. The regime's first full-fledged show trial was staged in the summer of 1922, with 32 socialist revolutionary leaders charged with conspiracy for treason and assassination.[25]

The intolerance of alternative organizational tools for manipulation of the masses was not limited to political organizations. The Bolsheviks regarded the Russian Orthodox church as a potentially potent foe and set about to find a way to destroy its autonomy and appeal without arousing mass sympathy for the church. This was accomplished by a remarkable political tactic. The entire Volga basin was suffering in 1921 from a devastating famine, mainly as a result of the civil war. Museums and churches were ordered to turn over any inessential property to the state for the purposes of relief, and they complied with this decree. A second decree of February 1922, however, ordered the confiscation of all church property, whether in use in services or not, again for the purpose of famine relief. The patriarchate predictably refused, with the result that it could be portrayed as sabotaging the government's relief work. In the course of 1922, 8,100 clergymen were killed or imprisoned in clashes with the regime, including Patriarch Tikhon himself, whose office remained unfilled until 1943.[26]

The nobility and the most prominent bourgeoisie had to be extirpated. Administrative change proceeded more rapidly and was more thorough in the countryside than in the city. The dominance of the prerevolutionary landed nobility in provincial government, and the importance of land redistribution, necessitated the thorough destruction of provincial administration and its replacement by the system of rural soviets.[27]

Too, the old ruling class was disenfranchised and dispossessed. Victor Kravchenko poignantly describes the case of Clavdia:

Clavdia went to live with an old aunt, in a dark garret room of what had been their own family mansion. Theirs was the bitter, half-illicit existence of "former" people, the declassed and outlawed. Young Clavdia had neither the right to school nor the right to work. They sustained themselves by selling hidden remnants of their old possessions.[28]

The totalitarian roots of the Bolshevik Party lay not only in the prerevolutionary conspiratorial period but also, perhaps even mostly, in the civil war and the exceptional savagery with which that conflict was fought.[29] The civil war led to the militarization of state and Party from the very first days of the revolution. The civil war was the stimulus for the initial forced requisitions of grain from the countryside and in general for the nationalization of the economy. There was a pervasive influx of military men and military methods of administration in the post–civil war Soviet bureaucracy. This infiltration was particularly marked in the secret police and left the permanent mark of the military ethos on that organization.[30]

From his first stroke in May 1922 until his death on January 21, 1924, Lenin's authority within the Party had been declining, more than he was aware himself, and more than history has appreciated. A recent article in the Soviet press, for example, recounts that Lenin had insisted that *Pravda* publish a controversial and inconvenient article he had written on reorganizing *Rabkrin* (worker's and peasants' inspectorate) and that Kuibyshev had jokingly suggested making up a single issue of *Pravda* containing the article, just to placate Lenin.[31]

When Lenin's pronouncements contradicted his policy, Stalin suggested that "this is not the *Vozhd'* [leader] talking, this is the *Vozhd's* illness talking."[32] The same article reports that a circular letter was sent to all Party organizations, signed by Stalin, Zinoviev, Kamenev, Trotsky, Bukharin, Feliks Dzerzhinsky, and others, to the effect that Lenin did not understand what was going on in public affairs and that they were to pay no heed to anything he said or wrote.[33]

There is no need to review in great detail here Stalin's battles with the left and right oppositions in the half decade after Lenin's death. The "triumvirate" of Stalin, Kamenev, and Zionviev succeeded in the political defeat of Trotsky (later dropped from the leadership and forced into exile), but no sooner than this was done Stalin made a switch to the right, inventing the Left Opposition. The Left Opposition, the artifact of Stalin's manipulation, subsequently became the real United Opposition (Trotsky, Zinoviev, Kamenev, Lenin's widow Nadezhda Krupskaia, Yurii Piatakov, and others), which by the end of 1925 had been disgraced. In plenary sessions of the Central Committee in the summer and fall of 1926, Zinoviev and Kamenev were expelled. Kamenev's public repentance at the Fifteenth Congress in 1927 did not gain him reelection to the Politburo.

Having defeated the Left Opposition, in alliance with Bukharin and the Right, Stalin fabricated a Right Opposition consisting of Nikolai Bukharin, Mikhail Tomsky, and Aleksei Rykov. By November, 1929, Bukharin and Tomsky had been forced out of the leadership, followed by Rykov a month later. By the end of December, 1930, Stalin had a compliant Politburo consisting for the most part of men who owed him their positions, and therefore their loyalty. These were: full members Kliment Voroshilov, Lazar Kaganovich, Mikhail Kalinin, Stanislav Kossior, Valerian Kuibyshev, Viacheslav Molotov, Yan Rudzutak, and Sergo Ordzhonikidze; and candidate members Anastas Mikoyan, Vlas Chubar', and Anatoly Petrovsky.

The relative calm of the mid to late 1920s period served, in a real sense, as a camouflage under which the Party, already centralized and subject to discipline within, established itself as the sole legitimate force in Soviet society, consolidating within itself all decision-making authority and eliminating the possibility of mass resort to any kind of group protection against the arbitrary power of the state. This process of atomization went largely unnoticed, or at least unremarked, because of the illusion of the permanence of the benign political and economic conditions of the NEP. Some high-ranking members of the leadership who would have been repulsed by foreknowledge of what was to come, and who perhaps should have known better, shared the illusion.

Bukharin, at least by 1928, did not. The Trotsky Archive contains Kamenev's notes on a conversation with Bukharin in Kamenev's apartment on July 11, 1928. Kamenev asked Bukharin, "Is the struggle really serious?" to which Bukharin replied:

That's just what I wanted to talk about. We feel that Stalin's line is ruinous for the whole revolution. We could be overthrown on account of it. The disagreements between us and Stalin are many times more serious than the disagreements we used to have with you.... I have not spoken with Stalin for several weeks.

He is an unprincipled intriguer, who subordinates everything to the preservation of his own power. He changes his theory according to whom he needs to get rid of. . . . Now he has made concessions, so that he can cut our throats. We understand this, but he maneuvers so as to make us appear to be the schismatics.[34]

Stalin manipulated Party membership in his struggle with the opposition, carrying out massive purges of organizations where the oppositionists were strong, followed by mass recruitment to provide votes for his group.[35] Stalin's overall strategy in forging his personal dictatorship, however, was centered around the placement of personnel. In his position as general secretary he had considerable opportunity to manipulate personnel assignments and to place men who owed their careers to him in influential positions. Clientelism, for reasons I will discuss in Chapter 7, was rife in the early years of Soviet power, and Stalin used it masterfully.[36]

Stalin, as "patriarch," was aware of the potential power of his "organizational weapon," and that the basis of his power was located in his ability to manipulate factions. He was wary, therefore, of men who built patriarchal subsystems of their own. A leader with a large "tail" was problematical for Stalin in at least two ways: he could be refractory at best, and at worst a threat to Stalin's position, or so it might have seemed to Stalin, for whom "coalition" betokened "conspiracy." It is noteworthy that the men Stalin felt compelled to destroy—Bukharin and the other Old Bolsheviks, for example—were men who had substantial personal followings. It is remarkable that most of the men around Stalin who survived—Georgii Malenkov, Andrei Andreev, Lazar Kaganovich, Andrei Zhdanov, Nikolai Patolichev, Nikita Khrushchev, and so on—did not. Those who did, such as Lavrentil Beria, had only small networks of clients safely distant from Moscow.[37]

Stalin's men had another intriguing characteristic: most of the late 1930s Politburo belonged to a clique that has been called the *Nizhnenovgorodskoe zemliachestvo* (Nizhnii Novgorod landsmen), all having participated in the revolution and having been associated with the Nizhnii Novgorod (now the city of Gorky) Party organization at one time or another. These included Anastas Mikoyan, Viacheslav Molotov, Andrei Andreev, Lazar Kaganovich, Georgii Malenkov, and Andrei Zhdanov.

A. I. Mikoyan reports in a recently published memoir that in the early 1920s Stalin was regarded as the voice of moderation in the Party. No one considered him a potential dictator, and they supported him for that reason in preference to more authoritarian and high-handed men like Trotsky:

Looking back, I don't think any of them saw in Stalin a serious rival, a pretender to the role of *vozhd* of the Bonapartist type. Therefore, we preferred to rapidly confirm him, so as not to be stuck with one of the leaders more authoritarian than Stalin, because he wouldn't impose his will but would conduct collective leadership. Today, this seems not only strange but even unbelievable, but in my opinion that's the way it was.[38]

Kamenev was rudely and noisily shouted down when, at the Fourteenth Party Congress in December 1925, he said, "I have arrived at the conviction that Comrade Stalin cannot fulfill the role of unifier of the Bolshevik staff."[39] Stalin himself continued to emphasize collegiality, at least outwardly. At the same congress, he insisted in clear terms that there would be no repression of top Party leaders: "We are against the policy of decapitation. This does not mean that the leaders will be allowed to do what they like in the Party. Oh no, there will be no kowtowing to the leaders. If any one of us goes too far he will be called to order.... Collegiate leadership—that is what we need now."[40]

The men whom Stalin brought into the top leadership of Party and state were men of a coarser moral and intellectual breed than the Old Bolsheviks they replaced, though some, such as Ordzhonikidze, were talented and dedicated. Kaganovich, it is said, was barely literate. Most (again with notable exceptions such as Kirov and Ordzhonikidze) were disliked; jokes involving an obscene pun on Kuibyshev's name were circulated after his death in 1935.

Stalin's selections of individuals for important Party posts were sometimes made in a most casual way. A. A. Andreev wrote in his memoirs that Stalin approached him during the Fifteenth Congress in 1927 and said, "What would you say to being sent to the North Caucasus as *kraikom* first secretary? Our leadership there is weak."[41] He did go, his most important task there to oversee collectivization.

Aleksei Chuianov, later to be Stalingrad first secretary during World War II, relates in his memoirs an episode that took place in 1937 when he worked for the Central Committee Department of Leading Party Organs. Part of his responsibility was to vet candidates for positions in industrial enterprises. Ordzhonikidze called him one evening and gave him the names of more than ten men he wanted approved as mine directors, and he wanted them confirmed by morning. Chuianov worked all night—for 15 hours—calling various mines, *partkoms*, and *gorkoms*. When he explained to Burmistenko the next morning the lengths to which he had gone, Burmistenko said laughing, "Foolish lad, all you had to do was send it to the Secretariat and say that Sergo had asked for immediate confirmations."[42]

Not long after that, Chuianov was summoned to the office of Central Committee secretary Andreev and informed that he was going to Stalingrad as *obkom* first secretary.

At that time a Politburo courier came in with a packet; taking it, Andreev said, "Here is the Politburo decision." I didn't know what to say to these words.

"And so, think of yourself as a future secretary of a Party *obkom*," he continued, "you can't go in an old student's suit." He got the administrator of affairs to the Central Committee on the phone. "I'm sending Comrade Chuianov to you. Dress and shoe him, like a future *obkom* secretary, at Central Committee expense. He has no money."

And then to me again: "You have to leave today, don't even go home. Call your wife, have her meet you at the station, give her the old suit. Try to quickly familiarize yourself with everything, and get down to the business of the conference. Andrianov is working as second secretary. He was sent there not long ago. A firebrand. Having some success."

So within hours, I closed out business at the Central Committee department, changed clothes, and without stopping at home went to the station. There my wife met me with our six-year-old son Vladimir. "Why in such a hurry, that you couldn't even go home? What happened?" "Nothing happened," I said. "It simply must be."[43]

Although writing about the year 1946, N. S. Patolichev too gives an example of how Stalin made personnel decisions himself in the name of the Central Committee:

Stalin continued pacing, then he stopped in front of me and asked, "How old are you?"
"Thirty-seven."
Stalin looked at me closely. "When did you join the Party?"
"1928."
Stalin paced some more, then stopped in front of me again. "What do you say we make you a secretary of the Central Committee?" He looked at me, then renewed his pacing. When he turned his back to me, I looked at Zhdanov and Kuznetsov. Zhdanov, smiling, shrugged his shoulders as if to say, "Make up your own mind." Turning to me, Stalin said, "Well, say something!" "Comrade Stalin, do what you think is best" was my answer.
Stalin then went to the telephone, dialed a number and said, apparently to Poskrebyshev, "Write down a second point for the draft Central Committee decision: confirm Comrade Patolichev as a secretary of the Central Committee."[44]

The period of the NEP, designed to allow the economy to recover after seven years of international and civil war and revolution, was a period that allowed some limited small-scale free enterprise and in particular marked the end of forced requisitions of grain from the countryside that had marked "War Communism." The peasants were to be allowed to increase their productivity, indeed, as echoed in Bukharin's famous phrase, to "enrich themselves,"[45] in the hope that a prosperous and taxable rural economy would eventually provide the capital for industrialization. The opposite point of view, the left position, was that there was no alternative to "primitive socialist accumulation"—originally a thesis of Yevgeny Preobrazhensky[46]—and that the peasantry must be forced to underwrite rapid industrialization.

The "Great Debate" of 1924 to 1928 centered around just this question of how, at what pace, and at whose expense industrialization should be accomplished. Stalin, until the very end, always emerged from these debates as the moderate, the voice of reason, while the left and right demanded each other's blood. A master of organizational politics, Stalin cynically but brilliantly maneuvered between the left and right in the course of the Great Debate, now allying with one side to isolate and defeat the other, then nimbly switching sides to defeat his erstwhile allies. At the same time, working with Kaganovich, he used *Orgotdel'* to place men useful, and loyal, to him in strategic posts throughout the country. Stalin was straightforward about his methods in manipulating personnel: "To be a leader and organizer means, first of all, to know your Party cadres, to be able to grasp their strengths and weaknesses . . . and second, to know how to assign them."[47] A chilling adumbration of the purges still to come occurred at the funeral of Commissar of War Mikhail Frunze, who had died during surgery, when Stalin said, "Perhaps this is the way, just this easily and simply, that all the old comrades should be lowered into their graves."[48]

The Thirteenth Party Congress of 1924 returned Stalin, Rykov, Kamenev, Zinoviev, Tomsky, Bukharin, and Trotsky as full Politburo members and Molotov, Kuibyshev, Kalinin, and Dzerzhinsky as candidate members. Stalin also enlarged the membership of the Central Committee from 27 to 40 members, selecting the new members carefully. He justified this as a measure to bring in new people free from personal influences and the factionalism that had developed in the central leadership.[49] Stalin continued to enlarge subsequent Central Committees until 1927 (the Fifteenth Congress) when 71 full and candidate members were elected; the membership remained stable after that until 1952. Stalin's strategy was to dilute the influence of his opponents by bringing in ever more members loyal to him, without taking the premature political risk of trying to force his foes out of the Central Committee.[50] Truly dramatic enlargement of the Central Committee only began in 1952, and it continued throughout the Khrushchev and Brezhnev periods.

Membership turnover on the Central Committee, defined as the percentage of members of a given Central Committee who are being elected for the first time, is a direct measure of stability. Turnover among candidate Central Committee members was always much higher during the Stalin period than that among full members, hovering around 50 percent. Among full members, after 1921 the turnover remained stable at between 4 percent and 17 percent until the Eighteenth Congress in 1939, at which 66 percent of full and 97 percent of candidate members were elected for the first time, reflecting, of course, the purges between the Seventeenth and Eighteenth Congresses. Membership renewal was almost as high at the Nineteenth Congress, with 63 percent of full and 88 percent of candidate members elected for the first time. Turnover at the Twentieth Congress was 30 percent for full members; Krushchev's renewal did not become dramatically evident until the Twenty-second Congress in 1961, when 46 percent of full and 77 percent of candidate members were newly elected.

Stalin also dramatically increased rank-and-file Party membership; 203,000 new members were inducted in the "Lenin enrollment" of the spring of 1924, a 50 percent increase. Within a few months, 200,000 more new members were admitted. The effect of this was to reduce the Old Guard—those who had jointed the Party before 1917—to a minority of Party membership and, of course, thereby to reduce their influence. This is shown in the distribution of year of Party entry of delegates to all Union Party congresses, if delegate status can be considered an indication of membership in the Party's trusted *aktiv* (activists); as early as 1920, more than half of delegates had joined the Party after the civil war, and by the time of the Seventeenth Congress in 1934 this proportion had risen to three-fourths. By 1934, 90 percent of all Party members had joined the Party after the Bolshevik victory in the civil war. In spite of this fact, however, Old Bolsheviks and civil war veterans continued to dominate Central Committee membership throughout the NEP period and beyond, still comprising 67 percent of full and candidate members elected at the Seventeenth Congress.

THE CULTURAL REVOLUTION

The new system required more than a political elite, of course. Technical intelligentsia in all areas of industry and agriculture were needed. Since the first generation of top Soviet leaders and technical specialists came from essentially the same class—the intelligentsia—it would be well to make some distinctions between them. The Russian words *intelligentsia* and *intelligent* have no precise English equivalents. The term came to be used in the Nineteenth century to refer to social critics. It has lost this meaning in Soviet usage, however, and today simply refers to individuals engaged primarily in mental, as opposed to purely manual, labor. It carries no connotation of critical or creative thought as does the English word "intellectual." "Technical intelligentsia," as I will use the term, refers to specialists in industrial fields possessing higher specialized education and who are active in industry.[51] This includes both "line" personnel, such as managers, directors, technical directors, or chief engineers, and "staff" personnel, such as engineers who have advisory or consulting and planning functions but no managerial responsibilities. The Soviet designation for this group of individuals is *inzhenerno-tekhnicheskie rabotniki* (engineering-technical workers), usually shortened to ITR.

Those members of the ITR available after the revolution had been trained, and most had become active in their careers, well before the revolution. Few, if any, identified themselves with the proletariat or looked upon the revolution or the Bolshevik seizure of power with sympathy. Many of the tsarist technical intelligentsia took up arms against the Bolsheviks or emigrated. Stephen Timoshenko, an engineer and professor trained before the revolution, relates in his memoirs the circumstances of his emigration in 1920:

The next morning we went to talk to the ataman. The general received us very graciously, set forth in simple terms his opinion about the position of professors. He believed that the struggle against bolshevism would be a long one, but that, when it was over, the new Russia would need its men of science. These people were of no value at all in the present fight, but in migrating to Yugoslavia they would preserve for the future Russia the traditions of Russian science.[52]

Even before the Bolshevik takeover, beginning with the decree on workers' control of November 1917, factory committees of workers had the right to participate in all aspects of factory management, and this contributed to more or less continual conflict between the workers and the ITR over the control of production.[53] After October 1917 the Bolshevik leaders were reluctant to interfere with workers' control, occupied as they were with the civil war, and content to have nationalized only the "commanding heights" of heavy industry and finance. Only a loose control was maintained through the Council of the National Economy (VSNKh). The grievances of the ITR were related to their commitment to a capitalist form of industrial organization, to their fear that mismanaged Russian industry would fall under German, British, or U.S. control (depending on the uncertain outcome of the war), and significantly, as Nicholas Lampert emphasizes, to their "injured professional self-esteem."[54] Because of their uncamouflaged capitalist orientation and the fact that they had been trained and had worked under tsarism, they soon acquired the pejorative Bolshevik label "bourgeois specialists."

During the civil war and after, the bourgeois specialists were in a difficult situation. They were subject to the hostility of virtually the entire working class (as their former bosses) and of radicals within the Party. "Specialist-baiting" (*spetseedstvo*) remained a serious problem until the early 1930s; they were harassed, sometimes beaten, and occasionally murdered. They had some protectors in the elite: Rykov, Bukharin, the writer Maksim Gorky, and most especially Lenin. Lenin had respected them and considered their services essential to the survival of the regime, as he constantly exhorted. By the end of the civil war, and with the coming of NEP, most of the bourgeois specialists remaining in the Soviet Union were working for the regime; as managers and engineers in production, and even in central and local agencies of the government. With the nationalization of much of industry, workers' control was weakened, and the authority of the ITR was somewhat restored.

The relationship between the Party and the bourgeois technical intelligentsia, then, was one of uneasy and fitful accommodation. In order to provide at least some Communist supervision of the bourgeois specialists, the Party had decided in the early 1920s to provide part-time "Red Directors" courses for industrial managers. These were administered by the Moscow *Gorkom*, and in April 1925 the first cohort of 134 students began work. Over the next several years, "Red Directors" courses were established in many major industrial cities, full-time instruction was inaugurated, and the course was gradually lengthened from one to four years.[55] An additional, and significant, means of creating loyal managers was the system of Industrial Academies (*Promakademii*), established in 1927 under VSNKh at Kuibyshev's initiative. By the end of the First Five-Year Plan, there were 14 *Promakademii* with 3,000 industrial managers studying in them.[56]

In 1928 the uneasy *modus vivendi* between the regime and the bourgeois specialists changed drastically. Having overcome most of his opponents within the leadership, Stalin inaugurated the First Five-Year Plan (which envisaged rapid, forced-pace industrialization and the collectivization of agriculture) and with it the complex of policies that at the time was called the cultural revolution. The cultural revolution was a confrontation between the Communists, championing and to a progressively greater degree comprises of, the proletariat, and the "bourgeois" intelligentsia.[57] The confrontation was described, with the early Bolsheviks' incomparable candor, as class war.

The Bolsheviks had found themselves in an unenviable position for successful revolutionaries. Having carried out an avowedly "proletarian" revolution—that is, based upon and putatively in the interests of the urban working class—and aspiring to industrialize the country, they found in the 1920s that they were dependent upon the bourgeois engineers and technical specialists who were trained and became affluent under tsardom. After years of the Great Debate, Stalin finally endorsed the view (ironically, earlier associated with Trotsky) that the peasantry would have to underwrite industrialization; to effect this, private agriculture was brutally collectivized during the First Five-Year Plan.

What is of greater interest here, however, is Stalin's determination to create a new proletarian intelligentsia, promoted from the working class. The result of this was unprecedented upward mobility for tens of thousands of people: peasants became workers, unskilled workers became skilled technicians, skilled workers became engineers and managers. It is sometimes tempting, from our Western perspective, to assume that Stalin must have been unpopular because of his repressive policies and the Great Purges of the 1930s. But in terms of personal mobility and advancement, in industry and in the Party and state apparatus, the people whose support counted benefited from these policies, whereas the sentiments of those who were dispossessed, purged, exiled, imprisoned, or murdered did not count, at least not to Stalin. This is inherent in the nature of purges.

During the NEP, the apolitical stance of the bourgeois specialists had been tolerated. With the beginning of the First Five-Year Plan, however, the attitude of the regime changed. From 1928 until mid-1931 the bourgeois technical intelligentsia—along with the cultural intelligentsia—became once against the object of a vicious campaign on Stalin's part to depict them as not merely bourgeois, but as class enemies and counter-revolutionaries.

The event that signaled the beginning of the cultural revolution was the Shakhty affair, a show trial of bourgeois mining engineers from the Shakhty coal-mining region in the Donbas, then in the North Caucasus. Show trials were a common means of manipulating public opinion and intimidating particular groups of people and had been employed since the earliest days of the revolution. But the Shakhty trial was so far the largest and most spectacular of these, and it attracted international attention (not least because five of the arrested engineers were German nationals). It served Stalin so well that the show trial was to become a favorite technique in the decade to come.

But the Shakhty affair was not directed against political opponents of Stalin, real or imagined. It was, rather, a declaration of class war. One of the western reporters who witnessed the trial wrote:

We wrote of evidence and witnesses and judicial rulings, fortifying the illusion that this was, in a rough and strange way, a tribunal of justice. All the time I knew, as those around me knew, that the innocence or guilt of these individuals was of no importance. *It was the indubitable guilt of their class that was being demonstrated.*[58]

The trial began on May 18, 1928, in Moscow and lasted for six weeks. Extraordinary efforts were made to publicize it: present were movie cameras, Soviet and foreign newspaper reporters,[59] and a gallery of Soviet citizens, including school children. It has been estimated that more than 100,000 Soviet citizens watched some part of the trial in person before it was over.[60] The trial was particularly popular with workers, who resented the better working conditions and higher pay and privileges, as well as the perceived "arrogance," of their bourgeois masters.[61] Andrei Vyshinsky, the former Menshevik who was to preside over the show trials of the 1930s and later became the Soviet representative at the Nuremburg trials, presided over the collegium of five judges. The prosecutor was Nikolai Krylenko, a zealous Old Bolshevik, who shaved his head and wore sporting clothes at the trial.[62]

Fifty Russian engineers and three Germans (the other two arrested having been released) were tried. Many of these held high and responsible positions in the coal industry; they were all "bourgeois," in that they had worked as engineers before the revolution. They were accused of conspiring with former owners of the mines, now abroad, and engaging in systematic sabotage and "wrecking." Why the former owners would want their mines wrecked is never made entirely clear; by the terms of the conspiracy, they would be returning to reclaim them. The conspiracy was aimed ultimately at aiding the foreign military intervention in the USSR said to be planned by the capitalists. The conspiracy was said to extend to foreign intelligence agencies and to have sympathizers even in the ministerial apparatus in Moscow—a hint perhaps meant to extort support for Stalin from highly placed skeptics in the Party and government who considered the charges ridiculous.

The original accusation—that the Shakhty engineers were in contact with the former mine owners, now abroad and planning sabotage—was met with considerable skepticism in Moscow, first on the part of the Osobennoe Gosudarstvennoe Politicheskoe Upravlenie (OGPU) chairman, V. R. Menzhinsky, and later on the part of Rykov and Kuibyshev. As evidence, the OGPU representative in the North Caucasus, Efim G. Evdokimov, had presented letters from the former owners to the engineers. Since the letters contained nothing incriminating, Evdokimov insisted that they were written in code. Menzhinsky ordered him either to decode the letters before making any arrests or to forget the matter. The matter might then have been dropped but for Stalin's intervention. He gave Evdokimov and the North Caucasus OGPU carte blanche to prosecute the case and obtain confessions.[63]

Ten of the defendants confessed and implicated others, some retracting their signed confessions at the trial. Six made partial confessions. The rest, including the Germans, pleaded innocent. No documentary evidence of any kind was presented by Krylenko—the prosecution's case stood solely on the strength of confessions extracted during lengthy, exhausting nighttime interrogations, if not torture. On several occasions Krylenko attempted to engage in technical disputation with the engineer-defendants, to his own embarrassment. At the end, Krylenko demanded the death sentence for 22 of the defendants. Vyshinsky sentenced 11 to death, 6 of which sentences were commuted to life imprisonment as reward for turning state's evidence, and the remainder were sentenced to terms of from one to ten years. One of the Germans was acquitted, and the other two were given suspended sentences,[64] a predictable conciliatory gesture, since Stalin depended heavily on Germany for industrial material and assistance.

In 1935 a prominent Soviet sociologist could interpret the significance of the trials as follows:

In July 1928 Comrade Stalin in his report to the Leningrad *aktiv* said: "The lesson to be drawn from the Shakhty trial is this: we must accelerate the tempo of education, the creation of a new technical intelligentsia from people of the working class, dedicated to the business of socialism and capable of assuming technical leadership of our socialist industry."[65]

Several other interpretations of the significance of the Shakhty affair are possible. One is that Stalin needed the services of the bourgeois technicians, which he certainly did, but they, like the Right Opposition, were opposed to his policy of rapid industrialization on the grounds that it was inefficient or technically infeasible, or both. If the technicians could not be convinced of the rightness of Stalin's policies, then they had to be terrified into submission. Their unity and esprit de corps must be broken to prevent even the possibility of organized opposition. The trial, therefore, was a warning to the bourgeois engineers. This interpretation is very close to that of Nicholas Lampert, who emphasizes that the campaign constituted

a drastic assertion of the primacy of *political* definitions of the situation against the intellectual's claim to authority on the basis of *specialised knowledge*. This was part of an attempt, directed at the intelligentsia as a whole, to undermine existing professional commitments and thereby to establish a closer harmony between the activities of intellectuals and the currently interpreted interests of the state.[66]

In addition, Lampert suggests that Stalin was irked by the ITR's professional skepticism of his ambitious plans for rapid industrialization and he promoted an image of Bolshevik enthusiasm and willpower—the Bolsheviks' ability to overcome obstacles by sheer revolutionary élan—and counterposed this to the technicians' "philistinism."[67] This may have been at least a part of Stalin's motivation, but it was not the result of the trial; some engineers became passive and quiescent, avoiding responsibility, but most did not, necessitating another show trial in 1930, discussed below.

A second possible interpretation is that the message was directed to the masses to demonstrate to them the necessity of constant political vigilance and loyalty because, even 11 years after the revolution, international conspiracies of bourgeois wreckers and saboteurs were still active in their midst. The engineer-wreckers could also serve as convenient scapegoats for the shortages, inefficiencies, and blatant inanities, of the Stalinist economic system. The masses could be terrified into willingness to make even greater sacrifices by the implicit threat of international conspiracies and even of imminent foreign military invasion.[68] Again, this may have been, and probably was, a part of Stalin's motivation. If so, then again there is evidence that the outcome did not measure up to the hope. Eugene Lyons reports that in private, "in a guarded phrase or a politically off-color joke or in tense silences," people betrayed their doubts.[69]

On the other hand, there is also evidence that the charges were believed, at least by some. Kravchenko writes regarding both the Shakhty trial and the *Prompartiia* trial, to be discussed below, that "though the picture was full of absurdities, I believed it, as the majority of the country did."[70]

Later, however, Kravchenko writes, with respect to the purges of the 1930s, "Though we banished such knowledge to remote regions of our minds, some of us Communists knew well enough that hordes of men and women were being herded into prisons and forced labor camps. We explained it to ourselves as "preventive" action—or we evaded the moral problem altogether by refusing to look at it through undimmed eyes."[71] In spite of their quaintly polemical title, Kravchenko's memoirs are honest and balanced, and thus provide a wealth of insight into the Stalinist 1930s and 1940s. In emigration, Kravchenko successfully defended himself against the charge of two French journalists that his book had been written by the U.S. secret services.[72]

Kendall Bailes, while not rejecting any of these interpretations, sees an additional contributing factor in Stalin's attitude toward the bourgeois specialists. He never trusted them, even in the early 1920s when Lenin constantly urged the necessity of relying on them. Their opposition to rapid industrialization paralleled that of Bukharin, Rykov, Tomsky, Kuibyshev, and other members of the Right Opposition. Furthermore, all these individuals with the exception of Bukharin defended the Shakhty engineers in the course of the pretrial investigation. Thus, the Shakhty affair can be seen as a maneuver within the general context of Stalin's struggle with his opponents on the right.[73] Robert Conquest also interprets the trial in this light.[74]

Beginning in 1930, there were numerous trials and executions of members of the intelligentsia in fields such as bacteriology (organizing a horse epidemic), the food industry (sabotaging the food supply—which became a standard explanation for food shortages), state farm officials (wrecking), officials of the Agriculture Commissariat (spying), *Gosplan* officials (wrecking), and numerous others.[75]

The next great trial of bourgeois engineers was the trial of the "Industrial Party," or *Prompartiia*, as it is invariably called in Russian. This was another show trial, held November 25 to December 7, 1930, with Vyshinsky again presiding and the indefatigable Krylenko, still in sporting clothes and head shaven, arguing for the prosecution. Both men had found their niche in the Stalinist system. About 2,000 engineers (fully one-fifth of the graduate engineers working in the Soviet Union at that time) were arrested in connection with the alleged conspiracy, but only 8 percent were in the dock.[76] Two indictees, Pyotr A. Pal'chinsky, the supposed founder of the Industrial Party, and A. S. Khrennikov, both engineers, were dead. Pal'chinsky was shot by the OGPU after refusing to confess to wrecking activities in the gold and platinum industry; Khrennikov died during the pretrial investigation—Solzhenitsyn believes it was not a natural death.[77]

As in the Shakhty case, the trial was put on like a theatrical production, with cameras, newspaper correspondents, and an audience of Soviet citizens. A Greek chorus was provided as outdoors, in managed demonstrations, half a million Soviet workers marched through the streets and around the Hall of Columns where the trial was being held, shouting "Death to the wreckers!" "Kill the agents of imperialism!" "Death! Death! Death!"

Also as in the Shakhty trial, the charges were transparently absurd and the evidence, except for the testimony of other prisoners who hoped to save their lives by cooperating with the prosecution, nonexistent. All the accused confessed; the alleged crimes were detailed by the first defendant, Leonid Ramzin. According to Ramzin's confession, and corroborated by the other defendants, the Industrial Party was born in 1925 and had 2,000 engineers as members by 1929. They plotted to take over the government of the Soviet Union and gave detailed lists of the engineers who were to fill particular government posts. They were to be assisted in this by foreign military intervention, and they were in constant contact with the French general staff, Balkan military men, and rich émigrés abroad. When, according to his testimony, Ramzin was supposed to have talked to Lawrence of Arabia in London, the colonel was not in Britain at all. One of the émigrés, Pavel P. Riabushinsky, who was elated to be premier, had been dead for years before the *Prompartiia* supposedly came into existence, as had another of the alleged émigré conspirators.[78]

The type of government Ramzin was talking about came to be called technocracy a few years later, and quite a few figures in the West argued passionately either for or against it. Here are Ramzin's words, in a section of the transcript ominously labeled by the editor "All Power to the Engineers":[79]

I might also note still another, maybe secondary, but no less important detail, which characterized the general mood in engineering circles at that moment. Pal'chinsky in particular propagandized the idea, which had tremendous popularity in engineering circles, namely—the contemporary state, relying upon highly developed technology, must deal with engineers as the representatives of this technology, that is, a leading role in governing the country, in managing the economy, must belong to the engineers. If you like, this is a parallel of the ancient Greek idea: as in ancient Greece they believed that the leading role must go to philosophers, so in today's state with its developed technology, it was imagined that the leading role must go to engineers.[80]

As sometimes is the case, there was a small kernel of truth at the heart of all the nonsense. Engineers *had* been talking about technocracy, and resenting their loss of privilege and income with the revolution and gradually losing their influence to the hastily educated proletarian "Red Directors" now coming out of the institutes, no doubt many fantasized about taking over the state. They certainly emphasized publicly their own importance to the industrialization process. In 1929 the Scientific-Technical Administration of VSNKh published a series of proposals for reform in industry, which would have given a greatly expanded role to engineers in decision making and used dangerous language such as "the future belongs to managing-engineers and engineer-managers."[81]

Furthermore, the engineering profession was still opposed—on technical, not political, grounds—to Stalin's Five-Year Plan, especially to the opening up of technical education to Communists in large members. Later in the 1930s Stalin linked the Right Opposition, and especially Bukharin, to the *Prompartiia*.

"Cadres," Stalin had concluded, "decide everything."[82] In 1928 he acted on that conviction with the decision to open wide the doors of higher education to workers and adult Party members who had demonstrated their political reliability. They were to make up Stalin's new proletarian intelligentsia, which he had become convinced was indispensable. Whether he fully believed it or not, Stalin argued that the bourgeois engineers had been able to carry out their sabotage because the Communists, including the "Red Directors," lacked technical education and skills and could thus be easily fooled by their nominal subordinates, the bourgeois specialists.[83] He believed that it was necessary to create, from the beginning, a new proletarian intelligentsia. Asking rhetorically, "And what does this mean?" Stalin argued in 1931 that

it means that our country has entered a phase of development in which *the working class must create its own industrial and technical intelligentsia*, one that is capable of upholding the interests of the working class in production as the interests of the ruling class. No ruling class has managed without its own intelligentsia. There are no grounds for believing that the working class of the U.S.S.R. can manage without its own industrial and technical intelligentsia.[84]

In other words, it was necessary to send proletarians to school. The policy had its desired effect in terms of numbers, if not of technical

competence. By 1937 there were 105,000 Communists with higher education, ten times the number in 1927, attributable, according to
Fitzpatrick, to the First Five-Year Plan policy of enrolling Party members,
since there were relatively few Party admissions in the intervening
years.[85] Stalin's desire to replace the bourgeois technicians with Communist, proletarian ones was embodied in a resolution of the July 1928
Central Committee plenum. No less than 65 percent of admissions in
the fall of 1928 were to be workers, and it was foreseen that this percentage would rise to 80 percent within a few years. A thousand experienced Communists were to be sent to the VTUZy, and the *rabfaki* were
to admit an additional 3,000 workers.[86]

The workers and Communists who were sent to school in the First
Five-Year Plan were referred to as *vydvizhentsy*, meaning roughly the
"promoted ones" or the "ones put forward." Of the *vydvizhentsy*, adult
Communist Party members who were selected and dispatched in groups
of 1,000 to higher education by Party and government organizations
became known as "thousanders" (*tysiachniki*). To be eligible for selection
as a thousander, Party members were required to be 35 or younger and
have five years of Party experience. By far, most of them were sent to
engineering schools, many in Moscow. In all, in the course of the First
Five-Year Plan approximately 20,000 *tysiachniki* were sent to VUZy and
VTUZy.[87]

Like all campaigns, the cultural revolution eventually ran its course
and began to die down after the 1931–32 academic year. There were
only so many individuals intellectually capable of joining the *vydvizhentsy*,
and so the qualifications of entering classes dropped drastically in 1931–
32. The hasty technical education of *vydvizhentsy* also had its predictable effect, and once again there were complaints from industrial
managers about the poorly trained engineers. So the organized mobilization of workers and Party members to higher education ended in
1932.

On the surface, at least, the effort to create a proletarian intelligentsia
bore fruit. In the decade of the 1930s, 868,000 specialists with higher
education, and 1,529,000 with secondary specialized education, entered
the work force.[88] Of this new intelligentsia, 28.9 percent had higher
education; 72 percent of them had been workers before the revolution,
and nearly all (97.4 percent) were Communist Party members.[89] The
vydvizhentsy were the raw material from which Stalin would forge a new,
transformed political elite. To make room for them, the old elite had to
be destroyed.

THE GREAT PURGES

The term "purge" was never applied to police terror, show trials of
oppositionists, or political terror in general. The commonly used term

"Great Purges" is actually a misnomer when applied to the *Ezhovshchina*.[90] The word "purge" (*chistka*, cleansing) had a very specific meaning, that of removing from the ranks of the Party opportunists, careerists, passive hangers-on, "class-alien" or bourgeois elements, the corrupt, and those who abused their position: generally people deemed unworthy of Party membership. There was a real necessity for this, given the periodic wholesale enrollments to Party membership and the apparent ease with which individuals could claim Party membership under almost any ruse. The deplorable state of Party record keeping at all levels contributed to this problem. Such purges, sometimes called "reregistrations" (*pereregistratsii*) or "verifications" (*proverki*) were conducted in 1919, 1921, 1924, 1925, 1928, 1929, 1930, 1933, 1935, and 1936; the last was an "exchange" (*obmen*) of Party cards. Except for the purges of 1919 and 1921, which expelled 10–15 percent and 25% of Party members respectively, these operations expelled as a rule less than 5 percent of those undergoing review.[91] J. Arch Getty provides a detailed discussion of the mechanics of Party purges. These purges tended to follow periods of mass enrollment into the Party. Until 1933, they were conducted by the Central Control Commission; in that year, however, a new Central Purge Commission was created, including in its membership Yan Rudzutak, Lazar Kaganovich, Sergei Kirov, Nikolai Ezhov and others, with regional and local purge commissions subordinated to it.[92]

Getty emphasizes that two-thirds of the victims of the 1933 purge had joined the Party since 1928, and hence it could hardly have been a purge directed at oppositionists.[93] In a long-standing practice, local Party officials, reluctant to part with the few skilled administrators they had, obstructed the implementation of these purges to various degrees and deflected the brunt of the casualties away from the Party bureaucracy and onto the rank and file.

The purges of 1929, however, had a special significance. In that year Stalin carried out a massive purge of the state bureaucracy. The insinuation of Communists into the state apparatus had proceeded at a snail's pace throughout the 1920s, and by 1928 only 18 percent of state officials were Party members. As Stephen Sternheimer notes:

In retrospect, it may well have been alarm at the regime's singular inability to Bolshevize the state apparatus to a meaningful degree that led Stalin and his aides to introduce a wholesale purge of the state bureaucracy in 1929. Simple projections reveal that if the average rate of politicization achieved in 1924 and 1928 had continued, the Party would not have been able to call any commissariat "ours" before at least 1933. And for the majority of commissariats for which data is available, no Communist majority would have emerged before 1947.[94]

In the early to mid-1930s, discontent with the harsh environment created by collectivization and industrialization was seething throughout the country, on the part of workers, peasants, the intelligentsia, and the Party. According to one account, even the OGPU was demoralized, its officers experiencing doubt and anxiety about the future.[95] An oppositional appetite had seized the Party and the youth; Trotsky's name was being revived, copies of Lenin's "Testament" were circulating, and anti-Stalinist graffiti were beginning to appear. There were rumblings of discontent among Old Bolsheviks, who remembered the comparatively democratic times of Lenin. We cannot, of course, know what was in Stalin's mind, but it seems not unreasonable to assume that he must have been alarmed by all this, and that the idea of a new and massive purge must have been in his mind as the Seventeenth Party Congress came and went.

Stalin dubbed the Seventeenth Party Congress, held from January 26 to February 10, 1934, as the "Congress of Victors," proclaiming in his speech to the Congress the Party's victory in its struggle against the kulaks and for the collectivization of agriculture, for the industrialization of the country, and for the attainment of socialism in one country.[96] Stalin said to the assembled delegates that "there is nothing more to prove and, it seems, nobody to beat."[97] Of the several thousand people who heard these disingenuous words, half were to die in the coming holocaust.

A victory over the countryside had indeed been achieved, if victory is interpreted narrowly as the imposition of the Party's will on the peasantry at any cost. Having liquidated, exiled, or subdued those elements of the peasantry that most energetically opposed collectivization, and having collectivized a little more than three-fourths of the remaining peasant families, repressive measures were relaxed in the countryside toward the end of 1933. The human and economic cost of the collectivization campaign was staggering; even Stalin admitted at the congress that agricultural production fell in 1933 over the 1929 level,[98] and he later admitted privately to Winston Churchill that the collectivization of agriculture had been an ordeal exceeding in horror the war against the Nazis.[99]

The successes in industry were similarly exaggerated. Gains were made in the First Five-Year Plan, to be sure, but the original indices of the plan were grotesquely overoptimistic and had repeatedly to be revised downward.[100] Bolshevik élan indeed accomplished much, but, contrary to Bolshevik faith, it could not accomplish the impossible. Although Stalin boasted of material gains—even in consumer goods, the most blatantly false of these claims—John Armstrong is probably correct in his assessment that the real significance of the First Five-Year Plan was in its laying the basis for future Soviet industrial self-sufficiency; indeed, the largest share of outlays up to 1934 had been in capital investment and the importation of foreign machinery and technical assistance.[101]

Finally, and sadly, Stalin's faith in the success of "socialism in one country" turned out to be premature. He was no doubt correct in his assumption (derived in fact from Lenin's earlier dictum that capitalism had entered a temporary phase of retrenchment) that there was no immediate threat to the Soviet Union's security in the late 1920s and early 1930s, his public rhetoric (the "war scare") notwithstanding. His isolationism, however, and his tendency to view foreign policy through a rigidly deterministic ideological lens, caused him tragically to overlook the menace posed by Hitler. Were it otherwise, his near destruction of international communism through his cynical manipulation of the Comintern and his emasculation of the Red Army on the eve of the Soviet Union's severest test simply elude explanation altogether.

The Seventeenth Party Congress appeared on the surface to be a personal victory for Stalin over his rivals; his most powerful and outspoken opponents, most notably Bukharin, Kamenev, and Zinoviev, were forced publicly to recant their views at the congress and to acknowledge the correctness of Stalin's policies, and given what we know of Stalin's personality, this must have been particularly gratifying to him.

The outwardly celebratory atmosphere of the Congress of Victors, however, belied tension beneath the surface. The evidence shows that there were sentiments among the leadership in favor of reducing Stalin's power or of deposing him altogether. In fact, the congress did change his designation from general secretary of the CPSU to merely secretary, on a par with the other members of the Secretariat. The immense popularity of Sergei Kirov, the first secretary of the Leningrad *obkom*, must have been particularly unsettling for Stalin.

His fears were not groundless. Reportedly, there were 292 votes cast *against* Stalin at the elections for a new Central Committee at the congress. Anton Antonov-Ovseenko reports, without attribution, that Kaganovich had 289 of these ballots burned and that in 1957 the summary report of the Central Committee's investigation showed 936 voting delegates when there should have been 1,225—that is, 289 ballots were missing.[102] The record showed three votes against Kirov and three against Stalin. A number of sources indicate that there was a move at the congress to replace Stalin, and that the Central Committee had offered the position of general secretary to Kirov.[103] A. I. Mikoyan confirms this.[104]

Kirov was a Party and journalistic pseudonym. Kirov's real name was Kostrikov. He was born March 27, 1886, in Urzhum in Viatka *guberniia*. Some documents show his birth date as 1888; in fact this was a ruse on the part of members of a revolutionary organization in Tomsk during the revolution of 1905. Kirov had been arrested, and when his birth date was "corrected" to 1888, he was classified as a minor and received a considerably reduced sentence.[105]

One of the perennially puzzling aspects of the Great Purges is the relationship they bear to the assassination of Kirov on December 1, 1934.

Stalin certainly had grievances against Kirov. The vote of the Seventeenth Party Congress was merely the final straw in a series of irritations that Kirov gave to Stalin. Kirov actively supported ex-oppositionists, including Bukharin, and he vociferously rebutted Stalin's allegation that Leningrad still seethed with Zinovievites. He took a conciliatory line on the peasants. He (among others) opposed Stalin on the execution of M. I. Ruitin and on the fate of other Communists. In general, Kirov represented a softer line than Stalin. It seems clear that Kirov was a serious obstacle to Stalin, and later historians confirm that a "Kirov line" was gaining favor in the Party.[106]

Kirov's assassin was Leonid Vasilevich Nikolaev, apparently a disgruntled Communist who had developed a fanatical hatred of the bureaucracy and a belief that he had been badly treated by it. It seems, however, that his act of murder was facilitated by the Leningrad People's Commissariat of Internal Affairs, generally known by its Russian acronym, NKVD. Nikolaev had been arrested *twice* by Kirov's bodyguards, and each time he had in his possession a gun and a map of Kirov's peregrinations around Leningrad. Each time, when Nikolaev was turned over to Leningrad NKVD deputy director Ivan Zaporozhets, Zaporozhets phoned Genrikh Yagoda in Moscow and then allowed Nikolaev to go free and to take his revolver with him.

On the evening of December 1, Kirov arrived at the Smolny Institute and went up to his office. His personal bodyguard, Borisov, remained in the car. Building security guards usually present on each floor were curiously absent, and Nikolaev got in the building without difficulty, waited for Kirov, and shot him in the back of the neck as he rounded a corner in the corridor.[107]

The circumstantial evidence strongly suggests (and Krushchev averred at the Twentieth Party Congress in 1956) that Stalin had instructed Yagoda to allow Nikolaev to go ahead with the assassination. It would otherwise be very difficult to explain the two releases of the assassin and the absence of the guards at the Smolny. Roy Medvedev reports that there had been several attempts on Kirov's life in 1934 and also gives a detailed account of the anomalies of the case.[108]

Stalin's ultimate use of the case was to destroy the remaining ex-Zinovievites in Leningrad and Moscow. In his own hand he drew up lists of members of the "Leningrad Center" and the "Moscow Center" of oppositionists, most of whom had been, and admitted having been, Zinovievites. Nikoleav, who apparently had been promised his life in return for his testimony, confessed to having killed Kirov on the orders of the "Leningrad Center." All were shot, including Nikolaev. Zinoviev and Kamenev themselves were arrested and received ten- and five-year terms, respectively, in subsequent trials; they were later to die, of course. The murder of Kirov, the investigation into it and trials associated with it, and the strengthening of the police apparatus as a result of it laid the basis for the Great Purges of 1936–1938.

As essential key to Stalin's purges was control over the secret police. The *CheKa*, reconstituted as the Gosudanstvoe Politicheskaia Upravlenie (GPU), was subordinated to the NKVD between February 1922 and July 1923. After this, as the OGPU, it was organizationally subordinate to the Council of Peoples' Commissars, directed by Dzerzhinsky until his death in July 1926. It was during this period that the secret police began to come under Stalin's control.[109] Stalin's principle contacts in the service were Genrikh Yagoda and Vyacheslav Minzhinsky, the latter having proved his serviceability in concocting the evidence against the Shakhty mining engineers. On Dzerzhinsky's death, Minzhinsky became OGPU chairman, with Yagoda as deputy.[110] Stalin controlled the secret police through his "secret chancellery," the *Osobyy sektor*, or Special Sector, headed from 1928 until 1952 by Stalin's personal secretary Aleksandr Poskrebyshev.[111]

Yagoda was fired in September 1936, was later arrested, and subsequently stood trial with Bukharin and the other defendants in the third Moscow trial in 1938. Yagoda, who helped prepare the cases against Zinoviev and Kamenev, now was accused of being a Zinovievite.[112] His replacement was Nikolai Ezhov. Ezhov was a good-looking man, at least judging from his photograph, with a face that seems gentle and sensitive, but from all reports he was a repulsive, sadistic, and unintelligent sociopath.[113] Ezhov was an Old Bolshevik—barely, having joined the Party in March 1917—who moved up rapidly under Stalin, entering the Central Committee in 1927.[114] Ezhov reportedly sent out by telegram quotas of "enemies of the people" to be exterminated by local NKVD chiefs.[115] Included among these victims was Ezhov's personal friend, the writer Isaac Babel.

A directive had been issued at Stalin's initiative on the day of Kirov's murder, without approval by the Politburo (which was informed only two days later), signed by Abel Enukidze, secretary of the Presidium of the Central Executive Committee. The directive, later dubbed the "Lex Kirov," was clearly designed to facilitate Stalin's coming terror:

1. Judicial bodies were directed to speed up bringing to trial those accused of plotting or carrying out terrorist acts.

2. The Courts were directed not to postpone the execution of death sentences for crimes in this category, to eliminate the possibility of a pardon. The Presidium of the Central Executive Committee of the USSR was not to consider appeals for pardon in these cases.

3. The NKVD was instructed to carry out the execution of those sentenced to death for crimes in this category immediately following the sentencing.

4. The entire investigation of such cases was to be accomplished in ten days or less, and the indictment presented to the defendant one day before the trial.

5. Attorneys for the defense were not to be permitted.[116]

In a further preparation for the terror that was to come, on April 7, 1935, a law was published decreeing that children age 12 or older guilty of stealing and other crimes were liable to the same punishments as adults, including the death penalty.[117] Alexander Orlov reports that from at least 1932, on Stalin's secret orders, masses of children caught plundering railway cars and stealing food had been shot.[118] Therefore, the law was not needed, as Stalin said it was, for fighting the problem of stray children.

In order to be able to execute Kamenev, Zinoviev, and the others, Stalin needed their unequivocal confession that they killed Kirov and intended to kill him, too (not just their admission of "political and moral responsibility"). To extract such confessions, and even more implausible ones from future victims, he had to be able to threaten their families and children. Orlov reports that opposition leaders on trial on January 1935 had been threatened with the deaths of their children but did not believe the threats. The publication of the new law made the threats credible.[119] Ezhov apparently also authorized the arrest of children on political charges; Orlov reports the arrest in 1937 of a ten-year-old boy, who finally confessed after a nightlong interrogation to having been a member of a fascist organization since he was seven years old.[120]

Chuianov provides an indication in his memoirs that the NKVD could not act with total impunity, at least toward the end of the terror. Apparently, a list of arrests had to have the signature of the *obkom* first secretary in addition to those of the provincial NKVD chief and procurator. The NKVD chief of administration Sharov came to Chuianov in June 1938 with a list of enemies of the people. Chuianov reflects at length about a Central Committee plenum resolution of January 1938 condemning false arrests, expulsions from the Party, and other repressions. The January plenum directed all Party and state organs to liquidate the remnants of gross violations of socialist legality. The NKVD chiefs who came to Chuianov said it was an urgent matter, but that it would take little of his time. They said that he had to sign a protocol concerning a few enemies of the Party and people. The affair had been checked over, and he could take the phone and ask the procurator if he wished. Chuianov said that he would not sign it right then, but to leave it with him and to bring to him all the materials on the convicted, and they would unhurriedly go over them together. They were irked, but at 10 P.M. the junior chief came back with the materials, and they pored over them until 5 A.M. Chuianov refused to sign the protocols because the investigations contained violations of Soviet law and were in contradiction of recent Party and state decisions. He ordered them to close the case and immediately release any of the accused still under investigation. He received a call from Georgy Malenkov about it. Malenkov told him to carefully review his decision from all sides, for he would be held responsible for any incorrect decisions. Chuianov later called Malenkov and said, "Conscience does not allow me to change my decision about the falsely arrested. Either send a responsible worker of the CC here to oversee the case, or believe me and agree that they all should be released."[121]

The centerpiece of the Great Purges were three show trials conducted in Moscow in 1936–1938. The first was the "Case of the Trotskyite-Zinovievite Terrorist Center," August 19–24, 1936. The defendants at this trial were:

G. E. Zinoviev	E. S. Goltsman
L. Kamenev	I. I. Reingold
G. E. Evdokimov	R. V. Pikel
I. N. Smirnov	V. P. Olberg
I. P. Bakaev	K. Berman-Iurin
V. A. Ter-Vaganian	Fritz David (I. I. Krugliantsky)
S. V. Mrachkovsky	M. E. Lurie
E. A. Dreitzer	N. Lurie.

All were sentenced to death, and the sentences were carried out immediately.

The second major show trial was the "Case of the Anti-Soviet Trotskyite Center," January 23–30, 1937. The defendants were:

E. L. Piatakov	S. A. Rataichak
K. S. Radek	B. O. Nerkin
G. Ia. Sokolnikov	A. A. Shestov
L. P. Serebriakov	M. S. Stroilov
N. I. Muralov	I. D. Turok
Ia. A. Livshits	I. I. Hrasche
Ia. N. Drobnis	G. E. Pushin
M. S. Boguslavsky	V. V. Arnold.
I. A. Kniasev	

All were shot except Arnold (who received a ten-year term) and Stroilov (who got an eight-year term).

The third trial was the "Case of the Anti-Soviet Bloc of Rightists and Trotskyites," March 2–13, 1938. The defendants were:

N. I. Bukharin	A. Ikramov
A. I. Rykov	F. Khodzhaev
G. G. Yagoda	V. F. Sharangovich
N. N. Krestinsky	P. T. Zubarev
K. G. Rakovsky	P. P. Bulanov
A. P. Rozenglots	L. G. Levin
V. I. Ivanov	D. D. Pletnev
M. A. Chernov	I. N. Kazakov
G. F. Grin'ko	V. A. Maksimov-Dikovsky
I. A. Zelensky	P. P. Kriuchkov.
S. A. Bessonov	

All were shot except Pletnev, who was given a 25-year term, and Rakovsky and Bessonov, who received 15-year terms.[122]

These trials attracted great publicity, and it was intended that they would. They also were given widespread credence both in the Soviet Union and among some circles in the West. They were a red herring in a sense, in that they diverted attention away from the real terror that was going on at the same time and contributed to the misconception that the victims of the purges were mainly political oppositionists. They were not, of course. The effect of the Great Purges was to liquidate a very large portion of the top- and middle-level political elite of the country, though other strategic elites were destroyed also, including the cultural and technical intelligentsia.

At the highest ranks of the Party apparatus, purge victims included 8 of 15 members of the Politburo elected at the Seventeenth Congress, 78 percent of the Central Committee members elected at that Congress, one-half of the delegates to the Seventeenth Congress, 90 percent of *obkom* and *gorkom* members in the Russian Republic, and upwards of 80 percent of the delegates to Republican Party Congresses and members of Republican Central Committees. The Ukrainian and Georgian Party organizations were particularly hard hit.

Purge victims in the state apparatus included two-thirds of members of the Council of People's Commissars and 80 percent of *oblispolkom* and *gorispolkom* members in the RSFSR. Industrial managers were another group particularly hard hit by the purges. Victims included all top administrators of the Main Administration of the Metallurgical Industry and 117 of 151 directors of the largest factories under the Commissariat of Ferrous Metallurgy. By the end of 1938, most of the directors of the biggest machine-building plants had been arrested.

On the eve of the purges, A. F Khavin published a statistical breakdown of the commanding staff of Soviet heavy industry. The data were based on a survey of 1,271 leading men in industry, including 495 enterprise directors, 76 construction site chiefs, 240 technical directors, and 460 shop chiefs. Khavin, a highly respected academic industrial sociologist, published his data in response to expressions of concern in the Soviet press—which hindsight indicates were not without political significance—concerning the qualifications of high industrial managers. Khavin emphasized that three "facts" clearly emerged from his data. The "first fact" was that fewer than 4 percent of all shop heads, 5 percent of technical directors, and 15 percent of enterprise directors had less than three years' experience in their branch of industry. The "second fact" was growing stability of personnel in the enterprises, with most managers having worked five to seven years in the same enterprise. Only 8 percent of directors in 1935 began supervisory work in 1918–1921, whereas 58 percent had assumed supervisory roles in the period of reconstruction (that is, after the civil war) and 42 percent during the First and Second Five-Year Plans.

Khavin's "third fact" was that all these top-heavy industry personnel had close knowledge of foreign technology; hundreds of them had gone abroad to study how work was organized in analogous plants.[123] In a later article, Khavin provides useful biographical information on the most prominent industrial managers of the Stalin period;[124] Khavin's data also indicated that only a little more than one-fourth of the directors had entered the Party before the revolution and that the prerevolutionary social standing of fully 72.4 percent of them was worker.[125] The import of Khavin's data, and very likely Khavin's intent, was to show that another shake-up of the top levels of industrial management was not necessary.

From the scientific and artistic intelligentsia, all 13 secretaries of the Academy of Sciences, one-third of the members of the Writers' Union, and the majority of the editors of central, republican, and *oblast* newspapers were arrested. Victims from the military included 35,000 officers—fully one-half of the officer corps—all 11 deputy commissars of war, 75 out of 80 members of the Supreme Military Council, 110 out of 195 division commanders, and 90 percent of generals and 80 percent of colonels. Along with many others, the civil war veterans and officers not of proletarian or peasant background were destroyed. Finally, most of the highest-ranking members of the Yagoda and Ezhov NKVDs, including Yagoda and Ezhov themselves, were executed.

Although the political leadership, the intelligentsia, and the military comprised the main bulk of the victims, it is by no means true that these were the only victims. By late 1937 the entire population was vulnerable to arrest on the flimsiest charges—factory workers, peasants, office workers, shop girls.[126] Of Western estimates of the number of victims of the Great Purges, that of Robert Conquest is the most carefully and judiciously derived. Conquest estimates about 7 million arrests in 1937–38, with about 1 million directly executed. An additional 2 million died in the camps. For late 1938, he estimates about 1 million in prison and about 7 million in camps (including 4 million already there at the end of 1936).[127] These figures do not include the victims of collectivization, the artificial famines, and the post–World War II terror. Citing recent Soviet sources, Conquest estimates the dead for the whole Stalin epoch at 20 million (not including another 20 million war dead), and the "repressed" at 40 million, about half from 1929–1933 and half from 1937–1953.[128]

Apparently to cover up statistical evidence of the scope of the purges and other unnatural deaths, the 1937 census was suppressed and never released for publication. The director of the Central Statistical Administration and some of his subordinates were shot in 1938, according to *Pravda* for January 19, 1939, for "plotting to underestimate the population of the Soviet Union." A German source suggested that tampering with the 1939 census had occurred, estimating that that census exceeded the 1937 census by more than 25 million, vastly more than the population could have naturally increased in two years.[129] Helene Carrere d'Encausse reports, without attribution, that the 1937 census showed a population of 164 million, 16.7 million fewer than the 180.7 million forecast by the Second Five-Year Plan.[130] Steven Rosefielde estimates that excess deaths in the period 1929–1953, attributable to forced labor, collectivization, and terror, exceeded 20 million.[131]

Not counting World War II deaths, then, approximately 40 million people—nearly one-fourth of the population—paid for Stalin's program, half with their lives, and the other half with most severe diminution of their life chances.

A purge on this scale is elite transformation *in extremis*. The period 1937–1939 was a period of the greatest turnover of political personnel in the country's history; indeed, in any country's history. Not even the Nazi takeover of Germany involved such a thoroughgoing transformation of the elite. Stalin was able to report to the Eighteenth Congress (March 10–21, 1939) that in the five years since the Seventeenth Congress, "the Party succeeded in promoting to leading state and Party posts over 500,000 young Bolsheviks."[132] This is a very large figure. It vastly exceeds the 194,000 Party posts mentioned by Stalin in his famous analogy to military ranks.[133] To be sure, he mentions state and Party posts; if we assume there were as many state as Party posts, the total is still less than 500,000 by 112,000, which must then represent only nominally "state" posts in the economy.

The Party was also thoroughly transformed in its membership by the end of the purges. Malenkov reported to the Eighteenth Party Congress that of the 1,589,000 members of the Party in 1939, only 8.3 percent had entered the Party before 1920; 80 percent of those who entered in 1920–1921 and 75 percent of those recruited in 1921–1928 disappeared in the purges, as did 50 percent of those who entered in 1929–1930.[134]

Table 4.1
Mean Year of Party Entry and Age at Election (by CC)

Congress		Mean Party Entry Year, Full/Candidate	Age at election Full	Candidate
VI	(1917)	1903	36.4	36.9
VII	(1918)	1903	36.5	39.0
VIII	(1919)	1903	39.4	37.9
IX	(1920)	1903	38.0	40.9
X	(1921)	1904	38.9	35.1
XI	(1922)	1905	39.1	34.5
XII	(1923)	1906	38.9	38.9
XIII	(1924)	1907	39.3	36.4
XIV	(1925)	1907	40.5	36.7
XV	(1927)	1908	42.0	37.8
XVI	(1930)	1910	43.2	39.6
XVII	(1934)	1911	44.7	44.3
XVI	(1939)	1920	45.1	40.1
XIX	(1952)	1927	50.0	48.5

Source: Author's database.

The rank-and-file membership of the Party was wholly postrevolutionary, post–civil war, and post-NEP.

This overwhelming transformation of the rank and file is reflected in Central Committee membership. Table 4.1 shows that Old Bolsheviks had dominated the Central Committee until the Eighteenth Congress. In terms of age, we can see Central Committee members gradually becoming older; this reflects reelections except after the Seventeenth Congress. It also reflects the increasing availability of individuals with more experience as time went by. Although the average age of full members at the Eighteenth Congress, at 45, is right in the progression of increasing age, the average age of full members elected for the first time at the Eighteenth Congress—for example, the replacements of those who perished—was younger, at 42. This distribution is skewed heavily to the left, however; 54 percent of them were younger than 38. The mean is pulled up by a handful of new members over age 50; if these are disregarded, the average age of the replacements becomes 37, almost a decade younger.

Membership of the Central Committee had remained very stable after some fluctuation in the period 1917–1921. Turnover of full members did not exceed 17 percent until the Eighteenth Party Congress in 1939, when 66 percent of full members and 97 percent of candidate members were elected for the first time, reflecting, of course, the purges of the 1930s. Turnover was almost as high at the Nineteenth Congress in the last year of Stalin's life, with 63 percent of full members newly elected and 88 percent of candidate members. Khrushchev's first Central Committee, elected in 1961, experienced unusually high turnover, too. After 1961, turnover stabilized at around 15–20 percent for full members.

As would be expected, radical change occurred between the Seventeenth (1934) and Eighteenth (1939) Congresses. One of these directly measurable changes is the year of joining the Party. Old Bolsheviks bore the main brunt of Stalin's purges at the leadership level. Of the 139 full and candidate members of the Central Committee elected at the Seventeenth Congress, 93 (67 percent) had joined the Party before the revolution. By contrast, of the Central Committee elected in 1939, more than one-third had joined the Party between 1921 and 1930, and 52 (38 percent) had joined the Party after Lenin's death in 1924.

A large share of the people destroyed in 1936–1938 were supporters of Stalin in the 1920s. The fact that he was apparently planning another purge when he died suggests that he might have been pursuing a long-term strategy of simply renewing the cadre once every decade or so to prevent coalitions against him from growing and maturing. This is only an interpretation and cannot in any way be proven. T. H. Rigby has shown that contrary to Stalin's having been a "disloyal patron," at least with respect to his closest associates, the closer individuals were to Stalin and the longer they had been among his supporters, the better were their chances of surviving the purges and that most of his 1934 Politburo survived.[135]

The men and women destroyed in the Great Purges did not include only Old Bolsheviks; they did include a significant proportion of the thousanders educated by Stalin in the late 1920s. The newly educated technical intelligentsia—the *vydvizhentsy*—began in the middle to late 1930s to be increasingly recruited into the Party. By the Eighteenth Party Congress in 1939 the last barriers to the recruitment of intelligentsia to the Party had been dropped, and the proletarian contingent of Party membership began a long decline. At the level of the leadership, the men who replaced the victims of the Great Purges—the Brezhnev generation—moved rapidly into positions of responsibility and rose as rapidly in the hierarchy of the political elite. Marshall Shatz characterizes the beneficiaries of the purges not as marking the emergence of a "new class," but as "the triumph of plebeian Russia," and he refers to the members of the new elite as "the Khrushchevs" because Khrushchev was typical.[136]

This cohort, men who first accepted a Party-government post in the period 1936–1940, had a mean year of birth of 1908 (Brezhnev's year of birth was 1906). This was a particularly auspicious time for an aspiring political leader to be born. Men born less than a decade earlier were destroyed in large number in the Great Purges. Men born a decade later were decimated at the fronts of World War II; those of this cohort who survived the war were deprived of the opportunity to acquire the education requisite to joining the elite because they were needed as manual laborers in postwar reconstruction. They constitute a "missing generation" in the Soviet elite,[137] which was simply not available to step into top positions as the Brezhnev leadership began visibly to age in the 1970s.[138]

The men of the Brezhnev cohort joined the Party several years later than earlier cohorts, at a mean age of 23. Their mean year of graduation from four-year technical institutes was 1937. They spent very little time— a year or less on average—working in their technical specializations before accepting a full-time political post in the mean year of 1938. The standard deviation for that statistic is one year: the accuracy of the nickname "class of '38," often applied to this generation, is striking. This generation dominated the post-Stalin era, and its concerns—industrialization, defense, and maintenance of the leading role of the Communist Party—dominated the Soviet political agenda into the early 1980s. It was not finally replaced until the second elite transformation, begun under Mikhail Gorbachev in the late 1980s and still ongoing.

The atavistic character, crudeness, and low moral consciousness of the bureaucracy put in place by Stalin would not have surprised Mosca. Mosca argued that the bureaucracy is always recruited from the middle class—the second stratum of the ruling class. The moral level of the bureaucracy will correspond to the moral level of the ruling class. If the ruling class has long traditions of honor and probity, the moral level of the bureaucracy will be high. However,

the level will be lower when the ruling class is of more recent date and stems either from rustling, bustling and lucky adventurers, or from families of peasants and shopkeepers who have acquired, at best, the first rudiments of manners and education. Even if such people have developed a certain competence, they are still often without a spark of idealism and retain an inveterate and sordid greed for large, and even for petty gains.[139]

In attempting to examine the Stalin period from a structural standpoint, one is struck by the degree to which this period, more than any subsequent period, was shaped by an individual's will. Despite our structuralist lens, Stalin's personality and character, and his personal agenda, still dominate the period. Nonetheless, it was also the result of a conjuncture: the conjuncture of a thoroughgoing plebeian revolution and a crisis caused by years of international war, revolution, and civil war. Michael Reiman argues that a key consideration in understanding Stalinism is that "it was not a product of positive social development or the positive development of a social doctrine or conception, but the result of a deep and all-embracing crisis; it evolved as a special kind of instrument or means of finding a way out of this crisis."[140]

The means of finding a way out of a problematical reality was to attempt to restructure reality on a massive scale. The total breakdown of the group structure of the society, the imposition of a novel new way of organizing and commanding the economy, and the creation of a wholly new, wholly postrevolutionary political elite were not merely side effects of Stalin's program, but its intent. The means of accomplishing this was terror and oppression on an unprecedented, truly Faustian, scale. When looked at from the standpoint of any individual victim, or any discrete grouping of victims, the terror unavoidably appears arbitrary, inhumanly cruel, and senseless, and it is difficult to imagine its serving any kind of remotely positive social function. But it did accomplish its aim of restructuring the society. This hardly justifies it, and I am not suggesting in any sense that it does; the cliche that holds that you can not make omelets without breaking eggs may be true, but there are surely better ways of breaking eggs than crushing them under a booted foot. The means used were chosen because they were available to Stalin and his men, who were not repelled by them.

NOTES

1. Harold D. Lasswell, Daniel Lerner, and C. Easton Rothwell, *The Comparative Study of Elites: An Introduction and Bibliography* (Stanford, CA: Stanford University Press, 1952), p. 6.

2. Gaetano Mosca, *The Ruling Class*. Trans. Hannah D. Kahn (New York: McGraw-Hill, 1939), p. 65.

3. Ibid., pp. 65–66.

4. Suzanne Keller, *Beyond the Ruling Class: Strategic Elites in Modern Society* (New York: Random House, 1963), pp. 125–26.

5. See Robert D. Putnam, *The Comparative Study of Political Elites* (Englewood Cliffs, NJ: Prentice-Hall, 1976), pp. 169–70.

6. Don K. Rowney, *Transition to Technocracy: The Structural Origins of the Soviet Administrative State* (Ithaca, NY: Cornell University Press, 1989), p. 13.

7. See Stephen Sternheimer, "Administration for Development: The Emerging Bureaucratic Elite, 1920–1930," in Walter M. Pintner and Don K. Rowney, eds., *Russian Officialdom: The Bureaucratization of Russian Society from the Seventeenth to the Twentieth Century* (Chapel Hill: University of North Carolina Press, 1980), pp. 316–54, esp. pp. 343–45.

8. Crane Brinton, *The Anatomy of Revolution* (New York: Vintage Books, 1965).

9. Leonard Schapiro, *The Communist Party of the Soviet Union* (New York: Random House, 1960), p. 231. Schapiro cites *Bol'shaia sovetskaia entsiklopediia*, vol. 11, p. 531.

10. Ibid.

11. *Bol'shaia sovetskaia entsiklopediia*, vol. 11, pp. 531–32.

12. Schapiro, *Communist Party of the Soviet Union*, p. 236.

13. Graeme Gill, "Institutionalisation and Revolution: Rules and the Soviet Political System," *Soviet Studies* 37, no. 2 (April 1985):217.

14. Sheila Fitzpatrick, "The Bolsheviks' Dilemma: Class, Culture, and Politics in Early Soviet Years," *Slavic Review* 47, no. 4 (Winter 1988):605.

15. Gill, "Institutionalisation and Revolution," p. 218.

16. E. H. Carr, *Socialism in One Country, 1924–1926* (Harmondsworth, England: Penguin Books, 1970), vol. 2, pp. 221–23. Gill states that what appears to be the first step to formalizing *nomenklatura* is in *Devyatyi s"ezd RKP(b) Mart-aprel' 1920 goda* (Moscow, 1960), pp. 425–26.

17. Gill, "Institutionalisation and Revolution," p. 219.

18. *Kommunisticheskaia partiia sovetskogo soiuza v rezoliutsiiakh i resheniiakh s"ezdov, konferentsii i plenumov Ts. K.*, vol. 1 (Moscow, 1953), p. 46.

19. Gill, "Institutionalisation and Revolution, p. 216. The new rule can be found in *Ustav kommunisticheskoi partii sovetskogo soiuza* (Moscow, 1982), p. 31.

20. S. V. Utechin, "The Origin of the Ruling Class in Soviet Society," PhD dissertation, Oxford, 1958. Cited by Schapiro, *Communist Party of the Soviet Union*, p. 237.

21. Robert V. Daniels, "Evolution of Leadership Selection in the Central Committee," in Pintner and Rowney, *Russian Officialdom*, p. 358.

22. *X s"ezd RKP(b): stenograficheskii otchet* (Moscow: Gospolitizdat, 1963), p. 573.

23. Ibid.

24. C. Bettelheim, *Class Struggle in the USSR, First Period: 1917–1923* (Hassocks, NJ: Harvester Press, 1976), pp. 286–88.

25. See Vera Broido, *Lenin and the Mensheviks: The Persecution of Socialists under Bolshevism* (Aldershot, Hants, England: Gower Publishing Co., 1987), pp. 159–62.

26. Alexander Shtromas, *Political Change and Social Development: The Case of the Soviet Union* (Frankfurt am Main: Verlag Peter D. Lang GmbH, 1981), pp. 40–43.

27. Don K. Rowney, "Structure, Class, and Career: The Problem of Bureaucracy and Society in Russia, 1801–1917," *Social Science History* 6, no. 1 (Winter 1982):108.

28. Victor Kravchenko, *I Chose Freedom: The Personal and Political Life of a Soviet Official* (New York: Charles Scribner's Sons, 1946), pp. 66–67.

29. See Joel Carmichael, *Trotsky: An Appreciation of His Life* (New York: St. Martin's Press, 1975), pp. 241ff, for an account of some of Trotsky's harsh policies during that conflict.

30. Roger Pethybridge, *The Social Prelude to Stalinism* (London: Macmillan, 1974), pp. 99ff. Trotsky also affirms this in *The Revolution Betrayed: What Is the Soviet Union and Where Is It Going?* (New York: Pathfinder Press, 1972), pp. 89–90.

31. G. Popov, "Kommentarii glavnogo redaktora," *Voprosy ekonomiki*, no. 8 (1988):99.

32. Ibid.

33. Ibid.

34. Robert V. Daniels, ed., *A Documentary History of Communism* (Hanover, NH: University Press of New England, 1984), vol. 1, pp. 207–8.

35. T. H. Rigby, *Communist Party Membership in the USSR, 1917–1967* (Princeton, NJ: Princeton University Press, 1968), p. 176.

36. See T. H. Rigby, "Early Provincial Cliques and the Rise of Stalin," *Soviet Studies* 33, no. 1 (January 1981): 3–28.

37. On Beria's clients, see Charles H. Fairbanks, Jr., "Beria, His Enemies, and Their Georgian Clientele" (Washington, DC: Kennan Institute for Advanced Russian Studies Occasional Paper no. 119, n.d., but ca. 1980). Ilya Dzhirkvelov says of Stalin's men: "For us working in the KGB, and for many other people as well, it was no secret that Stalin's favorites were Malenkov, Khrushchev, and Bagirov, Secretary of the Communist Party in Azerbaidzhan." Ilya Dzhirkvelov, *Secret Servant: My Life with the KGB and the Soviet Elite* (London: William Collins' Sons, 1987), p. 142. Stalin, according to Roy Medvedev, was given to prankstering with the men he liked, furtively putting a tomato or a cake on their seat before they sat down, or pushing them into the pond on walks around his dacha. Roy A. Medvedev, *On Stalin and Stalinism*, trans. Ellen de Kadt (New York: Oxford University Press, 1979), p. 156.

38. A. I. Mikoyan, "V pervyi raz bez Lenina," *Ogonyok*, no. 50 (December 13, 1987):5.

39. Kamenev, "Speech to the Fourteenth Party Congress, December, 1925," in Daniels, *A Documentary History of Communism*, p. 186.

40. I. V. Stalin, *Socheneniia* (Moscow, 1950), vol. 6, pp. 390–91.

41. A. A. Andreev, *Vospominaniia, pis'ma* (Moscow, 1985), p. 168.

42. A. Chuianov, *Na stremnine veka: zapiski sekretaria obkoma* (Moscow, 1976), pp. 40–41.

43. Ibid., pp. 41–43.

44. N. S. Patolichev, *Ispytanie na zrelost'* (Moscow, 1977), pp. 283–84.

45. N. Bukharin, "O novoi ekonomicheskoi politike i nashikh zadachakh," *Bolshevik*, nos. 9–10 (1925):4–5.

46. Preobrazhensky's thesis was set forth in *Novaia ekonomika*, published by the Communist Academy in 1924. See his discussion of criticisms of the thesis in E. A. Preobrazhensky, *The Crisis of Soviet Industrialization: Selected Essays*, ed. Donald A. Filtzer (White Plains, NY: M. E. Sharpe, 1979), pp. 54–74.

47. I. V. Stalin, *Socheneniia* (Moscow, 1950), vol. 9, p. 192.

48. Ibid., vol. 7, pp. 250. Boris Bazhanov was convinced that Frunze was deliberately killed on Stalin's orders; see G. R. Urban, ed., *Stalinism: Its Impact on Russia and the World* (Cambridge, MA: Harvard University Press, 1986), p. 11.

49. Robert V. Daniels, *The Conscience of the Revolution* (Cambridge, MA: Harvard University Press, 1960), pp. 190–97.

50. Daniels, "Evolution of Leadership Selection," p. 362. The size of the Central Committee has increased at every Congress since then, probably for the same reason.

51. I borrow here the distinction made by Nicholas Lampert, *The Technical Intelligentsia and the Soviet State: A Study of Soviet Managers and Technicians, 1928–1935* (London: Macmillan, 1979), pp. 7–8.

52. Stephen P. Timoshenko, *As I Remember* (Princeton, NJ: D. Van Nostrand,

1968), p. 183. Timoshenko went on to the United States and eventually became a professor of engineering at Stanford University.

53. P. Avrich, "Workers' Control," *Slavic Review* 22 (1963):47ff.

54. Lampert, *The Technical Intelligentsia*, p. 14.

55. P. M. Mikhailov, "Iz istorii deiatel'nosti kommunisticheskoi partii po podgotovke rukovodiashchikh kadrov promyshlennosti v period sotsialisticheskoi rekkonstruktsii narodnogo khoziaistva." *Voprosy istorii KPSS*, no. 10 (1976):80.

56. A. F. Khavin, "Kapitany sovetskoi industrii 1926–1940 gody," *Voprosy istorii*, no. 5 (May 1966):4.

57. See Sheila Fitzpatrick, "Cultural Revolution as Class War," in Sheila Fitzpatrick, ed., *Cultural Revolution in Russia, 1928–1931* (Bloomington: Indiana University Press, 1984), p. 8.

58. Eugene Lyons, *Assignment in Utopia* (New York: Harcourt, Brace & Company, 1937), p. 120 (emphasis added). Lyons, an American and a Communist sympathizer although not at Party member, was a United Press correspondent in Moscow at the time.

59. Among the foreign newsreporters present was the *New York Times* correspondent Walter Duranty; see his account of the trial in *The Curious Lottery* (Freepoint, NY: Books for Libraries Press, 1929), pp. 135–237. An account by Lyons is on pp. 114–33. Unlike later show trials, no stenographic record of the Shakhty trial was published, although it was extensively reported in the newspapers. Most accounts of the trial agree in most respects, with the odd exception of the number of defendants, which rages from 49 to 55.

60. Kendall E. Bailes, *Technology and Society under Lenin and Stalin: Origins of the Soviet Technical Intelligentsia, 1917–1941* (Princeton, NJ: Princeton University Press, 1978), p. 90.

61. A not uncommon attitude of the time; compare the line attributed to Stalin in Rybakov's novel about the 1930s: "The Party must control *all* the country's administrations, including the economic, and above all the industrial machine, which has at its disposal the most independent, most educated, and most arrogant personnel." *Anatoly Rybakov, Children of the Arbat* (Boston: Little, Brown, 1988), p. 372.

62. Krylenko edited and published a collection of documents from the trial: *Eknomicheskaia konto-revoliutsiia v Donbasse, itogi shakhtinskogo dela: stat'i i dokumenty* (Moscow, 1928).

63. Abdurakhman Avtorkhanov, *Stalin and the Soviet Communist Party: A Study in the Technology of Power* (New York: Praeger, 1959), pp. 28–29.

64. Lyons, *Assignment in Utopia*, p. 131.

65. A. Khavin, "Komandiry tiazheloi promyshlennosti," *Za industrializatsiiu* no. 24 (January 1935):4.

66. Lampert, *The Technical Intelligentsia*, p. 38.

67. Ibid., p. 48.

68. Solzhenitsyn leans to this interpretation; see *The Gulag Archipelago* (New York: Harper & Row, 1973), vol. 1, p. 398. A strong proponent of the scapegoat hypothesis is the former Soviet diplomat and counterintelligence chief Alexander Orlov; see *The Secret History of Stalin's Crimes* (New York: Random House, 1953), pp. 293–94.

69. Lyons, *Assignment in Utopia*, pp. 132–33. Lyons believed that the men

had been guilty either of sabotage or apathy so great that it amounted to the same thing; he rejects only that it was part of a conspiracy. See p. 132.

70. Kravchenko, *I Chose Freedom*, p. 56.

71. Ibid., p. 153.

72. See *Protsess V. A. Kravchenki: sudebnyi otchet* (Paris: Russkaia mysl', 1949).

73. Bailes, *Technology and Society*, pp. 71ff.

74. Robert Conquest, *The Great Terror* (London: Macmillan, 1968), pp. 549–51.

75. Ibid., pp. 551–52.

76. These were Sergei Kupriianov (textile engineer), Nikolai Charnovsky (professor of metallurgy), Ksenofont Sitnin (whose own son demanded his death; a similar incident occurred at the Shakhty trial), Aleksandr Fedotov (textile engineer), Ivan Kalinikov (engineer), Leonid Ramzin (fuel and energy engineer), Viktor Larichev (oil industry engineer), and Vladimir Ochkin (engineer). See the transcript of the trial, *Prostess "Prompartii" (Moscow, 1931)*.

77. See *Protsess prompartii*, p. 8n, and Solzhenitsyn, *The Gulag Archipelago*, pp. 375 and 376. Similar trials in this period included the Menshevik trial in 1931 and the trial of the Metro-Vickers engineers in 1933.

78. Lyons, *Assignment in Utopia*, p. 376. Ramzin's initial testimony is in *Protsess prompartii*, pp. 48–87. There were numerous such trials in the late 1920s and early 1930s. There is an English translation of the similar Metro-Vickers trial of April 1933: *The Moscow Trial: Authentic Report* (New York: Workers' Library Publishers, n.d., but ca. 1933 or 1934).

79. "*Vsia vlast' inzheneram!*" It was ominous because it mocks Lenin's 1917 slogan "All power to the soviets" (*Vsia vlast' sovetam!*), a phrase that still had considerable emotional and legitimating power.

80. *Protsess prompartii*, pp. 53–54. Five death sentences were handed down (one to the star witness, Ramzin) but were soon commuted to ten years' imprisonment. Ramzin was allowed to continue to work and teach in prison and was subsequently pardoned and released, to return to his Moscow professorship and to win a Stalin Prize in 1943. None of the others are known to have been pardoned.

81. Cited by Kendall E. Bailes, "The Politics of Technology: Stalin and Technocratic Thinking among Engineers," *American Historical Review* 79, no. 2 (April 1974):457.

82. Stalin's famous quote is in "Reche na vypuske akademikov Krasnoi Armii" (May 4, 1935), in I. V. Stalin, *Sochinenniia*, ed. Robert H. McNeal, 3 vols. (Stanford, CA: Stanford University Press, 1967), 1(14):61.

83. Sheila Fitzpatrick, "Stalin and the Making of a New Elite, 1928–1939," *Slavic Review* 38, no. 3 (September 1979):379.

84. J. V. Stalin, "New Conditions—New Tasks in Economic Construction," *Problems of Leninism* (Peking: Foreign Language Press, 1976), pp. 546–47.

85. Sheila Fitzpatrick, *Education and Social Mobility in the Soviet Union, 1921–1934* (Cambridge: Cambridge University Press), pp. 241–42.

86. A. I. Lutchenko, "Rukovodstvo KPSS formirovaniem kadrov tekhnicheskoi intelligentsii (1926–1933 gg.)," *Voprosy istorii KPSS*, no. 2 (February 1966):32.

87. Ibid., p. 36; Fitzpatrick, *Education and Social Mobility*, p. 186.

88. Khavin, "Kapitany sovetskoi industrii 1926–1940 gody," p. 5.

89. Ibid., p. 6.

90. See J. Arch Getty, *Origins of the Great Purges: The Soviet Communist Party Reconsidered, 1933–1938* (Cambridge: Cambridge University Press, 1985), p. 38.

91. Ibid., p. 46.

92. Ibid., pp. 50–51.

93. Ibid., p. 53.

94. Sternheimer, "Administration for Development," p. 338. Sternheimer also argues that Stalin may have foreseen difficulty implementing his "revolution from above," since so many of the state bureaucracy sympathized with the Right Opposition, p. 339.

95. Orlov, *The Secret History*, pp. 29–30.

96. *XVII s"ezd Vsesoiuznoi Kommunisticheskoi Partii (b) 26 Ianvaria—10 Fevralia 1934 g.: stenograficheskii otchet* (Moscow, Partizdat, 1934), p. 28.

97. Ibid.

98. Ibid., pp. 19–20.

99. Winston S. Churchill, *The Hinge of Fate* (Boston: Houghton Mifflin, 1950), p. 498.

100. Alec Nove, *An Economic History of the U.S.S.R.* (Harmondsworth, Middlesex, England: Penguin Books, 1982), pp. 189–90.

101. John A. Armstrong, *The Politics of Totalitarianism* (New York: Random House, 1961), p. 5.

102. Anton Antonov-Ovseenko, *The Time of Stalin: Portrait of a Tyranny* (New York: Harper & Row, 1981), p. 80.

103. For example, L. Shaumian, who had been a delegate at the Seventeenth Congress, in "Na rubezhe pervykh piatiletok: k 30-letiiu XVII s"ezda partii," *Pravda*, February 7, 1964; translation in T. H. Rigby, ed., *The Stalin Dictatorship: Krushchev's "Secret Speech" and Other Documents* (Sydney: Sydney University Press, 1968), pp. 109–12.

104. A. I. Mikoyan, "V pervyi raz bez Lenina," *Ogonyok*, no. 50 (December 13, 1987):5–7. Medvedev confirms it also: Roy Medvedev, *Let History Judge: The Origins and Consequences of Stalinism* (New York: Columbia University Press, 1989), p. 331. This was hinted at in a 1962 textbook edited by Boris Ponomarev: *Istoriia KPSS* (Moscow, 1962), p. 486; cited by Medvedev, *Let History Judge*, p. 331.

105. A. A. Kirilina and Iu. A. Lipilin, comp., *S. M. Kirov i Leningradskie kommunisty, 1926–1934* (Leningrad: Lenizdat, 1986), p. 7n.

106. Roy Medvedev, *On Stalin and Stalinism* (Oxford: Oxford University Press, 1979), p. 94. Also, Medvedev, *Let History Judge*, p. 334.

107. Robert Conquest, *Stalin and the Kirov Murder* (New York: Oxford University Press, 1989), pp. 8–9.

108. Medvedev, *Let History Judge*, pp. 336–46.

109. George Leggett, *The CheKa: Lenin's Political Police* (Oxford: Oxford University Press, 1981), p. 364.

110. On the NKVD, see Robert Conquest, *Inside Stalin's Secret Police: NKVD Politics, 1936–39* (Stanford, CA: Hoover Institution Press, 1985).

111. John J. Dziak, *Chekisty: A History of the KGB* (Lexington, MA: Lexington Books, 1988), p. 60. Also see Niels Erik Rosenfeldt, *Knowledge and Power: The*

Role of Stalin's Secret Chancellery in the Soviet System of Government (Copenhagen: Rosenkilde & Bagger, 1978), pp. 63ff.

112. Because, at least according to Orlov, a scapegoat was necessary because of suspicion of NKVD complicity in the murder of Kirov. Orlov, *The Secret History*, pp. 249–50.

113. Conquest, *The Great Terror*, pp. 14–15.

114. *Pravda*, Sept. 26, 1936.

115. Dziak, *Chekisty*, pp. 67–68, quoting Vladimir and Evdokia Petrov, *Empire of Fear* (New York: Praeger, 1956), pp. 73–74. Vladimir Petrov had been an officer of the NKVD.

116. *Sbornik materialov po istorii sotsialisticheskogo ugolovnogo zakonodatel'stva* (Moscow, 1938), p. 314; cited by Medvedev, *Let History Judge*, p. 341.

117. "O merakh bor'bys prestupnost'iu sredi nesovershennoletnikh," *Izvestia*, April 7, 1935, p. 1.

118. Orlov, *The Secret History*, pp. 39–40.

119. Ibid., pp. 40–41.

120. Ibid., p. 246.

121. Chuianov, *Na stremnine*, pp. 43–48.

122. Borys Lewytzkyj, *The Stalinist Terror in the Thirties: Documentation from the Soviet Press* (Stanford, CA: Hoover Institution Press, 1974), pp. 26–27.

123. Khavin, "Komandiry tiazheloi promyshlennosti," p. 4.

124. Khavin, "Kapitany sovetskoi industrii," p. 6.

125. Ibid., p. 6.

126. Robert Conquest cites recent Soviet materials that document the extent to which the purges included ordinary, nonpolitical people. See *The Great Terror: A Reassessment* (New York: Oxford University Press, 1990), pp. 257–58.

127. Ibid., pp. 485–86.

128. Ibid., p. 486.

129. W. Von Poletika, "Annulierte Volkszahlung und Bevolkerungsstand in der Sowjetunion," *Allgemeines Statistisches Archiv*, no. 28 (1939):322–56. Reported by Iosif G. Dyadkin, *Unnatural Deaths in the USSR, 1928–1954* (New Brunswick, NJ: Transaction Books, 1983), p. 8.

130. Helene Carrere d'Encausse, *Stalin: Order through Terror* (London: Longman, 1981), p. 44.

131. Steven Rosefielde, "Excess Mortality in the Soviet Union: A Reconsideration of the Demographic Consequences of Forced Industrialization, 1929–1949," *Soviet Studies* 35, no. 2 (July 1983):402. Rosefielde provides a detailed response to his critics in "Incriminating Evidence: Excess Deaths and Forced Labour under Stalin: A Final Reply to Critics," *Soviet Studies* 39, no. 2 (April 1987):292–313.

132. J. V. Stalin, "Report to the Eighteenth Congress of the C.P.S.U.(b) on the Work of the Central Committee," *Problems of Leninism* (Peking: Foreign Language Press, 1976), p. 922.

133. I. V. Stalin, *Socheneniia* (Moscow, 1950), vol. 13, pp. 107–8. I do not mean here to impugn much precision to Stalin's famous estimates, but rather to use his own figures to emphasize the scope of the Great Purges.

134. Malenkov speech at Eighteenth Congress.

135. T. H. Rigby, "Was Stalin a Disloyal Patron?" *Soviet Studies* 38, no. 3 (July 1986):311–24.

136. Marshall Shatz, "Stalin, the Great Purge, and Russian History: A New Look at the 'New Class,' " *Carl Beck Papers in Russian and East European Studies* (University of Pittsburgh), paper no. 305 (1984), p. 14.

137. Jerry F. Hough, *Soviet Leadership in Transition* (Washington, DC: Brookings Institution Press, 1980), pp. 9–10.

138. A quantitative study of the Brezhnev generation by a Soviet sociologist was published in the USSR: B. Ts. Urlanis, *Istoriia odnogo pokoleniia* (Moscow: Izdatel'stvo "Mysl," ' 1968).

139. Mosca, *The Ruling Class*, p. 408.

140. Micheal Reiman, *The Birth of Stalinism: The USSR on the Eve of the "Second Revolution"* (Bloomington: Indiana University Press, 1987), p. 115.

Chapter 5

Elite-Society Relations

The future belongs to bureaucratization.

Max Weber

The broad topic of elite-society relationships, or as it is sometimes called, elite-mass linkages, covers the nature of the political elite from the standpoint of its relationship to the larger society that it governs. From a very broad perspective, one could perhaps argue that all elite studies boil down to elite-mass relationships, and so depending on the perspective one chooses to take, there is a little or a great deal of ambiguity about what should be subsumed under that topic. In this chapter, I will discuss the concept of exclusivity of elites, the question of bureaucracy and its relationship with society—and in the process, develop a theory of non-Weberian bureaucracy—the interesting question of technocracy, and finally the "new class" debate.

In all societies, the essence of the relationship between elites and society is captured in the concept of exclusivity: elites are exclusive along a number of dimensions from society. Gaetano Mosca, although he does not use the term "exclusivity," makes the point very clearly that ruling minorities are distinguished from the masses by certain prized qualities.[1]

Exclusivity in general empirical terms can apply, following Mosca, to any traits that are "highly esteemed and very influential," that is, to any kind of elite. For modern societies, I posit two classes of traits that set apart political elites in particular: (1) functional exclusive traits, which I

define as those necessary for the leadership of a modern industrial society; this would include a certain level and type of education and experience, and, arguably, membership in a more or less privileged social
stratum (the "middle class," Mosca would insist)—these tend to be common to all such societies; and (2) essential exclusive traits: those specific
to a particular society. This might include and in the case of the Soviet
Union does include Communist Party membership, membership in certain cliques, certain personality attributes (lack of sentimentality, a busi-
nesslike mien, and so on), and certain ascriptive attributes such as
membership in a particular social caste, a certain ethnic identification,
or a favored gender (virtually always, it needs no argument, male).

Exclusivity also connotes separation and social distance. Elites, even if
conspicuous to the public, operate in arenas inaccessible to nonelites.[2]
Their habitat, lifestyle, privileges, and social venues are separate. As
Raymond Aron wrote, "the structure of the elite is not merely a reflection
of the structure of society."[3] Finally, exclusivity carries with it a presumption of superiority. Structurally, of course, this is merely social
superiority, but there is a tendency to assume that this extends to physical, intellectual, and moral superiority as well.

This exclusivity of the elite vis-à-vis the society is embedded in Soviet
political culture. In the words of one former member of the Soviet elite:

This division of Soviet society [between elites and masses] is unquestioned, and
moreover, in the case of the elites, the process of becoming removed from Soviet
society is entirely natural. Nobody ever voices any doubts concerning its legitimacy; after all, Lenin said that universal equality did not mean a leveling out
of everybody. In other words, even in the Soviet state there must be rulers and
ruled.[4]

In his discussion of the concept of marginality, Peter Ludz provides
a gloss on exclusivity as it applies in Communist societies:

On the whole the crucial conflict lies between the rigidity of the insulated leadership bodies (i.e., their maintenance of an impassable zone between themselves
and society) on the one hand, and their adaptation to and metamorphosis into
industrial organization forms, on the other. Marginality, or distance from society,
thus appears to be a "constant" for Communist political systems, even under the
conditions imposed by an industrial society.[5]

THE NATURE OF POWER IN THE SOVIET UNION

The deep social structure of Russian society on the eve of the revolution was not one that was created in the process of industrialization;
it was one that was at least two centuries old, very feudal in the Russian

sense, and reinforced constantly by tsarism. It was a structure built on a mass peasant base, with a thin stratum of aristocracy over it. Mutual expectations were well defined in this structure. The revolution did not destroy this infrastructure, and the definition of what the peasant had a right to expect and the obedience he owed to superiors remained the same, only called by different names. The NEP to the peasant was the fulfillment of the revolution. 1928 and 1929 were seen by the peasants as a violation of noblesse oblige and as such was resisted. What Stalin needed to destroy was the perceptual infrastructure; destroying individuals in large numbers (in part directly and in part artificial famines) and collectivization were the means of doing so. Some kind of neologism, perhaps "straticide," is needed to describe this unique ambition. Genocide, and even ethnocide, are familiar to us, but I am not aware of another historical example of a leadership intent on the physical annihilation of a social class. Although Stalin's brutal policies achieved quiescence in the countryside, the peasantry as a social stratum was not destroyed.

Since the industrialization process had not had the "opportunity" naturally to create a society with the class structure expected by Marxism, such a structure had to be created artificially. The Bolsheviks believed that workers would have the attitudes and orientations that Marxism requires of the "working class." They were wrong in this. The vast preponderance of new workers who manned the new factories going up were former peasants—that is, they came to the cities *as adults*—and the import of this is that they had undergone rural socialization; they brought with them the centuries-old deep structure of a peasant society.

In a society where the means of production have been nationalized, it is true, as Aron wrote, that there are no classes in the Marxism sense because these are defined by Marx in terms of a relationship to the means of production.[6] The power of the Soviet rulers does not flow from their control of the means of production, rather, they control the means of production because they have the power to do so.[7]

Whence, then, comes their power? It derives from a structure of domination in which effective power is associated with position; this structure of domination is a deep structure, and it survived the revolution intact. Those who became powerful in the Russian or Soviet system understood this structure of domination and used it to their own ends. This deep structure is a purely Hobbesian one: the twin keys to power in this structure are violence and control over scarce goods—the prosaic ability to punish or reward. Command of the levers of coercion can be second or third hand—it extends from local first secretaries through the entire hierarchy to the top. So long as a local tyrant can count on the support of his superiors, he can do virtually anything. Woe, however, betide him whose superiors do not back him up. However, this support is usually implicit—the unusual situation is when it is withheld, as in periodic anticorruption drives.

In a system of this type (which I will call a "Hobbesian political culture"), *legitimacy* is not really an appropriate concept; acquiescence in a system of domination stemming from recognition of helplessness against the rulers is not the same thing as voluntary compliance with an authority structure that is widely deemed right and proper.

The necessary condition for the maintenance of the Party's position as an exclusive ruling elite has been the coercive prohibition of voluntary associations and of any means of entry into the ruling class independently of the gatekeepers' will. The Party maintained its position by co-opting all societal functions. The result of this is that an *artificial elite*—in the sense of an elite that was not naturally selected in a competitive social environment—has come into existence. In all societies other than state-socialist societies, the elite comes from the highest socioeconomic categories. The important point here is that the socioeconomic category is *prior* to, and causative of, political power. In state-socialist societies, the reverse is true. Access to the political elite comes only through co-optation. There is no way to enter from below through one's own efforts or to force one's way in—one has to be selected.

An artificial elite runs serious risk of becoming very dysfunctional: if we assume that in some sense a social system "selects" structures to perform functions necessary to system maintenance, the presence of an artificial elite short-circuits that process. The pressure of unfulfilled needs increases until such a time as the leadership, faced with crises it cannot finesse, goes into decline or is replaced. However, I want to avoid giving too prominent a place to a self-correcting system maintenance assumption here. Unfulfilled needs can remain unfulfilled for a very long time before this occurs; societies are remarkably tolerant of inept leadership.

One of the consequences of Gorbachev's liberalization and the relaxation of Party dominance will be the emergence of strategic elites with autonomous powers beyond the ability of the Party to co-opt or control. A divided elite means the end of the Party as a ruling elite, since it can no longer control entry into positions of dominance.

For the present, however, the Soviet Union is a classless society in the limited sense that there is no one who has a base of power independent of the state (based on ownership of property, for example); there is no "natural elite." A classless society is a "mass society" in William Kornhauser's famous image: the masses have no means of legal, organized defense against the elite. Power comes about only through incumbency in state positions. The source of the power that comes with official position, leaving aside violent coercion, is the ability to create dependencies.

The precondition for the exercise of this particular type of power is scarcity; in an environment of economic plenty, there would be access to the necessities and the luxuries of life other than through the mediation of a Party secretary or the chairman of a soviet.

Power over rewards and punishments is personalistic power; for it to be meaningful, its exercise has to be largely up to the discretion of the individual powerholder. To the extent that it is institutionalized, it limits the discretion of the officeholder. If the official's power is no more than that of determining which rule applies and applying it in an automatic way, then that is not power at all. To the extent that the rules of office become institutionalized and predictable, discretionary power is diminished.

In what may at first gloss seem odd, discretionary power of this type in the Soviet system is greatest at the middle levels of the hierarchy. The process of the institutionalization of the powers of office (that is, the diminution of discretion), seems to have gone the farthest at the level of the CPSU general secretary (without gainsaying the ability of an outstanding—and rare—individual such as Mikhail Gorbachev to bend them); discretion increases as one proceeds down the hierarchy and appears greatest at the level of regional (*obkom* and *kraikom*) first secretaries. Below that level, the scope of the resources at the command of the leader diminishes rapidly. Even at the lowest level, however, this power is considerable: the power of the chairman of a village soviet to skim off the village's surplus is precisely his control over, for example, a position on a waiting list for a new apartment or other prosaic scarcities.

In a system of domination based on personal discretion over access to scarce resources, relationships of exchange are important and clientelism is a natural form for intraelite relationships to take. Patron-client networks permeate the political system. For a patron-client system to operate, two conditions have to pertain: the patron's contribution to the relationship is to give the client access to a political post, not to give him something of substance; the client gives to the patron above him political support, but also part of the spoils of his satrapy. The benefit to the client is his ability to use his post to skim off the spoils of *his* clients in turn below him. A system of domination of this type I will call non-Weberian bureaucracy.

NON-WEBERIAN BUREAUCRACY

In Marxist-Leninist thought, "bureaucracy" is conceived as an ill peculiar to capitalist societies; among the salutary effects of the socialist revolution was to be its final smashing. Vladimir Ilych Lenin wrote:

The possibility of this destruction is guaranteed by the fact that socialism will shorten the working day, will raise the people to a new life, will create such conditions for the majority of the population as will enable everybody, without exception, to perform "state functions," and this will lead to the complete withering away of every form of state in general.[8]

One of the earliest explicit, *internal* complaints that the Soviet Party and state were becoming "bureaucratized" came from the United Opposition, a union of the Trotskyist and Zinovievite opposition to Stalin that was formed in 1926, after the political defeat of both. In an appeal directed to the rank and file of the Party, the United Opposition urged that the Lashevich affair merely proved "the bureaucratic perversion of the Party apparatus."[9]

Since the revolution, the term "bureaucracy" has always been used in Soviet discourse in its pejorative sense. A "bureaucrat" in Soviet parlance is a Party or state official who behaves in a rigid, formalistic, insensitive, or otherwise objectionable way. It is never used to refer to administrators in a neutral way, nor is it used, as it is in the West, to distinguish appointed from elected officeholders. Here, the term "bureaucracy" will be used, in a normatively neutral way, to refer to the structure of both state *and* Party posts (since the distinction between elected and appointed officials is spurious in the Soviet context), and the term "bureaucrats" will refer to the holders of such posts.

The authority of Max Weber's thought in Western social science is so great that his typologies are sometimes applied uncritically, with Procrustean results. Many, if not most, Western scholars have characterized Soviet politics as involving authority based on charisma, for example, as a residual category, since it clearly is neither traditional nor rational-legal. Noting this problem, Alex Simirenko proposed that "ersatz charisma" or "pseudo-charisma," based not on personal devotion but on artificial manipulation of followers, might be more appropriate characterizations.[10]

Weber distinguishes two contrasting kinds of domination. One arises from monopolistic control of economic resources in the marketplace; the other, form the authority of office. Domination in the marketplace is indirect, through the mediation of commodities and resources. People are free to act in accord with rational self-interest; no one is expected to obey merchants or bankers out of duty. However, everyone must obey constituted authority without regard to interest.[11]

But clearly Weber wants to equate even authoritarian domination with legitimacy.[12] Commands are obeyed "as if the ruled had made the content of the command the maxim of their conduct for its very own sake."[13] And "the merely external fact of the order being obeyed is not sufficient to signify domination in our sense; we cannot overlook the meaning of the fact that the command is accepted as a 'valid' form."[14]

As Frank Parkin points out, this means that authority structures that rely more on coercion than on voluntary compliance are excluded from Weber's typology.[15] Weber apparently assumes that regimes cannot last long by coercion alone, but require some substantial measure of legitimacy. This is puzzling, because elsewhere Weber argues that the state is based on power (defined as violence): "Sociologically, the state cannot be defined in terms of its ends. . . . Ultimately, one can define the modern state sociologically only in terms of the specific *means* peculiar to it . . . namely, the use of physical force."[16]

For our purpose, it is best to assume, as is standard in modern political science, that the power of the state is *ultimately* based on a monopoly of force and that states vary in the degree to which domination is based on coercion, as opposed to authority grounded in legitimacy. It is important to go beyond Weber and insist, however, that domination can be based simply, or primarily, on coercion. For this to be true does not require daily violent confrontations between citizens and the state; when citizens have learned that defying the state is futile, it would be erroneous to confound their coerced compliance with voluntary compliance based on legitimacy.

Weber's ideal type of bureaucracy has become both the empirical and normative standard by which bureaucratic organizations are defined, described, and measured. It will be worthwhile here to describe Weber's paradigm in some detail. Weberian bureaucracy—as an ideal type, it bears emphasizing—has the following characteristics:

1. Officials are free, occupying the office by a free contractual relationship, and subject to authority only with respect to their well-defined impersonal official obligations.
2. There is a clearly defined hierarchy of offices, each with a clearly defined sphere of competence.
3. Officials are appointed (not elected) on the basis of technical qualifications ascertained by examination or diploma.
4. Officials are reimbursed by fixed salaries in money, and the office is the incumbent's sole, or at least primary, occupation; it constitutes a career, with promotion by superiors on the basis of seniority and/or achievement.
5. The official is separated entirely from the ownership of the means of administration, and he cannot appropriate his position—that is, he does not "own" it and cannot use it for his private ends or profit.
6. The official is subject to strict and systematic discipline and control.[17]

The image of bureaucracy given by Weber is of a highly structured, hierarchically organized *machine* (a simile he used himself), which is impersonal and divorced from the private means and ends of the individuals staffing it. Apparently so that there could be no ambiguity about it, Weber emphasized the element of impersonality repeatedly and in a variety of ways, for example: "Bureaucracy develops the more perfectly the more it is 'dehumanized,' the more completely it succeeds in eliminating from official business love, hatred, and all purely personal, irrational, and emotional elements which escape calculation."[18]

"Social action," for Weber, is action in which the actor takes into account the interpretations that others may place on it. This encompasses everyday social interaction. Elsewhere, Weber refers to this as "communal action" and makes a distinction between the latter and "institutionally commanded action" (*Anstaltshandeln*). The latter kind of action is structured by rules designed by others, in other words, institutionalized.[19] In its purest form, it removes the personal element and all personal discretion and meaning to be attributed to action. This impersonality is one of the most criticized aspects not only of bureaucracy but of modern social life in general. It is seen as dehumanizing by ordinary people, and it is criticized as such by writers as diverse as Karl Marx, Herbert Marcuse, and Jurgen Habermas. As unfortunate as this may be in human terms, it is essential if "rationally organized action" in Weber's understanding—action oriented to the achievement of goals that transcend those of individuals—is to be possible.

In another functionalist argument, Weber is emphatic about the staying power of bureaucracy once established. For Weber, and the emphasis is his,

once fully established, bureaucracy is among those social structures which are the hardest to destroy. Bureaucracy is *the* means of transforming social action into rationally organized action. Therefore, as an instrument of rationally organizing authority relations, bureaucracy was and is a power instrument of the first order for one who controls the bureaucratic apparatus.... Where administration has been completely bureaucratized, the resulting system of domination is practically indestructible.[20]

Weber observed only capitalist societies, and his sociology has the structure of capitalist societies woven thoroughly through it. His sociology is at its best, furthermore, when applied to democratic societies—the only nondemocratic society he looked at was Prussia. The reason for this is that the structure that underlies Weber's sociology is the market, conceived in broad terms. To some degree, bureaucracies behave in Weberian ways because such behavior is shaped by the capitalist and democratic context in which they are situated. This is, of course, a functional argument, but its purpose is to highlight the fact that Weberian forms, when translated to noncapitalist contexts, may behave in non-Weberian ways.

It is important to note, too, that the alternative form of administration, to which Weber contrasted bureaucracy, was not noncapitalist economically or nondemocratic politically but, rather, economically preindustrial and premodern and politically patriarchal or patrimonial. Bureaucracy in the Weberian sense was not only unnecessary in these contexts; it was really not possible. Since everything depended on the will of the chief or patriarch, predictability and rationality was not possible, nor even desirable from the patriarch's point of view. Patrimonial office, for Weber, lacks the distinction between "private" and "official" spheres; the office is part of his personal property, and his exercise of power is purely discretionary.[21]

Weber's conception of the ideal type is somewhat similar to Plato's "forms." Empirical species of the ideal type can be expected to deviate from the ideal in various ways, but the essence of the type remains identifiable. Weberian bureaucracies—if they adhere to the ideal type— should be unaffected by the culture in which they are found. An alternative statement of this assumption is that when they do deviate, the deviations are due to and colored by the culture. Communist bureaucracies allow greater latitude for culture to affect their operation. Both Soviet and Chinese bureaucracy have the characteristics of Communist bureaucracies, but there is greater difference in operation between Soviet and Chinese bureaucracies than between, say, French and German, and the difference is due to the greater latitude for cultural characteristics to manifest themselves in the operation of Communist bureaucracies.

The Weberian bureaucracy theory does not describe Soviet bureaucracy very well. In Paul Hollander's words, "Weber has no conceptual framework for the strange amalgam of rationality and irrationality, neutrality and ideological commitment, expertise and political reliability, that has entered into the formation of Soviet bureaucracy."[22]

When I discuss non-Weberian bureaucracy, what is envisioned is not a system of administrative organization that merely deviates from the Weberian ideal type. No actual organization adheres perfectly to its ideal type, as Weber first of all would insist. By a non-Weberian bureaucracy is meant one that looks, at first gloss, like a classical bureaucracy—that is why it is so called, rather than something else; it is crypto-Weberian— but that is in fact premised on quite different, in fact contrary, principles. A brief return to the concept of deep structures will help elucidate this.

Fault lines, or perversions, can be expected to occur in societies that experience "collapsed development." That is, in a society in which a modernizing elite "collapses" the process of development—jumps over "stages" and attempts to impose modern institutions on a traditional society—the feudal deep structure persists. When institutions are not allowed to evolve gradually, they will not be congruent with underlying, and governing, structures. The result is likely to be a crypto-modern society, that is, one that has superficially modern characteristics but in fact maintains a feudal substructure. Authority relations in such a society will be predominantly patrimonial and/or charismatic, rather than rational-legal. The paradigm of this phenomenon was Weimar Germany. A democratic shell was superimposed over a society in which a feudal deep structure supported a feudal class structure; unsurprisingly, Weimar's democratic institutions did not function as they were supposed to, and the society was unable to resist the totalitarian onslaught.

Deep structures have been long in the making and can, in fact are likely to, persist stubbornly in spite of superficial surface changes. This is why societies in which revolutions occur, or that try to make a rapid transition to modernity (such as the newly independent countries in the 1960s), are very likely to suffer relapse or worse. Deep structures are also preserved in part because the peculiar practices and expectations that result from the amalgamation of a feudal substructure and superimposed modern institutions perversely themselves become institutionalized.

This is what occurred in the Soviet Union. The institutions of the new Soviet state were too new, their jurisdictions and purposes *ad hoc* and poorly defined. The institutional system devised by Lenin was sui generis; how it was to operate and the relationships of its parts to one another had not matured and become institutionalized over time. The state and Party structure sprang full-blown from Lenin's head, almost as an afterthought, and its actual functioning had yet to be defined or to define itself. The deep structure of Russian society in 1917 was feudal, and so the authority relations that developed were, at root, feudal. Unavoidably too, because of the chaos of the revolution, civil war, and world war, extremely wide personal discretion was woven into the framework of political institutions. As the 1920s progressed, Stalin's relationships with his lieutenants, and Party secretaries at various levels with theirs, came to resemble far more Weber's model of patrimonial rather than bureaucratic officialdom: one in which the official's position arises strictly from personal submission to the ruler, and not to impersonal requirements of the office.[23]

In spite of his dislike of unilinear, developmental schemes of historical development, Weber assumed that rationality and bureaucracy (one was the direct consequence of the other) increased historically. Weber, then, unlike Karl Marx or Lenin, did not believe that socialism would do away with bureaucracy. On the contrary, bureaucracy would become even more important in socialist societies, requiring as they do even more planning and administration than capitalist societies.[24]

My argument is that bureaucratic officialdom will also exhibit patrimonial features when the bureaucratic structure is new (its role structures incompletely crystallized and routinized) or is grafted over a feudal substructure. A not completely institutionalized society is hence vulnerable to the effort of a strong and determined leadership to bend it to its own purposes. Under the iron hand of the despotic leadership, how-ever, it does eventually become routinized and institutionalized, retain-ing its irrational aspects long after the demise of the despot in spite of the most noteworthy efforts to reform it.

The technocratic thinkers of the 1930s (Burnham and Veblen, e.g.) tended to stress the *indispensability* of technical expertise as the factor that would transform the bureaucracy into a new ruling class. If this were so, then presumably at a certain stage of technical progress (or industrialization), technocracy would come into being. This does not take into account that the *structural* relationship of bureaucracy to the social system of which it is a part is a means—a purely technical instru-ment in someone else's hands.[25] For it to become an end in itself would require not just the increasing complexity of technology but a structural transformation of the social system—a rather profound rearrangement of its parts and their relationships to one another not likely to come about through a mere process of evolution.

Helen Constas, however, argues that through quite another dynamic having nothing to do with technology, bureaucracies can become ruling classes. "The bureaucratic ruling class of Soviet Russia," she urges, "did not come to power by any 'managerial revolution' based on their technical indispensability."[26] In a comparative study of pharaonic Egypt, Inca Peru, and the USSR, Constas concluded that a different social structure existed in these societies, a structure that could not be classed as slavery, feudalism, or capitalism and that she termed "bureaucratic society":

Certain institutional fundamentals characterized these societies: the state exer-cised total control over social, political and economic life; private property was either weak or absent; and the economy was administered by a bureaucratic ruling class which, through its monopolistic control of the state, was dominant over all other sectors of society and controlled them in classical totalitarian fashion.[27]

Constas argues that Weber actually used two types of bureaucracy, legal-rational and charismatic, which he never fully distinguished from one another. Weber failed to see the possibility of bureaucracy as a ruling class, always assuming it was a tool of some other group: always a means, never an end.[28] Weber recognized the difference, but he believed that charismatic bureaucracy would ultimately transform itself into the ra-tional-legal type. By contrast, Constas argues that they came about in different historical circumstances, "institutionalizing charisma in a bu-reaucratic direction." Therefore, she urges, they are "radically different historical forms." Because of the presence of charismatic elements in such a bureaucracy, according to Constas, the bureaucratic recruitment function is impaired:

To the degree that charismatic elements are present, ideological commitment, as well as technical competence, must necessarily figure in bureaucratic recruitment. It may even supersede it. Hence, purges, orthodoxy, and hewing to the Party line will inevitably arise at every level in a charismatic bureaucracy and in the most diverse fields of work.[29]

In a study outstanding for its method, in which he wished to determine the degree to which the territorial governing elite in tsarist Russia deviated from Weber's ideal type, John Armstrong proposed five "criteria of bureaucratic regression," each criterion being essentially the negation of one of Weber's rules:

1. Recruitment to governorships through family connections.
2. Minimization of training required for entrance.
3. Formal education in open educational institutions.
4. Absence of a specific civil career pattern for gubernatorial service.
5. Attachment to a specific loyalty.[30]

Armstrong was primarily interested in the ways in which the old regime governors maintained their autonomy from the ruler. Although that might be a fruitful research problem with respect to Soviet Party officials, it is not the purpose here, and Armstrong's criteria do not fit the non-Weberian model very well. Criterion 1 might be applicable if patronage, rather than family connections, were emphasized. Armstrong was looking at deviations from the Weberian model, rather than constructing a non-Weberian model.

I wish to do more here than, on the one hand, present a narrow model of specifically *Soviet* bureaucracy and, on the other, simply to subsume it under Weber's broad residual category of patrimonial bureaucracy. Hence, I wish to devise a model that is particular enough to explain Soviet reality and general enough to explain other Communist societies and, more importantly for comparative politics, can potentially be useful to describe and explain the phenomenon of bureaucracy in societies that arrived at modernity under the influence of the same historical imperatives.

Table 5.1 highlights the most significant differences between Weberian and non-Weberian bureaucracy.

Soviet non-Weberian bureaucracy, as discussed earlier, is crypto-Weberian; it *looks* Weberian to the observer, but the actual operational code is non-Weberian. One of the most impressive sources of power of an individual operating in this context is his ability to switch the context at will, that is, to change the ground rules in the middle of an interaction. In a non-Weberian bureaucracy, the functionary can at his discretion act in a social manner in the disposition of goods (to treat a good that

Table 5.1
Weberian and Non-Weberian Bureaucracy

	Weberian	*Non-Weberian*
Source of duty:	official, pre-existing rules	personal obligation ad hoc, often ex post facto
Scope of duty:	fixed and predictable	fluid, subject to whim
Scope of jurisdiction:	fixed	flexible
Accountability:	to an institution	to an individual (patron)
Criterion for office-holding:	meritocratic (qualifications)	clientelistic (loyalty)
Nature of office-holding:	trusteeship	benefice
Structure of chain of command:	hierarchical	mixed horizontal and hierarchical, or dual, or fragmented
Applicability of norms:	universal	particularistic
Role of client:	applicant	supplicant
Relationship of official role to private life:	separate	fused
Method of disposition of cases:	rule-guided	command-guided

comes from the state as his personal gift to the client) or behave in an institutional manner in the preemption of goods (what he is appropriating for his own use he appropriates in the name of the state).

A striking characteristic of Soviet non-Weberian administration is the presence of plural subordination and parallel, even competing, hierarchies of control and responsibility. In spite of repeated invocation of the principle of "one-man control" (*edinonachalie*) in industry, Soviet chains of command are confused and contorted. Originally meant to enhance control, this practice has had the opposite effect, making it easier to shift or evade responsibility and even to lose it irrevocably in a maze of overlapping jurisdictions.

Non-Weberian (in particular, Soviet) bureaucracy is also exemplified by an undeveloped control function—a great deal of autonomy is left to the local bureaucrat. Rules exist, but they are not always, or are only sporadically, enforced. "Control Commissions" (which have appeared in various incarnations over the Soviet period) are ineffective because they are limited in their investigative authority.

Among other ways, Communist non-Weberian bureaucracies differ from Weberian bureaucracies in their relations with clients. Clients are not at the center of Communist bureaucracies because the latter's norms are socially oriented; their predisposition is to subordinate individual to social needs. The subjects of bureaucratic action are usually *things*, not people, and this is consistent with Marxism. Middle- and lower-level bureaucracies in fact find themselves adjudicating the claims and demands of individuals, however, and without norms and procedures spelled out in fair detail, much is left to the bureaucrat's discretion.

The rules and procedures themselves explicitly seem to give great latitude to discretion—perhaps intentionally so, perhaps due to laziness or lack of experience to specify them—and a great deal of implicit trust in the right motives and superior consciousness of Communists: "[The issue] is to be settled in a socially conscious and just manner." Communist bureaucracies allow great latitude for the influence of individual quirks, petty squabbles, personality, and other phenomena regarded as dysfunctions in Western bureaucracies. There is nothing in this conception to distinguish Communist bureaucracies from other non-Weberian forms, such as Third World bureaucracies.

Weber's most basic distinction between the bureaucratic and the patrimonial official is that the former, unlike the latter, does not regard office as a private property.[31] Wide discretion given to regional first secretaries, particularly when their regions are productive, simply amounts to creating a fiefdom in which the official does often enrich himself through abuse of his position. I shall have more to say about this in Chapter 7.

TECHNOCRACY

"Technocracy" is one of those terms in political science that keeps reappearing but is also frequently criticized. It is probably an easy target of criticism because it is so poorly defined. To what does it actually refer? In its extreme versions, it seems to refer to something that has never existed except in science fiction: political rule by technical experts. The term is almost always used, at least today, in a negative sense: undue political influence by technological experts is usually lamented as something that usurps decision-making power away from politicians (who represent the people), who can evade accountability. It is thus a threat to democracy. Interestingly, it is seen similarly in the Soviet Union.

Technocracy is usually discussed in reference to French civil servants; graduates of Ecole National d'Administration (ENA) and Ecole Polytechnique are exemplary technocrats. In education and outlook, however, the *científicos* of Brazil, Venezuela, and to a lesser degree Mexico are a similar breed.[32] A generalized definition based on these examples can be given, and then we can attempt to determine whether, and to what extent, it applies to Soviet elites.

Technocrats are rationalists, with an almost Victorian belief in progress, who have great confidence in the ability of scientific management to solve human problems. Efficiency and logical analysis are central to the technocrat's approach to any kind of problems. Depoliticization of problems is also; technocrats are hostile to ideologies (though it is tempting to argue that technocracy itself is an ideology), and they are devoted to the national interest and the Rousseauian general welfare, as against narrow sectional interests; the play of interests impedes the rational ordering of society. Finally, technocrats generally have an outlook favorable to an active, positive role for the state in economic development.[33]

French and Latin American technocrats have a number of elements of cohesion that suggest that it might be fruitful to question whether they might be regarded as a class in the C. Wright Mills sense. They have a common social background, upper or solid middle class. They also have common training, almost all of the French technocrats being graduates of the *grandes ecoles*; they thus have a common body of knowledge and a common ethos, as well as spirit of camaraderie and a shared sense of superiority. This cohesion is reinforced by the organization of the civil service into corresponding *grandes corps*.[34]

If the essence of technocracy is efficiency, then that surely refers to *means*, and the logical objection to technocracy would be that politics should concern itself with good *ends*. In this understanding, technicians can at best be only instruments; they can not be allowed to be rulers, at least not in their role as technicians.

The Soviet leadership has from the 1920s had a marked obsession, even a love-hate relationship, with technical specialists. This is because economic development was so central a part of the new regime's self-defined task. In an economically developing society, technical specialists are indispensable. The risk when there is an indispensable group is losing control over that group, or even to that group. This problem was particularly marked after the Bolshevik seizure of power because the existing technical intelligentsia were seen as belonging to a social class assumed to be hostile to proletarian hegemony. Therefore, there was always an imperative to control it. This was the origin of the famous, and tiresome, "Red versus expert" debate.

The fact of the matter is that the Soviet political elite is ridden through and through with the technocratic ethos, as defined above. Soviet writers do not recognize this, however, and when "technocratic tendencies" are identified in the elite, this is treated as an evil that must be extirpated. This is a simple matter of definition. "Technocratic tendencies" more often referred to as "economic forms of management," simply means management that is narrow-mindedly technical, with insufficient attention given to human feelings and needs, and/or sufficient attention given to political factors. Armstrong noted that the "engineering or technocratic approach to human problems" was more marked among Soviet than among West European administrators. To some of his West European informants, Soviet engineers in management positions seemed callous and unfeeling.[35]

In modern Soviet usage, in other words, "technocracy" is a matter of style. But it was not always so, and for most of the Stalin period the question of "rule by technicians" was extremely sensitive and the Soviet leadership was much vexed by it. Even more vexed were internal and external critics of the Stalinist regime, for whom the question of technocracy and the question of bureaucracy were inextricably bound up with the "new class" debate. They are separated here analytically, but it is well to remember that in fact they were often perceived, and discussed, as a single problem.

From the earliest days of the revolution, the "bourgeois specialists" (*spetsi*, in the pejorative usage of the time) were a knotty problem for the regime. On the one hand, they were needed; but on the other, it was feared that because they were bourgeois, and because they had served under and been well rewarded under the tsarist regime, they would inevitably be disloyal to the proletarian regime. Lenin did not share this fear. He makes a distinction between bureaucrats as agents of parasitic structures of control and accounting (these must be smashed), and technical experts (who can be utilized by the workers):

The question of control and accounting should not be confused with the question of the scientifically trained staff of engineers, agronomists, and so on. These gentlemen are working today in obedience to the wishes of the capitalists, and will work even better tomorrow in obedience to the wishes of the armed workers.[36]

The idea of technocracy, political rule by technologists, by its nature is one that could not have been seriously entertained much prior to the beginnings at least of the Industrial Revolution. Perhaps the earliest literary image of technocracy was Francis Bacon's unfinished utopian novel *New Atlantis*.[37] Jean-Antoine de Caritat Marquis de Condorcet,[38] and Henri Saint-Simon in many of his writings,[39] were also early writers on the subject. The great utopianist H. G. Wells began in 1902 to advocate the rule of scientists,[40] and the idea reappeared frequently in his writings over the years until 1928, when he repented of technocracy and urged the importance of generalists.[41]

A number of works on technocracy, both optimistic and pessimistic, appeared in the 1930s (and some earlier), particularly in the United States, most notably including James Burnham,[42] Thorstein Veblen,[43] Stuart Chase,[44] Allen Raymond,[45] and a group of engineers organized as Technocracy, Inc.[46] The topic became popular again in the 1970s and 1980s, and new works appeared, most but not all pessimistic and critical, with an emphasis on ethical and moral issues surrounding technocracy.[47]

Since the earliest writers on the subject, technocracy has implied a particular notion of the nature of political power and authority:

Power is ultimately the power of nature itself, released by the inquiries of science and made available by the inventive organizing capacity of technics. All other sources of political power—wealth, public support, personal charisma, social standing, organized interest—are weak by comparison. They are anachronisms in a technological age and will ultimately decline as scientific technology and the people who most directly control its forces become more important to the workings of society.[48]

A key concept here is the supposed indispensability of technologists to a technological society. The masters of technology are perhaps essential to the operation of technology, but fears (or hopes) that they will thereby become the masters of society seem to have been ungrounded. Garbage collectors are essential to an industrial society too, but they are a long way from ruling one. Weber caustically writes that if the "indispensability of a group automatically lent it social or political power, then in slaveholding periods the slaves themselves should have ruled."[49]

The reason, perhaps, is that as a group they lack one or more of James Meisel's "three C's:" group consciousness, coherence, and conspiracy.[50] In spite of the impressive elements of coherence listed above, they are apparently not a class, do not think of themselves as one, and do not act on behalf of one.[51] For technocrats to belong to a power elite at all, it requires a society in which there is a heavy governmental role in economic planning and management, such as France or the Soviet Union. There is nothing remotely technocratic about the ruling political elite in the United States or Britain, where this state role does not obtain. Even in France, Brazil, and the Soviet Union, however, technocrats serve as tools of the interventionist state and do not control it. This was true in tsarist Russia as well: "Specialists or experts typically hold humble positions in generalist bureaucracies. The tendency in the prerevolutionary Russian civil administration was for socially elite generalists to occupy powerful and responsible positions in the bureaucracy, while experts who were necessary to organizational operations were inferior both organizationally and socially."[52]

As late as the 1950s in the Soviet Union, however, the mythical technocrat—who wants to take over the state—reappeared occasionally. The conservative writer Vsevolod Kochetov, in a novel that may have been occasioned by the publication of Vladimir Dudintsev's *Not by Bread Alone*, has a Soviet engineer make a statement that is unerringly evocative of the *Prompartiia* trial: "Our era is one of technology and science. Therefore, those in command of technology and science must become the leading, guiding force. Engineers, my dear, engineers! That is you and I—we!"[53]

The shadowy figure of the technocratic conspirer is a myth left over from the Stalinist past. Albert Parry argues that the fact that Soviet scientists, engineers, and managers are so reluctant to join the Party or to do tasks that the Party assigns indicates they are not in any mood to take over the state and become technocrats.[54]

A milder and more realistic form of the technocratic thesis is that the technicians do not actually rule in the sense of occupying top political posts; rather, they exercise disproportionate influence on public policy, either because of their "autonomous ability to dispose of vast resources,"[55] or because policy makers listen and pay attention to experts. Theodore Roszak, for example, defines technocracy as "that society in which those who govern justify themselves by appeal to technical experts who, in turn, justify themselves by appeal to scientific forms of knowledge. And beyond the authority of science, there is no appeal."[56] Ronald Hill found this aspect of technocracy to be a serious source of concern in the Soviet Union today:

There is emerging a more competent corps of professional administrators and the role of specialist advisers is also expanding. This raises the spectre of an alliance between highly trained administrators and intellectual advisers running the state as a technocratic elite. This is potentially a serious problem...and it has been given considerable attention in Soviet writings, with phrases such as "dictatorship of specialists," "regime of technocracy," and even a new coining, "acadocracy" or "scholocracy" (*uchenokratiya*) appearing in the literature.[57]

An interesting variation on the technocracy theme is Simirenko's suggestion of a "Therapogenic" model of Soviet society. In his conceptualization, the outstanding characteristic of the Soviet elite is that it has become "professionalized," not in the technical sense but in the sense that governing itself is seen as a profession with arcane skills not possessed by nonprofessionals. The profession of governing and the relationship of governors to the governed come to resemble the norms of professions, and citizens become "clients." The "therapy" metaphor comes from the elite's task of improving human material and creating the new man.[58]

Another, entirely separate, strain of thought with respect to technocrats is that which sees the Soviet technical intelligentsia not as a ruling class at all but as an oppressed class engaged in a struggle for political power with a *Partocratic* ruling class. This novel gloss was developed by Fedor Zniakov (a pseudonym) in a 1966 *samizdat* article that enjoyed wide influence among the Soviet intelligentsia in the 1960s and after.[59] Zniakov attributes the idea to George Orwell's *1984*, and it was picked up again by Andrei Amalrik.[60] In the West, the same idea appeared somewhat earlier—H. F. Achmanov wrote in the early 1960s that the technical intelligentsia are the "gravediggers of communism."[61] Along similar lines, Bohdan Harasymiw writes, "An open conflict over the elite recruitment system between the incumbent political elite and its challengers—the technical intelligentsia—requires only the organization of the latter into a self-conscious class."[62] Serge Mallet, too, sees a struggle between a fossilized bureaucracy and the technocrats—defined as a new class of economic directors—for control over the economy.[63]

This view of technocracy—to be sure, without the emphasis on class struggle—has much to recommend it. Technocracy in this view means the *depoliticization* of problems, the effort to arrive at rational and effective solutions rather than solutions based on or guided by ideology; a technocrat in this view refers, not to a member of an elite (ruling or not), but to someone who looks at policy problems in a certain way. Alexander Shtromas, in a work in which he contrasts "partocrats" to "technocrats," defines the "technocratic ideology" in terms of four maxims, paraphrased here:

1. Efficiency, quality, and productivity should form the basis of organizing the economy, not the dictates of socialism or other ideology.

2. Social and political issues should be subordinated to rationally definable national interest, instead of Communist ideology or the interests of a ruling group.

3. Professionals should be able to carry out their tasks with full personal responsibility, which implies personal initiative and independent decision making, rather than mechanical execution of orders from above.

4. All positions should be filled strictly according to skill and qualifications rather than political loyalty or reliability.[64]

Most scholars have noted a steady increase from the beginning of the Khrushchev period in the technical competence of Party officials. The Twenty-second Party Congress is sometimes called the "technocratic enrollment" because of the massive influx of specialists and technicians into the Party and into the Central Committee.[65] Robert Blackwell, however, dissents, finding in the Brezhnev period a slowdown, if not a reversal, of the recruitment of men with technical experience, at least at the *obkom* level.[66] Indeed, Gorbachev told a group of Party first secretaries in 1986 that it was necessary "to dispense with the technocratic approach to solving political and social problems."[67]

In counterpoint, articles have appeared in the press complaining about the declining role of engineers—they are given paper shuffling jobs—and the declining prestige of the engineering profession.[68]

Identifying individuals who have an orientation toward efficiency rather than toward politics is problematical, since this is a question of attitudes, and accessible demographic characteristics are a poor guide to attitudes. It might be possible, however, to identify *types* of individuals, based on their careers, who would be more likely to have such attitudes. The following remarks are directed toward this more limited end.

The orientation of the usual stereotyped breed of Soviet *apparatchik* is toward politics. This is so because the nature of the *nomenklatura* system is such that it encourages and rewards loyalty—even toadyism—more than competence and discourages innovation and risk taking. Making a career in the Soviet system thus obliges an official to pay close attention to politics even if he finds it distasteful, which no doubt many officials do. Many Party and industrial people must be privately frustrated with the inefficiency and waste of the system but perceive that they cannot do anything about it without political protection. Others are simply opportunist or careerist. Some have probably actually believed that political factors were indeed paramount. These we can call political bureaucrats.

The countertype, the technocratic bureaucrat, then, would be one who is more concerned about efficiency in production and management than he is about politics. We would expect these types to be in a minority in a sample of Central Committee elites, if for no other reason than that they would be less likely to have followed a Party-political career than the political bureaucrat. However, a beginning, at least, can be made toward identifying the type of functionary who would be most likely to have technocratic attitudes.

Socialization literature suggests that attitudes that persist for life are formed in early adulthood (about age 18 to 25), when the individual begins life independent of parents or of schools. This essentially means when the individual begins his career. It is at this time that he learns the unwritten rules, learning what brings rewards and what brings penalties. As the appropriate behavior brings rewards, the norms on which they are based are likely to become internalized. Thus, the organizational context in which the individual began his career and achieved his first successes is crucial for his socialization. If the individual began his career in a *raikom* and worked his way up the normal progression of a Party career, the orientation of the political bureaucrat would almost certainly be internalized.

In an organizational context that rewarded performance more than loyalty, one in which the engineering graduate could devote most of his energy to the thing he loves (presumably the technical aspects of the production process and how to make it better) without having to pay too significant a cost for his indulgence, then the technocratic orientation could take root and grow. This would be a career of the "engineer—head of shift—chief engineer—plant manager" type. Thus, an individual who spent five or ten years in production before assuming a Party or state political position would be more likely to become a technocratic bureaucrat.

Table 5.2
Central Committee Members by Years in Specialization (in percentages)

	Congress							
	19th	20th	22nd	23rd	24th	25th	26th	27th
5 yrs or more	41	41	56	62	66	67	65	71
10 yrs or more	24	30	35	46	51	48	47	51

Source: Author's database

Table 5.2 gives the percentage of members of each Central Committee who served five years or more, and ten years or more, in their specialization before assuming a full-time Party or government post. This table suggests that the proportion of technocratic bureaucrats (by my limited definition) has steadily increased over the period 1953 to 1986. More accurately, these data clearly indicate that over time, individuals who reach the Central Committee have spent longer apprenticeships in their specializations *before* assuming a full-time Party or government position and thus have increasingly been exposed at the onset of their careers to the socialization pressure of an organizational context I am presuming is more likely to produce a technocratic rather than a political orientation.

Most of the men (and the woman) that Gorbachev brought to top leadership positions in Moscow in the latter 1980s conform to this pattern, including some, like Egor Ligachev and Boris Yel'tsin, who subsequently lost his favor. Ironically, it is Gorbachev himself, trained in law and going immediately afterward into full-time Party work, who is the glaring exception.

DOES THE SOVIET UNION HAVE A RULING CLASS?

The political elite are those who rule. It can be asked whether the members of this group have anything in common other than the fact that they happen to rule. In the Soviet case, they have, at minimum, Communist Party membership in common, and the *nomenklatura* of the Communist Party is a "ruling elite." In the words of Peter Medding, "The classical ruling elite model is ... a model of politics in which the only political structures which are recognized as existing are those controlled by the elite. ... To demonstrate that the elite rules we would have to show that all existing political structures are controlled by the elite."[69]

The term "ruling elite model" originated with efforts on the part of James Burnham and C. Wright Mills to reconcile the elitism of Gaetano Mosca and Vilfredo Pareto with Marxism.[70] For a group to qualify as a ruling elite, it would have to meet three conditions: (1) identity, that is, consciousness of being a separate and ruling stratum, self-conscious of its right to rule; (2) control over entry into its ranks, not having entry to ranks forced upon it by any natural selection process (as would be the case for a natural elite); and (3) able to rule in its own interest, enjoying autonomy in decision making and unaccountable to any constituent group.[71] It can be seen that the "ruling elite" model is similar to Meisel's Three C's, mentioned above; consciousness, coherence, and conspiracy. There is little need here to belabor the point that the *nomenklatura* qualifies as a ruling elite. The question here is a knottier one: Is it, or any larger pool from which it is drawn—Party, intelligentsia, technical intelligentsia—a ruling *class*?

As was strongly emphasized above in the discussion of technocracy, historically the Party has been very sensitive about the question of whether it, or the intelligentsia in general, constitutes some kind of ruling class. It is not an idle question, but rather one that comes perilously close to issues of the legitimacy of the Party's ruling elite. The Party's justification for why it should rule—and brook no opposition—lies in a variant of what Weber called a "theodicy." "Theodicy" roughly means "God's justification"; in Weber's usage, it refers to the traditional insistence on divine sanction for earthly political authority. With rationalization, in Weber's scheme, came "disenchantment of the world" (meaning demystification) and the replacement of theodicies by legal authority. Soviet spokesmen insist, in fact, that the intelligentsia is not a class at all, but rather a "stratum" (*prosloika*), though the difference between a class and a stratum strikes me, at least, as subtle to the vanishing point. After noting that the intelligentsia make up one-fifth of the Soviet working population, a *Pravda* commentator writing in 1965 explains:

> In socialist society the intelligentsia is not a social stratum with interests different from the interests of the working class and peasantry. It does not enjoy any privileges in its relation with other groups of the population. The world view of the intelligentsia wholly corresponds to that of the workers and the peasants, and this excludes the possibility of setting itself up as a special caste.... The conditions of physical and mental labor are converging, and world culture is open to all, intellectuals, workers, peasants. The state has been transformed from a dictatorship of the proletariat to a state of all the people. It is therefore clear that in conditions of victorious socialism the Communist Party does not have a different policy in relation to intelligentsia as opposed to workers and peasants. The Party has to be the representative of the interests of all strata.[72]

Germane here are various theories to the effect that the Party, the bureaucracy, or the intelligentsia have become, in a perversion of Marxism, a new ruling and exploiting class. The earliest articulation of the "new class" thesis—or at least of a concept in which the "new class" thesis was implicit—is probably in Plato, in reference to the famous Guardians. The question of whether the Soviet Communist Party in particular constitutes a new class was of course made famous by the publication of Milovan Djilas's classic *New Class* in 1957. The idea, however, has a very long pedigree, going back as far as Michael Bakunin's debate with Marx in the latter nineteenth century.[73] By the 1920s the idea was given wide credence and was articulated by figures ranging from Karl Kautsky to Adolf Hitler.

As early as the 1870s the anarchist Bakunin adumbrated theories of the new class. Bakunin believed that Marx's "dictatorship of the proletariat" would of necessity lead to a new despotism. The working class might seize power, but—unable to master the arcana of "scientific socialism"—would have little choice but to hand it over to a new elite. In a passage uncanny for its prescience he identified that new elite as the Communist Party chiefs:

They will gather up the reins of government in a strong hand because the ignorant people need strong guardians; they will establish a single state bank, concentrating in their own hands all commercial and industrial, agricultural, and even scientific production; and they will divide the mass of the people into two armies, one industrial and one agrarian, under the direct command of state engineers, who will form a new privileged scientific caste.[74]

Even Mosca wrote of a new class in Russia consisting of the managers and governors of a collectivist society who control the fates of everyone and who, he believed, would find ways to pass their advantages to their children.[75]

Djilas, in his famous book, saw the new class as political bureaucracy, which collectively owns and controls not only the means of production but also the distribution of its products. Djilas was careful to point out that it is not a hereditary class; rather, it renews itself by co-opting new members committed to its norms.[76]

In the Soviet Union, the new class thesis is associated mainly with the heretical doctrine known as "Makhaevism" (*Makhaevshchina*). Jan Waclaw Machajski (1867–1926)[77] was a Russified Polish intellectual and revolutionary who spent some years in tsarist prisons and in Siberian exile. While in exile in 1898 he wrote, under the pseudonym of A. Vol'skii, a massive and difficult work entitled *The Intellectual Worker* (*Umstvennyi rabochii*). After circulating several years in hectographed form, *The Intellectual Worker* was published in Geneva in 1904–05. It has not yet been translated into English in its entirety. He also published two shorter works in Geneva: *Bourgeois Revolution and the Cause of the Workers* (*Burzhuaznaia revoliutsiia i rabochee delo*) and *The Bankruptcy of Nineteenth-Century Socialism* (*Bankrotsvo sotsializma XIX stoletiia*), the latter reprinted in St. Petersburg in 1906. He started two journals, *Workers' Conspiracy* (*Rabochii za-govor*, no. 1, September-October 1907, published in Geneva in 1908) and *Workers' Revolution* (*Rabochaia revoliutsiia*, no. 1, June-July 1918, published in Moscow that year). Only the first issue of each appeared.[78] After the Bolshevik seizure of power, Machajski, having returned from Paris to Moscow, worked quietly as a copy editor for a Soviet state publication until his death in 1926.

At the center of Machajski's doctrine is the thesis that socialism represented the interests, not of the proletariat, but of the intelligentsia. The concept of the intelligentsia as a "rising new class" had been advanced earlier by Kautsky.[79] Kautsky, however, believing that most of the intelligentsia stood above the class struggle and had no consciousness of itself as a class, could serve as an ally of and spokesman for the proletariat. Machajski decisively rejected Kautsky's view, a view also held by Bernstein and Lenin, arguing that the intelligentsia—defined as virtually anyone with an education and therefore not obliged to engage in manual labor—benefited as much as the capitalists from the oppression of the working class.[80]

The form of property owned by the intelligentsia, its "invisible capital" that enables it to exploit the working class along with the capitalists, is knowledge, or education. The intelligentsia are a hereditary class because they can pass their status on to their offspring by providing them with the leisure to obtain an education also. In Machajski's scheme, intellectual workers do not create value (Marx had maintained that they do); but they live instead off the surplus value produced by the proletariat. Machajski believed that they would continue to do so under socialism, and he saw the Bolshevik takeover as "a counterrevolution of the intellectuals."[81]

There is a clear congruence between Machajski's ideas and those put forward earlier by Bakunin in the latter's polemic with Marx, and some scholars believe that Machajski owes a substantial unacknowledged intellectual debt to Bakunin.[82] Bakunin argued that the intelligentsia have no interest in revolution because they cherish the comfortable position with which capitalism provides them.[83]

Machajski's ideas were widely known and discussed in social democratic circles in spite of the fact that his publications were few and appeared in limited editions. Some of the disciples and critics of Macahjski included Evgenii Lozinskii[84] and a Marxist writer named D. Zaitsev.[85] The question of the relationship of the intelligentsia to the proletariat and to Social Democracy was widely debated, sometimes bitterly, in the Russian underground, and Makhaevist groups appeared in several parts of Russia, but most strangely in Odessa and St. Petersburg.[86] A small Makhaevist party called the Workers' Conspiracy was active in St. Petersburg in 1906–07. In spite of deep antagonism to the intelligentsia on the part of the Russian working class, these groups remained small and ineffectual, though some anarchosynicalists not associated with Macahjski also published critiques of bolshevism very similar to his.[87]

There certainly was a marked intellectualization of the Party from the earliest days of the revolution. White-collar workers found it easier to gain admission to the Party, and once in the Party to become *apparatchikii*, than did workers or peasants, who were often illiterate.[88] At the Tenth Congress in 1921, the position of the Workers' Opposition—that Party enrollments should be manipulated to favor workers—was labeled Makhaevism (*Makhaevshchina*), marking the first official use of that term.[89] It was at the Tenth Congress that factionalism, intra-Party democracy, and so on, were stifled. Some members of the Workers' Opposition, notably Kollontai and Shliapnikov, had supported the Makhaevist view. Clara Zetkin wrote on July 3, 1925, to Nadezhda Krupskaia asking her to review a report she had written on the intelligentsia. In her answer, Krupskaia indicated three things: first, that there was still deep hatred for intellectuals on the part of the peasants and workers; second, that the Russian intelligentsia had not been affected by bourgeois ideology as much as those in the West because the Russian bourgeoisie had been so weak in Russia; third, "by now sabotage in the Soviet Republic by the intelligentsia has come to an end. Intellectuals intend to work jointly with the Soviet government in good faith."[90]

Stalin, who definitely represented an anti-intellectual strain in the Bolshevik Party and who sponsored the rise of intellectually mediocre men to the top, might have been predicted to have been sympathetic to Makhaevism, but he was not.[91] Stalin may have had his insecurities about his own intellectual stature in comparison to the Old Bolsheviks, but it cannot be said that he was anti-intelligentsia per se. He was opposed to the bourgeois intelligentsia and sought to destroy them, but only to replace them with a proletarian intelligentsia. Makhaevism continues to be castigated in the Soviet Union as "slanderous of the revolutionary intelligentsia."[92]

A dogged exponent of the "new class" thesis appeared outside the Soviet Union in the 1930s in the person of Bruno Rizzi.[93] Expanding the "new class" thesis rather impressively from a theoretical standpoint, Rizzi argued that industrialism brings into existence a new bureaucratic ruling class, the basis of whose power was not the ownership of property but control over the means of production, which are in fact owned by the state. "Bureaucratic collectivism," apparently Rizzi's original contribution to the debate, is a form of social organization that interpolated itself between capitalism and socialism. In one of the earliest articulations of convergence theory, Rizzi held that since bureaucratic collectivism is more efficient than capitalist forms of industrial organization, industrial societies will converge toward it. Rizzi predicted that Nazi Germany, fascist Italy, and the New Deal United States were converging in the late

1930s toward a bureaucratic collectivism of which the Soviet Union was the model. Rizzi deplored, rather than celebrated, this situation, warning the working class in a melodramatic style evocative of *The Communist Manifesto* that

the world is on the eve of a formidable historical turning point. We believe that Stalin will recall that he was a revolutionary before becoming a dictator, and will understand the terrible responsibilities which link him to the international proletariat. We judge only according to the facts and advise the workers to do the same. Europe and the world must become fascist or socialist. Capitalism has no further possibility of life. The USSR has become the pivot of world politics and will be the bastion of the proletarian revolution or else a trap for the world proletariat.[94]

Rizzi's thesis, although novel in certain respects, certainly came out of the tradition of technocratic and ruling-class theories that, as shown, has a long and convoluted history. Rizzi was not a scholar, but he was active politically and was familiar with the writings of at least the major Marxist critics of the Soviet Union, especially Leon Trotsky. He borrowed freely from these works, not always with attribution, but nonetheless vociferously asserting the originality of his ideas and accusing James Burnham of plagarizing him.[95]

Constas, criticizing Djilas rather than the earlier Rizzi and preferring to emphasize the routinization of charisma, argues that there is nothing new about the Soviet "ruling class." Such social structures, originating in the institutionalization of charisma in a bureaucratic setting, she calls "charismatic bureaucratic societies" and avers that it is one of the oldest historical structures known.[96]

In the 1970s and 1980s a number of critical Marxist discussions of class relations under communism began to appear not only in the West but in some East European countries as well: George Konrad and Ivan Szelenyi, *The Intellectuals on the Road to Class Power*; Jack Kuron and Karol Modzelewski, "An Open Letter to the Party"; Rudolf Bahro, *The Alternative in Eastern Europe*; Ferenc Feher, Agnes Heller, and Gyorgy Markus, *Dictatorship over Needs*.

Critical Marxist theories of the ruling class in state-socialist societies had, until the 1970s, been usually premised on the concept of state capitalism. Control over, rather than the actual legal ownership of, the means of production is what is important in this concept. This control is exercised in state-socialist societies by Party and state functionaries; their role—extracting surplus product from the working class—is identical to that of the bourgeoisie in capitalist societies.[97]

Some of the objections to the "new class" thesis were addressed by Kuron and Modzelewski, two Warsaw University professors who were later arrested:

It is said that the bureaucracy cannot be a class since the individual earnings of its members do not come anywhere near the earnings of capitalists; since no bureaucrat, taken by himself, rules anything more than his mansion, his car and his secretary; since entrance to the bureaucratic ranks is determined by a political career and not by inheritance; and since it is relatively easy to be eliminated from the bureaucracy in a political show-down. This is quite wrong. All of the above arguments prove only the obvious: the property of the bureaucracy is not of an individual nature, but constitutes the collective property of an elite which identifies itself with the state. This fact defines the principles of the bureaucracy's internal organization, but its class character does not depend on its internal organization or its mores, only on its relationship—as a group—to the means of production and to other social classes (above all the working class).[98]

Konrad and Szelenyi's *Intellectuals on the Road to Class Power* is a remarkable blend of technocratic, "new class," and Makhaevist traditions in critical Marxism. Konrad and Szelenyi acknowledged that Djilas's analysis of the new class was correct in the 1950s, but beginning with the reform movements of the 1960s intellectuals of all kinds began sharing power with the bureaucrats and even replacing them. They argue that for the first time in history, the intelligentsia in the East European Communist states and the USSR are becoming a class, a "government-bureaucratic ruling class" that have taken the lead in modernizing their countries.[99] Much like Machajski, Konrad and Szelenyi find the source of the intelligentsia's power in its claim to a monopoly on truth:

The definition of universal, eternal, supreme (and hence immutable) knowledge displays a remarkable variability over the ages, but in every age the intellectuals define as such whatever knowledge best serves the particular interests connected with their social role—and that is whatever portion of the knowledge of the age serves to maintain their monopoly of their role.[100]

Bahro makes a similar argument, but whereas Konrad and Szelenyi seemed to lament the development, Bahro is optimistic about it.[101] In a subsequent postmortem of their thesis, Szelenyi conceded that the process had stopped by the end of the 1960s. The humanist intelligentsia failed to merge with the bureaucracy, a devastating setback having been the 1968 Soviet invasion of Czechoslovakia.[102]

Feher, Heller, and Markus, in *Dictatorship over Needs*, reject all notions of state capitalism or a "transitional society" (the latter being the Trotskyist view) and argue instead that the political situation in the Soviet Union is characterized simply by the relationship between a "sovereign Party" and a powerless people. The Party is in their view not a ruling class but a corporate group of rulers with dictatorial control over the economy, its only purpose being to maintain itself in power.[103]

Trotsky, the sternest critic of the Stalinist bureaucracy, explicitly rejected the idea that it represented a ruling class, on the basis that although it certainly abused state office for its own benefit, it had no property as its own and could not pass on its privileges to its heirs.[104] Other rejections of the "new class" thesis are founded on this inability of its members to pass on their status to their offspring automatically.[105]

The question of whether the Soviet ruling class is hereditary or not seems to me to be a red herring; indeed, a burning nonissue. Clearly it is not, in the sense that landed noble status had been. However, as has often been pointed out, there are ways in which the elite can smooth the way into elite status for their children through access to elite schools, connections, influence, and money. But this is equally true in capitalist societies as well, which also have no hereditary aristocracy. The salient question is not so much whether elite status can be inherited as a birth-right as it is how easily elite parents can assure elite status for their offspring. The answer is that in aristocratic societies, it is so easy that it is automatic; in capitalist societies, it is not automatic, but still relatively easy; in Communist societies, it is relatively difficult, but still possible and becoming more common. It was in part to counter such familization of elite status that Nikita Khrushchev's educational reforms were de-signed.

It is worth noting that although the children of political elites usually find their way into elite occupations, they rarely pursue political careers. They go into arts, engineering or science, or academia. The only ex-ception to this pattern is diplomacy: about 16 percent (but as high as 30 percent in Moscow) of children of political elites have gone into diplo-matic careers,[106] no doubt because access to foreigners, to travel abroad, and to foreign goods is highly valued and is in itself, of course, a badge of status.

Under conditions of *glasnost'*, candid discussions of class and, in a roundabout way, of the "new class" thesis, have begun to appear in the Soviet press. An interview with the noted Novosibirsk economist Tatiana Zaslavskaia appeared in *Izvestia* in 1988. Her comments are remarkably reminiscent of Djilas. Asked whether *nomenklatura* stratum can be called a class, she replied:

Generally speaking, this stratum does possess the three characteristics of a class as listed by Lenin. It has a special relationship to the means of production (it possesses almost unlimited power to dispose of those means), it occupies a special place in the organization of social labor (it manages that labor), and it is set apart from the rest of the population by the share and sources of the wealth it receives. But these hallmarks do not exhaust the concepts of class. Lenin regarded the economic exploitation of some social classes by others as an important feature of class structure. What we have learned in the recent past about the structure and functioning of our society during the periods of Stalinism and Brezhnevism, it seems to me, is reason for talking, at least, about indirect exploitation by the *nomenklatura* stratum of the remaining mass of the population. (I want to put special emphasis on the point that what is involved here is indeed a stratum.) But even if we believe that this stratum has not managed to turn into a class once and for all, it has been confidently moving in that direction, in any case.[107]

Weber makes a distinction between "class situation" and "status situation." Class itself, he argues, is strictly determined by economic interests.[108] In contrast to a class situation, however, a status situation consists of "every typical component of the life of men that is determined by a specific, positive or negative, social estimation of *honor*," although he concedes that status situation is linked to class situation.[109] Status situation is always premised on distance and exclusivity: "Above all else a *specific style of life* is expected from all those who wish to belong to the circle."[110] With respect to the Soviet Union, some other category seems necessary, since "class situation" does not strictly apply there. What is needed is a category that accounts for domination and privilege that stems from the holding of official position in state or Party. We can call this a "power situation." It is the *state* that monopolized access to the economy. The key to control over economic resources—in free economies bestowed by membership in a class—is given by holding political office in command economies.

There has been a recurrent debate among contemporary Western scholars on whether the Soviet Union has a ruling class.[111] David Lane has clarified the terms of debate with reference to the question of a Soviet ruling class. Lane, as do most scholars, distinguishes between a ruling class, on the one hand, and individuals occupying positions of authority, on the other. The ruling class, he writes, is in a position to dominate, exploit, and appropriate for itself society's resources. Such ruling classes, in Lane's words, are "social entities which have an awareness (or consciousness) of their distinctive interests *vis-à-vis* other classes; they are oppositional rather than hierarchical; they are exploitative and privileged rather than stratified and unequal; they are dominant and illegitimate rather than authoritative."[112]

Lane concludes that there is no evidence of notion of *class* domination in the Soviet Union. Much as do Feher, Heller, and Markus, Lane sees the situation in state-socialist societies as the dominance of a privileged stratum in a hierarchical structure of social and political stratification.[113] Social relations are not determined by relationships to the means of production; power stratification, rather than class, is a more powerful analytical concept.[114] T. B. Bottomore, too, rejects the notion that high state officials are a ruling class.[115] Bottomore not only rejects the notion that there is a ruling class in the Soviet Union but insists that there are no ruling classes in industrial societies at all, the development of which, he argues, "can properly be depicted as a movement from a class system to a system of elites, from a social hierarchy based upon the inheritance of property to one based on merit and achievement."[116]

Weber did not speak of *class* domination, arguing sensibly that only individuals or small groups can run the state.[117] Elsewhere Weber does state that control over economic goods can be a consequence of domination as well as an instrument for *maintaining* domination.[118] Kautsky, commenting on the Bolshevik revolution, wrote, "We cannot speak of the dictatorship of a class, since a class . . . can only rule but not govern."[119] Without offering any counterargument, Lenin took fierce and despiteous issue: "That is a muddle, a disgusting muddle, Mr. 'Muddle-headed Counsellor'! It is altogether wrong . . . to say that a *class* cannot govern. Such an absurdity can only be uttered by a 'parliamentary cretin' who sees nothing but bourgeois parliaments and notices nothing but "ruling parties."[120] Amitai Etzioni also stressed the difference between ruling classes and elites: "Class is a status concept; elite is a role concept."[121]

The Russian revolution and Stalin's later "second revolution" were successful in one sense: they destroyed the class *structure* of the society. The society was left inchoate; it had no structure that was recognized. One had to be created; in particular, one had to be created that corresponded somewhat to Marxist ideas about the structure of society: hence a proletariat (but without concessions to real workers), a peasantry (but not the real one that existed), and an intelligentsia. A *fictional* class structure was imposed over a mass society. A ruling class, if one were to exist, would also have to be created, or at best to evolve slowly out of social processes that were being forced from above in the Stalin period.

In reference to capitalist societies, Marxism distinguishes sharply between a ruling class and a political, or power, elite. The domination of the former stems from its relationship to property and the means of production; of the latter, from its relationship to the political structure of the society—that is, the Party-state.[122] Since property and the means of production are owned by the state in socialist societies, implied is a fusion of ruling class and political elite. Beyond the purview of the Party-state, in theory at least, there should be little of significance to dominate. And in the absence of non-Party or nonstate bases of domination, the question of the relative autonomy of the state would be moot.

It seems clear to me that a ruling class is not coextensive with a governing, political elite. The political elite *may* be, but certainly is not necessarily, drawn from the ruling class, and it may govern in its own interests. Even in pluralist societies individuals can be drawn into politics from despised classes and work their way into the political elite, a phenomenon that was particularly notable during the age of political machines in the United States. In societies such as the Soviet Union that have, as I suggested, an "artificial elite," it is even more marked. There is a Soviet upper class defined in terms of prestige and income that is quite, if not entirely, separate from the political elite. Out of this group, as will be discussed in Chapter 8, will emerge "strategic elites" in Suzanne Keller's sense, with the increasing pluralization of Soviet society. If democratization and the elimination of *nomenklatura* continue, it is quite likely that the Soviet "artificial elite" will give way increasingly to an elite drawn largely from this privileged—or, if you will, ruling—stratum.

Characterizations of the Soviet system as "state capitalism" usually proceed from the assumption that private ownership of the means of production is the defining characteristic of capitalism. However, any viable notion of capitalism implies competition (or the market, which amounts to the same thing). It is competition among producers and sellers that drives the dynamics of capitalism: it eliminates inefficient producers and promotes efficient ones, it regulates the relationship between supply and demand, and it determines prices. A competitive market, and these effects of it, are conspicuously absent in the Soviet system. The hypothesis is not saved by substituting planning for competition. Socialized planning is not the functional equivalent of the market because, conceptual reasons aside, it does not in practice produce the same or even similar effects as the market does. Calling the Soviet system state capitalism is a textbook case of Giovanni Sartori's "concept of misinformation."[123]

A ruling class, it seems to me, exhibit more than Weber's "status situation." It also occupies (by definition, perhaps) a "class situation," and in societies of the Soviet type, a "power situation."

As a synthesis of the ideas discussed above, I would suggest criteria for the existence of something functionally equivalent to a ruling class. The first and second will find no disagreement, I am sure, among either Marxist or mainstream scholars; these are, respectively, control over wealth and the means of production, and internal coherence. The third criterion is that the state itself should be its tool, or at least partially so. The fourth criterion is some kind of intergenerational continuity, although this does not have to imply formal inheritance; I have discussed above the ways such intergenerational continuity can be maintained. Without continuity over time, a structuralist would have difficulty recognizing our ruling class; it would merely be a temporal conjunction of the powerful and privileged. The fifth criterion is a sense of self-consciousness as an elite *and* some mechanism of boundary maintenance *from within*. My final criterion is autonomy: a ruling class must exist independently of other forces in the society, and especially of the state. Without the fourth and fifth criteria, a "ruling class" would not be a "class;" without the sixth, it would not be "ruling."

With regard to the fifth criterion, ordinarily a combination of class and status situations (wealth and breeding) serves to maintain boundaries. In the Soviet Union these boundaries are permeable by virtually anyone who can acquire sponsorship, though a very efficient political gate-keeping mechanism does exist. It is difficult to measure attitudes, but from what is known of the *nomenklatura* it is almost certain that they are conscious of themselves as an exclusive elite. Mervyn Matthews remarks with respect to the Soviet elite that "the sharing of privilege and a common social distance from the masses must encourage at least a certain unity among them."[124]

It is less on the third or fourth than on the fifth criterion that the Soviet political elite fails as a ruling class. It is an artificial elite, as I have repeatedly stressed, and its status is derivative of, not determinative of, political power, coming either from state or Party position. If a Soviet leader loses his *nomenklatura* status, he simultaneously loses his membership in the ruling class. There is, therefore, no ruling class apart from the *nomenklatura*. This artificial class system affects class relations in the rest of society. Zaslavskaia remarks that "it is quite noteworthy that the popular mind pits not collective farmers against workers or those who do physical labor against members of the intelligentsia but, above all, the 'governors' against the 'governed.' "[125]

There are, of course, significant activities outside the purview of the state, including not only often highly remunerative black and grey markets but other *demimondes* as well of varying scope and scale. Often, perhaps more often than not, these overlap with the Party and the state through individuals strategically located in both arenas, via activities over which the state nominally claims monopoly of jurisdiction, or through the arrogation to such arena of resources belonging to the state. Thus, the state in socialist society (meaning the Party-state), it would seem, is not autonomous, not very well integrated, and, truth be told, rather weak.

Since it is not a mainstream assertion, the thesis of the essential weakness of the Soviet state deserves some amplification. Weak actors, to borrow some of the language of game theory, cannot marshal sufficient resources consistently to win within the game's rules. A weak actor can win only when it can restructure the game in such a way that its opponents are rule constrained while it is not. To use more prosaic language, weak actors cheat. A state that can maintain itself over time only by extraconstitutional coercion is weak. Structurally weak states require large internal police forces or powerful external patron states. Examples of the rapidity with which they fall when that is removed are legion: Vietnam in 1975, Nicaragua and Iran in 1979, the East European Communist regimes at the end of the 1980s, and the Soviet state itself in the summer of 1991.

NOTES

1. Gaetano Mosca, *The Ruling Class* (New York: McGraw-Hill, 1939), p. 53.
2. George E. Marcus, " 'Elite' as a Concept, Theory, and Research Tradi-

tion," in George E. Marcus, ed., *Elites: Ethnographic Issues* (Albuquerque: University of New Mexico Press, 1983), pp. 11–12.

3. Raymond Aron, "Social Structure and Ruling Class," *British Journal of Sociology* 1, nos. 1–2 (1950):130.

4. Ilya Dzhirkvelov, *Secret Servant: My Life with the KGB and the Soviet Elite* (London: William Collins' Sons, 1987), p. 126.

5. Peter Ludz, *The Changing Party Elite in East Germany* (Cambridge, MA: MIT Press, 1972), p. 34.

6. Aron, "Social Structure and Ruling Class," p. 8.

7. T. B. Bottomore, *Elites and Society* (New York: Basic Books, 1964), p. 79.

8. V. I. Lenin, "The State and Revolution," *Selected Works* (London: Lawrence & Wishart, 1969), p. 349. For an excellent comparison of Weber's and Lenin's views on the role of bureaucracy in the state, see Erik Olin Wright. "To Control or to Smash Bureaucracy: Weber and Lenin on Politics, the State, and Bureaucracy," *Berkeley Journal of Sociology* 19 (1974–75):69–108.

9. "The Declaration of the Thirteen," in Robert V. Daniels, ed., *A Documentary History of Communism* (Hanover, NH: University Press of New England, 1984), p. 189.

10. Alex Simirenko, *Professionalization of Soviet Society* (New Brunswick, NJ: Transaction Books, 1982), p. 14. Jeremiah Wolpert was the first to use the term "pseudo-charisma": "Toward a Sociology of Authority," in Alvin W. Gouldner, ed., *Studies in Leadership* (New York: Harper, 1950).

11. Max Weber, *Economy and Society: An Outline of Interpretive Sociology*, ed. Guenther Roth and Claus Wittich, 3 vols. (New York: Bedminster Press, 1968), pp. 943–46.

12. The German word is *Herrschaft*, translated by Roth and Wittich as "domination." Parsons and Henderson translate the term as "imperative control" in their translation of Part 1 of *Wirtschaft und Gesellschaft* (Max Weber, *The Theory of Social and Economic Organization*, Oxford: Oxford University Press, 1947.) Elsewhere Parsons urges that it should be translated as "authority" to avoid the coercive connotation of "domination." Talcott Parsons, "Review Article: Max Weber," *American Sociological Review* 24 (1960):750–52. In general, Parsons casts an integrative, functional gloss to Weber that the latter may not have intended. See Robert J. Antonio, "Weber vs. Parsons: Domination or Technocratic Models of Social Organization," in Ronald M. Glassman and Vatro Murvar, eds., *Max Weber's Political Sociology: A Pessimistic Vision of a Rationalized World* (Westport, CT: Greenwood Press, 1984), p. 162.

13. Weber, *Economy and Society*, p. 946.

14. Ibid., p. 946.

15. Frank Parkin, *Max Weber* (New York: Tavistock Publications and Ellis Horwood Ltd., 1982), p. 75.

16. Max Weber, "Politics as a Vocation," in H. H. Gerth and C. Wright Mills, ed., *From Max Weber* (London: Routledge, 1948), pp. 77–78.

17. Weber, *Economy and Society*, pp. 220–21.

18. Ibid., p. 975.

19. Max Weber, "Über einige Kategorien der verstehenden Soziologie," in Johannes Wincklemann, ed., *Gesammelte Aufsätze zur Wissenschaftslehre* (Tübingen: J. C. B. Mohr, 1968), p. 471.

20. Weber, *Economy and Society*, vol. 3, p. 987.

21. Ibid., pp. 1028–29.

22. Paul Hollander, "Politicized Bureaucracy: The Soviet Case," *Newsletter on Comparative Studies of Communism* 4, no. 3 (May 1971), p. 20. For another discussion of the differences between ordinary bureaucracy and the Soviet Party and state bureaucracy, see Leonard Schapiro, *The Communist Party of the Soviet Union* (New York: Vintage Books, 1971), pp. 622–24. Schapiro prefers to consider the Party and state as a form of traditional and, at times, charismatic authority, in Weber's sense. John A. Armstrong also discusses some differences between Soviet and Western bureaucracies: "Sources of Soviet Administrative Behavior: Some Soviet and West European Comparisons," in Frederic J. Fleron, Jr., ed., *Communist Studies and the Social Sciences: Essays on Methodology and Empirical Theory* (Chicago: Rand McNally, 1969), pp. 357–78. The original article is in *American Political Science Review* 49, no. 3 (September 1965):643–55.

23. Weber, *Economy and Society*, pp. 1030–31. Weber does allow elsewhere for a kind of crypto-Weberian bureaucracy: "Where there is a hierarchical organization with impersonal spheres of competence, but occupied by unfree officials—like slaves or *ministriales* who, however, function in a formally bureaucratic manner—the term 'patrimonial bureaucracy' will be used." *Economy and Society*, p. 221. In my model of non-Weberian bureaucracy, however, the spheres of competence are *not* impersonal and the officials, particularly first secretaries, are very free within their jurisdictions.

24. Talcott Parsons makes this point: *The Structure of Social Action* (New York: McGraw-Hill, 1937), p. 509.

25. Weber is explicit about this. See *Economy and Society*, pp. 987–88.

26. Helen Constas, "Max Weber's Two Conceptions of Bureaucracy," *American Journal of Sociology* 64, no. 1 (January, 1958):408.

27. Ibid., p. 400.

28. Ibid.

29. Ibid., p. 402.

30. John A. Armstrong, "Old-Regime Governors: Bureaucratic and Patrimonial Attributes," *Comparative Studies in Society and History* 14, no. 1 (January 1972):1–5.

31. Weber, *Economy and Society*, p. 1028.

32. See James D. Cochrane, "Mexico's 'New Científicos': The Diaz Ordaz Cabinet," *Inter-American Economic Affairs* 21, no. 1 (Summer 1967):61–72. The Brazilian counterpart of ENA is ESG (Ecola Superior de Guerra). The Brazilian technocrats are not autonomous; their control over the economy has been maintained by military governments; see Marcio Moreira Alves, "The Political Economy of the Brazilian Technocracy," *Berkeley Journal of Sociology* 19 (1974–75):110.

33. F. Ridley, "French Technocracy and Comparative Government," in K. L. Shell, ed., *The Democratic Political Process* (Waltham, MA: Blaisdell, 1980). Also see Jean Maynaud, *Technocracy* (New York: Free Press, 1969).

34. Ridley, "French Technocracy," pp. 466ff.

35. Armstrong, "Sources of Soviet Administrative Behavior," p. 374.

36. Lenin, "The State and Revolution," p. 478.

37. Francis Bacon, *Essays Civil and Moral and the New Atlantis* (Danbury, CT: Grolier Enterprises, 1980).

38. Jean-Antoine-Nicolas de Caritat de Condorcet, *Sketch for a Historical Picture of the Progress of the Human Mind* (New York: Noonday Press, 1955).

39. See Frank E. Manuel, *The New World of Henri Saint-Simon* (Cambridge, MA: Harvard University Press, 1956).

40. H. G. Wells, *Anticipations of the Reaction of Mechanical and Scientific Progress upon Human Life and Thought* (London: Chapman & Hall, 1902).

41. H. G. Wells, *The Open Conspiracy: Blueprints for a World Revolution* (London: Victor Gollancz, 1928).

42. James Burnham, *The Managerial Revolution: What Is Happening in the World* (New York: John Day, 1941) and *The Machiavellians: Defenders of Freedom* (New York: John Day, 1943).

43. Thorstein Veblen, *Engineers and the Price System* (New York: Harcourt, Brace & World, 1963; first published in 1921).

44. Stuart Chase, *Technocracy: An Interpretation* (New York: Macmillan, 1933).

45. Allen Raymond, *What Is Technocracy?* (New York: Holt, 1933).

46. The story of Technocracy, Inc., is told in Henry Elsner, Jr., *The Technocrats: Prophets of Automation* (Syracuse, NY: Syracuse University Press, 1967). Also see W. H. G. Armytage, *The Rise of the Technocrats: A Social History* (London: Routledge & Kegan Paul, 1965).

47. Daniel J. Boorstin, *The Republic of Technology: Reflections on Our Future Community* (New York: Harper & Row, 1978); Jack D. Douglas, ed., *The Technological Threat* (Englewood Cliffs, NJ: Prentice-Hall, 1971); Jeffrey D. Straussman, *The Limits of Technocratic Politics* (New Brunswick, NJ: Transaction Books, 1978); Frank Fischer, *Technocracy and the Politics of Expertise* (Beverly Hills, CA: Sage Publications, 1990); David Kipnis, *Technology and Power* (New York: Springer-Verlag, 1990); Michael Trowitzsch, *Technokratie und Geist der Zeit: Beitrage zu einer theologischen Kritik* (Tübingen: Mohr, 1988); Victor Ferkiss, *Technological Man* (New York: Braziler, 1969); though written earlier, Jacques Ellul, *The Technological Society* (New York: Vintage Books, 1964), also belongs in this category.

48. Langdon Winner, *Autonomous Technology: Technics-out-of-control as a Theme in Political Thought* (Cambridge, MA: MIT Press, 1977), p. 139.

49. Quoted, but without reference, by Thomas A. Baylis, *The Technical Intelligentsia and the East German Elite: Legitimacy and Change in Mature Communism* (Berkeley: University of California Press, 1974), p. 8n.

50. James H. Meisel, *The Myth of the Ruling Class: Gaetano Mosca and the "Elite"* (Ann Arbor: University of Michigan Press, 1958), p. 4.

51. Ridley remarks that "while technocrat civil servants occupy positions of power and form part of the 'power elite,' it would seen that they exercise that power as individuals, not as a class." "French Technology," p. 468. Winner (*Autonomous Technology*, p. 143) and Armstrong (*The European Administrative Elite*, Princeton, NJ: Princeton University Press, 1972, pp. 190–91) make the same point even more emphatically.

52. Don K. Rowney, *Transition to Technocracy: The Structural Origins of the Soviet Administrative State* (Ithaca, NY: Cornell University Press, 1989), pp. 92–93. Rowney suggests, however, that since virtually all of the Soviet elite have technical educations, it makes dubious the assumption that generalist politicians will always control the technical specialists; ibid., p. 7.

53. Vsevelod Kochetov, *Brat'ia Yershovy* (Moscow: Molodaya gvardiia, 1959), pp. 85, 298, 410.

54. Albert Parry, *The New Class Divided: Science and Technology vs. Communism* (New York: Macmillan, 1966), pp. 20–21.

55. This is one definition John Armstrong gives to technocracy: "Sources of Soviet Administrative Behavior: Some Soviet and West European Comparisons," in Fleron, *Communist Studies and the Social Sciences*, p. 374.

56. Theodore Roszak, *The Making of a Counter-culture: Reflections on the Technocratic Society and Its Youthful Opposition* (Garden City, NJ: Doubleday, 1969), pp. 7–8.

57. Ronald J. Hill, "The All-People's State and 'Developed Socialism,' " in Neil Harding, ed., *The State in Socialist Society* (Albany: State University of New York Press, p. 118). A useful survey of Soviet scholarship on Soviet management is Erik P. Hoffman and Robbin F. Laird, *Technocratic Socialism: The Soviet Union in the Advanced Industrial Era* (Durham, NC: Duke University Press, 1985). Also See Michael E. Urban, *The Ideology of Administration: American and Soviet Cases* (Albany: State University of New York Press, 1982).

58. Simirenko, *Professionalization of Soviet Society*.

59. Fedor Zniakov "Pamiatnaia zapiska," *Arkhiv samizdata*, no. 374 (1986):1–13.

60. Andrei Amalrik, "Will the Soviet Union Survive until 1984?" *Survey*, no. 73 (Autumn 1969):48–79.

61. H. F. Achmanov, *Die Totengräber des Kommunismus* (Stuttgart: Steinbruben Verlag, 1964), p. 150.

62. Bohdan Harasymiw, *Political Elite Recruitment in the Soviet Union* (London: Macmillan Press, 1984), p. 183.

63. Serge Mallet, *Bureaucracy and Technocracy in the Socialist Countries* (Nottingham, England: Spokesman Books, 1974), pp. 30–31; an early discussion of this conflict is Albert Parry, *The New Class Divided: Science and Technology versus Communism* (New York: Macmillan, 1966).

64. Alexander Shtromas, *Political Change and Social Development: The Case of the Soviet Union* (Frankfurt am Main: Verlag Peter Lang, 1981), p. 76.

65. Michael P. Gehlen and Michael McBride, "The Soviet Central Committee: An Elite Analysis," *American Political Science Review* 62, no. 4 (December 1968):1232–41; Michael P. Gehlen, "The Soviet Apparatchiki," in R. Barry Farrell, ed., *Political Leadership in Eastern Europe and the Soviet Union* (Chicago: Aldine Publishing Co., 1970), pp. 140–56; Jerry Hough, *The Soviet Prefects: The Local Party Organs in Industrial Decision-Making* (Cambridge, MA: Harvard University Press, 1969), p. 70.

66. Robert E. Blackwell, "Elite Recruitment and Functional Change: An Analysis of the Soviet Obkom Elite, 1950–1968," *Journal of Politics* 34 (1972):124–52.

67. *Pravda*, October 24, 1986, p. 1.

68. See, for example, *Pravda*, February 1, 1983, p. 3.

69. Peter Medding, "Ruling Elite Models: A Critique and an Alternative," *Political Studies* 30, no. 3 (September 1982):399.

70. Geraint Perry, *Political Elites* (New York: Praeger, 1969), p. 28.

71. Medding, "Ruling Elite Models," p. 405.

72. A Rumiantsev, "Partiia i intelligentsiia," *Pravda*, February 21, 1965, pp. 2–3. "Victorious socialism" was what Khrushchev declared the society had attained. Later, under Brezhnev, there was a transition to "developed socialism."

73. It goes back even further, of course, if we include the intellectual history of the idea of technocracy. The two ideas are closely intertwined, and as emphasized above, I am artificially separating them for analytical clarity only.

74. Michael Bakunin, "Statism and Anarchy," translated by Marshall S. Shatz, in Shatz, ed., *The Essential Works of Anarchism* (New York: Quadrangle Books, 1972), p. 166.

75. Mosca, *The Ruling Class*, p. 418.

76. Milovan Djilas, *The New Class: An Analysis of the Communist System* (New York: Praeger, 1957), p. 61. For a detailed critical discussion of Trotsky's and Djilas's views, see Michael M. Lustig, *Trotsky and Djilas: Critics of Communist Bureaucracy* (Westport, CT: Greenwood Press, 1989).

77. Two spellings of his name are used: Machajski is the Polish spelling, while "Makhaevism" is derived from the Russian spelling.

78. *Umstvennyi rabochii* was published in 1968 by Inter-language Literary Associates of Baltimore and New York. All citations are to this edition. This edition also contains *Rabochaia revoliutsiia* on pp. 350–409. A copy of *Rabochii zagovor* is in the library of the Hoover Institution at Stanford University.

79. Karl Kautsky, "Die Intelligenz und die Sozialdemokratie," *Die Neue Zeit*, nos. 27–29 (1894–95):42–48.

80. Makhaiskii, *Umstvennyi rabochii*, pp. 79–80.

81. Makhaiskii, *Rabochaia revoliutsiia*, no. 1 (June–July 1918), in the 1968 Western edition of *Umstvennyi rabochii*, p. 380.

82. Marshall S. Shatz, *Jan Waclaw Machajski: A Radical Critic of the Russian Intelligentsia and Socialism* (Pittsburgh: University of Pittsburgh Press, 1989), pp. 37ff.

83. Bakunin, "Statism and Anarchy," pp. 171–72.

84. Evgenii Lozinskii, *Chto zhe takoe, nakonets, intelligentsiia?* (St. Petersburg: "Novyi golos," 1907).

85. D. Zaitsev, "Marksizm i makhaevshchina," *Obrazovanie*, no. 3 (March 1908):57–61.

86. Shatz, *Jan Waclaw Machajski*, pp. 110ff.

87. For example, M. Sergven, "Puti revoliutsii," *Vol'nyi golos truda*, no. 4 (September 16, 1918):1. On Makhaevism, see Max Nomad, *Rebels and Renegades* (Freeport, NY: Books for Libraries Press, 1968), Chap. 5; and Nomad, *Dreamers, Dynamiters, and Demagogues: Reminiscences* (New York: Waldon Press, 1964); Paul Avrich, "What Is 'Makhaevism'?" *Soviet Studies* 26, no. 1 (July 1965):66–75; and L. Martov et al., *Obshchestvennoe dvizhenie v Rossii v nachale XX veka* (St. Petersburg, 1909–14), vol. 3, pp. 523–33. Also see the introduction in English by Albert Parry to Vol'skii, *Umstvennyi rabochii*, pp. 7–22. Other interpretations can be found in Marshall S. Shatz, "Jan Waclaw Machajski: The Conspiracy of the Intellectuals," *Survey*, no. 61 (January 1967):45–57; Shatz, "The Makhaevists and the Russian Revolutionary Movement," *International Review of Social History* 15, no. 2 (1970):235–65; Anthony D'Agostino, "Intelligentsia Socialism and the 'Workers' Revolution': The Views of J. W. Machajski," *International Review of Social History* 14, no. 1 (1969):54–89. Max Nomad, early a disciple and later a

critic of Machajski, accused James Burnham of plagiarizing Machajski's ideas: Max Nomad, *Aspects of Revolt* (New York: Bookman Associates, 1959), p. 15.

88. T. H. Rigby, *Communist Party Membership in the USSR, 1917–1967* (Princeton, NJ: Princeton University Press, 1968), pp. 108–9; Roger Pethybridge, *The Social Prelude to Stalinism* (London: Macmillan, 1974), pp. 280–81.

89. *X s"ezd RKP(b): stenograficheskii otchet* (Moscow: Gospolitizdat, 1921), p. 269.

90. Zetkin's report has been lost. The cover letter containing her request to Krupskaia, and Krupskaia's answer, are in *Political Archives of the Soviet Union* 1, no. 1 (1990):42–43.

91. For denunciations of Makhaevism in the 1930s, see *Partiinoe stroitel'stvo*, no. 17 (1931); "O postanovke partiinoi propagandy v sviazi s vypuskim *Kratkogo Kursa istorii VKP(b)*, "*Pravda*, November 15, 1938; "Chto takoe 'Makhaevish-china'?" *Pravda*, November 18, 1938.

92. See "Makhaevshcina," *Bol'shaia sovetskaia entsiklopediia*, 2nd ed. (Moscow: 1954), vol. 26, p. 544. Also: Aleksei Ruminatsev, "Partiia i intelligentsiia," *Pravda*, 21 February, 1965.

93. Rizzi (1901–1977) was an Italian traveling shoe salesman and dilettante Trotskyist conversant with members of the anti-Stalinist left.

94. Bruno Rizzi, *The Bureaucratization of the World* (New York: Free Press, 1985), p. 37. This belongs in an anthology of grand mispredictions.

95. Adam Westoby, "Introduction," in Rizzi, *The Bureaucratization of the World*, p. 17n. Westoby's introduction provides a detailed etiology of Rizzi's ideas and their subsequent history.

96. Helen Constas, "The U.S.S.R.—From Charismatic Sect to Bureaucratic Society," *Administrative Science Quarterly* 6 (1961–62):283. Constas's conception is very similar to that of Karl Wittfogel in *Oriental Despotism* (New Haven, CT: Yale University Press, 1957). The long historical existence of such societies was noticed by Djilas; see *The New Class Divided, pp. 54–55.*

97. For a classic examination of the state capitalism thesis from a Marxist standpoint, see Tony Cliff, *State Capitalism in Russia* (London: Pluto Press, 1974), written in 1948 and first published in 1955. The term "state capitalism" actually originated in the Soviet Union during the debate on the NEP. See A. A. Solov'ev, *S"ezdy i konfereentsii KPSS: Spravochnik* (Moscow, 1986), p. 151. This was deemphasized by the late 1960s.

98. Jack Juron and Karol Modzelewski, "An Open Letter to the Party," *New Politics 5, nos. 2–3 (1966):15.*

99. George Konrad and Ivan Szelenyi, *The Intellectuals on the Road to Class Power* (New York: Harcourt Brace Jovanovich, 1979), p. 3. For a critical discussion of the Konrad and Szelenyi thesis, see Timothy W. Luke and Carl Boggs, "Soviet Subimperialism and the Crisis of Bureaucratic Centralism," *Studies in Comparative Communism* 15, nos. 1–2 (Spring-Summer, 1982):95–124. Alvin Gouldner made much the same argument in *The Future of the Intellectuals and the Rise of the New Class* (New York: Seabury Press, 1979).

100. Konrad and Szelenyi, *Intellectuals on the Road to Class Power*, p 14.

101. Rudolf Bahro, *The Alternative in Eastern Europe* (London: New Left Books, 1978).

102. Ivan Szelenyi, "The Prospects and Limits of the East European New

Class Project: An Auto-critical Reflection on *The Intellectuals on the Road to Class Power*," *Politics and Society* 15, no. 2 (1986–87):114–17. A review of Konrad and Szelenyi and Bahro from a neo-Marxist standpoint can be found in Tom Long, "On the Class Nature of Soviet-Type Societies: Two Perspectives from Eastern Europe," *Berkeley Journal of Sociology* 26 (1981):157–188.

103. Ferenc Feher, Agnes Heller, And Gyorgy Markus, *Dictatorship over Needs* (New York: St. Martin's Press, 1983). A comprehensive review of "new class" theories can be found in Marian Sawer, "Theories of the 'New Class' from Bakunin to Kuron and Modzelewski: The Morphology of Permanent Protest," in Marian Sawer, ed., *Socialism and the New Class: Towards the Analysis of Structural Inequality within Socialist Societies* (Bedford Park, South Australia: Australasian Political Studies Association Monograph no. 19, 1978), pp. 3–15. Also see A. Ivanov, "Nomenkalturnyi klass," *Posev* (March 1973):34–36; T. H. Rigby writes that as far as he knows, Ivanov was the first to explicitly identify the new class with those holding Party-*nomenklatura* posts. T. H. Rigby and Bohdan Harta-symiw, eds., *Leadership Selection and Patron-Client Relations in the USSR and Yugoslavia* (London: Allen & Unwin, 1983), p. 10n.

104. Leon Trotsky, *The Revolution Betrayed: What Is the Soviet Union and Where Is It Going?* (New York: Pathfinder Press, 1972), pp. 249–50.

105. See, for example, Jean Ellenstein, *The Stalin Phenomenon* (London: Lawrence & Wishart, 1976), p. 179.

106. *Struktura sovetskogo obshchestva: informatsionnyi biulleten' Instituta Sotsial'nykh issledovanii AN SSSR* (Moscow, 1973). Cited by Ilya Zemtsov, *The Private Life of the Soviet Elite* (New York: Crane Russak, 1985), pp. 63–64.

107. "*Perestroika* as Social Revolution: Academician Tatiana Zaslavskaia Answers Questions from Readers," *Izvestia*, December 24, 1988, p. 3. Translation appears in *Current Digest of the Soviet Press* 40, no. 51 (January 18, 1989):1–4.

108. Weber, *Economy and Society*, p. 928.

109. Ibid., p. 932 (emphasis in original).

110. Ibid., p. 932 (emphasis in original).

111. See, for example, Alec Nove, "Is There a Ruling Class in the USSR?" *Soviet Studies* 27, no. 4 (October 1975):615–38. For comments on the article, see Maria Hirszowicz, "Is There a Ruling Class in the USSR—A Comment," *Soviet Studies* 28, no. 2 (April 1976):262–733; and Vladimir V. Kusin, "A Propos Alec Nove's Search for a Class Label," Ibid., pp. 274–75. Nove returned to the topic in "The Class Structure of the Soviet Union Revisited," *Soviet Studies* 35, no. 3 (July 1983):298–312.

112. David Lane, "Ruling Class and Political Elites: Paradigms of Socialist Societies," in David Lane, ed., *Elites and Political Power in the USSR* (Aldershot, Hants, England: Edward Elgar, 1988), p. 3.

113. Ibid., p. 10.

114. Ibid., p. 13.

115. Bottomore, *Elites and Society*, pp. 79–80.

116. Ibid., pp. 37–38.

117. Weber, *Economy and Society*, p. 985.

118. Ibid., p. 942.

119. Karl Kautsky, *Dictatorship of the Proletariat* (Vienna: Ignaz Brand, 1918).

120 V. I. Lenin, "Proletarian Revolution and the Renegade Kautsky," *Collected Works* (Moscow: Progress Publishers, 1965), vol. 28, p. 241.

121. Amitai Etzioni, *The Active Society: A Theory of Societal and Political Processes* (New York: Free Press, 1968), p. 113.

122. See Wlodzimierz Wesolowski, "Ruling Class and Power Elite," *Polish Sociological Bulletin* 1, no. 1 (1965):23.

123. Giovanni Sartori, "Concept Misinformation in Comparative Politics," *American Political Science Review* 64 (December 1970):1033–53.

124. Mervyn Matthews, *Privilege in the Soviet Union: A Study of Elite Life-Styles under Communism* (London: Allen & Unwin, 1978), p. 11.

125. Zaslavskaia, in *"Perestroika* as Social Revolution," p. 3.

Chapter 6

Elite Recruitment and Mobility

History is the essence of innumerable biographies.

Thomas Carlyle

Few govern. If there is a single unvarying generalization that can be made about all political systems, ancient and modern, democratic and authoritarian, it is this. That "from the many are chosen the few" is, in the words of Kenneth Prewitt, "probably the most written about axiom in all of political theory."[1] How those few are chosen exhibits greater variability.

The earliest-known scholar to offer a paradigm of political recruitment was Aristotle:

I will now inquire into appointments to offices. The varieties depend on three terms, and the combinations of these give all possible modes: first, who appoints? secondly, from whom? and thirdly, how? Each of these three admits of three varieties: (A) All the citizens, or (B) only some, appoint. Either (1) the magistrates are chosen out of all or (2) out of some who are distinguished either by a property qualification, or by birth, or merit, or for some special reason.... They may be appointed either (a) by vote or (b) by lot.[2]

This does not quite cover all possibilities, as shall be seen, but it comes close. Had he added bureaucratic appointment (by "only some," i.e., an oligarchy), he would have anticipated, by two and a half millennia, modern Communist systems' *nomenklatura* selection method. As Suzanne

Keller has pointed out, Aristotle's principles are still valid,[3] and, as is often the case, modern scholars owe a generally unacknowledged debt to Aristotle.[4]

Political recruitment is an essential aspect of the study of elites, and not merely because it is the process that ultimately determines who will govern. The "so what" question is particularly appropriate here. The process of recruitment affects the character, the orientation, and the agenda of elites. It is of interest at one level because we are interested in the life chances both of individuals and of social groups, and at another because the relationship between social structures and structures of authority and domination is a central question in political science. Often—and certainly in Mikhail Gorbachev's Soviet Union—political recruitment is itself a political issue,[5] and on its resolution will depend in large measure the success of Gorbachev's effort to restructure the society.

There are many aspects of the recruitment process that will reward inquiry. I will limit the discussion to four: (1) theoretical models of the recruitment process, (2) the selectorate (Who chooses, and how is the choice made?), (3) credentials (What are the criteria by which the choice is made?), and (4) channels (What are the paths to the top? What factors affect mobility?).

MODELS OF THE RECRUITMENT PROCESS

Ralph Turner has drawn a very useful distinction between "sponsored" and "contest" mobility.[6] Although Turner was discussing intergenerational mobility in terms of occupations, specifically focusing on democratic societies such as the United States and Britain, his concept can be given considerably wider application without much distortion. Turner relates his concepts to the school systems in each society. In Britain, a sponsored system, elites are chosen at a very early age and receive their training in the public schools. In the contest system of the United States, by contrast, selection into the elite comes at the end of the individual's education; elites are subject then to competition, and there is a larger pool from which to select.

Turner's concepts can be treated as ideal types of recruitment into the political elite rather than as types of intergenerational mobility. A sponsorship system is one in which elite members are selected from above; successful entry into the elite requires "sponsorship" by those who are already members. Whatever other push-and-pull mechanisms may be operative, elite status cannot be earned without sponsorship. The gatekeepers exercise a veto over admission to the elite and over advancement within the elite. Contest mobility, by contrast, pertains to societies in which gatekeepers, though they may play a greater or lesser role, cannot exercise a veto. Elite status is earned, so to speak, through successful competition. It is not conferred.

The contest pattern will be more functional in maintaining a qualified elite that is responsive to new tasks and adaptable to increasing differentiation and sophistication of society. The greatest functionality of the sponsorship pattern occurs under two sets of conditions. It is perhaps indispensable in a society such as Russia at the end of the 1920s, which has embarked on a massive program of transformation and in which the skills and orientations needed are not widely available in the society—an elite equal to the task must be created. Second, it is useful to an elite (not the same thing as functional for the society) that wishes to maintain ironclad control over elite recruitment and advancement or that places the highest value on preserving certain characteristics of the elite—noble status, for example, or upper-class education and upbringing. Sponsored mobility thus tends to produce a more homogeneous elite.

John Armstrong has suggested three logical models of the ways in which, in broad terms, societies can select their elites. In the first, which he calls the Maximum Deferred Achievement Model, no selection for leadership positions is made from a cohort until it reaches a specified age; all have equal access.[7] It seems certain that such a recruitment process would have to rely on contest mobility; some criterion (not excluding random selection) would be applied as each cohort reached the age for selection. As Armstrong notes, however, this model is mainly hypothetical, since no society has ever been known to select its elite in this way. It is reminiscent of Friedrich Engels's suggestion that as the "administration of people" is replaced by the "administration of things," anyone under communism could be an administrator.[8]

Model 2 Armstrong calls the Maximum Ascriptive Model. In this model, the elite is selected in infancy and socialized separately until it reaches the age to assume its leadership roles.[9] This is, of course, an aristocratic principle, preeminently based on sponsorship; although no modern system comes really close to Model 2, some approximate it to varying degrees.

In Model 3, the Progressive Equal Attrition Model, a proportion of the cohort is eliminated at equal time intervals until just the required number remains when the cohort reaches the appropriate age.[10] This evokes the image of a pyramid moving, as it were, through time. A system based on this model could take the form of either a contest or a sponsorship mobility system, depending upon whether selectorates' choices are made at each plateau, or whether progressively more rigorous competition occurs at each level. The U.S. leadership recruitment system is a contest mobility system that conforms closely to Model 3, as does the Soviet sponsorship mobility system.

Armstrong's three models are, of course, ideal types intended to rep-

resent the possible *principles* of elite selection rather than the actual process of political recruitment as it occurs in specific countries. Most models
of the political recruitment process that have been proposed, at least in
the North American literature, have been designated with democratic
political systems in mind, and more specifically concerned as they are
with electoral politics, they have focused on systems that stress contest
mobility. Most, in fact, refer to the United States.[11] Most of these conform
to Armstrong's broad Progressive Equal Attrition Model; that is, they
suggest a funnel that through stages gradually eliminates contenders
until the top elite is reached.

Two such models are of sufficient generality to be universal. Prewitt
suggests the image of Chinese boxes, each box containing a smaller one
and corresponding to the following seven categories: (1) the many who
are governed; (2) the legally qualified; (3) the socially eligible; (4) the
politically active; (5) the recruits; (6) the candidates; and finally, (7) the
few who govern.[12] Lester Seligman, in an influential monograph, also
suggests a series of stages of the process: (1) eligibility, sorting out the
activists from the eligibles; (2) selection (in a democracy, the winning of
elections); (3) role assignment; and (4) role performance.[13]

Following the same "progressive attrition" approach, Bohdan Harasymiw has combined and elaborated Seligman's and Prewitt's models,
adding dimensions to them to provide a model of political recruitment
in the Soviet Union upon which it would be difficult to improve.

At the first stage, initial recruitment, a pool of *eligibles* is drawn from the adult
population. Out of these eligibles, in turn, are drawn the *activists*, those with a
part-time involvement in politics. Full-time politicians, members of the *political
elite*, are selected from among the activists. Within the political elite, we may
speak of promotion, eventually into the *power elite*.[14]

The selection of eligibles (initial recruitment) in Harasymiw's model
is identical to recruitment into the Communist Party. The second stage,
recruitment proper, refers to the selection (to a large extent, in fact, self-
selection) of the Party *aktiv*, those Party members who, while holding
full-time jobs, involve themselves in part-time political activity. The Party
refers explicitly to the *aktiv* as the "reserve" from which future full-time
Party cadres are chosen; the *aktiv* consists primarily of Party committee
secretaries in enterprises and other institutions and secretaries of primary Party organizations. Promotion from the Party *aktiv*, however, is
not necessarily the springboard for elites whose careers are primarily in
the ministerial apparatus, as I shall discuss below.

Recruitment into the "political elite" refers to the person's first appointment to a full-time Party or government post, one which is on one
of the Party's *nomenklatura* lists—as a rule at a very low level in the

hierarchy, though there are also many lateral entrants at higher levels. Within the *nomenklatura*, then, mobility progresses with very considerable attrition at the district level.[15] The final stage is the promotion of the few into the "power elite" at the apex of the system.

Harasymiw identifies push-and-pull forces assumed to be operative at each of three levels of analysis. Push mechanisms at the individual level include motivation, ambition, and personality. Pulling forces at this level are limited to patronage (sponsorship, connections, and friendships). At the social level, push mechanisms are occupational role and status, and pull forces are political role and selectors' preferences. Push forces at the institutional level of analysis include organizational affiliations, and the structure of political opportunities constitute the pulling mechanisms at that level.[16]

This model describes the most typical pattern of political recruitment operative in the Soviet Union, namely, an individual starting at the bottom of the political hierarchy—often shortly after completing higher education—and progressing through a defined career sequence of posts until he reaches the highest level he is going to reach.[17] A Party career especially, as we shall see, is highly structured—similar to careers in closed hierarchies elsewhere such as military services, or the U.S. Foreign Service.

For the time being systematic samples of personnel corresponding to the categories in the model are simply unavailable; we have reasonably complete and reliable career data only on individuals who reach the CPSU Central Committee, that is, the few who make it to the top.[18] Elite biographies of members of Union Republic Supreme Soviets are published, but only a handful of these are available in the West. We are therefore unable to compile data on the careers of the many who succeed only modestly or do not succeed at all. Harasymiw does, however, skillfully use *aggregate* data to rough in some of the dimensions of the recruitment process.

THE SELECTORATE

In all political systems, incumbent political elites act as gatekeepers to elite positions. The advantage of the gatekeeper analogy is that it emphasizes that it is the choices of individual persons as much as, or probably more than, abstract reifications such as modernization pressures, an "economic imperative," or system needs that determine who will be selected. It is a mistake to assume that abstractions such as system maintenance functions are recognized as such by real-life members of the elite and become the basis of concrete policy choices. Elites may not know what needs to be done to preserve the system or, thinking erroneously that they do know, may pursue actions that are dysfunctional.

Like the top leadership of the late Brezhnev period, they may shorten their horizons to preserving the system for their own projected tenure, leaving serious problems for the next generation. Finally, elites are real people with all the shortcomings of that genus, and the criteria actually applied in elite selection may not be those that best serve the needs and interests of society, but those that preserve and protect their own privileged position in the society; indeed, it is not improbable that this will be the *first* among the gatekeepers' priorities.[19]

I wish to make a distinction, therefore, between "objective system needs" (which an omniscient and disinterested observer might impute) and "regime needs." The latter term will be used to refer to system needs as perceived and defined by incumbent elites, not excluding their own personal and political needs and preferences. This is of crucial importance in sponsored mobility systems such as those of Communist states, because in these systems, the gatekeepers' choices are decisive.

The structure and composition of the elite are thus not determined by modernization, nor by a functional need to maintain the system, nor by anything so automatic. It is shaped by conscious decisions made by specific people about who will be selected and promoted. If that coincides with a systemic need perceptible to outside social scientists, that does not belie the fact that it was a concrete choice, not a functional requisite. Had functional requisites been operative, the Brezhnev elite would have retired well before stagnation set in.

Regime needs are made explicit in a variety of forums, which include speeches of high-ranking Party officials, conferences and scholarly writings on cadre selection, and articles and editorials in the Party press. These obviously do not explicitly specify personal biases and preferences. The latter can, however, be inferred with some accuracy from the practices in personnel selection (nepotism, toadyism, preference for members of one's own nationality, "family circles," and various "*mafii*") that are constantly condemned at lower administrative levels by critics at higher levels, along with the knowledge we have of patron-client relationships based on existing studies by Western scholars.

During the Brezhnev period, a preference for *stability* at the top levels of the central elite was very marked; hence the policy of "stability of cadres" and apparently conscious efforts to "depoliticize" the process of elite circulation,[20] especially after Brezhnev's consolidation of power circa 1969. This was, however, manifestly a *political* criterion, as opposed to a rational-technical one, and, especially in the later Brezhnev period, was accompanied by a further political aim of preserving the monopoly of political power by the Party in the face of pressure from scientific, technical, and managerial elites. It is clear that such recruitment and promotional criteria may in fact be dysfunctional with respect to system needs, that is, with respect to the differentiation and adaptability of

political leadership in the face of economic modernization. Modernization and the resulting greater complexity of society brings to the fore
new political tasks of coordination and innovation, calling for new political institutions and roles. At a very minimum, system needs would
seem to call for a greater role in policy making for the technical intelligentsia. The definition of *regime* needs in terms of stability and the
maintenance of the old guard in power ensured that such systemic needs
would simply not be met.

CREDENTIALS

Gaetano Mosca and Vilfredo Pareto both defined elites as those who
have the most of some quality particularly valued in society, and Mosca
in particular predicts the demise of an elite that has lost its usefulness:
"Ruling classes decline inevitably when they cease to find scope for the
capacities through which they rose to power, when they can no longer
render the social services which they once rendered, or when the talents
and services they render lose in importance in the social environment
in which they live."[21]

This is a functionalist argument. It is likely, however, that there is a
qualitative difference between the character of political circulation in
pluralist societies, where advancement into the elite is at least partially
competitive, and that in societies in which sponsored mobility is the norm.
In the former, through the process of elections there is some latitude
for societal pressures to shape the elite. This is not true in a sponsored
system, in which the top elite selects itself and controls admission to and
advancement within the elite. Elite transformation will occur only as the
result of a conscious decision.

The most highly valued skills and attributes become the basis for elite
recruitment. Peasant societies value aristocracies, for example, for they
perform needed functions. But this is a two-way process: elites shape
societies and thus the skills the society values. The Zulu nation, single-
handedly shaped into a cohesive and regimented military society by the
redoubtable Shaka, not surprisingly continued to value military skills in
elite recruitment. Some skills are highly valued in any administrative
milieu: technical expertise, for example, and interpersonal skills—the
ability to persuade and mobilize, and to negotiate favorable compro-
mises.

In principle, it should be possible to determine whether or not those
who are promoted are distinct from those members of the pool who are
passed over and whether different selection criteria are applied at different times. One way to do this would be to break each Central Committee down into three groups: holdovers from previous Central
Committees, those who will be dropped at the next Central Committee,

and newly elected members. For a given Central Committee, character- istics of new members plus those of the holdovers should equal the criteria active at that time and should contrast with characteristics of those dropped at that Central Committee (controlling, of course, for simple aging).

Unfortunately, those characteristics that are most likely to be operative and interesting are not among the demographic background data that are accessible to us. Among objective credentials data in the database, Party membership,[22] the possession of higher technical education, being born male and Russian, and having substantive work experience are those that set the elite apart from the also-rans. Moreover, except for an increase in lateral entry (an indicator of the premium placed on experience) during the Khrushchev period, these broad criteria of se- lection do not change over time.[23]

A number of studies have attested to the increasing importance of meritocratic, or rational-technical, criteria in elite mobility. In an im- portant article, Philip Stewart and his colleagues found that economic performance and level of economic development of RSFSR *oblasts* ex- plained more variance in elite mobility than the patronage model as level of economic development increased.[24] Similarly, Jerry Hough, Joel Moses, Grey Hodnett, and William Clark have found career mobility significantly tied to the level of modernization of their *oblasts*.[25]

CHANNELS

We may speak of a "structured mobility system" as one in which there exists a definite, hierarchically ordered progression of career stages, from entry into the elite at a young age, through a somewhat fixed series of positions, culminating (for only a few, to be sure) in top offices that carry with them considerable prestige. A familiar example is the U.S. Foreign Service; Foreign Service officers follow a distinct career line, culminating (for a handful) in an ambassadorship. Another example is the military officer corps. There is a distinction between rank within the corps on the one hand and assignment to specific posts on the other. In structured mobility systems such as these, one cannot ordinarily jump ranks; one has to put in a number of years of successful performance at each stage before being promoted to the next. Generally, there are quotas for each rank, though the degree to which these are explicitly enforced varies. Somewhat more individuals will be promoted to a given rank than there are available posts that need to be filled by persons at that rank so as to provide an adequate pool for assignments.

Upward mobility within a structured mobility system is sponsored mobility. To be sure, there is competition for promotions, but selectors exercise a veto over the promotion of candidates in ranks below them.

In almost all structured mobility systems, there is an "up-or-out" norm: persons who fail to advance after some time in rank are retired from the career service—"rifted," in military terminology. The career chances of a person within a structured mobility system thus depend on a very high degree on the favorable evaluation of those in higher ranks and very little on any other factors. Socialization to organizational norms is therefore virtually automatic and extremely effective.

The advantage of structured mobility systems is that they provide a constantly available pool of qualified personnel, ready (and eager) to go where they are needed and eager to conform to organizational expectations. A high degree of personal identification with the organization is typical of members of structured mobility systems. They are encouraged in their socialization to believe that they, and they alone, are qualified for and capable of fulfilling their tasks. Typically, they think of themselves as members of a closed elite; they become protective of their jurisdiction and their prerogatives. In particular, they develop a strong resentment against bureaucratic outsiders who threaten their autonomy or their turf.[26]

The typical Party, and to a lesser degree state, political career in the Soviet Union can de facto be considered part of a structured mobility system, even though there is no a priori system of ranks. The hierarchical structure of the typical career is manifest on the surface (*oblast* secretaries rank higher than district secretaries, for example) but is complicated by informal considerations (secretaries of important industrial regions require more skills and carry more weight than those of minor agricultural regions, for example). The structure underlying—in fact, driving—the Soviet structured mobility system is the *nomenklatura* process. The individual's *nomenklatura* level is analogous to rank in other structured mobility systems.

Beginning in the Brezhnev period, there was a decline in the predominance of the "generalist" Party executive (characterized in large part by frequent rotation among assignments) and a corresponding rise in the technical specialist type (characterized by promotion and career path within the same task area, geographical region, and institutional organization), though there is little difference in education or background between them.[27] Earlier, T. H. Rigby had chided the profession for overemphasizing the "Red versus expert" dichotomy, arguing that Party secretaries and industrial managers received the same technical education and that their careers are interchangeable.[28]

It has been common in Western analyses to assume that the relative influence of an institutional group in Soviet society is proportional to its representation in leadership bodies. It is taken for granted, for example, that the membership of Yurii Andropov and Andrei Gromyko in the Politburo during the 1970s signified greater influence in policy making for the KGB and the Foreign Affairs establishment, rather than merely an increase in the influence of Andropov and Gromyko themselves, as individuals, in the policy-making process. This is a reasonable assumption provided we further assume that the attitudes and priorities of these men reflect those of the institutions they represent (which they might, given their long association with them) and that they view their role as one of representing the interests of their bureaucratic base on the Politburo. The latter assumption at least is open to some doubt. Andropov went to the KGB in 1967 after many years of service in the Central Committee, and it is likely that his role as chairman of the KGB was to impose *Party* norms on that organization. Darrell Hammer, for one, has raised doubts that representation in the leadership automatically means representation of a bureaucratic point of view: "What do we mean... by the 'army?' Are we justified in assuming that the army was somehow personified by Marshall Zhukov in such a way that the army's standing in the system rose and fell with his personal fortunes?"[29]

That one can make that assumption is the methodological premise underlying much of the writing on the USSR produced in the late 1960s and early 1970s by the "interest group" school of analysis.[30] As has been observed by many Western analysts, however, the evidence is that informal personal affiliations that cut across institutional boundaries are more important in influencing attitudes and behavior.[31]

Party versus State Careers

Most discussions of career types are of Party careers, and studies of state careers and the ministerial elite have been rare.[32] Zbigniew Brzezinski and Samuel Huntington, writing in the early 1960s, described the Party official as a "professional politician" and a "generalist" who dominated the unified Party and state hierarchy of the USSR. Brzezinski and Huntington identified political and governmental bureaucrats, commercial and industrial specialists, and government-technical specialists in addition to the professional Party politician. They emphasized, however, that the composition of the leadership was becoming less differentiated.[33] Seweryn Bialer referred to the combined Party-government generalist as a "multiple executive," agreeing with Rigby and others that it is futile to try to distinguish a Party career type from a governmental career type. Bialer further proposed six additional career types: economic executives, military executives, transnational executives, executives of coercion, propagandists, and common executives.[34]

Although it is true that there is a considerable degree of crossing over between state and Party positions, most of this crossing occurs between Party and soviet posts below the regional level.[35] At the all-union state level and the *oblast* Party level (that is, at the level of Party and state

Table 6.1

Central Committee Occupational Representation, 1956–1986 (in percentages)

Occupation	Full Members	Candidate Members	Auditing Commission
N=all CC members (1,770):			
All-Union Ministers	10.7	11.6	3.7
Obkom 1st Secretaries	30.1	20.1	12.2
N=Political elite only (1,366):			
All-Union Ministers	13.1	15.0	5.5
Obkom 1st Secretaries	38.1	26.0	18.0

Source: Author's database.

Note: The figures are for Central Committee *memberships*; same individual is counted each time he was elected.

posts on the CPSU Central Committee *nomenklatura* lists), however, my data show that only 7 percent of full Central Committee members in such posts spent more than 10 percent of their careers in both Party and state positions. It is apparent that frequent crossing over between Party and state posts inhibits mobility, since so few individuals whose early careers were so characterized reached the Central Committee. Careers destined for ultimate success tend to be confined mainly to one channel or the other.

In the late 1980s, however, a number of regional and republican secretaries did move directly into major government ministries. These included Vsevelod Murakhovskii (State Agro-Industrial Committee), Eduard Shevardnadze (Foreign Ministry), Aleksandr Vlasov (Internal Affairs), and Vladimir Kliuev (Light Industry).

Several writers have noted that all-union minister and *obkom* first secretary are the most commonly represented occupational categories in the Central Committee.[36] Also, most holders of these posts are Central Committee members. Table 6.1 gives the percentage of all Central Committee members who hold these posts and the percentage of political elites only in the Central Committee holding these posts for the Twentieth through the Twenty-seventh Congresses. The latter measure shows that more than half of the full Central Committee members have held one of these positions.

Career Patterns

There are distinct career types among both Party and state personnel. The stereotyped Western concept of the one-dimensional *apparatchik* was the product of a time when less was known than now about Soviet political career patterns. There are distinct subgroups of Soviet political cadres based on task specialization.[37]

A number of categorizations of career types have been proposed in the literature based on work histories given in biographical data in Soviet sources. Roger Pethybridge, for example, analyzing the 1957 "anti-Party" crisis, saw four groups in conflict: the Party *apparatchiki*, government bureaucracy, the economic elite, and the military.[38] Wolfgang Leonhard proposed five types, which he called the "five pillars of Soviet society." These were Party *apparatchiki*, economic managers and engineers, state officials, the army, and the secret police.[39] Vernon Aspaturian identified six principal power groups within the Soviet elite: the party apparatus; the government bureaucracy; economic managers and technicians; the cultural, professional, and technical intelligentsia; the police; and the armed forces.[40] Basing his classification on the type of job on which the individual had spent 60 percent or more of his time, Michael Gehlen found eight career types among the Soviet elite: Party *apparatchiki*, state bureaucrats, the military, scientists, writers, trade unionists, workers, and consumer advocates.[41] Gehlen was classifying Central Committee members rather than members specifically of the political elite.

Institutional groupings continued to form the basis of later differentiations among career types, and the number of such groupings proliferated. Frederic Fleron, for example, identified 14 institutional-occupational categories among Central Committee members: central Party apparatus, regional Party apparatus, central government apparatus, regional government apparatus, economic managers and planners, the military, the KGB and Ministry of Internal Affairs (MVD), Komsomol, trade unions and public organizations, scientific and academic workers, writers and artists, workers and farmers, foreign affairs specialists, and industrial plant managers.[42] Christian Duevel, in his analyses of Central Committee representation, employed 12 similar categories.[43] The most complex scheme was developed by James Nichol; classifying "career experiences" instead of individual careers, Nichol identifies 23 "pure career types."[44]

The proliferation of career types in elite analysis would seem to be based on the assumption that there are significant differences among such groups, either in their mobility or in the relative representation of such groups in the leadership over time, leading at least to the possibility of differences in influence. It turns out, however, that the narrower and more differentiated the classification of career types, the fewer significant variations can be found among them. The search for meaningful relationships is facilitated by a leaner classification scheme.

Joel Moses, for example, provides a lean but robust classification, part

Table 6.2
Functional Specializations of Soviet Political Elite

Category	Number	Percent
Party Careers:		
Party Agricultural	179	17.3
Party Industrial	311	30.0
Party Ideological	153	14.8
Party Cadres	22	2.1
Party Generalist	126	12.2
State Careers:		
State Agricultural	116	1.5
State Industrial	171	16.5
State Economics	19	1.8
State Coercion	9	0.9
State TU/Social Services	29	2.8

Source: Author's database.

of which I have borrowed. Moses examined the career patterns of 614 members of *obkom* bureaus in 25 regions of the RSFSR and Ukraine for the period 1953–1979. He found clear evidence that officials are not randomly assigned to different posts, but that there are distinct task specializations associated with subgroups of political cadres. Classified on the basis of internal consistency in the positions making up their careers, he distinguished five functional subgroups: agricultural specialists, industrial specialists, ideological specialists, cadre specialists, and mixed generalists.[45]

The careers of political elites in my database were assigned functional specializations based on the type of work in which the individual spent 60 percent or more of his political career (see Table 6.2). The assignment of individuals to functional specializations was based on the following criteria: type of education; type of occupation, if any, which the individual pursued prior to recruitment to the political elite; the individual's predominant institutional affiliations (i.e., Party or state); and finally, the type of task orientation that can be ascribed to most of the posts the individual held. Each case was judged individually. The first five categories represent primarily careers in the Party apparatus; the remaining six are state careers. The classification of functional specializations is based on 1,054 political elites in the Central Committee database.

Party Agricultural Specialist. The Party agricultural specialist is an individual who spent most of his career as a district or *obkom* secretary in a predominately agricultural region. Usually his nonpolitical specialization is agricultural, having completed an agricultural institute and trained as an agronomist. Judging from the frequent indication of "peasant" as the social class of his parents, it seems likely that many agricultural specialists grew up on a collective farm. It is rare to find men from large cities or of working-class or employee background pursuing an education in agriculture or a Party career as an agricultural specialist. It is not unusual to find the Party agricultural specialist also holding, at various times in his career, the post of *oblispolkom* chairman or first deputy chairman, posts in rural soviets that have primary responsibility for agriculture. The most frequent final career destination for agricultural specialists is *obkom* first secretary in a primarily agricultural region.

A typical representative of this functional specialization is Anatoly S. Drygin. Drygin (b. 1914), an ethnic Russian, graduated in 1935 from the Michirinsk Institute of Vegetable Crops. From 1935 to 1941 he worked as a researcher at a fruit experimental station. From 1941 to 1946 he served in the army. In the period 1946 to 1960 he held the following series of posts: director of an experimental base for the All-Union Institute of Plant Breeding, director of a state farm, chairman of a rural district soviet, secretary of a *raikom*, and first deputy chairman of the Leningrad *oblispolkom*. During 1960–61, he was a secretary of Leningrad *obkom*, and in 1961 he became first secretary of Vologda *obkom*. He held this post until he retired in July 1985.[46]

Party Industrial Specialist. The industrial specialist must have more rigorous technical knowledge and sophistication than any of the other Party specializations. Their careers frequently begin as an engineer, plant manager, or Party secretary in an industrial enterprise. Full-time political employment most often begins with a post as secretary in an industrial district, small city, or *obkom*. He will also spend time as *oblispolkom* chairman or first deputy chairman in the soviet of an industrial town, city, or region, as well as positions with trade union organizations. This career channel typically culminates in the first secretaryship of an industrial *obkom* or *gorkom* or assignment to the republican or all-union Central Committee apparatus. It almost never culminates with crossing over to the ministerial apparatus.

A very typical—indeed, classic—Party industrial career is that of Viktor G. Boiko. Boiko, a Ukrainian, was born in 1931 and joined the Party in 1954. He graduated from the Krivoi Rog Mining Institute in 1960 and worked for a year as a superintendent in the Krivoi Rog Coal Trust. From 1961 to 1970 he worked as an instructor and a department head in Krivoi Rog *gorkom*, then as a department head in Dnepropetrovsk *obkom*. He then spent four years as chairman of Dnepropetrovsk *gorispolkom*. After a two-year stint as Dnepropetrovsk *gorkom* first secretary, he became second secretary of Dnepropetrovsk *obkom*. Another two-year stint as chairman of Dnepropetrovsk *oblispolkom* was followed in 1983 by his election as first secretary of Dnepropetrovsk *obkom*.[47] He was elected a full member of the Central Committee at the Twenty-seventh Party

Congress. He was dismissed from this post for "serious errors" in March 1987 and transferred to diplomatic work.

Party Ideological Specialist. Ideological specialists are symbol manipulators, and so they occupy positions in journalism, in the agitation-propaganda apparatus of Party committees, and also in areas of life that require ideological supervision: movies, book publishing, education and culture, and in scientific research institutions. They also tend frequently to have been associated, at one time or another or permanently, with the Komsomol, the principle responsibility of Komsomol officials being the ideological tutelage of youth. Persons in this career channel tend not to acquire skills that are readily transferable to other sectors. As a career takes shape in this field of specialization, the individual becomes locked into it.

Viktor I. Mironenko is an exemplary case of a Party ideological career. Probably a Ukrainian, he was born in 1953 and graduated in 1975 from the Chernigov Pedagogical Institute, joining the Party in the same year. From 1978 to 1980 he was a secretary of the Chernigov *obkom* of the Komsomol. In the period 1980–1983, he served in the posts of department head, secretary, second secretary, and then first secretary of the Central Committee of the Ukrainian Komsomol. In 1986 he became first secretary of the Central Committee of the All-Union Komsomol and a candidate member of the CPSU Central Committee.[48]

Party Cadres Specialist. Cadres specialists tend consistently to hold positions involving responsibility for the selection, promotion, and demotion of Party personnel. Most frequently, these positions are cadres secretary (sometimes second secretary) of *raikoms*, *gorkoms*, and *obkoms* of the Party, or chairmen or deputy chairmen of the Organizational Party Work departments of these committees. They also serve as heads of organizational instruction departments in local and regional soviets, and may also serve in Control Commission, trade union, or Komsomol posts.

Consider the career of Georgy P. Razumovsky, from 1985 the head of the Organizational Party Work Department of the CPSU Central Committee. Razumovksy was born in 1936 and joined the Party in 1961. He graduated from the Kuban Agricultural Institute in 1958 and then worked for a year as an agronomist on a collective farm in Krasnodar Territory. Between 1959 and 1964 he worked first as a Komsomol *raikom* first secretary, then as an instructor and later a sector head in the Krasnodar Party *kraikom*. From 1964 he worked as a *partkom* secretary, a *raikom* first secretary, and a department head in the Krasnodar *kraikom*. From 1971 to 1973 he worked in the CPSU Central Committee *apparat*; then he returned to Krasnodar as chairman of the territorial *oblispolkom*. After spending two years in the USSR Council of Ministers *apparat*, he returned once again to Krasnodar in 1983 as *kraikom* first secretary.[49] He achieved national prominence in this position for his effective work against corruption among regional officials. He took over the Central Committee cadres post in 1985, where he became a firm supporter of Gorbachev and an advocate of *glasnost'* in cadres selection and training. Together with Egor Ligachev (until 1987), Razumovsky oversaw all of Gorbachev's personnel changes.

Party Generalist. This category is comprised of officials whose careers resist classification into one of the categories above; that is, there is no functional specialization category in which they have spent 60 percent or more of their careers. For many officials, this is merely a residual category (after all, the criterion of having spent 60 percent of their time in a given specialization is arbitrary; with a lower cutoff point, fewer would have ended up in the residual category, as more would have with a higher cutoff point). However, there is reason to believe that many of these are "troubleshooters"; that is, they specialize in assuming leadership positions in regions experiencing problems.[50]

This would appear to be the case with Vladimir Odintsov, a Russian whose career suggests that he functions as a nationality specialist. After 19 years of Komsomol and Party work in Stalingrad, he won a candidate degree in history from the CPSU Academy of Social Sciences. Subsequently, he served (1961–1965) as a department head in Kalmyk *obkom*, followed by five years in the CC-CPSU Organizational Party Work Department. From 1970 to 1979, he served as second secretary of Dagestan *obkom*, again followed by three years in the Central Committee apparatus, this time as head of the Caucasian and Transcaucasian Section of the Organizational Party Work Department. This was followed by a ten-year stint as first secretary of the North Ossetian ASSR.

Another generalist career of some interest is that of Aleksandr F. Gorkin, a career that spanned the entire Soviet period and was remarkable for the variety of posts and geographic areas in which he served. He joined the Party in 1916, and with only incomplete secondary education he held a variety of Party and state posts, becoming a secretary of the Presidium of the Central Executive Committee in 1937–38. From 1938 to 1957 he served as secretary and deputy secretary of the Presidium of the USSR Supreme Soviet, and from 1957 to 1972 as Chairman of the USSR Supreme Court.[51] He retired in 1972 from this post at his own wish.[52]

There is even more regularity and consistency in the careers of predominately state officials. Whereas Party officials frequently cross back and forth between Party and state posts, especially early in their careers, the careers of state officials are more exclusively located in the state apparatus. Although they are all Party members and their careers show linkages to the Party, they have distinctly different career paths. Only very rarely do they hold Party posts early in their careers; they are recruited either from technical institute graduates or from among individuals who have worked for some time in industry. The Party *aktiv* mentioned earlier is not a pool for the recruitment of state administrators. Except for state industrial specialists, opportunities for advancement to the CPSU Central Committee are very limited for individuals who pursue careers predominately in the state bureaucracy.

State Agricultural Specialist. Purely state agricultural specialists are few in the database, only 16 in number. Agriculture is an area in which there is more crossing over between Party and state careers than in other fields, and many who hold agricultural positions in the state apparatus also held similar positions in the Party apparatus. State agricultural specialists have graduated either from an agricultural institute or from one of several institutes specializing in the mechanization of agriculture (and hence, these men are engineers). They often work many years in some nonpolitical sector of agricultural industry. When their state career begins, it is most often as staff work in either a republican or the All-Union Ministry of Agriculture. The path for those who reach the summit, then, is deputy minister, first deputy minister, then finally agricultural minister, either on the all-union or the republican level.

Mikhail Porfirevich Georgadze (b. 1912), for example, worked from 1929 to 1934 as leader of a tractor drivers' brigade on a state farm, probably in his native Georgia. He graduated in 1941 from the Moscow Institute of the Mechanization and Electrification of Agriculture, after which he was employed in staff work in the USSR Ministry of Agriculture, advancing from engineer to head of a chief administration. From 1951 he served first as deputy minister, then as minister of agriculture for the Georgian SSR. After a year as deputy chairman of the Georgian SSR Council of Ministers, he served a two-year stint (1954–1956) as second secretary of the Georgian Communist Party. After a year as first deputy chairman of the Georgian SSR Council of Ministers, he became a secretary of the Presidium of the USSR Supreme Soviet, holding this post until his death in 1982.[53]

State Industrial Specialist. Among state careers, state industrial specialist is the most common functional specialization, which is not surprising. These men have almost exclusively technical educations, usually in engineering. Typically they are found in the post of chief engineer or deputy chief engineer in an industrial enterprise, sometimes becoming an enterprise director before assuming a state political position. On accepting a government post, they assume high staff positions within industrial ministries or in the Council of Ministers, become department heads within ministries, then deputy minister, and finally minister. They are highly specialized, most spending their entire career within the same ministry, or if in more than one ministry, in closely related ones. Only rarely do state industrial specialists spend more than 10 percent of their working careers in Party posts, and when they do, it is invariably early in their careers. Almost never do they hold posts in local or regional soviets (although they may be elected as deputies to republican or all-union Supreme Soviets). Holding full-time soviet posts is associated almost exclusively with Party careers. Finally, it is worth noting that over 75 percent of state industrial specialists spent virtually their entire careers working in Moscow.

Boris Evstaf'evich Butoma, a Russian, was born in 1907 in the town of Makhachkala. He started work at age 13 as a lathe operator in a ship repair yard in Sevastopol, where he worked until 1932. In 1936 he graduated from the Leningrad Shipbuilding Institute. From his graduation until 1948 he worked in a shipbuilding yard in Vladivostok, working himself up from engineer to deputy director. He began his state career in 1948, working as head of a chief administration of the USSR Ministry of Shipbuilding until 1952. During 1953–54, at the time of the ministerial reorganization, he worked as a member of the board of the USSR Ministry of Transport and Heavy Machine Building. From 1954 to 1957 he served as deputy minister and board member of the USSR Ministry of Shipbuilding. From 1957 to 1965 he was chairman of the USSR State Committee for Shipbuilding (attached first to the USSR Council of Ministers and then to the USSR Supreme Economic Council). From 1965 until his death in 1976 he was USSR Minister of the Shipbuilding Industry.[54]

State Economics Specialist. State economics specialists are found in economics, finance, and trade. They have graduated from financial institutes, engineering-economics institutes, pedagogical institutes, or universities. Their administrative careers, often after a period of specialized or managerial work in enterprises, almost always begins with staff work in an *oblast*, republican, or all-union State Planning Committee (*Gosplan*), Ministry of Trade or of Finance, or Council of Ministers. Again, those who reach the Central Committee have become ministers.

An example is Yury Brezhnev, the son of the late Leonid Brezhnev. Brezhnev, born in 1933, graduated from the Dnepropetrovsk Metallurgical Institute in 1955, and again in 1960 from the All-Union Academy of Foreign Trade (a correspondence school). From 1955 to 1957 he worked as a superintendent of the pipe-welding shop of the Karl Liebknecht Plant in Dnepropetrovsk. After completing the Foreign Trade Academy, he worked for six years with the USSR trade mission to Sweden. Following this, he worked for four years, first as USSR deputy representative and then as USSR representative for trade in Sweden. From 1970 to 1976 he was chairman of the All-Union Foreign Trade Association for the import and export of pig iron, ferro-alloys, steel wire, and metal products. He was USSR deputy minister of foreign trade from 1976 to 1979 and then first deputy minister from 1979 until his retirement "for reasons of health" (at age 53) in 1986.[55]

State Coercion Specialist. A small category, state coercion specialists are chairmen or first deputy chairmen of the KGB or men such as Geidar Aliev who assumed central political posts in Moscow after long service in republican State Security Committees.

State Trade Union and Social Services Specialist. Trade union work is the larger category in this specialization. Most Central Committee members in this category are secretaries of the All-Union Central Council of Trade Unions, although secretaries of the World Federation of Trade Unions also appear. Most commonly, these trade union secretaries come to this job after a long period of manual labor in industry, rather than through political or administrative careers; the careers of some of these workers, however, often include active trade union work while employed in industry. In a few cases, low-level Party workers have been diverted into predominately trade union work.

Social services is a small category of individuals who reach high positions in areas such as social security and public welfare or specialized committees such as the Soviet Women's Committee (former cosmonaut Valentina Tereshkova, for example) or Friendship Societies. A large proportion of social services specialists, and quite a few trade union secretaries, are women.

A timely example is Aleksandra Biryukova, appointed a secretary of the CPSU Central Committee in 1986. Born in 1929, Biryukova graduated in 1952 from the Moscow Textile Institute. From that year until 1959 she worked as a superintendent in a Moscow textile plant. Staff work in the Moscow city *sovnarkhoz* (economic council) followed until 1963. She then worked for five years as chief engineer in a large Moscow textiles *kombinat* (complex). From October 4, 1968, until her appointment to the CPSU Secretariat, she served as a secretary of the All-Union Central Council of Trade Unions.[56]

State Miscellaneous. This is a residual category, small in size, made up of individuals who cannot be classified in one of the previous five state specializations. It consists primarily of professionals (often Academy of Sciences functionaries) who would have been excluded from the analysis as "honorary appointees" but for their assumption of a political post toward the end of their careers, often as a deputy chairman of the Council of Ministers or chairman of the Presidium of a republican Supreme Soviet. Staff personnel such as aides to the CPSU general secretary also fall in this category.

It is worthy of note that there is no state generalist category, as there is for Party careers. State careers are usually narrowly specialized, and there is no career type similar to the Party "troubleshooter," adaptable to a number of functions and institutional positions.

Co-Opted Elites

As discussed earlier, technological modernization does not automatically call forth elites competent to deal with the more sophisticated demands and processes of an industrial society. The guidance of such a society requires substantive technical knowledge, and the lack of such knowledge among elites erodes their effectiveness and authority. As regime needs are defined by the incumbent elites, therefore, it always includes the need for new elites who have a mastery of technology. These needs are enunciated at the top levels of the leadership and are invariably perceived as threatening by defensive upper- and middle-level elites. In modernizing societies, then, there is often an essential tension among entrenched elites whose skills are becoming outdated, a rising elite that is more qualified but finds its upward advancement blocked, and frequently a counterelite, comprised of critical intelligentsia outside the ranks of the Party, seeking access to political power.

In seeking to acquire access to the skills and expertise required to maintain the Party's leading position in the society, without yielding power wholesale to the counterelite, the system resorts to co-optation of existing specialized technological elites.[57] Lateral transfers from non-political occupations to the Party and the ministerial elite are the principle mechanism by which this co-optation takes place. During the immediate post-Stalin period and the Khrushchev regime, resort to lateral co-optation was so marked that it would not be inaccurate to call it a technocratic "move-in." In the first decade after Stalin's death, counting only political careers (that is, deleting military and honorary members) of the full and candidate members of the Central Committee and Central Auditing Commission members, the representation of career politicians[58] dropped from 61 percent at the Nineteenth Party Congress to 48 percent at the Twenty-second Congress. In a closely related finding, Fleron states that the percentage of economic managers and planners who had been *recruited* into the Party elite (that is, without at least seven years working in their specializations) declined from 33.3 percent in 1952 to 13 percent in 1961. The percentage of managers and planners *co-opted* into the Party elite (lateral entrants after at least seven years in the specialization) increased from zero to 21.7 percent over the same period.[59] Very similarly, the Communist Party in East Germany institutionalized in the 1960s and 1970s a systematic exchange and rotation of leaders from enterprises to the Party and state apparatus and vice versa.[60]

The representation of professional politicians continued to decline more slowly (about 2 percent per congress, on average), reaching a low in the Central Committee elected at the Twenty-seventh Congress in March 1986 of 47 percent. In the full Twenty-seventh Central Committee *after* Gorbachev's April 1989 forced retirement of about 100 members and the promotion of candidate members to replace them, the representation of professional politicians fell to 38 percent. The salad days of the Party "hack" are clearly waning.

A number of important studies have been based on the explicit assumption that socialization within an organizational context early in an individual's career is of lasting importance as a shaper of an individual's orientation toward politics. Of particular significance in such studies has been the distinction between professional politicians and specialized technical elites. George Fischer perceived the USSR in terms of a "monist model," counterposed to the "pluralist model." In the former, all power is concentrated in the public sphere, the state, and control of the state places power in the hands of a single ruling group. In lieu of social autonomy of specialized groups, the monist mechanism

consists of the executives getting and then using enough technical skills in the various major spheres (most of all in the economic sphere) to *counteract* the proliferation of specialized activities, and the very real pressures these may set up for division of labor. As this mechanism fuses two kinds of skills—economic and political—we can call it a mechanism of *dual leadership skills*.[61]

Fischer defines "top executives" as officials holding high-ranking full-time jobs in the Party;[62] hence, his classification is concerned with Party officials and not with the ministerial apparatus. Fischer suggested four types of officials based on the skills of the person before assuming a full-time Party post. "Dual Executives" did extensive work both in the economy and in the Party before assuming a top post. "Technicians" did extensive technical work, but not Party work, before assuming the top post. "Hybrid Executives" had technical education, but did not work in the economy extensively before top post. Finally, "Officials" were individuals with neither technical training or extensive work in the economy.[63] Fischer noted an increasing trend toward the predominance of "Dual Executives."

Individuals who served seven or more years in a technical specialization before embarking on a full-time political career Fleron refers to as "co-opted" elites—these individuals are presumed to have had at least the opportunity to develop a professional orientation toward the field of their specialization and to have developed personal ties with specialized technical professionals. Recruited elites were found to be dominant at the top levels of the political leadership, and among "staff" as opposed to "line" officials. As the regime sought to bring technical expertise into the leadership system, without at the same time surrendering Party control, co-optation at lower levels was found to have gradually increased, from 25.6 percent of Central Committee members in 1952 to 44.0 percent in 1961.[64]

In a later series of studies of Fleron's thesis, Robert Blackwell refined Fleron's categories somewhat; looking at *obkom* first secretaries (not at Central Committee members), Blackwell defined a professional politician as lacking higher specialized technical education; what Fleron called a "recruited specialist" (with technical education but having spent less than

Table 6.3
Mean Apprenticeship Period by Functional Specialization (in years)

Functional Specialization	Apprenticeship
Party Agricultural	7
Party Industrial	9
Party Ideological	6
Party Cadres	5
Party Generalist	5
State Agricultural	13
State Industrial	16
State Economics	9
State Coercion	4
State TU/Social Services	10
State Miscellaneous	16

Source: Author's database.

seven years in his specialty) Blackwell terms as "adaptive specialist." His definition of a co-opted specialist remains the same. Blackwell found a decrease in the prevalence both of professional politicians and of co-opted specialists in the post-Khrushchev period and an increase in the prevalence of adaptive specialists.[65]

For lack of a better term, I will use "apprenticeship" to refer to the period of time an individual works in his profession (usually after graduation from an institute) and his first acceptance of a full-time political position. Table 6.3 provides mean periods of apprenticeship broken down by functional specialization. In general, Party careers follow much shorter apprenticeships than do state careers.

Among Party careers, those specializations requiring substantive skills, as opposed to innate talent, exhibit the longest apprenticeship periods. Similarly with state careers, those requiring substantive knowledge and experience exhibit longer apprenticeships. The apprenticeship period for state coercion specialists is short, since their are no nongovernmental positions involving coercion. ("State Miscellaneous" careers show long apprenticeships, since by definition these are individuals who assumed a high state post only at the end of a long career outside government.) In general, the greater the substantive knowledge a specialization requires, the more important is experience gained outside of the Party or the government apparatus.

Rate of Mobility

Fischer found that "Officials" and "Hybrid Executives" got to top posts early in their careers rather than later; "Dual Executives" and "Technicians" got to the top later in life.[66]

The rate of mobility—the speed with which individuals climb the career ladder—is, to some degree at least, a measure of the skills and qualities most highly valued, not so much by the society, as Mosca stated it, but by the selectors who make such decisions on behalf of the society. Those who are needed advance very rapidly. The rapid rise of men like Aleksi Kosygin, Nikita Khrushchev, and Leonid Brezhnev in the 1930s is legendary; in the aftermath of the purges, mobility was very rapid for men who had the right stuff and were in the right place. As we have seen, purges of greater or lesser scope follow the resolution of succession crises, and new men favored by the new leadership rise rapidly from obscurity: Andrei Kirilenko and Brezhnev under Khrushchev, Konstantin Chernenko, Dinmukhamed Kunaev, Vladimir Shcherbitsky and, indeed, Gorbachev under Brezhnev, and Gorbachev's "Siberian coalition" more recently.

In more settled times, however, such meteoric ascent is not the norm, and the rate of career progression settles down into a more paced and predictable pattern. From a structural standpoint, we can posit a number of axioms that must govern career mobility in a Progressive Equal Attrition system.

First, the ideal career, from initial recruitment through incumbency of the highest attainable office, must be possible: that is, it must fit within the working lifetime of a man of less than 50 years; considerably less than 50 years is perhaps less hypothetical and more realistic. Among post-Stalin era Central Committee members, individuals began their political careers on the average between the ages of 26 and 36 (the mean age was 33, with a standard deviation of eight years). With an average retirement age of 70, a political career spanning about 34 to 44 years is typical. I shall posit an average career as spanning 40 years.

In fact, this assumption may be too optimistic. Two *raikom* officials from Chernovtsy *oblast* in the Ukraine wrote:

Let us suppose that as a *raikom* instructor we are directed to select people up to age 30, with a higher education, with experience as a *partorg* secretary. A young person leaves school at age 17, studies five or six years at a VUZ, serves two years in the army, and takes two years to join the Party. These are optimal time periods, but they show that only at the age of 29–30 can he be selected as a *partorg* secretary. He's already beyond the age for beginning to work in the *raikom*. So it follows that, for a self-starting worker, a practitioner of the new thinking, having sufficient practical experience, he will not begin party work until he is 35–40 years old, and already considered an old man.[67]

Secondly, the structure of opportunities should be pyramidal: relatively few posts at the top, very difficult to attain, and larger numbers of posts progressively easier to attain as one moves downward. The recruitment and promotion system should be able to provide consid-

Table 6.4
Mean Tenure in Posts (in years)

Career Category	Entire Group	Congress				
		20th	22nd	23rd	24th	25th
I	11.6	11.4	11.3	13.2	13.0	10.2
II	8.7	7.9	8.7	9.5	9.2	8.7
III	7.7	7.7	7.8	7.6	7.3	8.8
IV	7.5	7.1	8.0	7.7	8.2	7.2
V	8.0	7.9	7.9	9.7	8.2	7.0
VI	10.8	9.8	12.9	13.7	10.2	8.8

Source: Author's database.

erably more qualified candidates at each level than there are positions available at each level to assure a pool large enough so that the likelihood is enhanced that highly qualified people can be found. Finally, there should be, if not fixed terms of office, at least mechanisms by which the tenure of officeholders, particularly at higher levels, can be limited. Cushion—the ability of the economy to absorb political losers and others who leave the elite—will considerably facilitate elite circulation.

Given the above assumptions, and given the opportunity structure of a pyramid with five levels corresponding roughly to levels of *nomenklatura* ranking, then for circulation of elites to continue to flow smoothly, the average tenure of officeholders at each *nomenklatura* level (not necessarily in each post) should be eight years. Average tenures markedly exceeding this are an indicator of clogged mobility channels. Excessively long tenure at one level will clog lower levels, though this can be corrected by shifting more individuals out of the elite at these lower levels to allow circulation to continue.

Table 6.4 presents the mean tenures of individuals in each of six career categories for individuals elected as full members of the Central Committee at the Twentieth through the Twenty-fifth Party Congresses. Career categories in this table correspond approximately to *nomenklatura* levels, I being the lowest level, and VI the highest.

Insofar as this database does not reflect promotions after 1980, the figures for individuals elected at the Twenty-fifth Party Congress are misleading; most of the individuals in that column will have been promoted or demoted again in the intervening years. It does, however, reflect generally increased lengths of time spent in posts at the Central Committee *nomenklatura* level, with individuals first elected at the Twenty-third Congress spending significantly longer at those posts (most of which are either ministerial posts or *obkom* first secretary posts) than

Table 6.5
Percentage of Cohorts Occupying Posts at Given Levels

Level	Administrative Time Period									
	A	B	C	D	E	F	G	H	I	J
Cohort 5: Began career in 1936-1940 time period:										
Inactive	97	91	74	52	6	5	2	2	23	37
Military	1	6	1							
Manual Labor	2	6	16	10						
Specialization	1	3	10	38	16	1				
Local Level	36	33	19	2						
Oblast Level	12	17	25	23	14	9				
Republic Level	10	13	18	20	17	9				
All-Union Level	19	25	35	53	44	44				
Cohort 6: Began career in 1941-1945 time period:										
Inactive	100	94	92	57	37	6	1	1	8	17
Military	1									
Manual Labor	6	7	9	2						
Specialization	1	34	52	8	7	2	2	1		
Local Level	38	34	8	1	1					
Oblast Level	18	22	30	23	17					
Republic Level	13	17	23	24	17					
All-Union Level	16	19	36	41	48					
Cohort 7: Began career in 1946-1952 time period:										
Inactive	100	97	91	62	39	20	5	4	12	23
Military	2	12								
Manual Labor	3	5	12	10	4					
Specialization	4	26	49	54	14	2	1			
Local Level	31	15	5	2						
Oblast Level	19	33	35	23						
Republic Level	10	14	14	11						
All-Union Level	21	35	32	40						

Source: Author's database.
Note: The time periods are as follows: A: 1900-16; B: 1917-21;
C: 1922-27; D: 1928-35; E: 1936-40; F: 1941-45; G: 1946-52
H: 1953-64; I: 1965-69; J: 1970-82.

at earlier posts and more than other cohorts spent at that level. This indicates some degree of "bunching up" in those posts near the end of the Brezhnev period.

Table 6.5, based on the same database, reflects a similar phenomenon. For this analysis, individuals were aggregated into "Party-government" cohorts, that is, according to the time period in which they first assumed a full-time Party or government position; the table shows the percentage of those cohorts occupying positions roughly corresponding to their level in the administrative hierarchy. Only Cohorts 5, 6, and 7 are presented here, since there is too much distortion in earlier and later cohorts for meaningful comparison.

This table shows that the two successive cohorts after the 1936 cohort has tended, with some aberrations, to spend successively longer periods of time at each administrative level at roughly the corresponding points in their careers. What these tables attest to is that there has been some "bunching up" during the Brezhnev period, especially in posts at the *oblast* level, but that this has not been dramatic.

A useful indicator of speed of mobility is the length of the "wait" between the individual's first acceptance of a Party or government political post and the individual's first election to the Central Committee, defining first election to the Central Committee (full, candidate, or Central Auditing Commission) as "success." For our purposes, I will use the term "seniority" to refer to this time period, or "wait." Since my database consists of Central Committee members only, it is not representative of the Soviet elite at large. It is not a sample; it is a universe of individuals who achieved "success" during the post-Stalin period. I have no way of judging the mobility of the vastly larger number of individuals who began a political career but did not achieve "success" in the form of election to the CPSU Central Committee. Comparisons, likewise, can only be made among "successful" elites.

Some trends in the mobility of elites over time are apparent. One is increasingly longer periods of time spent in a specialized occupation before joining the elite. These elites are "lateral entrants," and lateral entrants are particularly favored in terms of rapid mobility; this is one of the most striking bivariate relationships to emerge from the data (see Figure 6.1). There is a very significant inverse correlation ($-.524$ for Russians and $-.432$ for non-Russians) between the length of time spent in the specialized occupation and rapidity of advancement to the Central Committee once the individual joins the elite. This correlation holds for all time periods during the Soviet era.

What creates this statistical relationship is the odd fact that the mean age of attainment of Central Committee status remains constant at about age 50. Few elites achieve that status before age 50, and few who do not make it by age 50 ever make it at all. The relationship is not just a statistical artifact, however. It means that a co-opted official, or lateral entrant, will get to the Central Committee at the same age as the recruited official (the *nomenklatura* "lifer") no matter how late in his career he joins the elite.

Several structural factors account for this. First, lateral entrants do not begin at the bottom of the hierarchy; when they join the elite, they do so at a high rank. The lateral entrant has greater experience and

Figure 6.1
Trends in Seniority Patterns

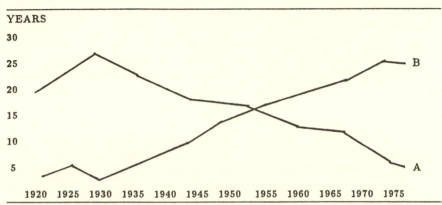

Legend: A: Years spent in specialization before taking first Party/Government post. B: Years between first taking a Party/Government post and first election to full Central Committee.

Source: Author's database.

maturity when he does join the elite; he is thus more valuable. Career politicians must gain this maturity and experience in low-level political posts.

A second structural explanation rests on the *nomenklatura* system. Non-political jobs in the economy are also on Party *nomenklatura* lists. A late lateral entrant is almost certainly co-opted into the political elite at the same *nomenklatura* level he held in the nonpolitical sector. The higher that *nomenklatura* level is, of course, the closer he is to Central Committee status. In other words, he differs from the lifelong politician only in that he acquired his seniority outside the political elite. But he has been upwardly mobile all along.

The career of Nikolai Sliunkov is paradigmatic of the lateral entrant. Sliunkov progressed from assistant master engineer at Minsk Tractor Works in 1950 to director of the plant. His political career began only in 1972, but he began as first secretary of Minsk *gorkom*, moving on from there to deputy chairman of USSR *Gosplan*, then first secretary of the Belorussian Communist Party, becoming a secretary of the CC CPSU in 1987.

There are some significant bivariate relationships between the mean "wait" for Central Committee status and other structural characteristics of the elite. Based on the entire post-Stalin elite sample of political careers ($N = 1079$), the mean wait for individuals with higher education (17.52 years, standard deviation 8.8) is almost 2.5 years shorter than the mean weight for those without higher education (19.83 years, standard deviation 9.6). Non-Slavic elite members had a mean wait (19.20 years, standard deviation 8.5) almost two years longer than Slavic elites (17.40 years, standard deviation 8.5). Those with a career predominantly in the state apparatus achieved CC status more than three years sooner than careers in the Party apparatus (15.35 years, standard deviation 9.5, as opposed to 18.56 years, standard deviation 8.5). Surprisingly, females moved up faster than males, with a mean wait of 12.12 years, standard deviation 6.4, compared with males at 17.82 years, standard deviation 7.9. However, such a small proportion of the sample, 36, or 3.2 percent, are women, that it is questionable how much significance should be attached to this. Co-opted elites, or lateral entrants (those with more than seven years spent in their specialized occupations before joining the elite), reached the Central Committee on average in 13.35 years (standard deviation 7.5), compared to 21.62 years (standard deviation 8.2) for recruited elites (those who spent less than seven years in a nonpolitical post before joining the elite).

The structural characteristics of elites that account for the greatest variance in mobility are number of years spent in the specialized occupation before joining the elite, sex education, attendance at a Party versus a non-Party higher-educational institution, and type of career. The latter can be dichotomized into higher education versus no higher education, Party versus non-Party education, and Party versus non-Party career. Among all the variables present in or computable from the database, multiple regression of these variables against mean wait for Central Committee status provides the best explanation of the variation in mean wait. Multiple regression analysis yields an equation of the form:

$$Y = a + b_1X_1 + b_2X_2 + b_3X_3 + b_4X_4 + b_5X_5 + e \qquad 6.1$$

where Y represents the waiting period in years between first accepting a Party-government position and first election to the Central Committee, a is a constant term, e is an error term, and $X_1 \ldots X_5$ represent the independent variables. The regression equation is

$$WAIT = 19.07 + 6.81(SEX) - 1.12(SCHOOL) - 0.91(EDUC)$$
$$- 0.59(CAREER) - 0.67(SPEC) \qquad 6.2$$

The residuals in this analysis are distributed on a nearly perfect normal curve. The F-test is 131.10336, with a significance of .0000. Standard error is 7.0, and adjusted R^2 is .38142. This means that these five independent variables account for 38 percent of the variance in waiting time for election to the CPSU Central Committee.

It is interesting to note that attendance at HPSs, the Higher Party Schools, seems to impeded, not promote, mobility; relatively few graduates of Party schools ever reach the central elite, most of them taking posts in teaching, the press, or radio and television or in the agitation and propaganda apparatus as one of the thousands of low-ranking lecturers. Of those who do go into politics, most are concentrated in lower-level positions in the state, rather than the Party, apparatus. They can be found most often as chairmen of autonomous republic, *krai, oblast, gorod,* and *raion* soviets. There is also impressionistic evidence, at least, that a Party education is considered remedial. I have been explicitly told this by several different Soviet citizens. It is also backed up in the secondary literature. One of Jeffrey Klugman's interviewees, for example, recounts the story of a woman who was a city Komsomol first secretary, not very good at her job and not well liked, whose position the subject undermined so as to get her job; she was sent to a Party school in Leningrad, and he got the job.[68] In another context, Werner Hahn writes of Stavropol' *kraikom* first secretary A. L. Orlov, who was fired by the Central Committee in 1946 for failure to perform his duties and was then sent to the Higher Party School.[69] In a previous study, I found reason to believe that a higher "price" for political advancement is exacted of non-Slavs than of Slavs in the form of postgraduate education and attendance at the Higher Party School.[70]

Graduates of Party schools who pursued a political career and eventually made it to the Central Committee experienced considerably slower advancement than those who eschewed Party schools. The mean wait for HPS graduates was 21.7 years; that for non-HPS graduates, 16.1 years. The Pearson correlation coefficient between HPS attendance and rapidity of achievement is $-.2842$.

Different types of functional specialization also experience different rates and outcomes of mobility. Armstrong found that Party secretaries in agitation and propaganda work in the Ukraine tend to remain in that field throughout their careers[71] and that agricultural secretaries experience little vertical mobility.[72] Table 6.6 provides the mean seniority, or wait, for Central Committee status for each of the functional specializations.

State agricultural and state industrial careers enjoy the shortest mean seniority. It will be remembered, however, that precisely these two career paths have the longest apprenticeships, as do state trade union and social services specializations, in large part accounting for their deviation from the remaining functional specializations.

It remains to discuss channels of career mobility, that is, the mean path of movement from one post to another. This suggests something similar to a Markov chains analysis. Grey Hodnett believes that the utility of Markov chains for career analysis is severely limited by technical constraints. Among other things, he argues that elite career patterns simply are not stochastic.[73] For Markov chains to be applicable, it would

Table 6.6
Mean Seniority by Functional Specialization (in years)

Functional Specialization	Seniority
Party Industrial	17
Party Ideological	19
Party Cadres	23
Party Generalist	22
State Agricultural	13
State Industrial	13
State Economics	21
State Coercion	25
State TU/Social Services	14
State Miscellaneous	14

Source: Author's database.

require that transition coefficients are the same for all persons and remain constant through time and that transition to the next state depend only on the previous state and not on anything that happened previously.[74]

The tables that follow (Table 6.7) are not strictly speaking Markov chains, insofar as they represent in the aggregate the probability that any position in Post A will be followed by any of the ten positions listed under Post B. A true Markov chain would represent states of a system at successive equal periods of time. The following set of tables, therefore, merely gives the probability distributions of Post B given Post A (i.e., held at any time, so long as they are successive).

What this table represents is likely career channels. For example, 61 percent of those holding a local soviet position (Post A) will go to a regional Party position (Post B) as their next posting. Of those holding a republican government position, 35 percent will go on next to a central government post; and for 22 percent, the republican government position will be their last posting. The highest probabilities under "terminate" indicate the most stable career channels, or, looked at another way, dead ends. A post in the central government, for example, is the lasting post for 79 percent of those who hold it, while a central Party post is the dead end for only 25 percent of those who hold it. Of those holding a central party post, roughly equal percentages go on to central government (14 percent), regional Party (17 percent), or to a nonpolitical posting (13 percent).

Another relationship that is worth noting is that between post marginality and career longevity. Post marginality refers to the likelihood that a political elite figure will lose his position within the first term of officeholding, however stipulated. Career longevity refers simply to the

Table 6.7
Job Transition Matrix

| POST A | POST B | | | | | |
	Non-Political	Local Party	Local Soviet	Central Soviet	Regional Party	Republic Party
Non-Political	0	24	4	4	11	3
Local Party	3	0	10	2	46	8
Local Soviet	1	5	0	0	61	1
Central Soviet	5	8	0	0	0	0
Regional Party	3	5	5	2	0	11
Republic Party	6	5	1	2	15	0
Republic Govt	10	4	2	2	10	14
Central Party	13	5	4	5	17	9
Central Govt	5	1	0	2	2	2
Komsomol	13	37	3	2	24	5

| POST A | POST B | | | | |
	Republic Govt	Central Party	Central Govt	Komsomol	Termination
Non-Political	5	3	16	5	26
Local Party	6	8	9	0	7
Local Soviet	9	2	10	0	10
Central Soviet	0	11	19	0	57
Regional Party	11	12	11	0	39
Republic Party	14	11	20	0	26
Republic Govt	0	2	35	0	22
Central Party	5	0	14	0	29
Central Govt	4	6	0	0	79
Komsomol	5	8	5	0	0

Source: Author's database.

length of one's political career. In competitive systems, as might be expected, these two indexes are inversely related: losers drop out early. William Welsh has noted, however, that in Communist systems, the relationship is the opposite: "Shorter careers tend to be characterized by a very small number of positions, each held for a relatively substantial length of time. Longer political careers are typified by frequent movement among a large number of positions, each occupied for a relatively short period of time."[75]

This relationship indeed does hold true, and the explanation for it can be found in the differences, once again, between contest and sponsored mobility systems. Push mechanisms predominate in contest systems; candidates who cannot win elections cease trying before very long. In sponsorship mobility systems, careers are structured careers (like the military or the foreign service): holding a post for a long period of time is a sign of lack of qualifications for promotion; those who do not move up after a period of time leave the elite.

CONCLUSIONS

At least until Gorbachev's 1989 restructuring of the political system, the appropriate models of the Soviet recruitment process are those of sponsored mobility and Armstrong's Progressive Equal Attrition Model, with the qualification that the attrition is less than equal: the elite is drastically pruned at the district level. It is a structured mobility system in that most individuals begin at the bottom and work upwards by means of relatively fixed channels. There are, however, lateral entrants: older individuals with lengthy experience in the nonpolitical sector who enter the elite at a high level.

The selectorate, or gatekeepers, are generally Party committee first secretaries, who have control over *nomenklatura* lists at that level. Regime needs, rather than system needs, guide their choices.

Credentials include Party membership, higher technical education, male gender, and either Russian ethnic identity or, for non-Russians, extensive assimilation into Russian language and culture. Measurable factors associated with rapid mobility include sex (male preferred), technical education acquired at institutes other than Party schools, an advanced degree, a Party rather than a state career, functional specialization in a technical career, and a lengthy period of work in the specialization before assuming a political post. It was demonstrated that these factors account for 38 percent of the variance in mobility.

NOTES

1. Kenneth Prewitt, "From the Many Are Chosen the Few," *American Behavioral Scientist* 13, no. 2 (November-December 1969): 170.

2. Aristotle, *Politics*, 1300a, 9–19.

3. Suzanne Keller, *Beyond the Ruling Class: Strategic Elites in Modern Society* (New York: Random House, 1963), p. 181.

4. For example, Lester G. Seligman lists the same three modes. *Recruiting Political Elites* (New York: General Learning Press, 1971), pp. 3–4.

5. Bohdan Harasymiw, *Political Elite Recruitment in the Soviet Union* (London: Macmillan, 1974), pp. 2–3. Representative theoretical treatments of political recruitment and mobility include Moshe M. Czudnowski, "Political Recruitment," in Fred I. Greenstein and Nelson W. Polsby, eds., *Handbook of Political Science* (Reading, MA: Addison-Wesley, 1975), vol. 2, pp. 155–242; David C. Schwartz, "Toward a Theory of Political Recruitment," *Western Political Quarterly* 22 (1969):552–71; Seligman, *Recruiting Political Elites*; I. William Zartman, "The Study of Elite Circulation: Who's on First and What's He Doing There?" *Comparative Politics* 6 (1974):465–88.

6. Ralph Turner, "Contest and Sponsored Mobility and the School System," *American Sociological Review* 25, no. 6 (1966):856–67.

7. John A. Armstrong, *The European Administrative Elite* (Princeton, N.J.: Princeton University Press, 1972), pp. 17–18.

8. Friedrich Engels, *Herr Dühring's Revolution in Science* (New York: International Publishers, 1935), p. 292.

9. Armstrong, *The European Administrative Elite*, p. 18.

10. Ibid., pp. 21–22.

11. For example, see Dwaine Marvick, "Continuities in Recruitment Theory and Research: Toward a New Model," in Heinz Eulau and Moshe E. Czudnowski, eds., *Elite Recruitment in Democratic Politics: Comparative Studies across Nations* (New York: John Wiley, 1976); Kenneth Prewitt, *The Recruitment of Political Leaders: A Study of Citizen-Politicians* (New York: Bobbs-Merrill, 1970); Lester G. Seligman, "Political Parties and the Recruitment of Political Leadership," in Lewis J. Edinger, ed., *Political Leadership in Industrial Societies: Studies in Comparative Analysis* (New York: John Wiley, 1976); Schwartz, "Theory of Political Recruitment"; and Herbert Jacob, "Initial Recruitment of Elected Officials in the U.S.: A Model," *Journal of Politics* 24 (1962):703–16.

12. Prewitt, "From the Many Are Chosen the Few," p. 169.

13. Seligman, *Recruiting Political Elites*, p. 3.

14. Bohdan Harasymiw, "Mosca and Moscow: Elite Recruitment in the Soviet Union," in Moshe E. Czudnowski, ed., *Does Who Governs Matter? Elite Circulation in Contemporary Societies* (DeKalb, IL: Northern Illinois University Press, 1982), p. 268 (emphasis added). Also see Harasymiw, *Political Elite Recruitment,* p. 26.

15. Armstrong reports that about 15,000 recruits reach district-level Party or government posts, but that turnover is very great at this level, since these low-level posts are regarded as a testing ground. *The European Administrative Elite,* p. 247.

16. Harasymiw, *Political Elite Recruitment*, p. 26.

17. No doubt, the "peter principle"—by which administrators are promoted until they reach the level of their incompetence—is operative in the Soviet Union, too.

18. Local and regional newspapers carry biographies of middle- and lower-level elites, that is, those who might or might not reach the top. For the time being, at least, these are unavailable in the West; in any event collecting these biographies for the whole country over a long time period would be an immense task.

19. I would go so far as to suggest that the true function of elections in democratic systems is not actually to permit voters to choose their leaders; it is, rather, to keep elites on their toes through having to compete for election at intervals, in other words, maintaining an institutionalized insecurity of tenure. Seen in this light, it does not matter who is elected; what matters is that an adequate level of competition is maintained. Only a sufficient amount of voter participation to maintain this level is needed. The democratic myth of voting—that each person's vote counts—serves this function.

20. R. Judson Mitchell, "Immobilism, Depoliticization, and the Emerging Soviet Elite," *Orbis* 26, no. 4 (Fall 1982):591–609; Seweryn Bialer, *Stalin's Successors* (Cambridge: Cambridge University Press, 1980); Robert Blackwell, Jr., "Cadres Policy in the Brezhnev Era," *Problems of Communism*, no. 28 (March-April

1979):29–42; Jerry Hough, *Soviet Leadership in Transition* (Washington, DC: Brookings Institution, 1980).

21. Gaetano Mosca, *The Ruling Class* (New York: McGraw-Hill, 1939), pp. 65–66.

22. Party membership is a sine qua non for admission to the political elite and advancement within it. All members of the regional and national elite are Party members.

23. James Nichol, who did an exhaustive quantitative analysis of such accessible variables for full Central Committee members, also found no significant change in selection criteria over time. "Political Selection and Life History Types in the Central Committee of the Communist Party of the Soviet Union," PhD dissertation, University of Washington, 1982, p. 505.

24. Philip D. Stewart et al., "Political Mobility and the Soviet Political Process: A Partial Test of Two Models," *American Political Science Review*, no. 66 (July 1972):1269–90.

25. Jerry Hough, *The Soviet Prefects: The Local Party Organ in Industrial Decision-Making* (Cambridge, MA: Harvard University Press, 1969), pp. 280–85; Joel Moses, *Regional Party Leadership and Policy-Making in the USSR* (New York: Praeger, 1974), p. 18; Grey Hodnett, *Leadership in the Soviet National Republics: A Quantitative Study of Recruitment Policy* (Oakville, Ontario: Mosaic Press, 1978), p. 391; William A. Clark, *Soviet Regional Elite Mobility after Khrushchev* (New York: Praeger, 1989), pp. 57ff.

26. Cf. John Armstrong: "What seems to be at work is a strong attachment to the concept of a defined career pattern. Anyone who reaches the top of the career ladder without having gone through the initiation stages is regarded as a threat, even if the material injury to career officials' chances is slight." *The European Administrative Elite*, p. 242.

27. Bialer, *Stalin's Successors*, pp. 120–23.

28. T. H. Rigby, "Traditional, Market, and Organizational Societies and the USSR," in Frederic J. Fleron, ed., *Communist Studies and the Social Sciences: Essays on Methodology and Empirical Theory* (Chicago: Rand McNally, 1971), pp. 182–83.

29. Darrell P. Hammer, "Statistical Methods in Kremlinology," Unpublished manuscript, Department of Government, Indiana University, n.d., p. 31.

30. Fleron, *Communist Studies*, pp. 120–21. Fleron discusses this problem further in a review in *Slavic and East European Studies* (Montreal) 10, nos. 3–4 (Fall-Winter 1965–66): 130–32.

31. See, for example, John A. Armstrong, *The Soviet Bureaucratic Elite* (New York: Praeger, 1959), p. 146; and T. H. Rigby, "Cryptopolitics," *Survey*, no. 50 (1964): 192.

32. However, see Karl W. Ryavec, *The Soviet Ministerial Elite, 1964–1979: A Representative Sample* (Amherst: University of Massachusetts, Program in Soviet and East European Studies, Occasional Papers Series no. 6, May 1981).

33. Zbigniew Brzezinski and Samuel P. Huntington, *Political Power: USA/USSR* (New York: Viking Press, 1965), pp. 161–63.

34. Seweryn Bialer, "The Soviet Political Elite: Concept, Sample, and Case Study," PhD dissertation, Columbia University, 1966, p. 154.

35. During the Khrushchev period and before, however, there was frequent

crossover between Party and state positions, at least at the republic level. See Armstrong, *The Soviet Bureaucratic Elite*, pp. 54, 144.

36. Robert V. Daniels, "Office-Holding and Elite Status: The Central Committee of the CPSU," in Paul Cocks, Robert V. Daniels, and Nancy Whittier Heer, eds., *The Dynamics of Soviet Politics* (Cambridge, MA: Harvard University Press, 1976), pp. 80–81; Nichol, "Political Selection and Life History Types," p. 543.

37. See Jerry Hough and Merle Fainsod, *How the Soviet Union Is Governed* (Cambridge: Harvard University Press, 1979), pp. 424–29, 445–48, and 497–505; Hodnett, *Leadership in Soviet National Republics*, pp. 130–36, 177–94, 224–302, and 395–96; Joel C. Moses, "Functional Career Specialization in Soviet Regional Elite Recruitment," in T. H. Rigby and Bohdan Harasymiw, eds., *Leadership Selection and Patron-Client Relations in the USSR and Yugoslavia* (London: Allen & Unwin, 1983), pp. 15–61.

38. Roger Pethybridge, *A Key to Soviet Politics: The Crisis of the Anti-Part Group* (London: Allen & Unwin, 1962), p. 17.

39. Wolfgang Leonhard, *The Kremlin since Stalin* (New York: Praeger, 1962), pp. 11–15.

40. Vernon V. Aspaturian, "Soviet Foreign Policy," in Roy C. Macridis, ed., *Foreign Policy in World Politics* (Englewood Cliffs, NJ: Prentice-Hall, 1964), pp. 169–75.

41. Michael Gehlen, "The Educational Backgrounds and Career Orientations of the Members of the Central Committee of the CPSU," *American Behavioral Scientist* 9, no. 8 (April 1966): 11–14.

42. Frederic Fleron, "Representation of Career Types in the Soviet Political Leadership," in R. Barry Farrell, ed., *Political Leadership in the Soviet Union and Eastern Europe* (Chicago: Aldine Publishing Co., 1970), pp. 108–39.

43. Christian Duevel, "The Central Committee and the Central Auditing Commission Elected by the 23rd CPSU Congress: A Study of the Political Survival of Their Members and a Profile of Their Professional and Political Composition," *Radio Liberty Research Paper*, no. 6 (New York: Radio Library Committee, 1966), pp. 17–20.

44. Nichol, "Political Selection and Life History Types," pp. 289–90.

45. Moses, "Functional Career Specialization," pp. 15–61.

46. *Pravda*, July 21, 1985, p. 2. Biographic details from *Deputaty Verkhovnogo Soveta SSSR*, 11th Session (Moscow, 1984), p. 136.

47. *Deputaty Verkhovnogo Soveta SSSR*, 11th Session (Moscow, 1984), p. 69.

48. *Ezhegodnik Bol'shoi Sovetskoi Entsiklopedii 1987* (Moscow, 1987), p. 577.

49. Ibid., p. 584.

50. Moses, "Functional Career Specialization," p. 22.

51. *Deputaty Verkhovnogo Soveta SSSR*, 8th Session (Moscow, 1970), p. 107.

52. *Pravda*, September 21, 1972.

53. *Pravda*, November 25, 1982, p. 5.

54. *Pravda*, July 13, 1976, p. 3.

55. *Ezhegodnik Bol'shoi Sovetskoi Entsiklopedii 1987* (Moscow, 1987), p. 569.

56. Ibid., p. 553.

57. For a discussion of the importance of co-optation as a means of raising

the skill levels of political elites, see William A. Welsh, *Leaders and Elites* (New York: Holt, Rinehart & Winston, 1979), pp. 73–74.

58. Defined as having spent less than seven years in a specialized occupation before taking a full-time political post.

59. Fleron, "Representation of Career Types," p. 129.

60. Thomas A. Baylis, *The Technical Intelligentsia and the East German Elite* (Berkeley: University of California Press, 1974), p. 170.

61. George Fischer, *The Soviet System and Modern Society* (New York: Atherton Press, 1968), p. 14.

62. Ibid., p. 19.

63. Ibid., p. 39.

64. Fleron's findings are reported in "Toward a Reconceptualization of Politics in the Soviet Union: The Political Leadership System," *Comparative Politics* 1, no. 2 (January 1969):228–44; "Cooptation as a Mechanism of Adaptation to Change: The Soviet Political Leadership System," *Polity* 2, no. 2 (Winter 1969):176–201; "Representation of Career Types"; and "System Attributes and Career Attributes: The Soviet Leadership System, 1952–1965," in Carl Beck et al., eds., *Comparative Communist Political Leadership* (New York: David McKay, 1973), pp. 86–153.

65. Robert E. Blackwell, "Elite Recruitment and Functional Change: An Analysis of the Soviet Obkom Elite," *Journal of Politics*, 34 (February 1972):124–52; "The Soviet Political Elite: Alternative Recruitment Policies at the Obkom Level: An Empirical Analysis," *Comparative Politics* 6, no. 1 (October 1973):99–121.

66. Fischer, *Soviet System and Modern Society*, pp. 52–53.

67. V. Voevodin and L. Slobodianik, editorial in *Pravda*, February 9, 1987, p. 2.

68. Jeffry Klugman, *The New Soviet Elite: How They Think and What They Want* (New York: Praeger, 1989), p. 62.

69. Werner Hahn, *Postwar Soviet Politics* (Ithaca, NY: Cornell University Press, 1982), p. 62n.

70. Kenneth C. Farmer, "Consociational Dictatorship or Imperium? Non-Russian Political Elites and Central Decision-Making in the USSR," *Nationalites Papers* 13, no. 1 (Spring 1985):52.

71. Armstrong, *The Soviet Bureaucratic Elite*, pp. 52–55.

72. Ibid., p. 96.

73. Hodnett, *Leadership in the Soviet National Republics*, p. 299.

74. Patrick Doreian, *Mathematics and the Study of Social Relations* (New York: Schocken Books, 1971), p. 137. However, Michael E. Urban, in an innovative study, was able to apply Markov chain analysis to the study of mobility in a way that does not seem to violate the assumptions: *An Algebra of Soviet Power: Elite Circulation in the Belorussian Republic, 1966–86* (Cambridge: Cambridge University Press, 1989).

75. Welsh, *Leaders and Elites*, p. 76.

Chapter 7

Venality

Power corrupts the few, while weakness corrupts the many.

Eric Hoffer

The point need not be belabored that power corrupts. A tendency to venality is probably a sufficiently universal part of human nature that when an opportunity to achieve gain through wrongdoing presents itself, there is always some who will take advantage of it. Hence, every political system has corrupt politicians.

Not all power corrupts absolutely, however (although Lord Acton was surely right about absolute power). We can rule out differences in national character (though not necessarily culture) as a differentiating factor, by assuming that human nature itself is universal. No nationality is inherently more prone to moral failing than any other. Nor is any political system, contemporary or historical, immune to corruption. Political systems vary in the degree and extent of corruption in them, and the differences are due in large part to structural factors: political systems vary in the degree to which they limit the power of politicians, and societies vary in the degree of opportunity they present. Virtue may well be, as has been suggested, a function of chronic lack of opportunity.

People will do pretty much what they want. When areas of social activity in which a sufficient (but undefined) "critical mass" of people wish to participate are proscribed legally and/or morally by the society as a whole, then "anarchic subsystems"—as I choose to call them—will emerge. Most societies, for example, proscribe prostitution, drug use, and, say, nude sunbathing, and so informal subsystems arise around these activities. They are anarchic insofar as they lie outside the law, but within themselves they have structure and norms, which are internally enforced. Political corruption[1] and *Seilschaften*[2] often constitute informal political systems of this type.

In this chapter, I will discuss three aspects of venality: corruption, clientelism, and executive style. Corruption and patronage, though analytically separable, go hand in hand and often have the same causes. Style is the analytical poor stepchild, so to speak, but it is as constant a refrain of criticism in the Party and in the press as the other two, and it has recently, under Mikhail Gorbachev, assumed great importance, and so it is appropriate to treat it here.

CORRUPTION

Gaetano Mosca did not fail to comment on corruption. In cases where the bureaucracy is recruited from recently resurgent lower classes, he remarks, its idealism, devotion to duty, and moral level in general are likely to be low:

In cases such as these bureaucratic organization yields its worst results. One notes brazen favoritism in superiors, base servility in subalterns and, in superiors and subalterns both, a tendency to exchange for favors of any sort such influence as their positions put at their disposal. In the more serious cases, bargaining turns into outright sale, and then we get a system of pecuniary corruption which disrupts and paralyzes every state activity once it has become common in the higher and lower grades of the bureaucratic scale.[3]

It would be tempting to apply this to the early Soviet bureaucracy, but for the most part it just is not applicable. In fact, the idealism and willing self-sacrifice of early proletarian officialdom was high; corruption did not become a problem until well into the NEP. Mosca was the champion of the middle class, a class whose incorruptibility he misread badly. Incorruptible regimes have been rare, but when they have occurred they have been in aristocratic regimes, where independently wealthy noble-bureaucrats had no need to covet anything from the public till.

James Scott defines corruption as "behavior which deviates from the formal duties of a public role (elective or appointive) because of private-regarding (personal, class, family, private clique) wealth or status gains; or violates rules against the exercise of certain types of private-regarding influence."[4] Corruption is deviation from the formal, legal norms of the society in which it occurs, rather than deviation from norms external to it. We may, if we wish, normatively insist that a political system is itself corrupt, but such an appeal to a universal norm implies nothing about the corruption of its members. Arnold Heidenheimer, for example, remarks on the prevalence of two conceptions of corruption: "the corruption of a bad policy," or the "decay of the moral and political order," the conceptions of corruption held by Thucydides, Plato, Aristotle, and Rousseau. Heidenheimer calls this the "institutional decay concept," distinguishing it from the narrower conception of "the acceptance of money or money's worth by public officials for misusing official powers."[5]

The extent of political corruption seems to be related to at least two structural factors: economic scarcity and the lack, or severe underdevelopment of, democratic political institutions. These two factors themselves seem to be interrelated; there are few affluent dictatorships. Just as a minimal degree of affluence is regarded as a prerequisite of democracy, it could be argued that scarcity is a prerequisite of authoritarianism: it limits the potential power of nonelites and expands the opportunities for elites to create dependencies.

Corruption and patronage go hand in hand.[6] Both phenomena are associated with countries marked by scarcities in material goods. The more scarce the goods and resources, the more power associated with control over them; it enables those who do control them to foster dependencies. In conditions of scarcity, and particularly in a command economy, public officials are advantageously positioned to control distribution and to arrogate goods to themselves. This is why officials in such systems have a stake in the perpetuation of scarcity and inequality of distribution, that is, underdevelopment, and this is exactly why underdevelopment is perpetuated. People who enter politics and reach positions of some power have entrepreneurial personalities; they are somewhat larger than life, and their expectations of rewards are similarly inflated. If the law does not permit sufficiently large incomes to politicians, then they can be expected to attempt to use their political power for personal gain. Under nondemocratic political conditions, where public approval or indignation are insignificant factors in the rise and demise of political leaders—and/or where a free press to mobilize such opinion is lacking—the political costs of corrupt and illegal activities are not very high. This is all the more true in countries where the legitimacy of the regime is low, for an embattled elite will close ranks and protect its own. Under such conditions, massive and publicized anticorruption campaigns risk the further erosion of legitimacy and will therefore rarely be resorted to, unless some higher political advantage can be gained thereby—a case in point was Yurii Andropov's effort to weaken Leonid Brezhnev in the latter's final year by exposing corruption among those close to him. The thoroughgoing purge of the corrupt under Gorbachev does not contradict this; Gorbachev is not concerned with preserving the legitimacy of the old system. If anything, he is seeking new bases of legitimacy founded on the destruction of the Stalinist vestiges of the old system and on democratic acceptance of the new.

The other side of this coin is the use of corruption as a potential weapon against recalcitrant officials or clients. Stalin used the lethal threat of accusation of "deviationism" as a means of keeping his men in line, and Khrushchev used the Damoclean sword of exposure as a Stalinist for the same end. It is difficult to ascertain whether corruption is used by Soviet leaders today in the same way, but it seems certain that it is. This is a very close parallel to the use of corruption as a mechanism of tension management that Marvin Zonis saw in the Shah's Iran:

Frequently members of the elite will be charged with corruption and removed from office, exiled or imprisoned when their offense was, in fact, entirely political. . . . [Some] suggest that corruption among the elite is used in exactly the same way as are the resignations submitted to the president of the United States by his cabinet secretaries as they assume the responsibilities of their office. When the chief executive determines that a secretary is no longer satisfactorily fulfilling his responsibilities, he may accept, with deep regrets, the resignation. It is alleged by some that His Majesty not only maintains a dossier pertaining to the improbity of each member of the elite, but actually countenances or even encourages their dishonesty in order to fatten their dossiers. When the proper moment arises, the elite can be confronted with the dossier and his resignation or exile demanded. Or if need be the materials therein can be used as the basis for successful judicial proceedings. Either way, the suspect or unwanted elite official can be politically neutralized.[7]

I propose that there are three genetic categories of corruption (by genetic, I mean that these are etiologies, classified according to origin; they have nothing to do with individual motivations for entering into corrupt activities). These are (1) residuary, (2) functional, and (3) opportunistic. I shall amplify each of these.

Residuary. This is admittedly an awkward word. The term "residual," however, seems to me to imply something of marginal importance left over when everything else is accounted for. By residuary corruption, I refer to carryovers from a traditional society that persist in a society undergoing a transition to a rational-legal, that is, modern, society. Practices such as bribery, nepotism, the skimming off of surplus, and so on— in general, the treatment of office as a personal patrimony—are in traditional societies part of the accepted practice and regarded as normal. In societies at least outwardly modern and rational-legal, they are inappropriate and so are considered corrupt. Kenneth Jowitt has pointed out that, ironically, Marxist-Leninist regimes tend to create institutions that in fact reinforce traditional values and ways of doing things.[8]

Such an anthropological interpretation of corruption in societies undergoing transition traces its origins in part to gift-giving practices that were prevalent—and not at all considered corrupt—in traditional societies, as described by Marcel Mauss.[9] Gift giving was not practiced in traditional rural Russian society to be the same degree and in the same way as in more primitive societies as described by Mauss. Nonetheless, the practice of making small gifts to officials (*prinoshenie*) as a mild form of bribe—to build up a reserve of good will more than to affect a particular decision—existed on a large scale and is still widely practiced in Soviet society. Outright bribery on a more serious scale is nearly as widespread.

Another explanation for corruption in traditional societies is kinship, and the primary obligation of individuals toward kin and the clear secondary status of obligations toward clientele or the larger society. This kind of corruption—nepotism, and a focus on kin and/or clan groups (*semeistvennost'*)—is widely observable in the Transcaucasian and Central Asian republics of the Soviet Union. Other similar practices include protectionism (*protektsionizm*), localism (*mestnichestvo*), and promoting one's friends (*podsazhivanie svoikh liudei*). These republics are "societies of amoral familists," in Edward Banfield's awkward but accurate terminology.[10]

Functional. By functional corruption, I mean forms of corruption that fulfill an instrumental function (other than mere enrichment). Corruption lubricates an inefficient, clumsy economic system that does not provide for rationalized production and distribution on its own. It insinuates de facto market relations into a command economy. Corruption in this view is functionally necessary to overcome structural rigidities and inefficiency of the system.

Just as the importance of government in underdeveloped states as a source of goods and employment is a structural factor encouraging corruption,[11] so it is precisely the same in the Soviet Union. In a command economy, the government owns all economic resources, and virtually everyone who works in the Soviet Union is employed by the state. Hence, any kind of economic activity that takes place outside the framework of the command economy is by definition corrupt.

A centralized economy with chronic shortages virtually guarantees a high level of illegal and quasi-legal economic transactions on the part of the population. A very large part of a structural explanation for corruption in the Soviet system is the planned economy. A planned economy creates a new category of crime that does not exist in a market economy. Speculation, buying and selling goods for a profit, covers the largest part of these activities, but it also includes private importation or production and sale of scarce goods—in general, a black market. Black market activities inevitably shade into activities that are universally criminal: stealing from the state, overcharging customers, embezzlement, and bribery pervade the Soviet system from top to bottom, and almost no one is innocent of some part in it on a large or small scale.

A command economy also create shortages; this is because a planned economy does not respond automatically to needs and demands, as a market-driven economy does, but rather to the plan. Therefore, needs and demands go unmet when the planners divert resources disproportionately to one or another sector, such as heavy industry or defense. Corruption, therefore, is functional in such a system; it serves important redistributive functions, and without it extreme instability could result from widespread unmet demands. Zygmunt Bauman goes further to argue that clientelism and patronage are "a systemic regulating feature of the Communist society, a functional equivalent of law and/or the impersonal market place."[12]

John Kramer emphasizes, rightly I think, that in the Soviet case it is necessary to distinguish between two types of corruption, that for private gain and that for bureaucratic gain—to enhance organizational performance and efficiency: "Such corruption especially manifests itself in Soviet production units in two ways: (1) use of illegal influence (*blat*, *tolkachi*); (2) false reporting of enterprise data."[13]

Corruption serves less concrete functions as well. Corruption is a means of elite integration, at least on a local scale. Participation in illegal acts, taking risks so that all involved are equally vulnerable, creates ties that bind and bond. Corruption cements patron-client ties; personal loyalties, both up and down the hierarchy, are strengthened when people are implicated together in marginal activities.

John Waterbury remarks that some "have pointed out that corruption may promote national integration, capitalist efficiency, capital formation, administrative flexibility, and a shift toward popular democracy."[14] Waterbury sees corruption as a "planned, cultivated, and vital element in assuring the survival of a regime" in Morocco.[15] Although in the Soviet Union it is probably not planned, there is considerable reason to believe that corruption has promoted all five of the salutary effects that Waterbury ascribes to corruption among Moroccan bureaucrats.[16]

James Critchlow, discussing corruption among native elites in Central Asia, similarly finds evidence of the functionality of corruption:

The record suggests that many "negative phenomena" have been tolerated up to now because they have helped to make the system work, by stimulating initiative, cementing working relationships, and easing popular dissatisfaction with the state controlled sector of the economy through the provision of goods and services that would otherwise be unavailable.[17]

Opportunistic. Opportunistic corruption is neither functional nor residuary—it comprises unconnected, individual violations of official norms for selfish, private gain. This, the form of corruption most familiar to us, perhaps, is almost most characteristic of modern societies.

I am suggesting here a model of the structure of the Soviet system as one in which local Communist Party satraps (first secretaries) are given relative autonomy in the use of the system for their own benefit in return for maintaining order and a certain level of economic productivity. Michael Urban, too, finds that subordinate officials "reveal a powerful tendency towards the personal appropriation of public office."[18] Merle Fainsod, in his examination of the Smolensk Archive, found evidence for this type of relationship between the center and the periphery:

Leaders tended ultimately to be judged in terms of their over-all success or failure in meeting the political and economic goals that the center set for them. As long as the *oblast* managed a margin of achievement which was roughly satisfactory, the center presumably was not inclined to inquire too closely into the methods used to obtain such results or even into the abuses that attended them.[19]

This is not at all unlike a *benefice* or dissimilar to a model of a regional prince who collects tribute from the masses: as long as the central rulers get their tribute (or whatever it is they need from him, including, perhaps, nothing more than local quiescence), the local satrap can skim off from the local population for his own use whatever he is able. As long as his corruption does not become so obvious or destabilizing as to threaten those above him, he will be protected. The position of the corrupt politician is in this sense similar to the position of the spy: if he is caught, he will not be claimed by the government he works for; if the satrap gets "caught," he will be prosecuted—this is not to keep the political elite clean, it is to protect it from being cleaned.

At the same time that there is a risk in denouncing and punishing corrupt politicians (the risk of collective loss of legitimacy on the part of the elite); there is also, oddly it might seem at first gloss, a benefit to be gained from constant, low-intensity exposure and denunciation. The kinds of newspaper treatments of corruption that have appeared for decades in the press always involve relatively low ranking individuals and always involve bribery, embezzlement, poaching, and defrauding customers: the kinds of venality that arouse moral indignation at local officials without calling the system itself into question. These newspaper treatments are a form of ritual "degradation ceremony"[20] and can serve as check on popular discontentment with the regime: *someone*, at least, is being punished. It is worth noting the similarity of this to the nineteenth-century popular belief, fostered by the autocracy, that the sufferings and injustices of the peasants were the fault of local bureaucrats and that when the "little father tsar"—far away—learned of it, he would surely punish the guilty.

Shortcomings in the work of executive personnel are frequently blamed on hasty and perfunctory examination of candidates' credentials. As merely one example of many such cases, Boris Konoplev complained in 1985 at a plenum of the Perm *obkom*:

In the past two years, more than 600 people who had earlier been confirmed in executive positions by the *obkom* have been replaced; of this number, 44 were relieved of their duties for failure to provide leadership or for compromising themselves. During the same period, 312 officials who had been confirmed by city and district party committees were removed for improper actions. Blunders of this sort . . . have become possible because of haste in promoting future organizers. Genuine study of their political and business qualities has been replaced by a cursory look at data on questionnaires.[21]

Konoplev also mentioned the habit of Party committees of protecting their own: "The Perm, Kungur, and Solikamsk city and the Berezovka district Party committees are especially fond of taking guilty executives 'under their wing.' "[22]

By the same token, in Rostov-on-Don,

there are frequent instances in which the guilty official is transferred from one position to another, or he is taken under someone's wing and shielded from punishment. Thus, over a period of two years criminal cases against dozens of officials were dropped because local soviets would not consent to have them brought to trial.[23]

Or, again, in Lipetsk,

People are firmly convinced of the dubious notion that the main thing is to make your way to a leadership post by any means; once there, you can work in a slipshod manner and you'll be protected, no matter what. In fact, even those who systematically abuse their authority, such as N. Yakhontov, the former chairman of the Lipetsk City Soviet Executive Committee, are openly shifted from one leadership post to another. On the other hand, numerous complaints (about 3,000 have been received by central agencies to date) indicate that personnel who dare to "wash dirty linen in public" lose their jobs and have ridiculous accusations made against them.[24]

The creation and nurturing of protective "family circles" went the farthest of all in the Central Asian republics. Beginning in the Khrushchev period, Central Asian elites emerged as virtual patriarchs in their regions, enjoying unusually lengthy terms in office. These men were Sharaf Rashidov (Uzbekistan), Dinmukhamed Kunaev (Kazakhstan), Turdiakun Usubaliev (Kirgizia), Mukhamednazar Gapurov (Turkmenia), and Dzhabar Rasulov (Tadzhikistan). By 1982 all of them except Gapurov (who assumed office in 1969) had been in office more than 20 years. Kunaev and Rashidov attained Politburo membership. Gorbachev complained that the autonomy of these Central Asian patrimonial satrapies had gone so far that they were "outside government control."[25] Critchlow argues that the real goal of the massive crackdown on corruption in Central Asia since 1982 has been to "halt processes of decolonization and de-russification which have jeopardized central control ...to recapture maverick party and state organs in the republics from partial control by ethnic and local-interest networks."[26]

The seriousness of the problem in Central Asia is reflected in the massive scope of the purges that Gorbachev carried out there, especially in Uzbekistan. Virtually all *obkom* and city first secretaries have been replaced, and by the Twenty-seventh Party Congress, more than half the *nomenklatura* officials in all of Central Asia had been replaced.[27]

CLIENTELISM

Clientelism refers to the prevalence of patron-client relationships in the political system. A patron-client relationship is a *personal* relationship between two political figures (i.e., it is not accounted for in the official hierarchy). It involves a direct exchange of goods—support and/or influence—and most analysts of clientelism insist that it is unequal.[28] The exchange of influence among political equals would not be anything different from ordinary political interactions. In the Soviet system, political leaders develop a following (a "tail," *khvost'*) of individuals ranking lower than themselves; the patron assures the steady promotion of his clients; in return, they owe him political support and, no doubt, a variety of minor ingratiations. The time-honored way of weakening or destroying a high-ranking political figure is to whittle away at his "tail," to weaken his support.[29]

No political system escapes *some* clientelism. Systems can tolerate a small to moderate amount without serious distortion of the political process. Clientelism is pervasive in the underindustrialized countries of the Third World. Where it is present to a significant degree in industrialized countries, such as the Soviet Union and Japan,[30] the explanation, as I shall show below, is partly structural—in that it is endemic to sponsored mobility systems—and partly cultural. The feudal substructure of Soviet society provides a fertile ground for the development of clientelist practices. It is not just a characteristic of political life: any Soviet citizen today can describe at length the importance of "connections" (*svyazi*) and "patronage" (*protektsiia*) for simply getting along in daily life. The feudal substructure of Soviet society emphasizes personalized relationships of reciprocal advantage over the kinds of impersonal norms that characterize Western society in all walks of life from the most mundane (getting theater tickets, for example) to high politics. T. H.

Rigby proposes a suggestive analogy with the ubiquitous black market: "Can we view the 'second economy' of the Soviet Union as being matched by a 'second polity,' centering on clientelist relationships?"[31]

As a middle-range theoretical concept, the study of patron-client relationships and clientelism took off in the 1970s, and a vast comparative and theoretical literature has grown up.[32] Rene Lemarchand gives a detailed definition of clientelism which best captures, I think, the nuances of the concept:

Patron-client ties involve dyadic bonds between individuals of unequal power and socioeconomic status; they exhibit a diffuse, particularistic, face-to-face quality strongly reminiscent of ascriptive solidarities; unlike ascriptive ties, however, they are voluntarily entered into and derive their legitimacy from expectations of mutual benefits. Asymmetry, diffuseness, and reciprocality are basic features of the type of social structure that had become associated with political clientelism.[33]

Clientelism in politics has a long history. Factional politics in ancient Rome were based on a complex horizontal and vertical network of social dependencies and affinities of the heads of noble households (the *patria potestas*). Vertical networks were called *patrocinia* and constituted patron-client networks. Horizontally, household heads were embedded in alliances with persons of equal ranks called *amicitia* (factions). The political power of a patron depended on the scope and depth of his affiliations and his ability to utilize them.[34]

Patronage as a political form is an exchange relationship that is always associated with extreme maldistribution of wealth and political power, and a society predicated on the notion of ranked social order and fixed place. Indeed, it seems to be a means of preserving a skewed distribution system. Landed gentry in Latin America depended on patronage to maintain discipline and social order, the conditions necessary for their continued privilege. For the same reason, they encouraged patronage in government because this helped fix the social hierarchy.[35]

Patronage as an effective device for enforcing loyalty and obedience requires that the withholding of patronage have devastating consequences for disloyal clients—hence, its frequent association with conditions of economic scarcity, where clients living near the margin can expect to pay a substantial material price for incalcitrance. This is why both middle-level and lower-level Party apparatchiks in the Soviet system have a stake in continued economic inefficiency and scarcity. It is the condition for clients' access to privilege and for patrons' political power stemming from the ability to perpetuate dependencies. Scarcity is a structure that guarantees their continued power and privilege; under conditions of abundance elites would have to compete for both.

The effects of a high level of clientelism on a political system are largely and for the most part negative, for three reasons. Most seriously, perhaps, it clogs promotion channels and undermines the principle of merit promotion; this cannot help but raise the level of mediocrity in the elite. Secondly, it encourages corruption by engendering self-protective "family circles." Finally, and consequent in part to that, it discourages overall elite integration; an elite marked by the prevalence of cliques is a fragmented elite.

Clientelism has some marginally good aspects. It helps, perhaps, to a small extent to identify talented political beginners. It also helps middle-level elites to build a coalition and therefore promotes a sort of crypto-pluralism where genuine pluralism is lacking. Finally, its disintegrative aspects to some degree attenuate the power of the elite as a whole; arguably, a bad elite perhaps *should* be fragmented.

Soviet political leaders at the top—inveterate players of the patron-client game themselves—sometimes make an effort to combat clientelism in the middle ranks, when its practice tends to make regional Party organizations insulated from the center. This condition came about as an unintended consequence of the Brezhnev practice of promoting individuals within their own functional sector and within the same region. Although purges are one means of dealing with this problem, in the latter 1980s Gorbachev began deliberately assigning people across functional lines, and among regions. He also resorted to bringing individuals to the center for a while, and then "parachuting" them into regional party organizations. It is very common to find in the political biographies of regional Party leaders that they had served for a period of six months or so as an "instructor" in the Central Committee.

In spite of the best efforts of reformers, however, patron-client ties remain remarkably persistent across institutional and geographical lines; in fact, their cross-institutional nature is one of the main advantages of clientelism, especially for clients. Clientelism depends on an individual patron's ability to intervene downward across layers of hierarchy and substantially limit the autonomy of other selectors. A non-Weberian bureaucratic structure, in which jurisdictions are vaguely delineated and formal and impersonal norms are weak, is certain to be a fertile soil for clientelistic practices to take root and grow.

Although political clientelism arose, for reasons I have discussed in Chapter 4, in the regional apparatus shortly after the revolution, at the level of the top leadership, it was Stalin who began the use of patronage to consolidate and keep his position. Lenin's authority and prestige was such that apparently he did not need to use it. According to Rigby:

Patronage was not a serious factor in Lenin's leadership at all. . . . [The] factor of self-serving calculation seems to have played little part in Lenin's relations with his followers. They were attracted to him because of his ideas, his policies, his methods, his dynamism—but not by expectations of personal advantage. Nor did *he* play the patronage boss, seeking to bind men to him by giving them preferential treatment.[36]

There were at least five factors or conditions that predisposed to the development of clientelism in earliest days of the revolution:

1. In the years preceding the revolution, local organizations and individuals in the underground certainly did develop fierce friendships and personal attachments, as well as, to be sure, animosities. These formed the nuclei of factional and friendship groupings after the seizure of power.

2. There was a natural tendency to appoint, and to seek out for appointment, people who were known and trusted. This meant appointing one's friends and former associates.

3. The conditions of work in regional party organizations also contributed to clientelism. Insufficient supplies and help, poor communications with the center, ambiguous and insufficient instructions—all these factors left local organizations to rely to a considerable degree on their own devices and on one another.

4. Because of the scarcity of resources, it was necessary often to circumvent or violate rules. Thus officials in the periphery became enmeshed in local conspiracies of corruption and malfeasance, which binded them together. There was a tendency toward corruption, too, in that because of general economic scarcity, Party membership and office carried advantages in acquiring the necessities of life.

5. The hostility of local populations to the Communists caused the latter to form self-protective supportive groups.

All of this took place entirely apart from formation of cliques on the basis of principle or factions centered around prominent people at the center. The Tenth Party Congress ostensibly banned factions and cliques, but they continued at the lower levels. Factional politics, of course, continued at the top, and numerous lower-level officials identified with one or another of these top men, but this was based on agreement with policy stances rather than on personal loyalties. In the course of the 1920s Stalin succeeded in coloring factional politics as left or right "deviations" from the general line, which, of course, was always *his* line.

At the same time, Josef Stalin himself was using clientelism to place his own men in strategic positions throughout the apparatus. By 1921 Stalin and Lazar Kaganovich were firmly in control of personnel assignment, however spotty and incomplete their records may have been. The practice was to move a Stalin supporter into an *oblast* (then still called a *guberniia*), whose first task would be to purge the local apparatus of members of the old clique. A good example of this was A. I. Mikoyan's experience in Nizhnii Novgorod.

Mikoyan was sent there in October 1920 to replace Vyacheslav Molotov, who had failed in his efforts to control the localist, working-class, Old Bolshevik clique that dominated the *guberniia* party committee (*gubkom*), consisting of sympathizers with the Workers' Opposition. Mikoyan relates in his memoirs that he presented himself to the secretary of the *gubkom*, Ivan Kremnitskii, and showed him his orders from the Central Committee assigning him to work in the Presidium of the Nizhnii Novgorod *gubkom*: "Kremnitskii greeted me and quietly explained that a plenum of the *gubkom* had abolished the post of chairman of the *gubkom* and created in its place a *gubkom* bureau, whose secretary was he, Kremnitskii, and that all the posts in the *gubkom* bureau were filled."[37]

Mikoyan states that the Nizhnii Novgorod Communists did not want a worker from the center in their midst, but they also did not want to directly violate a Central Committee decision, so they carried out an "organizational restructuring," easy enough to do in those days because there was no standard structure for local party organizations. Mikoyan told Kremnitskii—to the latter's surprise—that he would take any party position available, but that under no circumstances would he simply leave.[38] The *gubkom* met a week later and voted time after time, 10 to 2,[39] against providing him with a position. In the ensuing weeks he was treated most inhospitably; the Nizhnii Novgorod Communists regarded him as an "appointed general" (*naznachennyi general*) sent to "lord it over them" (*verkhovodit'*).[40] "Appointmentism" (*naznachestvo*) was a pejorative term local Party organizations used to refer to the Central Committee's growing practice of appointing people to local Party leadership bodies, arrogating their democratic right to elect their own leaders.

Finally, Mikoyan was given a post in the presidium of the *gubispolkom* and loaded down with detailed work in the hope that he would give up and leave. From that time until he became a Central Committee secretary in 1922, Mikoyan worked diligently to defeat the Workers' Opposition faction, and the smaller Trotskyist faction, in Nizhnii Novgorod. He recounts his surprise and dismay when, at the eleventh *guberniia* Party conference, Andreev showed up at the conference and came out in support of the Trotskyist platform.[41]

Another indication of lively patron-client politics in the Stalin period is given by N. S. Patolichev. Patolichev gives the distinct impression that he owed his advancement more to Andreev than to Stalin, and that Andreev had a fairly extensive clientele.[42] Stalin, in his disengenuous way, in his speech to the February-March 1937 Central Committee plenum, castigated certain party leaders transferred from one region to another for having dragged along their proteges.[43]

On the basis of all the foregoing, I suggest at least three general factors that explain the prevalence of clientelism in the Soviet Union:

1. Feudal remnants, analogous to the "residuary" category of corruption. I hesitate to use a term that is so resonant of Soviet ideological writings, but it is apt. The feudal substructure of the society persisted, as I have argued repeatedly, well beyond the revolution, and personalized patriarchal or patrimonial political relationships were woven into this substructure. Daniel Orlovsky states:

   > In prerevolutionary Russia (and in Muscovy) dyadic relations and larger networks or clienteles had their roots in the clan-based, highly personalized political culture of the Muscovite court and bureaucracy. In Russian history we may find the origin of not simply the domination of the "personal" over the "institutional," or the "legal," but of what might be more aptly seen as the institutionalization of the personal within a variety of political and legal structures.[44]

2. Structural characteristics of the Soviet system. The most important of these is the *nomenklatura* system. Where the *nomenklatura* right is located, with Party Committee first secretaries at all levels of the hierarchy, there is a node at which patron-client networks are almost guaranteed to sprout. With the right of appointing virtually anyone he chooses to subordinate positions, the temptation for the first secretary to appoint people whom he knows, likes, trusts, and has worked with in the past must be overwhelming.

3. Conditions of work in the Soviet system. These include endemic insecurity of tenure for officials (not always prevalent), lack of institutional protection for officials who fall out of favor with their superiors, and chronic resource shortages.

Another factor, suggested by S. N. Eisenstadt and L. Roniger, might be the closed nature of the Soviet elite and the fact that the social uncertainty that characterizes Soviet society encourages interpersonal relationships and sponsorship within the bureaucracy.[45]

Clientelism is so pervasive in the Soviet political system that it is doubtful that a person could get to the top of the Soviet elite, that is, into the Central Committee, without some help along the way. Unless an extraordinary degree of personal autonomous power is assumed for individual members of the elite, it is likely that *all* Central Committee members (except the nominal ones) are members of patron-client networks. A top leader in the Soviet Union does not have the advantage—unlike Western presidents and prime ministers—of being able to create his own cabinet and top-level aides. It takes time for a new Soviet leader to remove top-level people he cannot work with and to bring in his own reliable people.[46]

John Willerton studied patronage networks in the Brezhnev period, identifying Politburo and Secretariat members as potential patrons, and members of the Central Committee and Central Auditing Commission as potential clients. His criteria for identifying a potential network were that two political figures worked together at the same time in the same locale on at least two occasions, and that there were at least two occasions when an interrelationship could be shown in their careers, that is, two career promotions under the patron's supervision. In addition, common military experience or educational experiences were considered indicators of a possible link.[47]

As Willerton points out, the Brezhnev governing coalition included not just Brezhnev's personal following but a network of interconnected patron-client systems, bridged by personal alliances, which lent stability to the personnel system and permitted the enactment of a coherent policy program.[48] Over 30 members of the Central Committee and Central Auditing Commission at the end of the 1970s have been identified as members of Brezhnev's Dnepropetrovsk clientele.[49] Joel Moses found that some 75 percent of Brezhnev's proteges from Dnepropetrovsk were promoted beyond the Ukraine, compared with only about 18 percent of Podgorny's clients from Lvov and Kharkov.[50] Willerton identified five networks at the Politburo and Central Committee level that influenced elite politics:

(1) the Brezhnev network, at the heart of which was the so-called "Dnepropetrovsk mafia"; (2) the Suslov-Pel'she-Ponomarev group, headed by the long-time party *eminence grise*; (3) a Khar'kov (Ukrainian) group, headed by Nikolai Podgorny and including Vitalii Titov and Petr Shelest; (4) a Belorussian group, forged during the Second World War and headed by Kirill Mazurov, while including Petr Masherov and Mikhail Zimyanin; and (5) a Moscow-based group, headed by Ivan Kapitonov and including Viktor Grishin and Petr Demichev.[51]

Jerry Hough also found an enhanced rate of mobility for officials that had been associated with Kirill Mazurov in Belorussia, with Aleksey Kosygin in Leningrad, and with Nikolai Podgorny in Kharkov.[52] Similarly, on the basis of a close examination of political biographies, looking for past associations, Gyula Jozsa provides a list of likely and possible clients of 20 top-ranking leaders as of 1981.[53]

Critchlow, in the article cited above with respect to corruption, also remarked of the Central Asian first secretaries in the 1960s and 1970s that their long tenure "enabled them to put their personal stamp on the republican machinery as in a fiefdom, appointing their followers to senior posts at republican, oblast, and raion levels."[54]

William Clark believes that the clientelist model is outdated: "Put succinctly, to the degree that Sovietologists have correctly abandoned the totalitarian assumptions of an outdated paradigm, the idiosyncratic and personalistic elements of patron-client explanations are becoming increasingly anachronistic and invalid for a larger percentage of the *nomenklatura*."[55]

Clark argues that patron-client relationships exist "only by being superimposed upon a rational-technical system that over the long run colors the climate of expectations and affects the 'career chances' of elites."[56] The difficulty with this argument is that this is not the way clientelism comes about, at least not in the Soviet Union, as I have argued above. As the system modernizes and democratizes, no doubt clientelism will correspondingly decrease, but it is stupifying to read a statement that the clientelist model is "anachronistic" within such short memory of Brezhnev's Dnepropetrovsk Mafia and the play of factional rivalries in the extended succession to Brezhnev.

Even if, as Philip Stewart and his coauthors showed might be the case, rational-technical criteria, most especially performance, are increasingly important in recruitment and promotion of political elites.[57] Even if, as is altogether likely, its importance continues to increase, it is likely that clientelism will also remain important. William Reissinger and John Willerton believe that it will remain decisive:

In this context, rational-technical criteria may be of importance, yet the decisive factor would involve an aspirant's "connections" with the selectorate power elite. These connections, or patronage linkages, are often the necessary condition for recruitment because they assure the best prospects for political reliability in a subordinate.[58]

Mikhail Voslensky, in a recent series of interviews, while not denying that patronage and clientelism are pervasive and important, expressed skepticism about Western approaches to the study of patron-client groups:

Very often this principle [career biographies] is considered . . . a bit formalistically. "They worked together on the same part committee. Aha!" But maybe they were enemies. Also . . . being promoted by a certain person is insufficient by itself as a criterion for establishing factional affiliation. For instance: Ligachev, Ryzhkov, Vorotnikov, and Solomentsev all came from the *apparat* of the RSFSR and they had at one time or another been promoted by Kirilenko. However, Kirilenko was an organizational secretary. . . . So if everybody has been promoted by Kirilenko, it does not mean that all of them had been picked up by Kirilenko personally.[59]

EXECUTIVE STYLE

Scott emphasizes that corruption is only one manifestation of "bureaucratic self-serving." Other manifestations are an emphasis on status and rank rather than productivity and achievement; ritualization of procedures: paperwork and routine as an end, not a means; the absence of commitment to policy objectives; and failure to monitor the implementation of decisions.[60] All these are matters of "style," a term I choose because it covers undesirable actions or characteristics of leaders that do not fall into the category of corruption, malfeasance, or even, necessarily, incompetence. As much as, and perhaps more than, corruption, style is a subject of constant exhortation.

The flavor of this concern is well captured in a *Pravda* editorial entitled, appropriately enough, "Improve the Style of Work":

Improving Party agencies' style of work is closely connected with the comprehensive development of collective decision making. However, such decision making has nothing to do with meeting-mania, endless discussion of clear-cut questions, and needless paperwork. We must rebuff freeloading and localism and reject attempts to cover up errors in work with the well-known ploy of claiming "objective reasons." Instances in which desired results are passed off as the real thing are particularly intolerable.[61]

At the very top of the hierarchy, the general secretary sets the tone for his administration. Of the many unsatisfactory aspects of Nikita Khrushchev's leadership, style was not the least.[62] Khrushchev's ouster was followed by energetic demands for a return to a Leninist style of leadership. Khrushchev was coarse and crude in his public statements, and he was given to theatrics that, at least as far as is colleagues were concerned, embarrassed the Soviet Union. The *Pravda* article announcing his forced retirement attributed to him "hare-brained scheming, hasty conclusions, and rash decisions and actions based on wishful thinking, boasting, and empty words."[63]

Infractions under the rubric "style and methods of leadership" should be conceptually distinct from those under the category "corruption," although they sometimes shade into one another. Ineptitude, incompetence, "serious shortcomings," insensitivity, bureaucratic "formalism," drunkenness, even some kinds of petty abuse of position such as favoritism and nepotism are certainly grounds for censure and demotion, but unlike more serious occasions of corruption they are not *criminal* activities. Almost always, though, in the ritual degradations in the Soviet press reporting and condemning instances of official venality, accusations of the former are tacked on to more serious accusations. Vladimir Shcherbitskii reported in a *Pravda* interview in 1984, for example, that the deputy chief of the Ukrainian Civil Aviation Administration had been dismissed from his post and from the Party for "abusing his position, and unseemly conduct."[64] One is inclined to wonder whether either transgression alone would have resulted in his dismissal. In fact, the pattern of these degradations is that the transgression that led to the leader's demotion of firing is listed first, and then every other accusation that can be thought of to bring against him is added. This is why I classify these announcements as "degradation ceremonies," rather than as routine announcements of a leader's dismissal along with the reason for it.

A constantly recurring theme in Party press discussions of leadership style is the distinction between "political" and "administrative" methods, or styles, of leadership. The former is much preferred, while the latter universally criticized. Specialists brought into party leadership positions are sometimes criticized for their "administrative methods" and "insensitivity." This has begun to be called "micromanagement" in the West, that is, rather than general oversight and supervision of organizations within the Party official's jurisdiction, actually performing tasks or making decisions *for* that organization. This stifles initiative and responsibility on the part of the organizations or enterprises in question.[65]

Although not involving a political leader, a most interesting instance of this occurred in late 1985 at the Irbit Chemical-Pharmaceutical Plant in Sverdlovsk *oblast*. *Pravda* reported that a shop chief, Vadim Bakharov, noted for his initiative and efficiency, but also for a nature that is "not as smooth as honey," was removed by the plant director from his post and censured, indeed recommended to be dropped from CPSU membership, by the plant's Party bureau. Among the accusations against him was that he exhibited an "autocratic management style." In fact, his dismissal, at least according to *Pravda's* reporter, was the result of a concerted smear campaign on the part of individuals in the plant who believed that they had been harmed by Bakharov's highhandedness. After a series of investigations and appeals that went as high as the *obkom* first secretary, he was ordered reinstated in his position with back pay, although in the end he was not reinstated.[66]

Another aspect of "administrative methods" is excessive bureaucracy. The term "bureaucracy" is never used in Soviet commentary in a neutral way to refer to the structure of an organization—the term "apparatus" is generally used in this meaning. The term "bureaucracy" in the Soviet context is similar to its pejorative use elsewhere to refer to officials who place greater emphasis on paperwork, minute attention to petty details, formalistic application of rules, and the personal or career interests of the bureaucrat himself than on service to clientele or fulfillment of the organization's broader missions. Bureaucracy is, in the words of a *Pravda* editorial,

A fierce obstacle to broad participation by the popular masses in the affairs of management. It fetters lively ideas, encourages indifference, and produces paper necessary to no one. The creation of paperwork must be decisively and persistently eradicated. The task lies in working not with paper but with people, and knowing and taking into account how they work and live, what they think about, and what their problems and attitudes are.[67]

Similar to "administrative methods" is the "technocratic approach." This appears from time to time in the pronouncements of top leaders; Gorbachev, for example, told a conference of republican and provincial Party leaders that it was necessary to "dispense with the technocratic approach to solving political and social problems."[68] The term "technocracy," as discussed in a previous chapter, is always used in a pejorative sense, although its reference has changed over time. In recent decades it has referred to a narrowly technical kind of high-handed social engineering, without regard to nonmaterial human needs or the social and political consequences of administrative action and practices.

Discussions of the necessity for a new style of leadership began before Brezhnev died. In the fall of 1982 *Izvestia* published an article calling for *glasnost'* and praising Pavel Artemovich Leonov, then first secretary of Kalinin *obkom*, for his style of "open leadership." The *obkom* had recently begun to

establish a style of work characterized by frank discussion, openness, and truthful information on all matters. The tone is set by . . . [Leonov, who] wants people to raise the most urgent, difficult and tricky problems. He answers them honestly and openly, being convinced that one doesn't win trust by silence, equivocation or evasion.[69]

Gorbachev's brief and unpopular antialcohol campaign of 1985–86 was aimed as much or more at Party leaders and administrators as at the masses. The Central Committee passed a resolution enjoining Party and Soviet officials to "eradicate drunkenness, fight resolutely against harmful traditions and customs, and set an example in establishing a sober way of life."[70] On recommendation of the CPSU Party Control Committee, a number of Party and Soviet officials were stripped of their positions and expelled from the party for abuses as seemingly innocuous as serving alcoholic beverages at a supper organized *after* a *raikom* meeting.[71]

The language of official announcements of disciplinary action against leaders is often vague; the most common reasons given for dismissal of managers and lower-level party executives are "serious shortcomings in his work"—which would seem to refer to technical incompetence—and variations on shortcomings of character such as "having compromised himself" (probably, it is my sense, by public drunkenness, accepting bribes, or turning a blind eye to transgressions on the part of subordinates), "un-Partylike behavior," or "abuse of powers." Collectively, such failings are often subsumed under the bland euphemism "negative phenomena." The language of newspaper reporters is more colorful: "Toadying, obsequiousness, and hypocrisy before the 'powers that be' bloomed like a luxuriant poisonous flower. At the same time, Khan-like manners and overblown conceit with regard to 'underlings' flourished as well."[72]

Cited in Krasnodar were "abuse of office, favoritism, careerism, subjectivism and favoritism in promotions, report-padding, hoodwinking and embezzlement, disrespectful attitude toward subordinates, windbaggery, and windowdressing."[73]

Faults of elites relating to style, and frequently denounced publicly in journalistic ritual degradation ceremonies, include toadyism (*podkhalimstvo*), ingratiation (*ugodnichestvo*), political myopia (*politicheskaia blizorukost'*), indifference (*bezpechnost'*), parading (*paradnost'*), "eyewash" (*ochkovtiratel'stvo*), slovenliness (*razgil'diaistvo*), loafing (*rotozeikstvo*), and formalism (*formalizm*).

Concern for the moral and emotional health of executives has been expressed as well. The soulless, compulsive day-and-night workaholic of the past is criticized; one author urges that executives need to learn how to relax:

We need to learn about relaxation from Lenin. We can see this in his letters to his relatives and comrades-in-arms. In many of them he tells of long walks and bicycle rides, ice skating, theater productions, books he was reading, get-togethers, acquaintances, etc. Even during the most tense times of decisive revolutionary activities, Vladimir Ilyich went hunting and listened to Beethoven's "Moonlight Sonata."[74]

During the Gorbachev period, but in fact as early as the last years of Brezhnev's life, the Soviet media and propaganda organizations have strived to present in various media the image of the new Party executive, contrasting him with the old, discredited type. This did not always meet with approval; a review in *Pravda* in 1982 criticized a number of novelists for portraying "old guard" leaders as backward, "self-willed feudal lords."[75]

A play by Aleksandr Misharin entitled *Four Times Bigger than France* (*Ravniaetsia chetyrem Frantsiiam*), performed in 1982 simultaneously in two separate theaters, deliberately contrasted the old type of party executive with the new. The hero is Shakhmatov, *kraikom* first secretary of a *krai* "four times as large as France." Contrasted with him is Serebrennikov, a secretary of the same *kraikom*. The reviewer writes:

It seems to me that the character of Shakhmatov is interesting because first of all he depicts the new type of party executive that has appeared in the last few years. He is a scholar, a prominent and talented engineer, a solid person.... The image of Shakhmatov as party *kraikom* executive is that of an outstanding member of the Soviet intelligentsia, a person with a complex *persona*. He is an educated man with a doctorate, knows three languages, has the intellectual's trait of independent thought and distrust of stereotypes, and shuns any diminishment of human dignity.[76]

Serebrennikov is but a subtle contrast. He is an experienced and respected party official of the era of "strong-willed leadership," that is, of
the late Stalin period. He is energetic and unselfish, but all aspects of
his manner betray a man "who once moved time . . . but has since come
into conflict with it."[77] The climactic scene of the play involves a ship
that runs into trouble at sea. Serebrennikov, who, it is hinted, is responsible for the ship's poor preparation for the journey, orders the
captain to send out an SOS. Shakhmatov counters the order, since it is
up to the captain himself to decide whether to do so. The virtues this
act represents are decidedly modern: a faith in people and in progress,
and especially the encouragement of independence, initiative, and responsibility on the part of people on the job.

A novel by Georgii Markov, at the time of its publication the first
Secretary of the USSR Writers' Union, entitled *To the Oncoming Age*
(*Griadushchemu veku*, Moscow, 1981) was reissued and given a television
reading in May 1985. The hero of the novel, Sobolev—an *obkom* first
secretary in a fictional Siberian *oblast*—presented, according to Soviet
reviewers, "a vivid portrait of our contemporary, the outstanding Party
leader."[78] Oddly enough, the same fictional Party leader, Sobolev, reappeared in another work by Markov (in collaboration with Eduard Shim),
a play entitled *From Today's News* (*Iz novostei etogo dnia*), published in *Novy
mir*.[79] Anton Sobolev is portrayed quite a bit larger than life, in the
tradition of Stalinist socialist realism, but this time with preferred modern traits: he is efficient, committed to economic and political reform,
unostentatious, genuinely democratic (travels about Sinegorsk, his city,
by public transport rather than private car), is familiar with the latest
industrial technology, cosmopolitan in taste (Scotch rather than vodka),
has extensive knowledge of and contacts with the West while retaining
his Soviet *and Russian* patriotism—he is familiar with scriptures and with
nineteenth-century and 1920s literature and poetry. He is so "close to
the earth," in fact, that he recalls having eaten a handful of Sinegorsk
soil to prove his love for his bride.

NOTES

1. James C. Scott, *Comparative Political Corruption* (Englewood Cliffs, NJ:
Prentice-Hall, 1972), p. 2.

2. Gyula Jozsa, "Political *Seilschaften* in the USSR," in T. H. Rigby and Bohdan Harasymiw, eds., *Leadership Selection and Patron-Client Relations in the USSR
and Yugoslavia* (London: Allen & Unwin, 1983), pp. 139–73.

3. Gaetano Mosca, *The Ruling Class* (New York: McGraw-Hill, 1939),
pp. 408–9.

4. Scott, *Comparative Political Corruption*, p. 4; Scott attributes the sense of the
definition to J. S. Nye, "Corruption and Political Development: A Cost-Benefit
Analysis," *American Political Science Review* 61, no. 2 (June 1967): 416.

5. Arnold J. Heidenheimer, "Introduction," in Arnold J. Heidenheimer, Michael Johnsston, and Victor T. LeVine, eds., *Political Corruption: A Handbook* (New Brunswick, NJ: Transaction Books, 1989), p. 5.

6. On the overlap between patronage and corruption, see Edward Van Roy, "On the Theory of Corruption," *Economic Development and Cultural Change* 19 (October 1979):86–110.

7. Marvin Zonis, *The Political Elite of Iran* (Princeton, NJ: Princeton University Press, 1971), pp. 66–67.

8. Kenneth Jowitt, "An Organizational Approach to the Study of Political Culture in Marxist-Leninist Regimes," *American Political Science Review* 67, no. 3 (September 1974):1171–91.

9. Marcel Mauss, *The Gift: Forms and Functions of Exchange in Archaic Societies* (New York: W. W. Norton, 1967).

10. Edward C. Banfield, *The Moral Basis of a Backward Society* (New York: Free Press, 1958), p. 83.

11. Scott, *Comparative Political Corruption*, p. 12.

12. Zygmunt Bauman, "Comment on Eastern Europe," *Studies in Comparative Communism* 12, nos. 2–3 (1979):184–89.

13. John M. Kramer, "Political Corruption in the USSR," *Western Political Quarterly* 30, no. 2 (June 1977):213–24; the citation here is from the reprint of the article in Heidenheimer, Johnsston, and LeVine, *Political Corruption*, pp. 453–54. James Critchlow makes a similar observation: " 'Corruption,' Nationalism, and the Native Elites in Soviet Central Asia," *Journal of Communist Studies* 4, no. 2 (1988):144.

14. John Waterbury, "Endemic and Planned Corruption in the Monarchical Regime," *World Politics* 25, no. 4 (July 1973):533–55; in Heidenheimer, Johnsston, and LeVine, *Political Corruption*, p. 340.

15. Ibid.

16. On the thesis that corruption can perform important functions that the political system fails to perform, see David Bayley, "The Effects of Corruption in a Developing Country," *Western Political Quarterly*, no. 19 (December 1966):719–32; Nye, "Corruption and Political Development," pp. 448–57; Gabriel Bendor, "Corruption, Institutionalization, and Political Development: The Revisionist Theses Revisited," *Comparative Political Studies*, no. 7 (April 1974):63–83.

17. Critchlow, " 'Corruption' Nationalism, and Native Elite," p. 144.

18. Michael Urban, "Centralization and Elite Circulation in a Soviet Republic," *British Journal of Political Science*, no. 19 (1989):1.

19. Merle Fainsod, *Smolensk under Soviet Rule* (Cambridge, MA: Harvard University Press, 1958), p. 85.

20. Harold Garfinkel, "Conditions of Successful Degradation Ceremonies," *American Journal of Sociology* 61, no. 5 (March 1956):420–24.

21. *Pravda*, March 28, 1985, p. 2.

22. Ibid.

23. *Pravda*, June 9, 1984, p. 2; *Current Digest of the Soviet Press* (*CDSP* hereafter), no. 23 (July 4, 1984):19.

24. *Pravda*, December 11, 1983, p. 2.

25. *Pravda*, January 13, 1988.

26. Critchlow, " 'Corruption,' Nationalism, and Native Elites," p. 142.

27. Ibid., pp. 146–47. Other important works on official corruption in the USSR include Konstantin Simis, *USSR: Secrets of a Corrupt Society* (London: J. M. Dent & Sons, 1982); Ilya Zemtsov, *La corruption en Union Sovietique* (Paris: Hachette, 1976); Ilya Zemtsov, *Partiia ili mafiia: razvorovannaia respublika* (Paris: Les Editeurs Reunis, 1976).

28. See S. N. Eisenstadt and L. Roniger, "Patron-Client Relationships as a Model of Structuring Social Exchange," *Comparative Studies of Society and History* 22, no. 1 (1980):42–77.

29. A classic example of this is Brezhnev's destruction of Podgorny's political base in Kharkov. See Michel Tatu, *Power in the Kremlin: From Khrushchev to Kosygin* (New York: Viking Press, 1970), pp. 500–502.

30. See Shugo Minagawa, "Political Clientelism in the USSR and Japan: A Tentative Comparison," in Rigby and Harasymiw, *Leadership Selection and Patron-Client Relations*, pp. 200–228.

31. T. H. Rigby, "Early Provincial Cliques and the Rise of Stalin," *Soviet Studies* 33, no. 1 (January 1981):4.

32. Representative studies on clientelism include N. Abercrombie and S. Hill, "Paternalism and Patronage," *British Journal of Sociology* 27, no. 4 (1976):413–29; J. Boissevain, *Friends of Friends: Networks, Manipulators, and Coalitions* (Oxford: Basil Blackwell, 1974); Luigi Graziano, "A Conceptual Framework for the Study of Clientelistic Behavior," *European Journal of Political Research*, no. 4, (1976):149–74; Ghita Ionescu, "Patronage under Communism," in Ernest Gellner and John Waterbury, eds., *Patrons and Clients in Mediterranean Countries* (n.p.: Duckworth, 1977), pp. 97–102; Robert P. Kaufman, "The Patron-Client Concept and Macropolitics: Prospects and Problems," *Comparative Studies in Society and History* 16, no. 3 (June 1974):284–308; Keith Legg, "Interpersonal Relationships and Comparative Politics: Political Clientelism in Industrial Society," *Politics* (Australia) 7, no. 1 (1972):1–11; Keith Legg, *Patrons, Clients, and Politicians: New Perspectives on Political Clientelism* (Berkeley: University of California, Institute of International Studies, Working Papers on Development no. 3, n.d.); Rene Lemarchand and Keith Legg, "Political Clientelism and Development: A Preliminary Analysis," *Comparative Politics* 4, no. 2 (1972):149–78; J. H. Oliver, "Turnover and 'Family Circles' in Soviet Administration," *Slavic Review* 32, no. 3 (1973):527–45; T. H. Rigby, "The Need for Comparative Research on Clientelism," *Studies in Comparative Communism* 12, nos. 1–2 (Summer-Autumn 1979):204–11; John F. Willerton, "Clientelism in the Soviet Union: An Initial Examination," *Studies in Comparative Communism* 7, nos. 2–3 (1979):159–83; E. R. Wolf, "Kinship, Friendship, and Patron-Client Relationships in Complex Societies," in M. Banton, ed., *The Social Anthropology of Complex Societies* (London: Tavistock, ASA Monographs, 1966), vol. 4, pp. 1–22.

33. Rene Lemarchand, "Comparative Political Clientelism: Structure, Process, and Optic," in S. N. Eisenstadt and Rene Lemarchand, eds., *Political Clientelism, Patronage, and Development* (Beverly Hills, CA: Sage Publications, 1981), p. 15.

34. Horst Hutter, *Politics as Friendship: The Origins of Classical Notions of Politics in the Theory and Practice of Friendship* (Waterloo, Ontario: Wilfrid Laurier University Press, 1978), p. 35. On clientelist politics in the classical world, also see Lily Ross Taylor, *Party Politics in the Age of Caesar* (Berkeley: University of Cal-

ifornia Press, 1949), especially Chap. 2; and W. Robert Connor, *The New Politicians of Fifth-Century Athens* (Princeton, NJ: Princeton University Press, 1971), especially Chaps. 1 and 2.

35. Richard Graham, *Patronage and Politics in Nineteenth Century Brazil* (Stanford, CA: Stanford University Press, 1990), p. 42.

36. T. H. Rigby, "Political Patronage in the USSR from Lenin to Brezhnev," *Politics* (Australia) 18, no. 1 (1983): 87.

37. A. I. Mikoyan, *V nachale dvadtsatykh* . . . (Moscow: Izdatel'stvo politicheskoi literatury, 1975), p. 27.

38. Ibid., pp. 27–28.

39. His supporters were Taganov and Ikonnikov; four of his opponents were Chelyshev, Khanov, Khramov, and Vorob'ev. The other four are not named. See Ibid., p. 31.

40. Ibid., p. 32.

41. Ibid., pp. 73–74. Andreev later rued of this in his memoirs, as Mikoyan, *V nachale dvadtsatykh*, reports on p. 74n.

42. N. S. Patolichev, *Ispytanie na zrelost'* (Moscow, 1977), p. 42.

43. I. V. Stalin, *Socheneniia*, ed. Robert H. McNeal (Stanford, CA: Stanford University Press, 1967), vol. 1 (14), pp. 230–31.

44. Daniel T. Orlovsky, "Political Clientelism in Russia: The Historical Perspective," in Rigby and Harasymiw, *Leadership Selection and Patron-Client Relations*, p. 178.

45. S. N. Eisenstadt and L. Roniger, *Patrons, Clients, and Friends: Interpersonal Relations and the Structure of Trust in Society* (Cambridge: Cambridge University Press, 1984), p. 158.

46. John P. Willerton, Jr. "Patronage Networks and Coalition Building in the Brezhnev Era," *Soviet Studies* 39, no. 2 (April 1987): 175.

47. Ibid., pp. 177–78.

48. Ibid., p. 176.

49. Ibid., p. 183.

50. Joel C. Moses, "Regional Cohorts and Political Mobility in the USSR: The Case of Dnepropetrovsk," *Soviet Union* 3, no. 1 (1976):82.

51. Willerton, "Patronage Networks," p. 183.

52. Jerry F. Hough and Merle Fainsod, *How the Soviet Union Is Governed* (Cambridge, MA: Harvard University Press, 1979), p. 540.

53. Gyula Jozsa, "Political *Seilschaften* in the USSR," in Rigby and Harasymiw, *Leadership Selection and Patron-Client Relations*, pp. 151–52.

54. Critchlow, " 'Corruption,' Nationalism, and Native Elites," pp. 145–46.

55. William A. Clark, *Soviet Regional Elite Mobility after Khrushchev* (New York: Praeger, 1989), p. 17.

56. Ibid., p. 18.

57. Philip D. Stewart et al., "Political Mobility and the Soviet Political Process: A Partial Test of Two Models," *American Political Science Review* 66, no. 4 (December 1972):1269–94.

58. William M. Reisinger and John P. Willerton, Jr., "Elite Mobility in the Locales: Towards a Modified Patronage Model," in David Lane, ed., *Elites and Political Power in the USSR* (Aldershot, Hants, England: Edward Elgar, 1988), pp. 99–126.

59. Uri Ra'anan and Igor Lukes, *Inside the Apparat: Perspectives on the Soviet Union from Former Functionaries* (Lexington, MA: D. C. Heath, 1990), p. 21. It should be noted, however, that all analysts of patron-client relationships in the USSR are conscious of and explicit in their recognition of these and other limitations.

60. Scott, *Comparative Political Corruption*, p. 78.

61. *Pravda*, January 29, 1983, p. 1; translation in *CDSP* 35, no. 4 (February 5, 1983):4.

62. Jerome M. Gillison, "New Factors of Stability in Soviet Collective Leadership," *World Politics* 19 (1967):568.

63. *Pravda*, 17 October 1964, p. 5.

64. *Pravda*, August 5, 1984.

65. *Pravda*, June 25, 1986, p. 1.

66. *Pravda*, April 20, 1986.

67. Ibid.

68. *Pravda*, October 24, 1986, p. 1; *CDSP* 38, no. 43 (November 26, 1986):21.

69. *Izvestia*, September 18, 1982, p. 3; *CDSP* 34, no. 38 (September 19, 1982):9.

70. *Pravda*, March 14, 1986.

71. *Pravda*, March 14, 1986.

72. *Pravda*, October 24, 1986, p. 3; *CDSP* 38, no. 43 (November 26, 1986):2.

73. *Pravda*, April 1, 1985, p. 2; *CDSP* 37, no. 13, (April 24, 1985):16.

74. V. A. Bobkov, "Partiinie kadry: opyt, problemy, suzhdenie," *Voprosy istorii KPSS*, no. 5 (May 1987):21.

75. *Pravda*, July 5, 1982, p. 7; *CDSP* 34, 27 (August 4, 1982):9, 13.

76. Feliks Kuznetsov, *Literaturnaia gazeta*, December 8, 1982, p. 8.

77. Ibid., p. 8.

78. Editorial, *Literaturnaia gazeta*, no. 28, 1985, p. 8.

79. *Novy mir*, no. 7 (July 1985):102–331.

Chapter 8

Iron Teeth:
The Gorbachev Transformation

We *will* grow up!

James M. Barrie
Peter Pan

In perhaps his most quoted passage, Alexis de Tocqueville writes that "the most perilous moment for a bad government is one when it seeks to mend its ways."[1] Tocqueville's comments, written more than 135 years ago, have more than a little import for the situation Gorbachev finds himself in today. Relatively sudden decompression—the abolition of censorship, the lifting of controls on voluntary associations, and the partial legalization of private enterprise—have made the country more, not less, difficult to govern and have raised expectations beyond the regime's ability to satisfy them.

Russian and Soviet history does not bode well for would-be reformers. Alexander Yanov observes that all 14 of the major reformist attempts since the 1550s have ended either in "reversal by a counter-reform" or have "faded into political stagnation."[2] This is true as far as reforms per se go, but leaders outstanding for their energy and ruthlessness—Ivan the Terrible, Peter the Great, Catherine the Great, and Josef Stalin (who compared himself to Ivan the Terrible)—have *transformed* the country, for better or for worse.

In this final chapter, I will examine the process of the succession to Leonid Brezhnev, Mikhail Gorbachev's ongoing effort to shape an elite congenial to his reformist goals (and in the process effecting a transformation of the elite), and the prospects for the emergence of genuine strategic elites.

THE POLITICS OF THE EXTENDED SUCCESSION

As Brezhnev's life and career drew to a close, so, with equal reluctance, did that of the entire "class of 1938." The extended succession of 1982 to 1985 was not just a political but also—and even more critically—a generational transfer of power. The Brezhnev cohort, vigorous by Soviet standards in 1964, held stubbornly onto power at high levels, yielding it only at last to the Grim Reaper. Part of the reason for this is demographic: a "missing cohort"—that born around 1920—was largely slaughtered in World War II, and of those who survived, many were needed as laborers in postwar reconstruction and could not be spared the luxury of the higher education necessary for advancement into the elite. It was Cohorts 7 and 8, born around 1930, of whom Gorbachev (b. 1931) is exemplary, that was in a position to succeed the superannuated Brezhnev generation.

From 1969, when he emerged clearly as the dominant Soviet leader (especially vis-à-vis Aleksi Kosygin), through about 1977, when he ousted Nikolai Podgorny and assumed the protocol-rich post of chairman of the Presidium of the Supreme Soviet (and also the year his cherished new Soviet Constitution was promulgated), Brezhnev was at the top of his form. He had modernized the Soviet military and had pulled even with, even surpassed, the United States in nuclear weapons—détente to Brezhnev and the Soviet leaders meant, more than anything, that the United States had now conceded that it must take the Soviet Union seriously. In 1975, the country had begun extending its power into the Third World, Africa, and later, Afghanistan. Brezhnev's foreign policy had brought military strength and international influence to the Soviet Union.

A pillar of Brezhnev's domestic policy was the continued leading role of the Party, and he defended the Party's role against Kosygin's effort to decentralize decision making in industry. But combined with the enhancement of its leading role, he also constantly exhorted the Party to modernize itself, acquire modern managerial skills, and accept responsibility for results. "Developed socialism"—a Brezhnev ideological innovation—replaced Nikita Khrushchev's frenetic goal of achieving communism within a couple of decades: it envisioned the USSR as a developed industrial society, prepared now for the application of the "scientific-technological revolution."[3] The Party was expected to take the lead in this.

"Stability of cadres" was the centerpiece of Brezhnev's personnel policy. In contrast to Khrushchev's capricious tinkering with the apparatus and constant, destabilizing shuffling of personnel, Brezhnev held out the promise of stability of tenure for officials in return for their support of his regime goals.[4] His approach to leadership emphasized consensus, the balancing of institutional forces through co-opting the leaders of important institutional interests into the Politburo itself, and bargaining and compromise in place of Khrushchev's confrontational style. The practice of the late 1980s of referring to the Brezhnev period as the "era of stagnation"[5] is not totally fair. It really applies only to the last half decade of the Brezhnev period. Prior to that time, whatever one may think of the substance of Brezhnev's policies, his style was vigorous. At the Twenty-fifth Party Congress in 1976, some Western observers detected signs of genuine warmth and affection in the ritual tributes paid to Brezhnev.[6] Had Brezhnev retired at the Twenty-fifth Congress, besides setting a healthy precedent, he would have ensured himself a lasting reputation as the best Soviet leader since Lenin.

The last years of the Brezhnev era, however, were marked by immobilized leadership on the part of superannuated men of failing health and imagination. Stability of cadres gave way to stagnation of elite circulation, with frustrated, relatively young, better-educated, and more cosmopolitan and sophisticated elites bunched up at middle-elite levels, watching the Soviet Union being badly mismanaged by septuagenarians who refused to give up power.

Abroad, the country's armed might was being squandered in a way unpopular with the elite as well as the populace, and the much-prized nuclear parity was threatened with diminishment by a U.S. president intent on military renewal and in a nasty confrontational mood.

At home the mood was one of malaise, even outright cynicism. Corruption pervaded the system from top to bottom. Soviet agriculture was still stagnating, and the productivity of Soviet industry was steadily declining, but the illusion of growth and prosperity was maintained by imports from the West and by cutting investment. The Brezhnev economic strategy was to buy both guns and butter today at the cost of tomorrow's butter. Shifting costs to a future generation is not an uncommon policy of great political leaders; that cost is being borne in the Soviet Union today, of course.

The problem of the succession to Brezhnev was complicated by the characteristics of the Politburo, in particular its advanced age, and the consequences of Brezhnev's patronage politics. There were very few individuals eligible to succeed Brezhnev. Long practice, if nothing else, dictates that individuals are eligible for succession to the post of general secretary only if they have long experience in Party politics in Moscow, have significant foreign affairs experience, are ethnically Russian, and are senior secretaries, that is, holding a position on the Politburo *and* on the Central Committee Secretariat.[7]

Brezhnev had followed a personal patronage policy of destroying the careers of high-level figures who showed any inclination to challenge his authority. Podgorny in 1965 was removed from the Secretariat and promoted to the politically emasculated post of chairman of the Presidium of the Supreme Soviet; he lost this post in 1977 when, apparently out of vanity, Brezhnev decided to take it for himself. Aleksandr Shelepin, a vigorous contender in the mid-1960s, was demoted to successively less important posts and forced out of the Politburo by 1975. Petr Shelest and Gennadii Voronov were forced out in 1973, and Dmitrii Polianskii and Kirill Mazurov were ousted in 1978.

Brezhnev's policy of stability of cadres also gave most of his colleagues a stake in his political survival, and thus few were inclined to rock the boat by challenging him. Hence, until Brezhnev began openly supporting Konstantin Chernenko as his successor near the end of his life, there were not many heirs apparent. In the late 1970s, Andrei Kirilenko was regarded as a likely successor, but he did little to tout himself as such. Suffering a debilitating heart attack in the spring of 1982, he was effectively out of the running, whatever his chances might otherwise have been. Mikhail Suslov, the behind-the-scenes kingmaker, was 79 years old and not interested in the post. Arvid Pel'she was a non-Russian token member of age 83. Viktor Grishin, Moscow *gorkom* first secretary, had aspirations for the successions but was not on the Secretariat and had no foreign affairs experience. Foreign Minister Andrei Gromyko and Minister of Defense Dmitrii Ustinov would play a role in choosing the successor, but neither had the power base in the Party to push his own candidacy. Vladimir Shcherbitskii was non-Russian, not on the Secretariat, and isolated from the Moscow scene. Exactly the same was true of Kazakhstan first secretary Dinmukhamed Kunaev. Although a Russian, Grigorii Romanov was also isolated in the traditionally suspect Leningrad Party organization. Chairman of the Council of Ministers Nikolai Tikhonov was too old (age 77) and had no Party power base. Central Committee secretary for agriculture Mikhail Gorbachev was too young and too green in Moscow to have a viable hope. KGB chairman Yurii Andropov was not on the Secretariat and was also seemingly tainted by association with the secret police.

According to the traditional criteria of eligibility, then, this left only Konstantin Chernenko, Brezhnev's favored heir. Chernenko was neither a lion nor a fox, but rather a man of manifest unintelligence and proven mediocrity. His entire political career was spent in subservient positions—he never held a position involving the need for real leadership qualities. The general consensus in the Soviet Union and abroad is that

Chernenko was not qualified for a responsible leadership position. However, one émigré scholar, Ilya Zemtsov, maintains that Chernenko's mediocre image was a guise that permitted him to work his way to the top, and that Chernenko was indeed a talented leader. By his own admission, Zemtsov's analysis is based on hearsay, intuition, and Chernenko's "own" writings (which were almost certainly ghostwritten).[8] Chernenko had been associated with Brezhnev from the time of their service together in Moldavia in 1950, and Brezhnev had pulled him up with him as he rose in the hierarchy, in 1965 making him chief of the Central Committee General Department. In 1976 he became a Central Committee secretary, and from 1977 to 1978 a candidate member of the Politburo, becoming a full member in 1978. Simultaneously he served as Brezhnev's personal secretary and aide; as Brezhnev became more ill and frail, Chernenko was constantly at his side, assisting him physically at times.

It can probably be assumed that Chernenko had, in addition to Brezhnev's support, the support of Tikhonov, Shcherbitskii, Pel'she, Kunaev—staunch Brezhnevites—and possibly Grishin, who had his own ambitions.[9] He did not have Suslov's support, however. Suslov disliked Chernenko and openly supported Kirilenko, and this accounts for Kirilenko's apparent fall from Brezhnev's favor.[10] The remaining Politburo members (Andropov, Gorbachev, Romanov, Gromyko, and Ustinov) were determined not to allow the succession to fall by default to Chernenko, primarily, no doubt, because they regarded him as incompetent, but also because a Chernenko general secretaryship would just prolong Brezhnevite stagnation. But they faced the problem of finding a viable alternative; subsequent events indicate that they had settled on Andropov no later than the end of 1981.

Andropov's strategy in pushing his own candidacy was Machiavellianism at its most exemplary. He went for Brezhnev's soft underbelly, capitalizing on the general secretary's weaknesses and vulnerabilities.[11] Certain events, much written about, showed distinct evidence of KGB involvement in attempting to discredit Brezhnev and, by association, Chernenko. There was the peculiar incident of the implied aspersion on Brezhnev in an allegorical story in the Leningrad journal *Avrora*.[12] More bizarre were the attempts to link Brezhnev's family to charges of corruption. Brezhnev's daughter, Galina Churbanova (whose husband Yurii Churbanov, in a nice irony, was first deputy minister of Internal Affairs—in other words, the nation's second highest-ranking policeman) became linked, along with her alleged lover from the Bol'shoi Opera, Boris "The Gypsy" Buriatia, in a jewelry theft, as well as with additional instances of corruption in the Moscow Circus.[13] In a move at the diabolical brilliance of which one can only wonder, Andropov assigned the investigation of the case to the first deputy chairman of the KGB, Brezhnev's brother-in-law Semen K. Tsvigun, thus guaranteeing that a scandal would result. In charge of protecting the public reputation of the elite, Suslov apparently called Tsvigun in and reprimanded him severely. Tsvigun died within a few days, by all rumors a suicide, and Brezhnev pointedly did not sign his obituary.[14]

Charges of corruption were brought against members of Brezhnev's *khvost'* in the regional apparatus as well. The colossally corrupt first secretary of Krasnodar *kraikom*, Sergei Medunov, was dismissed and replaced by Vitalii Vorotnikov,[15] whom Brezhnev had exiled to Cuba as USSR ambassador in 1979. Konstantin Rusakov, another Brezhnev associate, was dismissed as *obkom* first secretary in Kuibyshev.

The event that really signaled the beginning of the succession struggle was the death of Suslov on January 25, 1982. With the kingmaker out of the way, the contenders began to square off. Andropov's public appearances increased, and Chernenko, hoping to steal some of Andropov's thunder, began paraphrasing and claiming for his own entire passages from Andropov's speeches.[16] Since, by the unwritten rule, Andropov would have to become a Central Committee secretary to be eligible for the succession, he put himself forward to succeed Suslov. And since this required a Politburo recommendation, it is virtually certain that someone—possibly, even probably, Gorbachev—organized a Politburo coalition to advance Andropov's candidacy. He was formally elected a Central Committee secretary by a plenary session of the Central Committee on May 24, 1982.[17] As his successor in the KGB, he appointed Vitalii Fedorchuk, head of the Ukrainian KGB. Fedorchuk was evidently a compromise choice between the two first deputy KGB chairmen, Georgii Tsinev, a Brezhnev protege, and Viktor Chebrikov, a client of Andropov. A compromise candidate may have been necessary to avoid politically polarizing the KGB.[18]

Andropov

Brezhnev died on the morning of November 10, 1982. More than 24 hours passed before his death was publicly announced, and another 24 hours passed before the official announcement that Yurii Andropov had been chosen as the new general secretary. In the full Politburo, Andropov's supporters included Minister of Defense Dmitrii Ustinov, Foreign Minister Andrei Gromyko (who by all reports despised Chernenko), Grigorii Romanov, first secretary of the Ukrainian Party organization Vladimir Shcherbitskii, and as a virtual certainty, Mikhail Gorbachev. Chernenko's supporters seem to have been limited to Kazakh Party first secretary Dinmukhamed Kunaev, chairman of the Council of Ministers Nikolai Tikhonov, and Moscow *gorkom* first secretary Viktor Grishin. By the time of the November plenum that elected Andropov, Kirilenko was no longer a major force on the Politburo. It is not known how the 83-year-old Arvid Pel'she voted, or whether he took part at all.

The reasons for the support of Andropov were varied, but three were probably paramount. First, he promised vigorous, no-nonsense leadership and some unspecified degree of reform, and this was attractive after the soporific final years of Brezhnev. Second, he was respected by the military, and probably also by Gromyko, as a conservative patriot who would maintain the country's preeminence in the world. Finally, he appealed to Gorbachev and people like him as a leader who would reinvigorate the Party, retire deadwood, and bring in more youthful and energetic elites. On the whole, he seemed to be a Paretian fox.

Furthermore, as Donald Kelley stresses, Andropov was probably the only viable senior secretary around whom a stop-Chernenko coalition could be forged.[19] If Gorbachev and Romanov had pressed their own candidacy, it would have left Chernenko with a plurality. This may be putting too fine an edge on it, however; the Central Committee would have had to make the final decision. For the Politburo to go before the Central Committee split three ways, or without a clear collective choice of a candidate, would have risked losing control over the succession decision to the Central Committee, a lesson well learned during the Khrushchev period.

Andropov moved quickly to begin the process of consolidating his position, but by no means with instant or complete success. At the November plenum that elected him, he managed to bring Geidar Aliev into the Politburo and to install him as first deputy chairman of the Council of Ministers. Aliev had been a sycophantic devotee of Brezhnev, but he correctly sensed the direction the wind was blowing in May 1982 and began praising Andropov.[20] He neatly sidelined Chernenko, at least for a time, depriving him of his portfolio for Party Organizational Work and for the Central Committee General Department.

Even though his political career at the center began with an important post in the Party Central Committee apparatus in 1957, Andropov's long tenure as KGB chairman (1967–1982) deprived him of the opportunity to build a substantial *Party* tail. He displayed notable resourcefulness in overcoming this disadvantage by co-opting the proteges of defeated leaders, beginning with those of Kirilenko. Andropov also showed a marked preference for technocrats in the men whom he brought into the central elite. Nikolai Ryzhkov, previous director of *Uralmash* (Urals Industrial Complex) and first deputy chairman of *Gosplan*, was appointed to the Secretariat at the November plenum. It is possible that by advancing Ryzhkov, Andropov may have blocked the rise of some younger Brezhnev appointees such as Vladimir Dolgikh. Grigorii Romanov, Leningrad *obkom* first secretary with a reputation for efficient industrial management, and a Politburo full member since 1976, was brought into the

Secretariat at the June 1983 plenum and given responsibility for defense-related industries. The promotions of Romanov and Aliev might have been motivated by no more than a desire to promote individuals whose career progression was stalled by Brezhnev's patronage practices.[21] Romanov was replaced in Leningrad by Lev Zaikov, later to be brought to Moscow by Gorbachev. Zaikov, a consummate technocrat, was an unusual choice in that he was leapfrogged into the post from the chairmanship of Leningrad *gorispolkom* over the head of the second secretary.[22]

Mikhail Solomentsev was relieved of his long chairmanship of the RSFSR Council of Ministers and made head of the Party Control Commission. Vitalli Vorotnikov, another industrial specialist, was brought into the Politburo as a candidate member and made chairman of the RSFSR Council of Ministers. Egor Ligachev, first secretary of Tomsk *obkom* with a reputation for efficiency and incorruptibility, was brought to Moscow by Andropov in April 1983,[23] replacing Ivan Kapitinov as head of the Central Committee's Organizational Party Work Department. There, with his deputy Evgenii Razumovskii and later with Gorbachev himself, Ligachev supervised personnel appointments. Ligachev had worked in the Organizational Party Work Department for the RSFSR in 1963–1965 under no other than Kirilenko.

Other Brezhnev men relieved of their posts by the fall of 1983 included Georgii Pavlov (Central Committee administrator of affairs), Sergei Trapeznikov (head of the Central Committee department for Science and Educational Institutions), Nikolai Pegov (head, Central Committee department for Cadres Abroad), Evgenii Tiazhel'nikov (head of Central Committee Propaganda Department), and Valentin Falin (first deputy head of the Central Committee International Information Department). Large numbers of gerontocrats (most aged 75 or older) were pensioned off that fall, including 15 Central Committee members.

Andropov promoted his former KGB subordinate, Vitalii Fedorchuk, from the KGB chairmanship to minister of internal affairs, replacing the notoriously corrupt Brezhnev associate Nikolai Shchelokov,[24] and moving Fedor Chebrikov into the KGB chairmanship. A number of other ministers and State Committee chairmen were dismissed that spring for corruption. Another future close associate of Gorbachev was advanced to the center of Andropov: Aleksandr Yakovlev, exiled to Canada by Brezhnev, was brought back to Moscow in 1983 (without doubt at Gorbachev's urging) to head the prestigious Institute of World Economics and International Relations (IMEMO), where virtually all senior diplomatic personnel receive their training.

Significant changes were made at the regional level as well. Andropov's practice was to break up regional Party organizations that had become inbred (and hence corrupt and protective) due to Brezhnev's policy of promotion within Party organizations.[25] Examples are the appointment of Nikolai Sliunkov (January 1983) as first secretary of the Belorussian Party, and of Lev Zaikov as Leningrad *obkom* first secretary to relieve Romanov. By the end of 1983 fully 20 percent of regional Party first secretaries were changed, cashiered either on charges of corruption or incompetence or retired because of advanced age and/or poor health. Gorbachev would continue this policy of breaking up family circles.

In fact, in contrast to Chernenko's insistence on strengthening the Party and the Party's ties to the people, Andropov tended to deemphasize the Party and to place increasing emphasis on the soviets. A peculiar aspect of his personnel policies was to promote soviet *oblispolkom* and *gorispolkom* chairmen to Party first secretaryships. Gorbachev continued Andropov's emphasis on state institutions, of course carrying it much further than Andropov had had time to do.

Andropov, a long-term diabetic with all the complications attendant to that cruel disease (one that reputedly also plagued the ascetic Suslov), suffered kidney failure as early as February 1983 and began dialysis.[26] He disappeared from public view in August, his absence at important events such as the November 1 parade explained by the anemic excuse that he had a "cold." He continued to run the country from his hospital suite, seen every day by Gorbachev and a few aides. He continued to issue statements and to respond to newsworthy events.

In spite of his illness, some high-level personnel changes were made. At the December 1983 plenum of the Central Committee, Solomentsev and Vorotnikov were promoted from candidate to full Politburo membership, Chebrikov attained candidate membership, and Ligachev joined the Secretariat. Still, this did not tilt the Politburo decisively in the favor of Gorbachev, Andropov's choice as his successor. Andropov died on February 9, 1984, before he had successfully set the stage for his young protege to succeed him.

Chernenko's Return

The next day, Chernenko was appointed head of the funeral commission for Andropov, a post that in past (and future) practice devolved upon the deceased's successor. The formal announcement of Chernenko's election did not come until a Central Committee plenum on February 13, indicating that the choice was not a foregone conclusion but, rather, involved debate and bargaining. The Brezhnevite faction alone could not have assured Chernenko's election; he had to have support from other quarters.

The most likely reason he was chosen, ironically, was precisely because he was aged and ill. The alternative candidates were considerably younger: Romanov (61), Gorbachev (53); even Shcherbitskii at 66 or Grishin at 69 were hale enough to be around for a half decade or more, and the younger men for as much as ten or fifteen years. Shcherbitskii, of course, had little chance, being Ukrainian. But if one of the younger factions were to move against Chernenko in 1984 and lose to the other, the loss would have been permanent.

Chernenko did have some advantages other than a short life expectancy. Andropov's anticorruption drive and his policy of aggressively pruning out political and administrative deadwood had put older and comfortably established members of the Party and administrative apparatus on guard. Too, the Central Committee, where the final decision would be made, was not Andropov's, in spite of his having replaced 19 regional secretaries. It has been elected at the Twenty-sixth Congress in 1981, before Brezhnev died, and consisted overwhelmingly of holdovers from previous Central Committees—that is, persons who owed their high positions to Brezhnev. Having seen under Andropov what even moderately aggressive reformism could mean for their careers, they must have regarded Chernenko as a comforting alternative. Since Gorbachev did emerge as second secretary during Chernenko's term, it is likely that such an arrangement was the price of Gorbachev's support. Gorbachev's status as unofficial "second secretary," that is, de facto heir apparent, was confirmed by his election as chairman of the Supreme Soviet Foreign Affairs Commission,[27] a post generally associated with that status.

Chernenko paid lip service to the continuation of Andropov's reformist and anticorruption policies, and indeed exposures and indictments of corrupt officials continued throughout Chernenko's term in office. Particularly in Uzbekistan did the anticorruption campaign become a scourge of the top leadership. Chernenko's only innovation, if such it can be called, was reemphasis on the leading role of the Party (as opposed to Andropov's desire to strengthen state institutions, especially the soviets) and his long-standing preference for strengthening ties between the people and the Party (rather than, for example, direct enforcement of labor discipline).

Although some personnel changes occurred at the regional level and below, there were no changes at the top. The anti-Chernenko faction was neither purged nor neutralized, nor were Chernenko's men advanced. Stasis of high-level personnel appointments seems likely to have been one of the conditions of Chernenko's elevation. Radio Liberty reports that in excerpts from his memoirs published in *Sovetskaia Rossiia*, Ligachev referred to Chernenko as "a virtuoso apparatchik" and wrote that he spent his entire 13 months in office "scheming against Gorbachev."[28]

Only two men, Romanov and Gorbachev, were senior secretaries near the end of Chernenko's life and thus in a position to succeed him. Romanov began to make himself more visible in the winter of 1984–85, among other things giving the keynote speech at the November 7 celebrations.[29] Romanov was respected as a tough and effective administrator during his long tenure as Leningrad *obkom* first secretary.[30]

Some observers believe that it was not Romanov who was being put forth against Gorbachev, but Grishin.[31] Many sources indicate that Viktor Chebrikov provided KGB dossiers to discredit Romanov and Grishin,[32] Grishin for mismanagement and corruption in the Moscow *gorkom*, and Romanov apparently for alcoholism. Another, secondhand, report indicates that Chebrikov let it be known that Grishin's son had married Beria's daughter in an effort to discredit him.[33]

Chernenko finally died on the evening of March 10, 1985, of heart failure associated with emphysema and cirrhosis of the liver. Perhaps the most pathetically unmourned demise of any Soviet leader, Chernenko's death was publicly announced the morning of March 12, followed in less than four hours by the announcement of Gorbachev's election.

Gromyko nominated Gorbachev for general secretary at a Central Committee session on March 11. Dusko Doder reports, secondhand, that Gromyko had said, "Comrades, this man has a nice smile, but he has got iron teeth."[34] The remark, if it occurred, was expunged from the officially published transcript of the speech.[35] Although Gromyko indicates in his memoirs that he nominated Gorbachev, he mentions nothing of the supposed remark.[36] The election was not unopposed, although it seems that Gorbachev had fairly wide support. It will be worth quoting at length Ligachev's comments at the Nineteenth Party Conference about that session:

The whole truth must be told: those were trying days. I happened to be at the center of those events, so I can judge them. An absolutely different decision could have been made. There was a real possibility of that. I want to tell you that, thanks to the firmly committed position taken by Politburo members Comrades Chebrikov, Solomentsev, Gromyko, and a large number of *obkom* first secretaries, the correct decision was made at the March plenum of the Central Committee.[37]

The import of this is that Gorbachev had, including himself, the votes of five full Politburo members (Solomentsev, Gromyko, Aliev, Vorotnikov, and his own; although Ligachev and Chebrikov may have been firm supporters, they were not full, voting Politburo members). Grishin and Romanov would have had four (their own, plus Kunaev and Tikhonov). Shcherbitskii was out of the country; his vote would have created a tie. Gorbachev had firm support in the Secretariat (rallied by Ligachev and Ryzhkov) and, as Ligachev indicates, great support among regional secretaries (as many as two-thirds of them, according to R. Judson Mitchell.)[38]

GORBACHEV AND THE SOVIET ELITE

It would be impossible in the space available here to discuss all aspects of Gorbachev's reform effort, along with his victories, near defeats, and Teflon resilience, nor is it necessary. Gorbachev has stimulated a vast Western scholarly production of studies on his still young reign.[39] Instead, the emphasis here is on the impact of Gorbachev on the administrative elite as a body; some familiarity with recent developments in the Soviet Union is therefore assumed.

Mikhail Sergeevich Gorbachev was born to a peasant family on March 2, 1931, in the village of Privol'noe in Stavropol *krai*. Although the Nazis occupied the North Caucasus for a few months, the winds of war did not rage so violently there, and the family seems not to have suffered as much as did citizens elsewhere in the country. Reportedly, Gorbachev did well in school, and he worked as a combine driver during the summers for a Machine Tractor Station.

In 1950 Gorbachev enrolled in the Moscow State University Faculty of Law, winning a Stalin Scholarship after a short while. He joined the Komsomol, becoming a *komsorg* (a Komsomol organizer), and then, in 1952, joined the Communist Party. The much-quoted Zdeněk Mlynář is the source of most of the information about Gorbachev's university days. Mlynář, from Czechoslovakia, was a classmate and close personal friend of Gorbachev at Moscow State University. Mlynář related that Gorbachev was a good Communist, but also astute, honest, not above uttering some mildly unorthodox political opinions, and of a cosmopolitan outlook remarkable for those Stalinist times.[40] While still a student, in 1954, Gorbachev married Raisa Maksimovna Titorenko, then a philosophy student living on the same floor of the spartan student dormitory as Gorbachev. Much later, in 1967, Gorbachev earned a second degree from Stavropol Agricultural Institute.

After graduation the Gorbachevs returned to Stavropol, and there his political career was confined until 1978 (see Table 8.1). His earliest patron appears to have been Vsevolod Murakhovskii, whose post as Stavropol Komsomol *kraikom* first secretary Gorbachev assumed when Murakhovskii moved to the Party apparatus. Gorbachev's principle patron and mentor, however, was Fedor Kulakov, Stavropol *kraikom* first secretary until 1964, when he went to Moscow to serve as Central Committee secretary for agriculture. His successor in Stavropol was Leonid Efremov, demoted to that post from the Presidium apparently because he was not a Brezhnev man.[41] Gorbachev continued to move up until he replaced Efremov in 1970. At the Twenty-fourth CPSU Congress, he was elected a member of the Central Committee at age 40, fully a decade younger than the norm. When Kulakov died in 1978, Gorbachev succeeded him as Central Committee secretary for agriculture. In 1979

Table 8.1
Gorbachev's Career Pattern

Dates	Position
1958:	Deputy Chief, Agitation and Propaganda Department, Stavropol Komsomol *kraikom*
1958-62:	2nd, then 1st Secretary,Stavropol Komsomol *kraikom*
1962-63:	Organizer, Stavropol *kraikom* Agricultural Production Association
1963-66:	Head, Stavropol *kraikom* CPSU Party Organs Department
1966-68:	1st Secretary, Stavropol CPSU *gorkom*
1968-70:	2nd Secretary, Stavropol *kraikom*
1970-78:	1st Secretary, Stavropol *kraikom*
1978-84:	Secretary, CPSU Central Committee
1979-80:	Candidate Member, CPSU CC Politburo
1980-91:	Full Member, CPSU CC Politburo
1984-85:	2nd Secretary, CPSU Central Committee
1985-91:	General Secretary, CPSU Central Committee
1989-present:	President of the Soviet Union

he became a candidate member, and in 1980 a full member of the Politburo.

Within a few years after Kulakov's death, Gorbachev came into Andropov's favor. Andropov was apparently impressed with Gorbachev's efficiency and lack of taint by corruption. Stavropol *krai* is the location of a number of vacation spas and sanatoria used by the central leadership, and Gorbachev would have met them there. Andropov's favorite retreat was at Mineral'nye Vody. Brezhnev, Andropov, Chernenko, and Gorbachev met at the train station in Mineral'nye Vody on September 19, 1978, as the leaders were on their way to Baku;[42] much written about after 1985, this meeting of four consecutive general secretaries had apparently been arranged for Andropov to introduce Gorbachev to Brezhnev, for Gorbachev was brought to Moscow in November as Central Committee secretary in charge of agriculture.

Gorbachev first really came into the public spotlight, in the USSR as well as in the West, during his highly publicized visit to Britain in December 1984 as head of a Supreme Soviet delegation. This visit, and the publicity it received, may have been arranged by Gromyko in anticipation of the succession.[43]

All the evidence indicates that unlike Brezhnev, Andropov, and Chernenko before him, Gorbachev was not indebted to the military or the KGB in attaining power. He did, however, have to contend with their objections to his policies and limit their leverage over state policy. Matthias Rust, that young West German pilot with more nerve than good sense, inadvertently provided Gorbachev with the opportunity to purge the highest ranks of the military. On May 28, 1987, Rust flew a light aircraft, apparently undetected, to Moscow and landed in Red Square. For the failure to detect him, the military high command was purged on May 30, 1987. Dmitri Yazov replaced Sergei Sokolov as minister of defense.

Withdrawal from Afghanistan, the fall of Communist governments in Eastern and Central Europe, and the appearance of peaceful cooperation with the United States have further limited the military's claim on resources and policy priorities. Gorbachev relies on a nonthreatening U.S. and NATO posture in order to maintain this advantage. The military conservatives in Russia had to shift from the bogeyman of an external threat to an internal one: the disintegration of the union itself with increasingly bold self-assertion among minority nationalities.

Gorbachev's intention to rejuvenate the leadership was made clear in the earliest weeks of his tenure. A *Pravda* editorial entitled "Improving Cadres Work" demanded "initiative and innovation" and insisted that only "practical results" would be the criterion by which cadres' work would be judged. The editorial pointedly referred to the March Central Committee plenum (at which Gorbachev had been elected) as authority for its demands.[44] Pointers in this direction had emerged even before Chernenko's death: "younger leaders, women, and rank-and-file workers" were to be promoted, although the proviso was added that these newly promoted leaders should "learn from the experiences of older generation."[45] This formula has all the earmarks of a committee decision, taken following a debate precisely on the question of generational turnover.

Transforming the Party Elite

Significant personnel changes were not long in coming. Gorbachev's ally, RSFSR premier Vitalii Vorotnikov, replaced the top leadership of the RSFSR Supreme Soviet Presidium and the RSFSR Council of Ministers with younger men, many of them earlier proteges of his own.[46] Gorbachev's allies in the early 1985 personnel shake-ups were always Vorotnikov, Ligachev, and Ryzhkov. Brezhnev had relied on a Ukrainian coalition of supporters, Dnepropetrovsk the source of the largest number of them.[47] Gorbachev was more eclectic in his choice of men to promote, but to the extent that there was a geographical pattern, he relied on (1) a North Caucasus coalition, mainly drawn from his associates in Stavropol and Krasnodar *krais*, and (2) a Siberian coalition, consisting in large part of former Kirilenko clients co-opted by Andropov and centered on Tomsk, Novosibirsk, and Sverdlovsk. The Siberian division of the Academy of Sciences at Novosibirsk has produced a number of Gorbachev's economic advisers, most notably Abel Aganbegian and Tatiana Zaslavskaia. The Sverdlovsk state and Party organizations, and the Urals Polytechnical Institute, have produced a very large share of the technocrats brought to Moscow by Andropov and Gorbachev, including Boris Yel'tsin, Yakov Riabov, Nikolai Ryzhkov, Leonid Bobykin, Lev Voronin, and Yurii Batalin.

All of these immediate changes took place well before public discussion of *glasnost'*, *perestroika*, and *demokratizatsiia* began. They are better interpreted, therefore, as consolidation of Gorbachev's power than as efforts to put in place a team that would implement his reforms. Later, however, as in the selection of delegates for the Nineteenth Party Conference on June-July 1990, Gorbachev on any number of occasions urged that delegates be chosen on the basis of their commitment to *perestroika*.[48]

The first changes in the Politburo occurred at the April 1985 Central Committee plenum. Ryzhkov, Ligachev, and KGB chief Chebrikov became full members, perhaps in reward for their support at the March plenum, and defense minister Sokolov became a candidate member. Viktor Nikonov, apparently a Vorotnikov protege from the RSFSR apparatus, became a Secretariat member, assuming Gorbachev's previous agricultural portfolio. Later, in June, Ligachev assumed the ideology portfolio[49] and Razumovskii assumed the chairmanship of the Organizational Party Work Department,[50] where he became Gorbachev's hatchet man. Razumovskii had taken over Krasnodar *kraikom* after Vorotnikov was elevated, and he had carried out a thoroughgoing purge there of the corrupt and superannuated.[51]

Major shake-ups occurred in the summer and fall of 1985. At a July 1 Central Committee plenum, Romanov was relieved of his duties and apparently went into hospital treatment for chronic alcoholism. Eduard Shevardnadze became a full Politburo member, and Boris Yel'tsin and Lev Zaikov became Central Committee secretaries. The next day Shevardnadze became foreign minister and the Supreme soviet confirmed Gromyko's election as chairman of the Presidium, or president, virtually certain a "promotion" he did not want.[52] On September 27 Tikhonov resigned as chairman of the Council of Ministers, to be replaced by Ryzhkov.

In late December of 1985 Yel'tsin replaced Grishin as Moscow *gorkom* first secretary, although Grishin was not removed from the Politburo until February 1986. Yel'tsin was promoted at that time to candidate membership of the Politburo. At the Twenty-seventh Party Congress (February 25–March 6, 1986), Lev Zaikov was named a full member of the Politburo, and Yurii Solovev and Nikolai Sliunkov were named candidate members. Vasily Kuznetsov and Boris Ponomarev retired.

Personnel changes at the regional level proceeded at a rapid pace in the 1985–1987 period. It was reported in mid-1987 that in the two years since Gorbachev's accession, 40 percent of republican and regional first secretaries, and half of the lower secretaries, had been replaced, along with similar proportions of soviet executives, ministers, and chairmen of state committees.[53] In the Central Committee elected by the Twenty-seventh Party Congress, about one-third of full members were elected for the first time; the real change was among candidate members, of whom 72 percent were new. From 1984 through 1988, I maintained a card file of personnel transfers (promotions, demotions, and lateral transfers), gleaned from *Pravda* and the *Current Digest of the Soviet Press*. The file was incomplete, and I never systematically analyzed it; it did indicate, however, that during that time period there were at minimum 5,000 personnel changes reported in the central press.

By 1987 Gorbachev had formulated and publicized his cadres policy. At the January 1987 plenum, he explicitly linked the success of *perestroika* to the transformation of cadres policy.[54] At the same plenum he put forth proposals for the competitive election of Party officials by secret ballot, called for the recruitment of non-Party people to responsible positions, and emphasized the decisive importance of executive style and the moral and attitudinal requirements of good leadership.[55] In an article detailing the shockingly low level to which the Party's prestige among the public and even among Party functionaries has fallen, *Pravda* urged that political leaders need "striking individuality, analytical thinking, detailed knowledge, [and] speaking skills."[56]

Gorbachev, who used the power of *nomenklatura* so effectively to transform the Party leadership, now endorsed its abolition in favor of competitive elections.[57] In sanctioning the dismantling of the *nomenklatura* system, Gorbachev dismantled his most potent personnel device. He apparently gambled that there is enough popular sentiment in favor of *perestroika* that voters will return politicians who share his views. It is too soon to judge the realism of this expectation, since it is not being implemented: nearly all changes in regional Party executives have been through the exercise of Central Committee *nomenklatura* procedures, rather than by popular election.[58]

A significant element of Gorbachev's personnel policy has been the breaking up of local cliques in *obkoms* and *raikoms* by deliberately assigning people to regions they had not worked in before[59] and bringing personnel to Moscow for a year or longer stint as a Central Committee instructor or inspector before assigning them to regional first secretaryships.[60] This breaks up horizontal patronage bonds and encourages vertical ones; it also promotes elite integration, but in a way that definitely enhances the center's control.

The frenetic pace of turnover was due to the impending Twenty-seventh Party Congress, scheduled for March 1986. As mentioned in an earlier chapter, many, perhaps more than three-quarters of Central Committee members are *ex officio*. To achieve a Central Committee to his liking, Gorbachev had to make personnel changes before the congress. As it happened, the Twenty-seventh Central Committee ended up by 1987 with 122 "dead souls": members still holding Central Committee seats who had in the interim lost the posts that had entitled them to their seats. Their continued presence in the Central Committee was intolerable for Gorbachev since, disgruntled, they could add substantially to a vote of the conservatives to oust him. Gorbachev had hoped that these would be retired at the upcoming Nineteenth Party Conference (the first such since 1941); according to rules, an interim Party Conference can replace up to 20 percent of Central Committee membership. Apparently, however, Gorbachev obtained the Central Committee's acquiescence in holding a conference only on condition that no personnel changes would be made. Most of the "dead souls" were finally forced to resign their seats at a Central Committee plenum on April 25, 1989.[61]

The Twenty-eighth Party Congress (July 2–13, 1990) was widely heralded in its immediate aftermath as Gorbachev's final victory over the Party's conservatives.[62] It was an important victory at the time, but it later proved to have been an ephemeral one.

The disposition of the delegates to the congress was initially hostile to Gorbachev, and the mood was colored by the very recent conference of Russian Communists (which had, quasi-legally, transformed itself into the founding congress of the Russian Communist Party), which witnessed a resurgence of loyalty to the Party as against the reformers. The delegation to the congress was overwhelmingly dominated by Party *apparatchiki* (more than 40 percent; for recent times, this is high, but not as high as during the Stalin period, when 50 percent and 60 percent of delegates were officials). The first four to five days of the congress witnessed a veritable frolic of reformer bashing—crude, loud, and unprecedentedly rude. Gorbachev was caught in a bind familiar to reformers: he was pummeled from the left for going too slow, and from the right for going too far. Although he sought to placate the right, he held to his position that the Party should abandon its leading role (i.e., be a "parliamentary" rather than a "vanguard" party).[63] He gradually wore down the most extreme conservatives; overall, his strategy seemed to be (although in reality he was probably playing it by ear) to divide the right, winning over leading moderates and making a show of unity with Yel'tsin and the left. In the end, Gorbachev was reelected general secretary, and imposed his own choice, Vladimir Ivashko, as deputy general secretary, defeating Ligachev's effort to attain that post.

Yel'tsin launched a vicious attack against the Party in his speech to the Twenty-eighth Congress. He pointed out that this congress was not discussing the process of *perestroika*; these issues were being decided outside the Party, by the Congress of People's Deputies. What the congress had to decide was the fate of the Party itself, especially the fate of the upper echelons of the Party apparatus. Unless the Party restructured itself, it would find itself in opposition to the people and ousted from power, with its property nationalized.[64]

Yel'tsin predicted that Party leaders at all levels could be put on trial, alluding ominously to the experiences of the Communist Parties of Eastern Europe. Averring that a multiparty system is inevitable in the USSR, Yel'tsin gave his prescription for how the Party could redeem itself: (1) organizationally codify the various platforms that exist within the Party; (2) change the name of the Party to reflect its commitment to democratic socialism; (3) adopt a general resolution on the transformation of the Party; (4) divest itself of all state functions, abolish the PPOs in state organizations, and leave the existence of PPOs in production facilities up to the workers themselves. Yel'tsin believed that steps in these directions would lead to the emergence of a parliamentary-type Party.[65]

Later, Yel'tsin, that "inexhaustible source of surprises," as a journalist later dubbed him,[66] announced his resignation from the Party, giving as the reason the incompatibility of the demands on him as chairman of the RSFSR Supreme Soviet with continued Party membership. Vladimir Shostakovskii, rector of the Moscow Higher Party School and a member of the Democratic Platform, did likewise. Both men were prompted to announce their resignations on learning that their names were on a list for election to the Central Committee.[67]

The congress abolished the distinction between full and candidate members of the Central Committee (but retained a Central Control Committee). Likewise, the distinction between full and candidate members of the Politburo was abolished; the Party statutes ratified by the Congress mandates that the Politburo consist of the general secretary, the deputy general secretary, and the first secretaries of the 15 union republic Communist Parties (a step in the direction of consociationalism). The statutes reinstituted the Secretariat, headed by the deputy general secretary, charging it with "the execution *in the Party*" of Party decisions and with oversight of the work of the Central Committee apparatus.[68]

The congress elected a Central Committee of 412 members, only 59 of whom (14 percent) are carryovers from the Twenty-seventh Central Committee. The mean year of birth of members of the Twenty-eighth Central Committee is 1940, compared to 1928 for the Central Committee elected at the Twenty-seventh Congress in 1986 (1925 for full members only). The new Central Committee is thus about eight years younger than the previous one was at the time of its election and, it bears remarking, younger than Gorbachev himself. Ages are distributed virtually normally around the mean age of 50.2, found in Chapter 6 to be the mean age for first election to the Central Committee. What is unusual is the high percentage of deputies (86 percent) elected for the first time. Most of these officials acquired the post that entitles them to Central Committee membership after 1985—that is, under Gorbachev.

Eighty-seven percent hold full-time Party apparatus jobs, 91 percent of them either All-Union postings (84 percent) or RSFSR postings (7 percent). Thus, only 9 percent hold state or Party jobs in the non-Russian republics. Six percent are women. One hundred ten (27 percent) are also people's deputies.

By the late summer of 1990 there was not a single holdover from the Brezhnev period (with the exception of Gorbachev himself) in the Politburo, the Central Committee Secretariat, the heads of Central Committee departments, the Presidium of the Council of Ministers, or in any of the *obkoms, kraikoms, oblispolkoms,* or *kraiispolkoms* (with two exceptions: Grigorii Shishin, first secretary of Tuva ASSR *obkom,* who has held that post since 1973, and first secretary since June 1982 of Iakut-Sakha SSR Yurii Prokop'ev), or in the posts of republican first and second secretaries. All members of the Central Committee elected at the Twenty-eighth Party Congress in July 1990 (except Gorbachev) joined the Central Committee after Brezhnev died. Gorbachev has accomplished what not even Stalin could: a virtually complete turnover of the political elite on the CPSU Central Committee *nomenklatura* lists, a turnover that is distinctly generational in nature.

Gorbachev's goal, although he could hardly make it explicit, has been substantially to weaken the Party, and in a sense he double-crossed the regional Party elite by leading them to believe otherwise; hence the sentiment for some sort of anti-Gorbachev coup before the Twenty-eighth Congress. No doubt, Gorbachev envisions the disappearance of the Party altogether in the future; he certainly has made it plain that he would like to see it compete with other parties for state power. It can be wondered why before the coup of August 1991, he did not abandon the Party altogether or lead its progressive members in a Bolshevik-like split. Probably it is because the Party, and even any hypothetical conservative rump, is simply too strong. It is nationally organized, and its tentacles reach into every nook and cranny of Soviet life. Gorbachev probably felt that he did not need a foe that powerful, so the next best tactic was to continue to dominate it as a means of limiting its influence, even at the cost of major concessions to the conservatives.

Transforming the State Elite

On the first day of the Nineteenth Party Conference, Gorbachev began
to recommend a radical restructuring of the organization of power and
administration, making it more democratic and clarifying the distribution of power between the Party and the state. He called first of all for
restoring the sovereignty of the soviets, stating as a principle that "no
state, economic, or social question can be decided without the soviets."[69]
The goal was to make the soviets absolutely independent in the solving
of problems in the territory under their jurisdiction and to give them
an adequate local tax base to do this.

Gorbachev proposed the creation of a Congress of People's Deputies
of the USSR (*S'ezd narodnykh deputatov SSSR*), consisting of 2,250 deputies, 750 chosen respectively from territorial districts and from nationalities by contested ballot; the remaining 750 seats were to be
reserved for central agencies, including 100 seats for the CPSU. The
deputies would serve five-year terms, meeting once a year.[70] The Congress of People's Deputies would elect from among its number a more
empowered standing Supreme Soviet of 400 to 450 members and a
chairman with enhanced executive powers.[71] The Nineteenth Party Conference included all these proposals, with others, in its resolutions.[72]

Elections for the Congress of People's Deputies were held on March
26, 1989. The procedure for nomination of candidates was awkward
and involved, and this afforded establishment officials some opportunity
to manipulate the nominations.[73] For the 1,500 seats that were to be
filled by competitive elections, 385 (25.6 percent) had only one candidate,
953 (63.5 percent) had two, and 162 (11 percent) had three or more.[74]
The competitive elections, as could be expected, favored liberals in spite
of reportedly widespread efforts of Party officials to tamper with it.
Yel'tsin won his Moscow constituency in a landslide. Party officials were
defeated as well in Leningrad, Minsk, Kiev, and Kishenev. Overall, one
of every five Party officials running was defeated. Even though 88 percent of the deputies elected were Party members, these tended not to
be Party officials, workers, or prominent conservatives. Gorbachev may
have been correct when he indicated at a Central Committee plenum
after the elections that the people did not reject Communists per se, but
bureaucrats, dogmatists, and conservatives.[75] Republican first and second secretaries tended to get elected, most in the contested election.
State officials are not well represented in the congress because of an
exclusionary rule in an amendment to the Constitution. Of 121 military
candidates, 79 were elected, as were 9 republican KGB chairmen.[76] The
Baltic popular fronts won handily, taking 74 percent of Lithuania's seats,
86 percent of Latvia's, and 71 percent of Estonia's.

The first session of the congress elected a 542-member Supreme Soviet

Table 8.2
Occupation of Supreme Soviet Members

Occupation	Number	Percent
Party officials	42	08.0
Soviet officials	52	10.0
State officials	53	09.8
Public organization	34	06.3
Industry, labor	73	13.5
Industry, managers	62	11.4
Agriculture, labor	40	07.4
Agriculture, managers	46	08.5
Military	5	00.9
Professionals	98	18.1
Retired	10	01.8
Unknown	27	05.0

Source: Author's database.

on May 27, 1989. To the disappointment of liberal deputies, it was elected as in the past on the basis of a single prearranged slate for every region. Although Yurii Afanasev bemoaned the election of a "Stalinist-Brezhnevite" legislature,[77] in fact only a few high-ranking party apparatchiks were elected, a group that had dominated Supreme Soviets of the past. Table 8.2 shows that fewer than 25 percent of the deputies occupy a political post of any kind, as opposed to 31 percent in the Eleventh (the last prereform) Supreme Soviet.

Among the Supreme Soviet deputies, the largest categories of academic training are technical (19 percent), agricultural (10 percent), and secondary specialized (8 percent). All other fields are represented by fewer—in most cases, much fewer—than 6 percent of deputies. Fifty-nine nationalities are represented: 39 percent Russians, 11 percent Ukrainians, 3.6 percent each for Belorussians and Azeris, and 3.4 percent each for Georgians and Uzbeks. All other nationalities come in with less than 3 percent, and most less than 1 percent. Seventy-two percent have higher education; 18 percent having an advanced degree. Eighty-two percent are male (up from 67 percent at the Eleventh Supreme Soviet), and 86 percent are Party members (72 percent of Eleventh Supreme Soviet deputies were Communists). Eighty-five percent of Supreme Soviet deputies who were elected to the congress from electoral districts are Party members, showing that competitive election in a district, or selection to the Supreme Soviet, did not militate against Party members as such. Twenty-six (about 5 percent) of the Supreme Soviet deputies are from the CPSU's 100 reserved seats.

The mean age of Supreme Soviet deputies is 46.2, but in fact this is a bimodal distribution with peaks at age 39 and age 50, and with remaining ages distributed about equally on either side. The age of deputies who were elected to the congress from districts, whom one could expect to be younger, is only a little younger, at 45.5; again, this distribution is bimodal, peaking at 39 and 49. Age 50 is the expected age for attainment of membership in a high decision-making body; those clustered around the younger modal age are fast-trackers.

The import of all this is that this is a very young body of legislators, almost none of whose members experienced World War II or the Stalin period as adults. Only the older of them, those whose ages are distributed closely around the age 50 peak, began their political careers even during the Khrushchev period. Not only did the accession of Gorbachev and his cohorts represent a generational turnover, but Gorbachev has implemented yet another generational change.

Transforming the Executive

To put some distance between himself and the Supreme Soviet, and probably to afford himself another opportunity to increase his powers, Gorbachev asked for, and the Supreme Soviet approved in February 1990, the creation of a new federal presidency. This was approved by the Congress of People's Deputies at the same time that it abolished the Communist Party's constitutionally enshrined leading role (Article 6), and on March 15 Gorbachev was sworn in as president. He was elected by the congress; subsequent presidents will be elected by direct popular election. Even though he ran unopposed, Gorbachev was not elected unanimously; he received 1,329 votes.

In becoming president, Gorbachev assured himself of at least five years of secure tenure. He could be toppled as Party leader at any time, and, with not a great deal more difficulty, as chairman of the Presidium of the Supreme Soviet. He could be impeached from the presidency, however, only by the Congress of People's Deputies, and only if it can be shown that he has behaved unconstitutionally. His powers include the declaration of a state of emergency (under specified conditions), the declaration of martial law, the dissolution (under certain circumstances) of the Supreme Soviet, a veto over legislation (which the Supreme Soviet can override by a two-thirds vote), and the power to issue decrees that, as long as they are not unconstitutional, are binding without having to be passed by the Supreme Soviet.[78]

Subsequent to that, Gorbachev revised his advisory system and his powers several times, always able to cajole the Congress of People's Deputies into approving his designs. In March 1990 he created a 15-member Presidential Council to assume the advisory functions of the

Politburo, as well as Council of the Federation to see to its implementation, but he found this inadequate to ensure implementation of his decisions in the periphery. In December 1990 he gained congress approval for the creation of a post of vice-president, a new Council of the Federation, a Cabinet of Ministers, and a Security Council. Gennadii Ianaev, a former trade union official, became the new vice-president. The old Council of the Federation was upgraded in December to a policy-making body whose decisions can be implemented by presidential decree. The Cabinet of Ministers replaces the old Council of Ministers, now abolished, and places the government, including the prime minister, directly under the authority of the president, somewhat on the French model. The Security Council is modeled directly on the U.S. National Security Council and will advise the president on matters of external and internal security.[79]

From the time of the Twenty-eighth Congress in July, 1990, Gorbachev began increasingly to court the right. He may have seen no alternative to this, given the mounting conservative opposition; he may have feared a military coup unless he responded to the demands of the right. This hypothesis would suggest that Gorbachev had not changed his views or his intent but was taking another step backward to preserve the option of future steps forward. Apparently, there was at least an implicit threat of a coup displacing him, likely led by Col. Viktor Alksnis, Gorbachev's new nemesis. Alksnis is a leader of the *Soiuz* (Union) group who has publicly demanded Gorbachev's resignation and who, with KGB chief Vladimir Kriuchkov, has made preservation of the union the issue on which they will stand and fight. This would indicate that no amount of purging of the military will redefine its institutional interests or very much curtail its ability to assert them.

An alternative explanation for Gorbachev's sharp veer to the right at the end of 1990, of course, is that he saw a real and present danger of the collapse of the union and voluntarily joined the conservatives to forestall it. It is difficult to choose between these alternative explanations because they are both consistent with what is known about Gorbachev as a political leader: his tactical wiliness and his strategic fixity of purpose.

At the December 1990 session of the Congress of People's Deputies, Foreign Minister Eduard Shevardnadze announced his resignation, warning that "a dictatorship is coming."[80] Shevardnadze's disenchantment with Gorbachev probably began with the violent crackdown on demonstrators in Tbilisi in April 1989. In his resignation speech, he referred to the machinations of "two colonels" (without question the allusion was to Alksnis and Nikolai Petrushenko) to oust him from his post. Shevardnadze may also have suspected that he was being set up as Gorbachev's flak-catcher, to deflect criticisms from the right.[81]

NASCENT STRATEGIC ELITES

Given the quality of the resources it had to work with—a rich natural environment and a diverse, talented and attractive people—the mediocrity of the Soviet achievement, to understate the case, is appalling. Communist Party mismanagement of Soviet society nears criminality in its magnitude. There are numerous explanations for this, some of which, having to do with personnel management, I have tried to elucidate in this book. The stifling of a society's potential is directly related to the stifling of the initiative and creativity of its best people. The CPSU strategy for controlling Soviet society has consisted in very large part of efforts to co-opt strategic elites.

Strategic elites are natural elites, in the usage I introduced in Chapter 5. Suzanne Keller's theory of strategic elites is explicitly grounded in a Parsonian functionalist view of the social process. However, she argues, healthily in my view, that societal requisites—goal attainment, adaptation, integration, and pattern maintenance and tension management—do not just fulfill themselves. Individuals who translate functional imperatives into workable rules constitute strategic elites.[82] As long as they are allowed to emerge naturally—not, that is, artificially through a mechanism such as *nomenklatura*—there will be competition among strategic elites within particular sectors sufficient to assure that at least some of the best of them will dominate. Functional system needs are, willy-nilly perhaps, met.

An artificial elite, on the other hand, is not selected through competition but through sponsorship. As a consequence, individuals enter the elite on the basis of loyalty and patronage and not, as a rule, on the basis of merit. Regime needs take precedence over system needs. There are no natural strategic elites in the USSR, not because there are no talented, creative, and principled figures in various sectors—manifestly, there are—but because those that exist are not permitted to exercise moral, spiritual, and cultural leadership. Under conditions of state censorship, and of the capture of creative activity by the Writers' Union, the Composers' Union, and the like, strategic leadership in these sectors is exercised by loyal Partocrats rather than by the best representatives of these sectors. Mediocrity or worse is perpetuated institutionally, and the society becomes not an aristocracy but nearly a kakistocracy—rule by the worst.

Gorbachev's and his lieutenants' vigorous defense of *glasnost'*, the abolition of censorship, and the tolerance from as early as 1986 of "informal groups" have created the conditions for a new pluralism from below on a scale not seen in the USSR since the 1920s. These are the conditions for the emergence of a civil society or, to say precisely the same thing in a different way, limited government. Before this separation of the proper division of responsibilities and prerogatives between state and society becomes firmly embedded in the political culture, however, democracy will remain a potential, not a reality.

Barring a conservative coup and the abortion of reform (not an unlikely contingency), it is from the informal groups (*neformal'nye gruppy*) that strategic elites will emerge. This will be an important precondition for democracy and, if Tocqueville is right, a condition for its maintenance:

No countries need associations more—to prevent either despotism of parties or the arbitrary rule of a prince—than those with a democratic social state. In aristocratic nations secondary bodies form natural associations that hold abuses of power in check. In countries where such associations do not exist, if private people did not artificially and temporarily create something like them, I see no other dike to hold back tyranny of whatever sort, and a great nation might with impunity be oppressed by some tiny faction or by a single man.[83]

Tocqueville states elsewhere that the more the state stands in lieu of private, voluntary associations, the more dependent will the people become on the state, and the more the morals and intelligence of the people will be endangered.[84] This usurpation of functions by the state and by the Communist Party is in fact what has transpired in the Soviet Union since the 1930s, and the effect it has had is another vindication of the great prognosticator's perspicacity.

Earlier voluntary associations were liberal and pro-Gorbachev, but as Aron Katsenelinboigen argues, *glasnost'* makes it possible not only for liberals to openly profess their views but for reactionaries to do so, too: nationalists and Russophiles such as *Pamiat'* and *Otechestvo* (Sverdlovsk), youth gangs such as the *Liubertsy*, and neo-Nazi organizations.[85]

Literally thousands of voluntary associations have arisen in the Soviet Union during the Gorbachev period; the Soviet press reported that there were 30,000 in 1988.[86] Some, of course, existed since the early 1960s as dissident organizations, hounded by the KGB. If one includes in this number the rock bands, soccerball clubs, punks, hippies, street gangs, vigilante groups, and Afghan veterans' clubs, the number of informals rises to nearly 150,000.

The earliest major association with political overtones was the Russian nationalist group *Pamiat'* (Memory), espousing at first an innocuous program of preserving historical monuments. Increasingly, however, it voiced quasi-fascist, anti-Semitic and integral nationalist themes. Other much less virulent associations advocating cultural preservation and ecological protection also appeared in the RSFSR and the other republics. In Moscow, the Democratic Union appeared in 1988, declaring itself an alternative to the CPSU and unremittingly hostile to Gorbachev. The

Democratic Platform, organized in January 1990, is a reformist group of Party members intent on either reforming the Party or splitting it.

In the Baltic states, the most successful voluntary associations were the popular fronts. These were actually proposed by CPSU members as a focus of cooperation between the Party and the informal groups. Lithuania's *Sajudis* and the Latvian and Estonian popular fronts were prepared to cooperate with the Party in support of *perestroika*. By 1989, however, they were espousing the cause of national independence, and the Communist Parties of the republics followed suit.[87] By the middle of 1989, popular fronts had been established in all the union republics. In the RSFSR, democratic associations began to address ethnic Russian issues when it became clear that no groups other than *Pamiat'* and *Otechestvo* (Fatherland) were addressing these issues.

One of the larger and more effective associations is the Interregional Group of Deputies, formed in June 1989, among the membership of the Congress of People's Deputies. At its height in October 1989, the group claimed 360 members.[88] It espouses a liberal program in support of further democratization and implementation of a market economy. A larger, better-organized, and more effective parliamentary group, however, is *Soiuz* (Union), created in February 1990. The first legal registration of parliamentary groups in December 1990 showed 730 members of the Communist group, 561 for *Soiuz*, and only 229 for the Interregional Group.[89] The *Soiuz* group's purpose is to prevent the breakup of the Soviet state that is threatened by centrifugal nationalist phenomena.

On October 9, 1990, the Supreme Soviet passed the Law on Public Associations,[90] after several proposed drafts had been subjected to criticism in the course of 1988 and 1990. Since the abolition of Article 6 of the Constitution discontinued the Communist Party's legal monopoly, this law effectively legalizes a multiparty political system for the USSR.[91] The law denies official registration for groups advocating the violation of the territorial integrity of the USSR by force, prohibits financial assistance by the government to any political party, forbids parties (but not other public associations) from receiving money from abroad, and requires that parties publish their programs and publicly disclose their financial activities.

Informal associations, and particularly political parties, pose a clear and immediate danger to the Communist Party's ability to maintain its dominance in the sociopolitical system. Party seminars have been held to discuss various strategies the Party might use to cope with the threat. Proposals have included the infiltration of informals by Party officials and, more scrupulously, the study of the platforms of the informal groups,[92] with an eye presumably to modifying the Party's platform, or at least its image, in order to make it more competitive.

In 1956 the Stalinist Molotov proved to be right when he darkly warned Khrushchev of the destabilizing effects that de-Stalinization would have. The conservative Ligachev's equally dark warning is evocative of that:

Recently, calls for a multiparty system have been heard. In the conditions of a federal state, which is what the Soviet Union is, this would be simply disastrous. A multiparty system would mean the breakup of the Soviet federation. This is clear, because the Communist Party is the only real political force uniting all the peoples of the country into a single Union of republics.[93]

Ligachev is right. The only justification for continued Russian tutelage of the minority nationalities is Marxism-Leninism. With the nearly complete erosion of the ideology, and the weakening of its organizational base, Russia is left as just another colonial power, facing the same outcome that history has seemingly prescribed for all the others.

It is not possible here to survey the ideological spectrum of the numerous voluntary associations and political parties that seem to have been appearing almost daily. What is important to note is that they are quickly learning the skills of party and interest-group politics and that some of the more robust of them, such as *Soiuz*, can command the ear of the president and alter outcomes. The development of political parties is still in an immature stage; small parties organized around a single issue have little hope of winning political power. The best hope for the emergence of a genuine multiparty system lies either in a split in the Communist Party, in which each faction takes with it part of the Party's infrastructure and property, or else in the large parliamentary groups in the Congress of People's Deputies and in the Supreme Soviet. Western political parties did, after all, originate in parliamentary factions in the British Parliament.

CONCLUSIONS

I argued in Chapter 1 that the underlying structure of Brezhnev's Soviet Union resembled the French *ancien regime* more than it resembled that of any other modern industrial state. I concede that this is an argument by analogy, but that is what comparative analysis comes down to, and I find the analogy compelling.

Soviet notables themselves saw the parallel with the French revolutionary situation. Nikolai Shmelev warned at the first session of the Congress of People's Deputies in 1989 that "this scenario was already written once—two hundred years ago!"[94]

Tocqueville was concerned with the growth in France of "equality," by which he meant the displacement of the aristocracy's prerogative of

Table 8.3
Political Substructure of Modern USSR and French *Ancien Regime*

FUNCTION	STRUCTURE	
	France/USSR	Tocquevillian Preference
Executive:	Centralized command	Central coordination
Legislative:	Pliant council	Autonomous parliament
Implementation:	Centralized	Decentralized
Enforcement:	Force, bureacracy	Authority, administration
Social structure:	Feudal, egoistic	Egalitarian, community
Social control:	Tyranny	Freedom
Economy:	Command	Market
Distribution of benefits:	Inequality	Equality
Recruitment:	Aristocratic succession	Meritocratic

rule through the encroachments of the bourgeoisie. The structural similarity between the party *nomenklatura* and Tocqueville's aristocracy, and between Tocqueville's bourgeoisie and the Party and non-Party intelligentsia, is manifest (see Table 8.3). The abandonment of the Party's leading role, the dilution of *nomenklatura* rights,[95] the legitimation of voluntary associations, the legalization of alternative political parties, and the conditions of *glasnost'* permitting strident nationalist self-assertion have created a fertile situation in that country which Tocqueville would recognize immediately as revolutionary.

The analogy between the French bourgeoisie and the Soviet Union's middle class comes through clearly in the remarks of a member of the Democratic Union:

The most active people today are those who were in some way linked to the old movement. They are usually well-educated people who have been denied professional status and who occupy no meaningful positions—their very lives a travesty of the slogan "the proletariat has nothing to lose but its chains." The Democratic Union's membership largely fits this description. An entire generation of the creative intelligentsia in Russia has worked as stokers, guards, and laborers. Unfortunately, their juniors seem to be completely apolitical. They have a long way to go before they reach the level of their Chinese or Bulgarian counterparts.[96]

Compare with this the remarks of Anatolii Strelianyi, the editor of *Novy mir*, in a speech to Komsomol activists at Moscow University: "The social base of perestroika consists of: highly qualified workers, parts of the scientific-technological intelligentsia, and parts of the lower-level Party apparatus and economic managers."[97]

The Soviet administrative elite is undergoing its second major transformation since the 1917 revolution. The Stalinist transformation created a narrowly technocratic elite of managerial modernizers. The elite that has been assuming its place since 1985 (and the process is by no means complete) is more diverse, more liberally educated, more cosmopolitan, and more pragmatic than the previous one. It is becoming an elite not of technocrats or managers, but an elite of politicians. Politicians are a product of contest, not sponsorship, mobility system. The widespread practice of competitive elections, assuming that they are genuinely democratic and immune to manipulation, will drastically curtail patronage and clientelism. Some patronage will survive, of course, as it does even in U.S. political machines, but it will not be made inevitably by a sponsorship mobility system. Perpetuation of scarcity as a source of power over the powerless will diminish as an imperative, once the powerless have the power of the ballot.

It is difficult to prognosticate the success of reform. It is likely that the peasant, feudal deep structure of consciousness discussed in Chapter 1 is still present to a considerable degree, partly because it has been reinforced and encouraged by communism, rather than eradicated by it. Further, the centralized economic system has created a "command culture" in which generations of people of all ranks have looked to the top for guidance in all matters and rewards have gone to those who obey orders from above. The modal Soviet personality type is not entrepreneurial, although it is true that irrepressible entrepreneurs have bent the system to their will through corruption and marginal economic activities. Except for a handful of such entrepreneurs, the Soviet workforce, industrial and agricultural, has not responded to the invitation to privatization; 75 years of communism has ensured that there is no knowledge or experience, or even memory, of how to function in other than a command environment.

Reform in the past, from Peter the Great forward, has been from above, forced on a reluctant and recalcitrant people by a determined ruler who has chosen a single goal (building a new capital city or military force, industrialization, or whatever), funneled all of the society's resources into the project, and allowed the chips to fall where they may. The resulting popular sociopsychological mental outlook so created has been ad hoc and not closely related to the outlook that developed in the West when these same processes occurred more naturally, that is, by pressures from below. In their reaction to the coup of the summer of 1991, however, the Soviets empowered themselves to take hold of their own destiny. In the USSR (or in Russia and the former republics of the USSR) the long-term prospects for real democracy are, I believe, good, if the short-term disappointment, resentment, anger, and conflict can be weathered.

NOTES

1. Alexis de Tocqueville, *The Old Regime and the French Revolution*, trans. Stuart Gilbert (Garden City, NY: Doubleday, 1955), p. 177.

2. Alexander Yanov, *The Russian Challenge and the Year 2000*, trans. Iden J. Rosenthal (Oxford: Basil Blackwell, 1987), p. 7.

3. On "developed socialism," see Donald R. Kelley, *The Politics of Developed Socialism: The Soviet Union as a Post-Industrial State* (Westport, CT: Greenwood Press, 1986).

4. For critical discussions of "stability of cadres," see Gail Warshofsky Lapidus, "The Brezhnev Generation and Directed Social Change: Depoliticization as a Political Strategy," in Alexander Dallin, ed., *The 25th Congress of the CPSU: Assessment and Context* (Stanford, CA: Hoover Institution Press, 1977); and R. Judson Mitchell, "Immobilism, Depoliticization, and the Emerging Soviet Elite." *Orbis* 26, no. 4 (Fall 1982):591–609.

5. This is a ritual practice in Soviet politics: Because policy is so inextricably tied to personalities, new leaders must pave the way for new policies by discrediting their predecessors. Tongue no doubt in cheek, Aleksandr Yakovlev called the Brezhnev period the "era of universal enchantment." A. N. Yakovlev, "Dostizhenie kachestvenno novogo sostoianiia sovetskogo obshchestva i obshchestvennie nauki," *Vestnik Akademii Nauk SSSR*, no. 6 (1987):53. With similar dry humor, M. A. Ulianov referred at the Nineteenth Party Conference to the Stalin, Khrushchev, and Brezhnev periods respectively as the era of the cult, the era of voluntarism, and the era of stagnation. *Current Soviet Policies* (Columbus, OH: Current Digest of the Soviet Press, 1990), p. 42. Future pundits may call the Gorbachev period the era of disappointment.

6. Jerry F. Hough, "The Brezhnev Era: The Man and the System," *Problems of Communism* 25, no. 2 (March-April 1976): p. 1.

7. See Grey Hodnett, "Succession Contingencies in the Soviet Union," *Problems of Communism*, no. 24 (1975):1–21.

8. Ilya Zemtsov, *Chernenko: The Last Bolshevik* (New Brunswick, NJ: Transaction Publishers, 1989), pp. vii–ix. This book abounds with errors, such as the assertion that Gorbachev headed the Novosibirsk Party organization in the 1970s: p. xv.

9. However, Zhores Medvedev writes that Kunaev and Shcherbitskii balked at working under someone they considered their junior. *Andropov* (New York: Penguin Books, 1984), p. 11.

10. Baruch A. Hazen, *From Brezhnev to Gorbachev: Infighting in the Kremlin* (Boulder, CO: Westview Press, 1987), p. 29.

11. Myron Rush, "Succeeding Brezhnev," *Problems of Communism* 32, no. 1 (January-February 1983):3.

12. Viktor Goliavkin, "Iubileinaia rech," *Avrora* (Leningrad), December 1981.

13. *New York Times*, February 22, 1982. On Buriatia, see the journalistic account by Stanley Lauden in *Galina Brezhnev and Her Gypsy Lover* (London: Quartet Books, 1989).

14. Jonathan Steele and Eric Abraham, *Andropov in Power: From Komsomol to Kremlin* (Garden City, NY: Anchor Press/Doubleday, 1984), p. 142. The story is

confirmed in its essentials by Medvedev, *Andropov*, pp. 95–96. R. Judson Mitchell, however, regards the story as improbable, that Suslov and Tsvigun "commiserated over their inability to suppress a scandal" and that Tsvigun was killed by a KGB hit squad. *Getting to the Top in the USSR: Cyclical Patterns in the Leadership Selection Process* (Stanford, CA: Hoover Institution Press, 1990), pp. 82–83.

15. *Pravda*, July 24, 1982.

16. Hazen, *Infighting in the Kremlin*, pp. 34–36.

17. *Pravda*, May 25, 1982, p. 1.

18. Donald R. Kelley, *Soviet Politics from Brezhnev to Gorbachev* (New York: Praeger, 1987), pp. 34–35.

19. Ibid., p. 47.

20. Hazen, *Infighting in the Kremlin*, p. 35.

21. Alexander Rahr, "Andropov Consolidates His Hold on the Central Committee Apparatus," RL 339/83 (September 9, 1983).

22. On this and related personnel changes, see Peter Taylor, "Personnel Changes in Leningrad," RL 287/83 (July 29, 1983).

23. *Izvestia*, April 30, 1983.

24. Shchelokov, stripped of his military titles, and seeing his son purged from the Komsomol, shot himself on December 13, 1984. *Frankfurter Allgemeine Zeitung*, December 17, 1984. Soviet politics can still be lethal.

25. Brezhnev explicitly boasted of this policy at the Twenty-fourth Party Congress: *XXIV S"ezd KPSS, Stenograficheskii otchet* 1 (Moscow, 1972), p. 124.

26. *Pravda*, February 11, 1983.

27. *Izvestia*, April 12, 1984, p. 1.

28. His memoirs are entitled *V kremle i na staroi ploshchadi*. Annotation in *Report on the USSR* 3, no. 11 (March 15, 1991):40.

29. *Pravda*, November 6, 1983, pp. 1–2.

30. See Blair A. Ruble, "Romanov's Leningrad," *Problems of Communism* 32, no. 6 (November-December 1983):36–48.

31. Mikhail Shatrov, "Neobratimost' peremen," *Ogonek*, no. 4 (1987):4–5. Cited by Archie Brown, "Power and Policy in a Time of Leadership Transition, 1982–1988," in Archie Brown, ed., *Political Leadership in the Soviet Union* (Bloomington: Indiana University Press, 1989), p. 181.

32. All these sources trace ultimately back to Zhores A. Medvedev, *Gorbachev* (New York: W. W. Norton, 1986), p. 172. Medvedev attributes it to a rumor, "probably deliberately leaked." The marital relationship is a fact; that Chebrikov used it at the March 10 meeting to discredit Grishin is the rumor.

33. Warren Shaw and David Pryce, *World Almanac of the Soviet Union: From 1905 to the Present* (New York: Pharos Books, 1990), p. 168.

34. Dusko Doder, *Shadows and Whispers: Power Politics inside the Kremlin from Brezhnev to Gorbachev* (New York: Random House, 1986), p. 267.

35. *Kommunist*, no. 5 (March 1985):6–7.

36. Andrei Gromyko, *Memoirs* (New York: Doubleday, 1989), p. 341.

37. *Pravda*, July 2, 1988, p. 11.

38. Mitchell, *Getting to the Top in the USSR*, p. 133.

39. Some of the better of these include Dusko Doder and Louise Branson, *Gorbachev: Heretic in the Kremlin* (New York: Viking, 1990); Baruch Hazen, *Gorbachev and His Enemies: The Struggle for Perestroika* (Boulder, CO: Westview Press,

1990); Kelley, *Soviet Politics from Brezhnev to Gorbachev* (New York: Praeger); Basile Kerblay, *Gorbachev's Russia*, trans. Rupert Swyer (New York: Pantheon Books, 1989); Roy Medvedev and Giulietto Chiesa, *Time of Change: An Insider's View of Russia's Transformation*, trans. Michael Moore (New York: Pantheon Books, 1990); Zhores Medvedev, *Gorbachev*; Mitchell, *Getting to the Top in the USSR*; Dev Murarka, *Gorbachev: The Limits of Power* (London: Hutchinson, 1988); Richard Sakwa, *Gorbachev and His Reforms, 1985–1990* (Englewood Cliffs, NJ: Prentice-Hall, 1991); and Stephen White, *Gorbachev in Power* (Cambridge: Cambridge University Press, 1990).

40. A lengthy summary of Mlynář's observations at various times is in *Mikhail S. Gorbachev: An Intimate Biography*, by the editors of *Time* magazine (New York: Time, 1988), pp. 52–70. Also see Mlynář's own book: *Can Gorbachev Change the Soviet Union? The International Dimensions of Political Reform* (Boulder, CO: Westview Press, 1990).

41. Zhores Medvedev, *Gorbachev* (New York: W. W. Norton, 1986), p. 60.

42. *Pravda*, September 21, 1978, p. 1.

43. Mitchell, *Getting to the Top in the USSR*, pp. 130–31.

44. *Pravda*, April 2, 1985.

45. *Pravda*, October 19, 1984.

46. *Sovietskaia Rossiia*, March 27, 1985, p. 1.

47. Joel C. Moses, "Regional Cohorts and Political Mobility in the USSR: The Case of Dnepropetrovsk," *Soviet Union* 3, no. 1 (1976):82.

48. For example, see *Materialy Plenuma Tsentral'nogo Komiteta KPSS*, January 27–28, 1987 (Moscow, 1987), p. 49.

49. Alexander Rahr, "A New Chief Ideologist in the Kremlin," RL 183/85.

50. Elizabeth Teague, "A New Man to Administer Party Appointments," RL 187/85.

51. See his own report in *Kommunist*, no. 4 (March 1985):29.

52. Gromyko mentions nothing of this in his memoirs, although he indicates that his retirement from the presidency in the fall of 1988 was at his own request: *Memoirs*, p. 345.

53. *Partiinaia zhizn'*, no. 12 (1987):12.

54. *Materialy plenuma Tsentral'nogo Komiteta KPSS*, January 27–28, 1987 (Moscow, 1987), p. 48.

55. Ibid. A good discussion of the aspect of the plenum relating to personnel selection is G. K. Kriuchkov, "Kadrovaia politika partii v usloviakh perestroiki," *Voprosy istorii KPSS*, no. 2 (February 1987):17–32. Also see Elizabeth Teague, "Gorbachev Discusses Personnel Policy," RL 38/87.

56. *Pravda*, October 16, 1989, p. 2.

57. See, for example, his comments before a conference of first secretaries on July 18, 1989: *Pravda*, July 19, 1989, p. 1.

58. *Pravda*, July 10, 1989, p. 2.

59. This was made explicit by Ligachev in his speech to the Twenty-seventh Congress; see *Current Soviet Policies IX* (Columbus, OH: Current Digest of the Soviet Press, 1986), p. 75.

60. Dawn Mann, "New Trend in Personnel Policy," RL 385/86.

61. Dawn Mann, Alexander Rahr, and Elizabeth Teague, "Gorbachev Cleans out Central Committee," *Report on the USSR* 1, no. 18 (May 5, 1989):8.

62. For example, see Giulietto Chiesa, "The 28th Congress of the CPSU," *Problems of Communism* 39, no. 4 (July-August 1990):24–38.

63. Gorbachev proposed this at a February 5, 1990, plenum; it was endorsed by the Central Committee on February 7 and passed into law by the Congress of People's Deputies on March 13, 1990. *Pravda*, March 14, 1990.

64. *Pravda*, July 8, 1990, p. 4.

65. Ibid.

66. E. Gonzales, *Izvestia*, July 13, 1991, p. 1.

67. *Pravda*, July 13, 1990, p. 3.

68. *Pravda*, July 18, 1990, pp. 1–2 (emphasis added).

69. *Pravda*, June 29, 1988, p. 4.

70. Ibid., p. 5.

71. Ibid. The Supreme Soviet ultimately consisted of 542 deputies.

72. *Pravda*, July 5, 1988, p. 2.

73. Sakwa, *Gorbachev and His Reforms*, p. 135.

74. Ibid., p. 136.

75. *Pravda*, April 27, 1989, p. 2.

76. Dawn Mann and Julia Wishnevsky, "Composition of Congress of People's Deputies," in Radio Liberty, *Report on the USSR* 1, no. 18 (May 5, 1989):1–5.

77. *Pravda*, May 28, 1990.

78. Elizabeth Teague, "The Powers of the Soviet Presidency," in Radio Liberty, *Report on the USSR* 2, no. 12 (March 23, 1990):4–7.

79. Alexander Rahr, "Further Restructuring of the Soviet Political System," in Radio Liberty, *Report on the USSR* 3, no. 14 (April 5, 1991):1–4.

80. *Izvestia*, December 21, 1990; *Current Digest of the Soviet Press* 42, no. 52 (January 30, 1991):8.

81. Suzanne Crow, "The Resignation of Shevardnadze," in Radio Liberty, *Report on the USSR* 3, no. 2 (January 11, 1991):7.

82. Suzanne Keller, *Beyond the Ruling Class: Strategic Elites in Modern Society* (New York: Random House, 1963), pp. 91–95.

83. Alexis de Tocqueville, *Democracy in America*, ed. J. P. Mayer, trans. George Lawrence (Garden City, NY: Anchor Books, 1969), p. 192.

84. Ibid., p. 515.

85. Aron Katsenelinboigen, "Will Glasnost' Bring the Reactionaries to Power?" *Orbis* 32, no. 2 (Spring 1988):217–30.

86. Vera Tolz, *The USSR's Emerging Multiparty System* (New York: Praeger, 1990), p. 10.

87. Ibid., pp. 20–21.

88. Elizabeth Teague, "The 'Soyuz' Group," in Radio Liberty, *Report on the USSR* 3, no. 20 (May 17, 1991):17n.

89. Ibid., p. 17.

90. *Izvestia*, October 16, 1990.

91. Vera Tolz, "The Law on Public Associations: Legalization of the Multiparty System," in Radio Liberty, *Report on the USSR* 2, no. 46 (November 16, 1990):1–3.

92. Vera Tolz, "A New Approach to Informal Groups," in Radio Liberty, *Report on the USSR* 2, no. 10 (March 9, 1990):1–3.

93. *Pravda*, July 21, 1989.

94. Quoted in Medvedev and Chiesa, *Time of Change*, p. 289.

95. In September 1990, the Secretariat did abolish some of the Central Committee's *nomenklatura* rights. Annotation in Radio Liberty, *Report on the USSR* 2, no. 36 (September 7, 1990), p. 29.

96. Valery Terekhov, in "From a Mob to a Nation: A Discussion with Four Activists from the Democratic Opposition," *Uncaptive Minds* 3, no. 5 (November–December, 1990):3.

97. Annotation in *Radio Liberty Research*, RL 321/87.

Selected Bibliography

Andreev, A. A. *Vospominaniia, pis'ma*. Moscow, 1985.

Armstrong, John A. *The European Administrative Elite*. Princeton, NJ: Princeton University Press, 1972.

————. *The Politics of Totalitarianism*. New York: Random House, 1961.

Avtorkhanov, Abdurakhman. *Stalin and the Soviet Communist Party: A Study in the Technology of Power*. New York: Praeger, 1959.

Bahro, Rudolf. *The Alternative in Eastern Europe*. London: New Left Books, 1978.

Bailes, Kendall E. "The Politics of Technology: Stalin and Technocratic Thinking among Engineers." *American Historical Review* 79 (1974):445–69.

————. *Technology and Society under Lenin and Stalin: Origins of the Soviet Technical Intelligentsia, 1917–1941*. Princeton, NJ: Princeton University Press, 1978.

Bobkov, V. A. "Partiinie kadry: opyt, problemy, suzhdenie." *Voprosy istorii KPSS*, no. 5 (May 1987):18–31.

Bottomore, T. B. *Elites and Society*. New York: Basic Books, 1965.

Breslauer, George. "Is There a Generation Gap in the Soviet Political Establishment? Demand Articulation by RSFSR Provincial Party First Secretaries." *Soviet Studies* 36 (1984):1–25.

Brown, Archie, ed. *Political Leadership in the Soviet Union*. Bloomington: Indiana University Press, 1989.

Burant, Stephen R. "The Influence of Russian Tradition on the Political Style of the Soviet Elite." *Political Science Quarterly* 102 (1987):273–93.

Chuianov, A. *Na stremnine veka: zapiski sekretaria obkoma*. Moscow, 1976.

Clark, William A. *Soviet Regional Elite Mobility after Khrushchev*. New York: Praeger, 1989.

Conquest, Robert. *The Great Terror: A Reassessment*. New York: Oxford University Press, 1990.

———. *Inside Stalin's Secret Police: NKVD Politics, 1936–39*. Stanford, CA: Hoover Institution Press, 1985.

———. *Stalin and the Kirov Murder*. New York: Oxford University Press, 1989.

d'Encausse, Helene Carrere. *Confiscated Power: How Soviet Russia Really Works*. New York: Harper & Row, 1982.

Doder, Dusko. *Shadows and Whispers: Power Politics inside the Kremlin from Brezhnev to Gorbachev*. New York: Random House, 1986.

Doder, Dusko, and Louise Branson. *Gorbachev: Heretic in the Kremlin*. New York: Viking, 1990.

Dziak, John J. *Chekisty: A History of the KGB*. Lexington, MA: Lexington Books, 1988.

Eisenstadt, S. N., and Louis Roniger. "Patron-Client Relationships as a Model of Structuring Social Exchange." *Comparative Studies of Society and History* 22 (1980):42–77.

Eisenstadt, S. N., and Rene Lemarchand, eds. *Political Clientelism, Patronage, and Development*. Beverly Hills, CA: Sage Publications, 1981.

Ellenstein, Jean. *The Stalin Phenomenon*. London: Lawrence & Wishart, 1976.

Evans, Peter B., Dietrich Rueschmeyer, and Theda Skocpol, eds. *Bringing the State Back In*. Cambridge: Cambridge University Press, 1985.

Feher, Ferenc, Agnes Heller, and Gyorgy Markus. *Dictatorship over Needs*. New York: St. Martin's Press, 1983.

Fitzpatrick, Sheila. "The Bolsheviks' Dilemma: Class, Culture, and Politics in Early Soviet Years." *Slavic Review* 47 (1988):599–613.

———. *Education and Social Mobility in the Soviet Union, 1921–1934*. Cambridge: Cambridge University Press, 1979.

———. "Stalin and the Making of a New Elite, 1928–1939." *Slavic Review* 38 (1979):377–402.

———., ed. *Cultural Revolution in Russia, 1928–1931*. Bloomington: Indiana University Press, 1984.

Foster, George M. "Peasant Society and the Image of Limited Good." *American Anthropologist* 65 (1965):293–315.

Getty, J. Arch. *Origins of the Great Purges: The Soviet Communist Party Reconsidered, 1933–1938*. Cambridge: Cambridge University Press, 1985.

Gromyko, Andrei. *Memoirs*. New York: Doubleday, 1989.

Hahn, Werner. *Postwar Soviet Politics*. Ithaca, NY: Cornell University Press, 1982.

Harasymiw, Bohdan. "Nomenklatura: The Soviet Communist Party's Leadership Recruitment System." *Canadian Journal of Political Science* 2 (1969):493–512.

———. *Political Elite Recruitment in the Soviet Union*. London: Macmillan Press, 1984.

Hazen, Baruch A. *From Brezhnev to Gorbachev: Infighting in the Kremlin*. Boulder, CO: Westview Press, 1987.

———. *Gorbachev and His Enemies: The Struggle for Perestroika*. Boulder, CO: Westview Press, 1990.

Heidenheimer, Arnold J., Michael Johnsston, and Victor T. LeVine. *Political Corruption: A Handbook*. New Brunswick, NJ: Transaction Books, 1989.

Hoffman, Erik P., and Robbin F. Laird. *Technocratic Socialism: The Soviet Union in the Advanced Industrial Era*. Durham, NC: Duke University Press, 1985.

Jowitt, Kenneth. *The Leninist Response to National Dependency.* Berkeley: Institute of International Studies, University of California, 1978.

———. "An Organizational Approach to the Study of Political Culture in Marxist-Leninist Regimes." *American Political Science Review* 67 (1974):1171–91.

Keller, Suzanne. *Beyond the Ruling Class: Strategic Elites in Modern Society.* New York: Random House, 1963.

Kelley, Donald R. *The Politics of Developed Socialism: The Soviet Union as a Post-Industrial State.* Westport, CT: Greenwood Press, 1986.

———. *Soviet Politics from Brezhnev to Gorbachev.* New York: Praeger, 1987.

Kerblay, Basile. *Gorbachev's Russia.* Translated by Rupert Swyer. New York: Pantheon Books, 1989.

Khavin, A. F. "Kapitany sovetskoi industrii 1926–1940 gody." *Voprosy istorii,* no. 5 (May 1966):3–14.

Kirilina, A. A., and Iu A. Lipilin, comps. *S. M. Kirov i Leningradskie kommunisty, 1926–1934.* Leningrad: Lenizdat, 1986.

Klugman, Jeffry. *The New Soviet Elite: How They Think and What They Want.* New York: Praeger, 1989.

Konrad, George, and Ivan Szelenyi. *The Intellectuals on the Road to Class Power.* New York: Harcourt Brace Jovanovich, 1979.

Kriuchkov, G. K. "Kadrovaia politika partii v usloviakh perestroiki." *Voprosy istorii KPSS,* no. 2 (February 1987):17–32.

Lampert, Nicholas. *The Technical Intelligentsia and the Soviet State: A Study of Soviet Managers and Technicians, 1928–1935.* London: Macmillan, 1979.

Lane, David, ed. *Elites and Political Power in the USSR.* Aldershot, Hants, England: Edward Elgar, 1988.

Levi-Strauss, Claude. *Structural Anthropology.* New York: Basic Books, 1963.

Lewytzkyj, Borys. *The Stalinist Terror in the Thirties: Documentation from the Soviet Press.* Stanford, CA: Hoover Institution Press, 1974.

Linden, Ronald H., and Bert A. Rockman, eds. *Elite Studies and Communist Politics: Essays in Memory of Carl Beck.* Pittsburgh: University of Pittsburgh Press, 1984.

Marcus, George E. " 'Elite' as a Concept, Theory, and Research Tradition." In *Elites: Ethnographic Issues,* George E. Marcus, ed. Albuquerque: University of New Mexico Press, 1983.

Matthews, Mervyn. *Privilege in the Soviet Union: A Study of Elite Life-Styles under Communism.* London: Allen & Unwin, 1978.

Mauss, Marcel. *The Gift: Forms and Functions of Exchange in Archaic Societies.* New York: W. W. Norton, 1967.

Medvedev, Roy. *Let History Judge: The Origins and Consequences of Stalinism.* New York: Columbia University Press, 1989.

Medvedev, Roy, and Giulietto Chiesa. *Time of Change: An Insider's View of Russia's Transformation.* Translated by Michael Moore. New York: Pantheon Books, 1990.

Medvedev, Zhores. *Andropov.* New York: Penguin Books, 1984.

———. *Gorbachev.* New York: W. W. Norton, 1986.

Meisel, James H. *The Myth of the Ruling Class: Gaetano Mosca and the "Elite."* Ann Arbor: University of Michigan Press, 1958.

Merelman, Richard M. "On Culture and Politics in America: A Perspective from

Structural Anthropology." *British Journal of Political Science* 19 (1989):465–93.

Mikoyan, A. I. *V nachale dvadtsatykh....* Moscow, 1975.

———. "V pervyi raz bez Lenina." *Ogonyok*, no. 50 (December 13, 1987):5–7.

Mitchell, R. Judson. *Getting to the Top in the USSR: Cyclical Patterns in the Leadership Selection Process.* Stanford, CA: Hoover Institution Press, 1990.

Mosca, Gaetano. *The Ruling Class: Elimenti di Scienza Politica.* Edited and revised by Arthur Livingston. Translated by Hannah D. Kahn. New York: McGraw-Hill, 1939.

Narodnye deputaty SSSR: Spravochnik serii Kto est' Kto. Moscow, 1990.

Nove, Alec. "The Class Structure of the Soviet Union Revisited." *Soviet Studies* 35 (1983):298–312.

Pareto, Vilfredo. *The Mind and Society.* 4 vols. New York: Harcourt, Brace & World, 1935.

———. *The Rise and Fall of the Elites: An Application of Theoretical Sociology.* Totowa, NJ: Bedminster Press, 1968.

Patolichev, N. S. *Ispytanie na zrelost'.* Moscow, 1977.

Pintner, Walter McKenzie, and Don Karl Rowney, eds. *Russian Officialdom: The Bureaucratization of Russian Society from the Seventeenth to the Twentieth Century.* Chapel Hill: University of North Carolina Press, 1980.

Protsess "Prompartii." Moscow: Sovetskoe zakonodatel'stvo, 1931.

Putnam, Robert D. *The Comparative Study of Political Elites.* Englewood Cliffs, NJ: Prentice-Hall, 1976.

Ra'anan, Uri, and Igor Lukes. *Inside the Apparat: Perspectives on the Soviet Union from Former Functionaries.* Lexington, MA: D. C. Heath, 1990.

Reiman, Michael. *The Birth of Stalinism: The USSR on the Eve of the "Second Revolution."* Bloomington: Indiana University Press, 1987.

Rigby, T. H. "Early Provincial Cliques and the Rise of Stalin." *Soviet Studies* 33 (1981):3–28.

———. *Lenin's Government: Sovnarkom, 1917–1922.* Cambridge: Cambridge University Press, 1979.

———. "Political Patronage in the USSR from Lenin to Brezhnev." *Politics* (Australia) 18 (1983):84–89.

———. "Was Stalin a Disloyal Patron?" *Soviet Studies* 38 (1986):311–24.

Rigby, T. H., and Bohdan Harasymiw, eds. *Leadership Selection and Patron-Client Relations in the USSR and Yugoslavia.* London: Allen Unwin, 1983.

Rosenfeldt, Niels Erik. *Knowledge and Power: The Role of Stalin's Secret Chancellery in the Soviet System of Government.* Copenhagen: Rosenkilde & Bagger, 1978.

Rowney, Don K. *Transition to Technocracy: The Structural Origins of the Soviet Administrative State.* Ithaca, NY: Cornell University Press, 1989.

Sakwa, Richard. *Gorbachev and His Reforms, 1985–1990.* Englewood Cliffs, NJ: Prentice-Hall, 1991.

Scott, James C. *Comparative Political Corruption.* Englewood Cliffs, NJ: Prentice-Hall, 1972.

Shatz, Marshall S. *Jan Waclaw Machajski: A Radical Critic of the Russian Intelligentsia and Socialism.* Pittsburgh: University of Pittsburgh Press, 1989.

———. "Stalin, the Great Purge, and Russian History: A New Look at the 'New

Class.' " *Carl Beck Papers in Russian and East European Studies*. University of Pittsburgh, Paper no. 305 (1984).

Simis, Konstantin. *USSR: Secrets of a Corrupt Society*. London: J. M. Dent & Sons, 1982.

Simonov, Konstantin. "Glazami cheloveka moego pokoleniia (razmyshleniia o I. V. Staline)." *Znamia*, no. 3:3–66, no. 4:49–120, no. 5:70–96 (1988).

Skocpol, Theda. *States and Social Revolutions*. Cambridge: Cambridge University Press, 1979.

Timoshenko, Stephen P. "The Development of Engineering Education in Russia." *Russian Review* 15 (1956):173–85.

Tocqueville, Alexis de. *The Old Regime and the French Revolution*. Translated by Stuart Gilbert. Garden City, NY: Doubleday, 1955.

Tolz, Vera. *The USSR's Emerging Multiparty System*. New York: Praeger, 1990.

Turner, Ralph. "Contest and Sponsored Mobility and the School System." *American Sociological Review* 25 (1966):856–67.

Urban, Michael E. *An Algebra of Soviet Power: Elite Circulation in the Belorussian Republic, 1966–86*. Cambridge: Cambridge University Press, 1989.

———. *The Ideology of Administration: American and Soviet Cases*. Albany: State University of New York Press, 1982.

Urlanis, B. Ts. *Istoriia odnogo pokoleniia*. Moscow: Izdatel'stvo Mysl', 1968.

Voslensky, Michael S. *Nomenklatura: The Soviet Ruling Class*. Translated by Eric Mosbacher. Garden City, NY: Doubleday, 1984.

Weber, Max. In *Economy and Society: An Outline of Interpretive Sociology*, Guenther Roth and Claus Wittich, eds. 3 vols. New York: Bedminster Press, 1968.

———. *The Methodology of the Social Sciences*. Translated by Edward A. Shils and Henry A. Finch. Glencoe, IL: Free Press, 1949.

Welsh, William A. *Leaders and Elites*. New York: Holt, Rinehart & Winston, 1979.

White, Stephen. *Gorbachev in Power*. Cambridge: Cambridge University Press, 1990.

Willerton, John P., Jr. "Patronage Networks and Coalition Building in the Brezhnev Era." *Soviet Studies* 39 (1987):175–204.

Yanov, Alexander. *The Russian Challenge and the Year 2000*. Translated by Iden J. Rosenthal. Oxford: Basil Blackwell, 1987.

Index

ABOUT THE AUTHOR

KENNETH C. FARMER is Associate Professor and Chairman of the Department of Political Science at Marquette University. He is the author of *Ukrainian Nationalism in the Post-Stalin Era* and numerous articles on Soviet nationalities policies and elites in the Soviet Union.